Thirza Vallois

D0171342

Around and About Paris

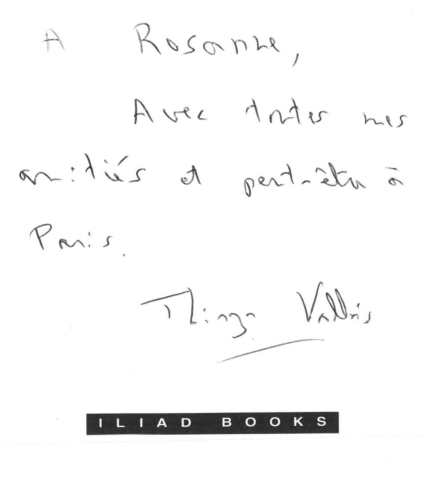

A Rosanne,

Avec tnter mes
amitiés et peut-êtu à
Paris.

Thirza Vallois

I L I A D   B O O K S

First Published in 1995

Reprinted 1999

Copyright ©

1995, Thirza Vallois

ISBN 0 9525378 0 X

Iliad Books
5 Nevern Road
London SW5 9PG
Tel: 0973 325 468
Internet: http://www.wfi.fr/vallois

Printed in Canada by Webcom Limited

VOLUME ONE

From the Dawn of Time to the Eiffel Tower

1st, 2nd, 3rd, 4th, 5th, 6th and 7th arrondissements

To my Parents and Nathaniel with love

◆ In memory of Ella ◆

◆ ACKNOWLEDGEMENTS ◆

My deepest gratitude to all my friends who, in one way or another, have contributed to this book and given me their support during this long adventure. They are listed in alphabetical order:

Valentin Beugin, Ingrid Cranfield, Baba Gamet, Danielle Michel-Chiche, Jeannette Molcho, Hilary Moore, Richard and Barbara Parkes, Ellis Santos, Masha Schmidt, Claudie Taieb, Brigitte Thiéblin, Barbara-Sue White, Sarah Wilkinson, Janice and Rebecca Williams, Elizabeth and Peter Wilson and also the students of cartography at the Lycée Adrienne Monnier in Paris and all the other friends who have helped me.

Special thanks to Gerry Silverman without whose encouragement and advice this book may have never been published.

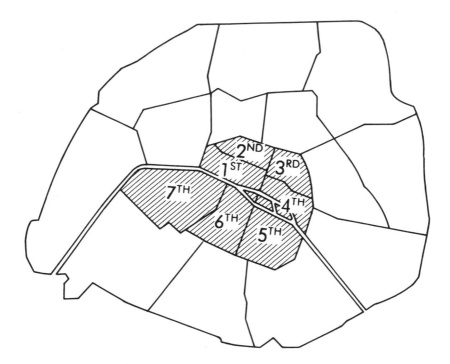

REALISATION CARTOGRAPHIQUE : GOFFIN R.   GEORGET N.

contents

INTRODUCTION

"Qui regarde au fond de Paris a le vertige."
("He who looks into the depths of Paris grows giddy.")
Victor Hugo

A journey into the depths of Paris is what this book is about, an invitation to scratch beneath its surface of dazzling vistas and imposing monuments and to probe into the souls and lives of the restless people, both high and low, who throughout the ages have never ceased to shape and reshape it. For Paris is a city of perpetual change, a hectic building site of destruction and reconstruction, of restoration and renovation, where fashions are no sooner created than forsaken, a city in perpetual motion whose rounds of pleasure are periodically broken by maelstroms of social fury and bloodshed and whose throbbing pulse has always exerted a magnetic power on creative minds from far and wide who have bequeathed to the world great schools of art and thought.

Continual waves of newcomers have come to Paris in search of livelihood, spiritual nourishment or political shelter. As the population of the city grew and craved elbow space, they helped to bring down its successive walls - from that built by Philippe-Auguste in 1190 to the last wall built by Thiers and demolished in 1919 - always pushing out the boundaries of Paris farther from its original nucleus, l'Ile de la Cité.

Thus developed the arrondissements which spiral outwards clockwise, like a snail shell, keeping Paris conveniently compact, yet endowing it with infinite potential for growth. In 1795 Paris was divided into 12 arrondissements, but in 1860 the number was increased to 20, when Baron Haussmann incorporated the bordering villages into the capital. This change, determined solely by administrative considerations, was part of the modernization that had started with the French Revolution.

The Paris created by Baron Haussmann during the reign of Napoleon III is, to a large extent, still the Paris of today. Supported by some, deprecated by others, he carved through the medieval city, doing away with many insalubrious streets to make room for the present bright broad avenues. By now, however, Haussmann's

1

INTRODUCTION

Paris is overlaid with the patina of time, medieval Paris is more of a film set than a reality and the fragments of 'villages' that the sharp observer can still spot here and there tend to blend into the more recent overall unity of their respective arrondissements. Today the administrative life of every Parisian, from birth to death, is regulated by and revolves around his arrondissement which, in a way, has replaced his old parish. Its centre of gravity is the monumental Mairie, where newborn babies are registered, children are enrolled in school and couples get married; where also social welfare is provided and sports and cultural activities are organized. Although Parisians still speak of old neighbourhoods such as the Marais, the Latin Quarter or Les Halles, they commonly refer in everyday contexts to their arrondissements. Each arrondissement now has its history, its own economic, social and cultural heritage and its own local colour and character, even though the uniformity of modernization has rendered the differences indistinguishable to the unpractised eye.

Because the arrondissements reflect the social, economic and cultural pattern of Paris, it is essential to focus on these in order to understand Paris thoroughly. This book is therefore organized by arrondissements, so as to allow the city to unfold little by little before your eyes. The names of streets, the geographic location of the city's monuments, the social and ethnic distribution of the population will become meaningful and coherent. You will understand that it is not pure chance that draws the wealthy to the 16th arrondissement or publishers to the 6th. You will find out how and why *haute couture* started in the 1st arrondissement and why it has recently shifted to the 8th. You will realize why the 5th has to some extent lost its soul and why embassies are often located in the 7th. Each arrondissement has compelling stories to tell and therefore none has been given priority. They tell stories of humble craftsmen and great rulers, of everyday tragedies and of outbursts of rejoicing or social confrontations; stories of adulation and scorn; of scandals, gossip, passion and crime. Some of the stories may be apocryphal, all are part of Paris lore.

Although the past has been searchingly unearthed, the ebullient present has not been neglected. The speed with which the French capital has leapt forward into the modern age is stunning. Never have so many architects and town planners had

2

their eyes riveted on the French metropolis, nor has its traditional way of life been so threatened. As chains of supermarkets replace small shops, as working women renounce fine cuisine in favour of pre-cooked frozen meals, as television replaces street entertainment, Paris can boast an ever-increasing number of high-rises, throughways, traffic jams, junk food and clothes shops.... The banks of the river Seine, once the home of fishermen and winos and the promenade of amorous couples, have been largely taken over by fast cars. Old-time homely French restaurants are hard to come by now that the colourful French working-class is all but extinct. In an upwardly mobile society a medley of Third World nationals have taken their place and introduced their own homely restaurants, equally colourful but not French.

If you long for bygone days, you may be grieved to see multitudes of fast-food restaurants and a riot of T-shirts in shop windows or dangling above street stalls. However, the picturesque open-air flower and food markets, the bird market, the book-stalls, the odd street organ are still there. Many French people still eat baguette and camembert, and men still like a good game of *boules*, even though they have long given up their basque berets. On the other hand, if you are a forward-looking optimist, you will appreciate that more and more young people are articulate in foreign languages.

By the time you have reached the end of your journey, it may strike you that Paris has always been a city in the making, born out of the latent or explosive tensions between the forces of reaction and the forces of progress, and out of the necessities of time. A city willed by authoritarian regimes but also the spontaneous emanation of its headstrong people, it is the very expression of the vitality of French society.

THIRZA VALLOIS

A NOTE ON THE TEXT

So as to facilitate the reading of French names and titles, the use of capital letters follows English rules. When they are italicized, however, French rules have been retained.

Because Paris is a city of change, some of the places or exhibits mentioned in the text may have since disappeared or been transformed. If this is the case, please bear with the author.

THE 1st ARRONDISSEMENT

At the heart of the 'snail-shell' (*l'escargot*), as the layout of Paris has come to be known, lies the 1st arrondissement, as to be expected from the orderly French. It was also the first to be settled by the Celtic tribe of the Parisi, the early inhabitants of Paris who in the 3rd century BC occupied l'Ile de la Cité, the original nucleus of Paris, now shared between the 1st and 4th arrondissements.

French society also had its origins here, from the king down to the pleb. Except for brief spells, this was the home of the kings of France, which made it the royal arrondissement *par excellence*, as its royal squares, monuments and other landmarks testify: Place Dauphine built in honour of the Dauphin, the son of Henri IV and future Louis XIII; Place des Victoires and Place Vendôme, which honour Louis XIV; the Palais-Royal, the palatial home of Richelieu, glamorous enough as an early childhood home for Louis XIV; the regal rue Saint-Denis, the 'Champs-Elysées' of medieval Paris, the sacred way through which the royal processions entered Paris, notably on their way to the cathedral of Notre-Dame after the king's coronation in Reims, and through which the kings were carried to their final resting place in the basilica of Saint-Denis, north of Paris.

From Notre-Dame it was but a stone's throw to the King's Palace on the site of today's Palais de Justice. In the 3rd century, the Roman Emperor Julian had already established his seat here, but it was only in the 6th century that the Merovingian king Childebert made it the permanent home of the kings of France. In the 13th century, the pious and beatified Louis IX built a private chapel adjoining the palace, la Chapelle Royale, now commonly known as la Sainte-Chapelle.

But above all, it was the Louvre, the subsequent residence of the kings of France, and, in the 19th century, the Palais des Tuileries which adjoined it to the west, that shone forth on the arrondissement, dazzling the rest of Europe, making her other courts green with envy:

> "He'll make your Paris Louvre shake for it, were it the
> mistress-court of mighty Europe,"
>> William Shakespeare/*Henry V*.

The Louvre of Henry V's time, was not the present building, but a medieval fortress, turned into a royal residence by Charles V in 1368. Initially it was no more than a defence tower, part of the fortification system that Philippe-Auguste had built in 1190 round the part of Paris that lay north of the Seine, before embarking on the Third Crusade. Wary of a potential threat from England by way of the Seine, albeit upstream (which is how the Norsemen had invaded the city three centuries earlier), he erected the Louvre on the right bank, at the western-most point of the fortification, facing the Tour de Nesle on the opposite bank. With the presence of the Plantagenets not so far down the river, at Gisors (in the Vexin in Normandy), and with the vague memory of that horrendous devastation of Paris by the Norsemen, he had good reason for concern: Philippe-Auguste had no illusions about the Plantagenet Richard the Lionheart's territorial designs, even though he was his brother-in-law and was to accompany him on his holy journey to Jerusalem. Soon a wall 3,000 metres long, 3 metres thick and 10 metres high encircled the right bank of Paris, complete with an adjoining fortress, just west of the present church of Saint-Germain-l'Auxerrois. Inside, a round keep, 19 metres in diameter, rose 31 metres above ground level - the initial Louvre. Upon his return in 1191, Philippe-Auguste deposited the Crown treasures and archives at the Louvre, which he considered the safest place in the capital, thereby adding to its prestige as *'la plus halte tor de Paris la citet'* ('the tallest tower in Paris the city'), the aura of symbolising the monarchy's power and glamour.

Charles V, though equally dedicated to the fortification of his capital, was also an enlightened king: besides making the Louvre his residence, he collected within its thick walls the kingdom's manuscripts and founded the first royal library of France.

François I, settling into a new period of peace, well being and refinement, decided to dispense with the defensive function of the Louvre and replaced the medieval fortress with a Renaissance palace - an ambitious project completed only by Henri IV. The people of Paris were quite upset by the sudden disappearance in 1528 of *'la Grosse Tour'*, where Charles V used to read and meditate. For François I, however, fortresses had unpleasant associations: he had recently been released from the fortress of Madrid where he had been kept captive by the Emperor Charles V, who had defeated him at Pavia in 1525. His overhauled Louvre now became the sumptuous backdrop of scintillating celebrations, of colourful tournaments and jousts which made show of the magnificence of a new, enlightened reign and meant to astonish its illustrious guests - in particular Emperor Charles V of Spain, who was to be dazzled and humbled during his visit to the Louvre in 1540. All the weather vanes had been gilded for the occasion, the window casements enlarged, the window panes coloured, the staircases and apartments illuminated with brass candlesticks.

But when the celebrations were over, and the silk hangings and tapestries taken down, the Louvre assumed its daily aspect, which was still largely medieval: François I had only had time to start the construction of the two sections that flank the south west angle of the Cour Carrée. On the other hand, he bestowed the artistic spirit of the Renaissance upon the Louvre, and he also started the painting collection that would one day make it the largest painting museum in the world. His was but an embryonic collection, comprising, nonetheless, the works of such great masters as Leonardo da Vinci, Raphael, Titian, among them, and probably, the most renowned painting in the Louvre, the *Mona Lisa*, which François I is believed to have transferred to Paris from Amboise (in the Loire Valley) after the death of da Vinci in 1519.

In 1593, four years after his accession to the throne of France, Henri IV agreed to barter his Protestant religion for Paris and put an end to the bloody strife between Protestants and Catholics: *"Paris vaut bien une messe"* ("Paris is well worth a mass") were his famous words. Paris meant first and foremost the Louvre. His ambitious schemes for it were already on his mind when he entered the capital on 22 March 1594. A Swiss visitor to the building site confirmed the King's ambition when he wrote that "the edifice is so pompous and so vast that once completed there will be no other like it in all Christendom". By then the Palais des Tuileries was facing the Louvre to the west, running perpendicularly to the Seine from north to south. It had been built by Catherine de Medici in 1564, the widow of Henri II and mother of three successive kings, François II, Charles IX and Henri III, as well as of Marguerite de Valois, his own wife. Henri IV set out to connect the Palais des Tuileries to the Louvre by means of a colossal wing of monumental grandeur - 470 metres long La Grande Galerie, also known as la Galerie du Bord de l'Eau ('waterfront gallery') since it ran along the Seine. It met the Palais des Tuileries at right angles and was completed by the elegant Pavillon de Flore. (The Pavillon de Marsan on the northern side of the Palais des Tuileries, was added only at the time of Louis XIV). This gigantic enterprise was a constant headache for his minister Sully, who had to squeeze segments of the population dry in order to raise the necessary funds.

The Galerie du Bord de l'Eau was built to house the best artisans and artists of the kingdom and thus realize the artistic mission Henri IV had set for the Louvre, which became the home of royalty, along with their 1500-strong army of servants (who were not all lodged there, however), and of a select artistic community.

Louis XIV was 14 when he settled in the Louvre in 1652, after the princely rebellion - *la Fronde* - had been quelled and it was deemed safe for him to return to Paris. He never liked the Louvre and in 1682 moved his court to the newly built palace at Versailles, leaving the Louvre to fall into decline. However, as long as he resided there, he channelled a lot of energy and money into completing the construction around the Cour Carrée; for the show had to go on and to exceed in flashy splendour that of his predecessors. His was the reign of glamour *par excellence*. Scintillating balls, ceremonial dinners, each consisting of a score of dishes, were succeeded by performances of plays by Corneille and Molière. His Majesty and his brother, Monsieur, were great lovers of this form of entertainment, unlike their grandfather Henri IV, who once confided to a woman friend, "Yesterday evening I saw the comedians play, when I fell asleep. It was midnight when they finished."

During the reign of Louis XIV the number of paintings in the Louvre increased from 200 to 2,000, thanks largely to his enterprising aides, particularly his minister Mazarin, who embarked on a feverish outburst of acquisitions for the royal art collection and library. Mazarin's successor, Colbert, also encouraged the development of the arts and sciences, supported by ample donations made by Nicolas Fouquet, the king's wealthy treasurer, before his disgrace. The five newly founded Academies were set up too at the Louvre but paradoxically contributed to its deterioration. The King's apartment, for example, left vacant when he moved to Versailles, became the premises of the Académie des Sciences, housing an elephant skeleton, a stuffed camel and various anatomical organs floating in alcohol-filled jars.

Worse was to come: booths and stalls soon crammed the courtyard, the magnificent halls were devastated, the panelling of the royal apartments torn off, the painted ceilings drilled into to make room for skylights or stove pipes. A motley population of artisans, parasitical courtiers and prowlers replaced the splendid members of the court who had moved to Versailles. Many courtiers had gone reluctantly, resentful at having to give up the independence they had enjoyed in the city, be it on the Faubourg Saint-Honoré, on the Faubourg Saint-Germain across the river, or in the remote Marais. Paris offered pleasure and gratification to the privileged, often in the form of the witty conversation and intellectual stimulation to be found in the literary *salon* of some enlightened lady. It was precisely in order to keep a close eye on this increasingly independent aristocracy that the astute monarch, asserting his divine right, transferred its members to the glorified "ghetto" of Versailles, where they were no more than glamorous lackeys in his service. Louis XIV had not forgotten the lesson of the princely rebellion which in 1650 forced him into exile at Saint-Germain-en-Laye, putting an end to his idyllic childhood at Palais-Royal, when little Marie, the daughter of his mother's chambermaid, played his queen.

Roughly a century after the move to Versailles, on 6 October 1789, the infuriated people of Paris transferred Louis XIV's great-great-grandson, Louis XVI, back to Paris. The days of absolutism were over and it was now the King's turn to be kept in check. Heading from Versailles to the Tuileries (the Louvre being too dilapidated to be inhabited), the royal coach was made to follow a long and strange procession of National Guards, royal troops, excited throngs of Parisians and carts of corn and flour escorted by sharp-eyed mutinous women. From then

8

on the Tuileries replaced the Louvre as the residence of the kings and emperors of France. This explains why, after his coup on 2 December 1851, Louis Napoleon promptly left the Republican seat of the Palais de l'Elysée (8th arrondissement) in favour of the Royal seat of the Tuileries.

Similarly, the nascent bourgeois Third Republic, wishing to cut off all links with France's monarchistic past, moved out of the 1st arrondissement in 1871, after its victory over the proletarian *Commune*, heading back west to the Palais de l'Elysée, the home of the Republic's Presidents ever since. The fire that had damaged the Tuileries during the civil strife of the *Commune*, had tolled the knell of the 1st arrondissement as the seat of power. In 1882, rather than restore the charred carcass of the Palais des Tuileries, the Third Republic razed it to the ground, securing irrevocably the definitive death of the monarchy.

With the Tuileries as the seat of power during the better part of the last century, its gardens attracted the fashionable set, and luxury hotels opened up in the vicinity, close to the beautiful *hôtels* (townhouses) of the nobility, catering predominantly to an affluent English clientele. Among them were the legendary Ritz on Place Vendôme and the prestigious Meurice opposite the Tuileries Gardens, at n° 228 rue de Rivoli, next door to the English bookshop, Galignani, at n° 224, where they would pop in to read the daily papers of their homeland. For their convenience too WH Smith opened a Parisian branch at n° 248. The English visitors also frequented the fabulous clothes and jewellery shops on rue de Castiglione, Place Vendôme and rue de la Paix (now in the 2nd arr.). In order to serve the Empress Eugénie and the other ladies of the Napoleonic nobility, the world of fashion concentrated in this area too. Thus French *haute couture* was born in the 1st arrondissement and the bordering 2nd in the second half of the 19th century and it was Charles Worth, the Empress's English *couturier*, who was its illustrious forerunner. It would take another century for its centre of gravity to shift gradually westward, to the 8th arrondissement.

But the 1st arrondissement was not only the crown of Paris: Emile Zola had dubbed its plebeian eastern parts 'the belly of Paris' a metaphor he used in 1873 for the title of one of his novels. For a year he had been haunting the central market of Les Halles at all times of day and night, imbibing the atmosphere and recording the ever-changing hues of this gigantic digestive apparatus of the capital: dark bluish-grey metal structures against a light grey sky in wet weather; sheets of gold on the hard-packed earth as the sun's rays penetrate through the grey atmosphere on a fine day; the glowing glass panes of the market's pavilions at sunset; the lights of gas lamps standing out against black roofs. Poultry, fish in wicker baskets, meat, cheese, butter and milk each had their own pavilion. Colourful vegetables, even glossier and brighter when washed by the rain; piles of artichoke stalks, cabbage leaves, carrot and turnip-tops – heaps of refuse waiting to be removed before fresh 'fodder' is poured into the city's belly, come two in the morning, when rattling carts converge on Les Halles, delivering the bountiful harvest of rural France. The neighing of horses, the braying of donkeys, the cries of coachmen, the occasional swish of the whip accompany this nocturnal procession. Peasant girls in headscarves now set to work, unloading the carts and forming piles of carrots, turnips, leeks, lettuces and cabbages. The smell of carrots, parsley and celery vie with the aroma of Provence - bouquets of thyme, laurel and garlic arrayed in neat rows at the foot of the church of Saint-Eustache.

Having watched at work *les forts des Halles* - the robust porters, 'all nerves and muscles' - Zola descended into the undisclosable underground depths of the market, where the shameful slaughter of fowl and other creatures was carried out nightly, a place reeking of blood and pestilence and overrun by rats. This underworld was unknown to the bourgeois and the artist, who, in the early hours of the morning, after a night spent in a cabaret or a theatre,would drift off to the market in search of strong emotions to be found, they believed, by mixing with the lower orders. The onion soup and the glass of wine at the typical zinc bar would be followed at the break of dawn by a chunk of baguette dunked in a *café crème* as a celebration of the new day and the never-ending cycle of life.

This world is gone. Deemed unsuitable for modern times, the market was transferred in 1969 to Rungis, south of Paris. You may be old enough to have seen it before its demolition and may have even dined in the early hours of the morning on a traditional *soupe à l'oignon* at Le Pied de Cochon at 6 rue Coquillère, or Au Père Tranquille at the corner of rue Pierre Lescot and rue Rambuteau, where in 1929 Evelyn Waugh also dined on onion soup. Many Parisians were appalled by the demolition of Victor Baltard's iron pavilions, considered an artistic testimony to the Industrial Age. One only of the 14 pavilions was allowed to survive, but was transferred to the suburb of Nogent-sur-Marne, east of Paris (RER, line A). Others also bemoaned the lost soul of Paris:

> *Il est un lieu de bonheur... la dernière image du naturel dans la Ville. Il est maintenant le Paradis Perdu.*
> (It was a place of bliss... the last vision of natural life in the City.
> It is now Paradise lost), as sculptor Raymond Mason put it.

Louis Chevalier, the superb social observer and poet of Paris, was more blunt:

> *La mort des Halles a sonné le glas de Paris.*
> (The death of Les Halles has tolled the knell of Paris.)

A surreal gigantic hole - *'le trou des Halles'* - replaced the 'belly' of Paris, then left gaping for a decade while ambitious politicians shilly-shallied about its fate. In 1979 the Forum des Halles rose out of the ashes of the picturesque central market. Undoubtedly the Forum can pride itself on being the largest pedestrian precinct in Europe, truly an achievement in a traffic-ridden city. Otherwise, it is barely more than yet another shopping centre, designed to squeeze in as many shops as possible (240), and generally gaudy.

When it first opened, a new generation of trendy young people settled on the terrace of the no less trendy Café Costes, (decorated by the up-and-coming Philippe Starcke, who has since introduced his designs in Manhattan and at the Palais de l'Elysée). Property prices in the vicinity rocketed, prompting the alert Japanese, in November 1989, to buy up one third of the Forum des Halles.

Meanwhile, the 'bowels' of Les Halles were converted to house the gigantic new central station of Châtelet-Les Halles, where the suburban north/south - east/west express lines of the RER (Réseau Exprès Régional) meet and connect with the urban Métro network. This, the largest station in the capital, was designed to facilitate life for commuters, and to enhance the cultural dimension of the centre of Paris, with the Georges Pompidou Centre in the nearby 4th arrondissement as its main pole. At the same time, however, it attracted the homeless and shiftless and social drop-outs, whose presence does not make this a safe area to stroll in, especially after dark; nor does the conspicuous, oppressive presence of the police make it a pleasant one.

Fortunately the western extension of the Forum, opened in 1986, and the gardens that lie between the two Forums enjoy a more benign atmosphere. Mothers are not afraid to bring their young off-spring to this traffic-free, sunny area, under the reassuring and maternal watch of the venerable church of Saint-Eustache.

While for centuries the area nourished the people of Paris, it also cared for them once departed. The Cimetière des Saints-Innocents, into which had been piled up the remains of generations of Parisians since Gallo-Roman days, stood on the corner of rue Berger and rue Saint-Denis.

By the late 18th century the stench of putrefaction and the danger of epidemics were so great that a general outcry arose, this time *against* the preservation of a site. Voltaire considered it a barbarity that placed the French below the Hottentots! But one journalist who opposed the demolition on religious grounds, was sent to the Bastille prison for an entire year. The transfer of the cemetery's occupants to the newly opened catacombs south of the city (now in the 14th arrondissement), began on 7 April 1786 and took 15 months. Night after night eerie processions carried draped remains from the different cemeteries of Paris to their new abode where six millions of them now rest. Today, the Square des Innocents, now Place Joachim Du Bellay, bustles with street performers and loitering crowds, who gather around the Renaissance fountain with its cascading water, unaware that they are treading the soil that once buried the innocent dead.

If life and death cohabited in the 1st, so did the lower orders and royalty who were still living side by side in the last century, an intimacy inconceivable today. The painter Auguste Renoir grew up in one of the lanes that then ran through the Esplanade of the Louvre and was one of the little street urchins to whom Queen Amélie's ladies-in-waiting threw sweets through the window when they made too much of a nuisance of themselves. Renoir's son, the celebrated film director, wondered "how successive kings could have tolerated such a seedy neighbourhood under their very noses".

This rubbing of shoulders between the classes contributed to a variety of contrasts which is more striking in the 1st arrondissement than in any other: the imposing Gothic mass of the Conciergerie, against the delicate and graceful architecture of the Sainte-Chapelle or Pei's seemingly weightless glass Pyramid of the Louvre. Rue Saint-Denis with its garish neon lights, provocative street-walkers and sex-shops, is a long way from the Palais-Royal, now a peaceful haven of elegant architecture, yet in the 18th century the stronghold of the city's prostitution. The busy, workaday area around Place du Châtelet, once a den of crime, has little in common with the gem-like Place Dauphine on the Ile de la Cité. Beyond it, at the western tip of the island, the charming little garden of Vert-Galant, enhanced by the beauty of the 16th-century Pont-Neuf, adds a ravishing romantic touch to the arrondissement.

WHERE TO WALK...

LES HALLES

The Forum des Halles is a convenient starting point, best reached by the RER or Métro. Get off at Châtelet-Les Halles station and head for Porte Lescot. Unless you make your trip off peak, your ascent into the outside world will be slow - an impregnable human fortress invariably obstructs the escalators, providing the visitor with ample time to take in the noise, the garish shops, the uninviting eating-places, often the conspicuous presence of the police... The atmosphere will improve as you step out into the Patio and its open-air terraces, highlighted by an enchanting merry-go-round and its nostalgic music, which will carry you back to the days when the central market of Les Halles stood here, Paris's pulsating lifeblood for nearly eight hundred years.

In 1135 Louis VI set up a primitive market on a piece of land allotted by the Bishop of Paris, against a return of a third of its revenue. Its name - Les Champeaux - may have derived from the marshy fields (*champs*) covered with market-gardens that surrounded it. In 1183 Philippe-Auguste replaced it with two stone buildings to shelter goods and vendors in bad weather, and secured them with locks to prevent thefts. In order to raise the funds for the project, he confiscated the possessions of the Jews.

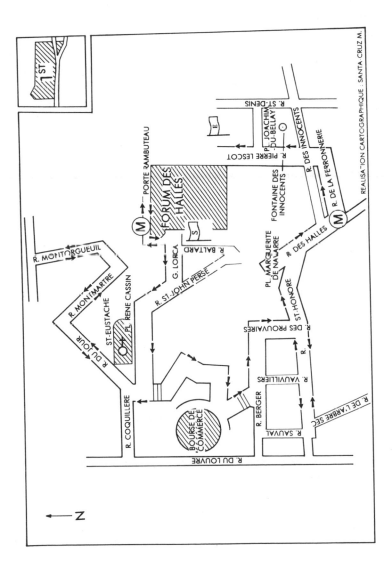

The new market became known as Les Halles, or *les alles*: *'pour ce que chacun y allait '* ('for everyone went there'), and it was this name that stuck. Economic prosperity and demographic growth in the 16th century led Henri II to rebuild and enlarge the market in 1553, an initiative repeated by Napoleon III three centuries later, for the same motives. By then France had entered the Industrial Age and iron often replaced stone. Impressed by Victor Baltard's newly-built Gare de l'Est, Napoleon III commissioned him to build the new market, commending the use of iron: *"Faites-moi des parapluies! "* ("make me umbrellas!"). 14 iron pavilions were thus erected between 1851 and 1857 and stood till 1969, when the central market was transferred to Rungis south of Paris and the pavilions were demolished, leaving Paris scathed. For not only was it deprived of a fine example of the architecture of the time, an artistic expression of the Industrial Revolution, but also of its life-giving core, which had its roots in the Middle Ages. A motley, clamorous, plebeian world, highlighted by the colourful, forthright language of its fishwives and other shrill female vendors, brilliantly summed up by François Villon in the *Ballade des Femmes de Paris*:

> *Quoy qu'on die d'Italiennes*
> *Il n'est bon bec que de Paris.*
> (Whatever be said of Italian women, the big
> mouths of Paris are second to none).

On special occasions these notorious *poissardes* were allowed into the King's Palace to pay their respects to the royal couple. Having been served a hearty meal, they would return to Les Halles and pass on proudly the latest Palace gossip to the entire eager neighbourhood. Despite a rigid social hierarchy, the physical proximity of high and low created a certain familiarity, a feeling of belonging to one and the same society. The *Dames des Halles*, as they were also called, felt personally involved in the goings-on in the Palace, which accounts for an astonishing letter, written by Femme Ladoucette to Marie de Medici, Henri IV's second wife, on 30 August 1608. Having introduced herself as *Dame des Halles* "from mother to daughter since Saint Louis", and a mother to four by her husband (which is a guarantee of moral integrity), she admits to a forthright tongue, but, she adds, it is no lying tongue... She then proceeds to complain to the Queen about her philandering husband, the King, a good fellow deep down but who fidgets at the sight of a coquette and scatters bastards around, although blessed with a most appetising Queen, so well conditioned to have little princes. If the King happened to wander through Les Halles, she pursues, she would give him a sound thrashing for the love of her Queen. Femme Ladoucette received no scolding for her bold letter - instead she was promoted *'fournisseuse* (purveyor) *royale '*!

With its ceaseless human tide, the market-place was picked out for public executions and punishments and the scaffold was part of the landscape from the 14th century on. Needless to say decapitations were preceded by the customary methods of torture and followed by the unrelenting mutilation of the bodies. Some of the victims were condemned to the pillory alone, and the King's pillory, the largest of them all, was a sizeable octagonal structure, with a pointed roof and weathervane, somewhat resembling a chapel. The ground floor was often inhabited by the King's Great Executioner, while the convicts were exposed in the tower above. The excited mob relished the sight, taunting the exposed victims, pelting them with rubbish and litter. There were no gallows, however, at Les Halles, the King conceding that this was no place for bodies to be left rotting on a rope.

If you wish to travel into a more recent past, visit the Musée Grévin at level -1. Twenty-one scenes from Belle Epoque Paris are on display in this wax museum, providing a kitschy and sketchy yet truly instructive idea of turn-of-the-century Paris and its representative figures - Victor Hugo, Emile Zola, Jules Verne, Pasteur etc. You will travel to the old village of Montmartre, to the fashionable Champs-Elysées, to the bustling market of Les Halles, obviously; you will admire the 1900 Universal Exposition and will be dazzled by the scintillating bourgeoisie at the Opera of Palais Garnier.

Also at level -1 is the Musée de l'Holographie, the most important of its kind in the world. Holography is an optical technique, originally invented by D. Gabor in 1948, for which he was awarded the Nobel Prize in 1971. On display are numerous examples of three-dimensional images, including a portrait of the famous jazz musician Herbie Hancock. It was done in 1985 when he stayed in Paris for the shooting of Bertrand Tavernier's *Around Midnight*. Good exhibitions are organised occasionally at the Pavillon des Arts, at Porte Rambuteau, while next to it, La Maison de la Poésie will be of interest to poetry lovers.

The new extension of the Forum can be joined through an underground Passage (head for Porte Saint-Eustache) but, if the sun has greeted you, walk through the peaceful gardens. The trees are still too young, but at least the area has been given over to the pedestrian and only cheerful children and occasional buskers will disturb the perfect tranquillity. If you long to bask in the sun, settle down on the terrace of *Le Jardin des Halles* facing south. For extra lazy southern atmosphere, order a *'Jardin des Halles'* salad. Once revived proceed towards the church of Saint-Eustache, the second largest church in Paris after Notre-Dame. This imposing, somewhat maternal 16th-century church, is a surviving witness of an age when it watched over the plebeian congregation of Les Halles. However, the names of the greats are also associated with this church, where Richelieu and the Pompadour were baptized, Louis XIII received his first holy communion, Lully was married and Rameau was buried. A plaque on the wall of the southern aisle informs you that the funeral service for Anna Maria Mozart was held here in July 1788. She had accompanied her son on his third and last visit to Paris, an unhappy visit which left Mozart both bereaved and embittered. No longer a *Wunderkind*, he was ignored by a shallow, unmusical society and had to share with his mother an insalubrious, draughty flat at n° 10 rue du Gros-Chenet (today's rue Sentier in the 2nd arr.). She took ill in June and died wretchedly on 3 July. Mozart gives a heart-rending account of this sorrowful event in his *Correspondence*. Resentful and contemptuous of Parisian society, he left the city the following September never to return.

The funeral service for the famous fable writer Jean de La Fontaine was also held here; so was Molière's, though in riotous conditions: it took the intervention of the King to persuade the clergy of Saint-Eustache to give this parishioner a Christian burial - the clergy did not like 'stage men' and did not admit them into its fold. All the more so because those ill-mannered louts would turn up in front of the church during Sunday morning mass to announce their forthcoming play - otherwise more exciting than mass - thus inevitably turning many souls away from God.

Because of its remarkable acoustics, the names of several illustrious musicians are associated with the church of Saint-Eustache. In 1855 Berlioz attended a performance of his uplifting *Te Deum* by 950 musicians and in 1886, Liszt's majestic *Grand Mass* was premiered here, also in the presence of its composer. The famous choir of Saint-Eustache was directed by no other than Charles Gounod, whose most outstanding pupil was a child by the name of Auguste Renoir. Gounod had built great hopes in young Renoir, who, however, felt a deeper urge to use his hands...

The strong musical tradition is still maintained and the church houses one of the most fabulous organs in Paris, the work of the Dutch establishment Peter Jan Van Den Heuvel. It was installed in 1989, while its beautiful case was designed in the 19th century by Victor Baltard, the architect of Les Halles. Equipped with both a mechanical and an electronic transmission system, this is the biggest double transmission organ in the world, most suitable for the performances of 20th-century music. As you make your way out through the northern aisle, you will notice in the wall a colourful niche, depicting the life of the central market of Les Halles - a touching tribute to its workers, the 'good people of Paris'.

Outside the church, rue du Jour, rue Montmartre and rue Montorgueil have retained some of this atmosphere. Although trendy boutiques are gradually taking over, they have not as yet ousted the colourful displays of food that spill into the streets (mainly on rue Montorgueil), ravishing the eye and delighting the palate. (Food shops are closed between 1 and 4pm, on Sunday afternoons and all day

Monday). At n° 6 rue Coquillère Le Pied de Cochon has preserved its Belle Epoque setting and still serves onion soup.

Retrace your steps to Porte du Jour and walk down the steps into the New Forum, in front of the rotunda of the Bourse de Commerce, of which more later. You could spend endless days at the Vidéothèque where the entire memory of Paris is preserved in video archives (both fiction and documentary), appropriately situated on the site where the organic heart of Paris once beat. To experience this vicariously, the viewer need only press a button and the city comes to life on the screen. Of late, private homes have had links installed to the Vidéothèque, sparing the owners the bother of going out, while at the same time disconnecting them from their real environment.

Next to the Vidéothèque, le Parc Océanique Cousteau is yet another world of visual illusion. In this gigantic aquarium, the video has replaced both the ocean's waters and its creatures so as to prevent the fish languishing in boredom in an artificial environment. The expensive technology entailed accounts, perhaps, for the exorbitant admission fees. The receipts, however, are used for the protection and improvement of the quality of life on our planet. The gift shop next door is run by the Cousteau Society, for the same cause. The New Forum also houses an auditorium, a snooker club and a large swimming-pool. A greenhouse with lush tropical plants helps to enhance this environment of artificial Edens.

Back in the fresh air retrace your steps to the Old Forum along rue Berger. Turn right into rue des Prouvaires which will lead you to rue Saint-Honoré. A major artery in pre-Revolutionary days, leading to the Louvre and to the Palais-Royal, the street is still lined with 17th- and 18th-century houses. For a brief period it was the sinister route of the tumbrils, on their way from the Conciergerie prison to the guillotine on Place de la Révolution (Concorde). Thus on 16 October 1793, the painter David was posted on the corner house balcony of rue des Prouvaires and 54 rue Saint-Honoré, on your right, from where he had a good view of Marie-Antoinette carried to her doom, her hands tied behind her back, a tragic sight he captured in his shattering portrait of the Queen. Turn right into rue Saint-Honoré. On the day of Marie-Antoinette's execution, the apothecary at n° 93 closed his shop Au bourdon d'Or as a sign of mourning. An earlier apothecary was trading here on 14 May 1610, when Henri IV was stabbed on the neighbouring rue de la Ferronnerie. The King was rushed here but could not be saved.

Continue to the corner of rue Vauvilliers where the first episode of the *Fronde*, the revolt against Louis XIV's mentor and Minister, Mazarin, began in August 1648. The corner house at 2 rue Sauval further down on your right, was the birth-place of Molière in 1622. The house was later demolished and replaced by the one still standing today, where Wagner stayed in 1839. At n° 115 was situated the pharmacy where the Swedish Marshal Fersen is believed to have obtained the invisible ink for his correspondence with Marie-Antoinette during her sequestration at the Conciergerie. A close friend of the royal family, Fersen had tried to help them escape. Evidence of the existence of the pharmacy goes back to 1715.

Retrace your steps and continue across rue des Halles, Place Marguerite de Navarre and walk into rue de la Ferronnerie, today a wide trendy street lined with clothes shops which cater to the young clientele of Les Halles. However, in the 13th century, this was the stronghold of the iron trade after which it was named, a narrow, congested street, cluttered with blacksmiths' and iron mongers' stalls. It was still much the same on 14 May 1610, when the royal coach was held up with the King aboard, on his way from the Louvre to the Arsenal, near the Bastille, where his minister Sully was residing. The King was absorbed in a letter when a man named Ravaillac jumped on to the coach and stabbed him. The assassin was declared mentally deranged but was nevertheless sentenced to be quartered on Place de Grève (today's Place de l'Hôtel-de-Ville), a sentence speedily carried out, thirteen days after the crime.

This was not the first murder attempt made on the life of the King; for while his early amorous adventures had gained him the affectionate nickname of le Vert Galant (the amorous youth), the charm faded as he grew older. The population resented the fact that he had dozens of bastard children scattered throughout the kingdom, which all but plunged France in civil strife yet again. Furthermore, he had expressed his intention to marry his favourite, Gabrielle - an outrage to the raison d'état. Only the latter's premature death prevented this infamy. In the kingdom of France, as Femme Ladoucette had expressed it in her letter to the Queen, one separated the sheep from the goats.

Turn left into rue Sainte-Opportune, past rue des Innocents to Place Joachim Du Bellay. Its impressive fountain, the only Renaissance fountain in Paris, was designed by Pierre Lescot and sculpted by Jean Goujon in 1549, the greatest sculptor of his time. Known as the Fontaine des Innocents, it commemorates the old cemetery of Paris, the cimetière des Innocents, that was here until 1787/8, when it was replaced by a colourful fruit, vegetable and herb market. The fountain, however, stood at the corner of rue Saint-Denis and the present rue Berger at the time, against the church of Saints-Innocents which was demolished when the cemetery closed down.

The fountain had three arcades and a balcony at the time, where prominent figures took shelter during royal processions. Indeed, it was inaugurated on 16 June 1549, on Henri II's solemn entry into the city. The market was demolished in 1855, the fountain shifted, altered and restored a couple of times, and today its dashing waters, the crowds of young people who gather around it, the street performers and the sunny terrace of Café Costes across the square, make this the most lively spot of the Forum.

La Fontaine des Innocents

FROM PLACE DU CHÂTELET TO THE SQUARE DU VERT-GALANT

The western part of Ile de la Cité is our next destination, but we shall set out from Place du Châtelet on the mainland. In its centre the fountain La Victoire, erected in 1808, commemorates Napoleon's Egyptian campaigns, following which Paris was seized by a feverish Egyptomania and set out to adorn her streets with pseudo-Egyptian art. Hence the four crouching sphynxes flanked to each side of its socle. The Théâtre du Châtelet (Théâtre Musical de Paris or TMP) and the Théâtre de la Ville on either side of the square were later additions by Davioud built in the 1860s, when the present square was opened as part of the Second Empire's scheme to rehabilitate what was hitherto a seedy slum.

To generations of French provincials between the 1860s and the 1960s, the name Châtelet was associated with the Théâtre du Châtelet, the highlight of their visit to the capital, specializing in sugary operettas such as *L'Auberge du Cheval Blanc (The White Horse Inn)*, which made their hearts throb and their eyes weep. Luis Mariano was their adulated star, sweeping the ladies off their feet with his schmaltzy *'Mexico'*. To contemporary Parisians the name Châtelet means more prosaically the inevitable central underground junction everyone is bound to hit upon occasionally. Few connect it with the ghastly prison of Le Grand Châtelet, which stood here for nearly a thousand years and was only demolished between 1802 and 1808. A plan of the Grand-Châtelet is engraved in marble on the façade of the Chambre des Notaires at 12 avenue Victoria, unnoticed by most passers-by.

In 870 Charles le Chauve erected a primitive wooden tower in front of the bridge (Pont au Change) to defend it against the Norsemen; it seems to have played its role effectively. Around the year 1130 Louis VI built a proper fortress to protect the Ile de la Cité (roughly on the site of today's TMP), and linked the two with a bridge - Le Grand Pont. The city walls erected by Philippe-Auguste in 1190 made this fortress superfluous and it therefore became the seat of the Paris courts of law, provostship and main prison. The governor of Paris (*Préfet* under the Romans, *Comte de Paris* in the early centuries of the French kingdom) was invested with military, financial and judiciary powers. At the beginning there was not always a clear-cut division between the king and the governor, and a couple of *Comtes de Paris* were also kings, notably Hugues Capet (987-996) who merged officially the two functions. In 1060, however, Philippe I delegated his powers over the city to a newly appointed *prévôt*, who, as a representative of the Crown, sat under a canopy decorated with fleurs-de-lis. Incidentally, the present heir to the French throne (in case of a restoration of the Monarchy) is also the Comte de Paris.

The prison of Le Grand-Châtelet was the most sinister prison in Paris, the mere sight of which chilled the passer-by. We shall spare the reader the details of the

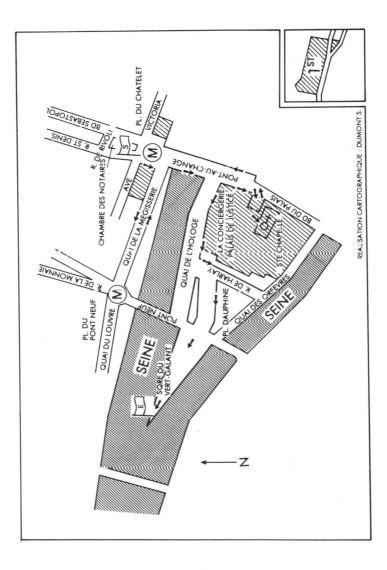

REALISATION CARTOGRAPHIQUE : DUMONT S.

perverse methods of torture afflicted upon the writhing prisoners inside, although their agony can be perceived through the lines of 16th century poet Clément Marot, who was locked up here for having eaten meat on Lent and who named his poem, significantly *L'Enfer (Hell)*.

The neighbouring streets were just as ghastly, filled with the stench, blood and screams of slaughtered animals (hence rue de la Grande-Boucherie, today's Avenue Victoria, rue de la Triperie, a small section at the beginning of rue Saint-Denis). The site of today's Théâtre de la Ville (in the 4th arrondissement) was a maze of foul alleys, bearing such evocative names as rue de la Tuerie (carnage), de l'Ecorcherie (skinning)... Another maze of dark alleys lay north of the square, the realm of cut-throats, villains and felons; even more threateningly to the authorities – a lair of political opponents and rioters, which determined Napoleon III's right-hand man, the Baron Haussmann, to reduce it to ashes. The broad artery of Boulevard Sébastopol replaced it, securing for the government forces full control over the rabble. But it was also as a health measure that Haussmann decided to clean up the area and, while he was about it, to turn it into a fashionable neighbourhood. Hence the new square and its two elegant theatres and the pompous inauguration of the Théâtre du Châtelet in 1862, with a magical performance of *Around the World in Eighty Days*. But the neighbourhood never attracted the fashionable set. Rather, it was a source of inspiration to the opening lines of T.S. Eliot's *Wasteland*.

Turn right into quai de la Mégisserie and continue to the bridge of Pont-Neuf through the bustling pet and flower market. The *quai* is named after the *mégissiers* (tanners) who had worked here for hundreds of years, slaughtering lambs and fowl and causing great ravage to the Seine. In order to remedy the situation Louis XIV ruled the tanners out of the city, transferring them to the remote banks of the Bièvre in the southern 5th and 13th arrondissements, where they caused as much damage, but out of his sight. Cross over and retrace your steps along the picturesque green bookstalls of the *bouquinistes*. These are a remnant from the time when the Pont-Neuf was a world of its own, crowded with strollers, pedlars, acrobats, prostitutes and riff-raff. When the bridge was cleaned up in the late 18th century, its hucksters spilled over to the *quais*, eventually settling into the book trade. Don't let them distract you from the impressive view of the Conciergerie across the river, even more spectacular when seen from the bridge of Pont-au-Change.

Continue along the bridge and onto Boulevard du Palais on Ile de la Cité, the border line between the 1st and 4th arrondissements. On your right, behind a beautiful 18th-century wrought-iron gate, is the Palais de Justice, on the site of the first residence of the kings of France, and before them of the Roman governors. Above all Julian who in 360 was proclaimed here emperor by his soldiers. Part of the Roman palace was still standing when the Merovingian kings (the first French dynasty) returned to the site in the 6th century. It is not quite clear whether Clovis, the founder of the dynasty, lived here, but all his followers did, throughout the 7th century. There is also evidence of the presence of the Carolingian kings (the second dynasty) - Pépin le Bref, Charlemagne, Louis le Debonnaire, Charles le Chauve. With the Norman invasion in the 9th century came total destruction, and it was not until a century later, once Hugues Capet had secured for himself and for his descendants the throne of France, that the reconstruction of the palace was envisaged. It took several generations to complete. In 1298 the extravagant Philippe le Bel ordered the reconstruction of a new palace, 'the most beautiful that anyone in France ever saw'. Its Great Hall has survived and is today's Salle des Pas Perdus on the first floor. It was a vaster palace too, which enabled him to concentrate the administration, treasury and justice of the kingdom in one place. The Salle des Gens d'Armes also dates from that time, while the Salle des Cuisines was added by Jean II le Bon around 1353. Both are open to the public but must be entered through the quai de l'Horloge.

There was no Boulevard and no wrought-iron gate at the time, but a moat and a drawbridge (some vestiges of this fortification can be seen in a tunnel at Métro Cité) secured its defence. These did not prove sufficient during the bloody revolt led by the provost of merchants, Etienne Marcel in 1357. With Jean II le Bon, the founder of the Valois dynasty, held captive in England, and reckoning on the support of the English, Etienne Marcel believed he could overthrow the monarchy. On 22 February the Dauphin (the future Charles V) was sitting with two of his counsellors when the provost's men erupted into the palace and slew his counsellors before his very eyes. The Dauphin was unhurt, but the gushing blood of the victims stained his clothes, an experience he was not going to forget. A prudent politician, deservedly known as *le Sage*, he left the palace one night stealthily by way of the river and moved to the more remote Hôtel de Saint-Pol in the Marais, meanwhile arranging for himself a residence within the safer walls of the Louvre, where he spent time from 1368 on. The kings of France never returned to the island and the premises were taken over by the the parliament, then the kingdom's court of justice.

The entrance to the Palais de Justice and la Sainte-Chapelle is through the courtyard, la Cour de Mai, so called because a May tree was planted here on May Day by members of the Basoche, the celebrated community of law students and clerks. The Basoche was founded in 1303 as a professional association, but it soon became an entertainment troupe, famous for its satirical performances. The celebrations of May Day were popular in the Middle Ages, to which testifies a painting showing the daughter of the Duc de Berry dressed in green as the Queen of May.

The arcade on the right was the entrance to the Conciergerie before 1825. During the Revolution 2,278 victims of the Revolutionary Tribunal passed through it to the jeers of delighted *tricoteuses* huddled on the perron.

The Palais de Justice is open to the public. Miles of underground corridors join the cells to the judges' offices, to Commissaire Maigret's memorable PJ (headquarters) on quai des Orfèvres, and also to the courtrooms. You can visit the Salle des Pas Perdus, where bustling lawyers in their black robes might remind you of the world of justice as depictedd by cartoonist Honoré Daumier. It dates from the 1870s, the previous one having been burnt down during the *Commune*.

In the Middle Ages, when this was the Great Hall of the palace, it consisted of two naves separated by eight pillars. It was a colourful hall, with a black-and-white chequered floor and polychrome walls. Sumptuous, Gargantuan meals were served on a huge marble table, which was also used as a stage for mystery plays, farces and other entertainments in vogue. Nobody seemed to mind the horrific skins of ferocious animals hanging from the vaulted ceilings; nor the barbaric goings-on literally next door, in the adjoining prison of the Conciergerie. The statues of the kings of France stood against the pillars, gloriously painted in azure and gold - 58 in all by 1618, when a fire burnt down the hall with all its contents. Even after the monarchy had deserted the palace, each new king had his statue added to its predecessors, the last one being Henri III, who used the last available space. The Great Hall led to the parliament hall, also built by Philippe le Bel. In 1502 Fra Giocondo embellished it with a magnificent coffered ceiling which disappeared during the Revolution, when the Revolutionary Tribunal sat here. Today this is the first chamber of the civil tribunal, restored roughly to its original aspect, without Giocondo's ceiling, however, and reduced in size.

The Sainte-Chapelle must be the highlight of this walk. So great is its aura that it has completely overshadowed the existence of an earlier royal chapel, la Chapelle Saint-Michel, which was built in the 12th century by Louis VII and where Philippe-Auguste was baptized. It was still standing in 1781 and has been commemorated since across the river, on the Left Bank: the Boulevard, Place, bridge, quai and fountain of Saint-Michel are all named after it. Admittedly, it was but a rudimentary rectangular structure with a flat roof, no match for the bejewelled Sainte-Chapelle, built by Saint Louis to house a piece of the Holy Cross and the Crown of Thorns. He had bought them from Baudouin II, the last Emperor of Constantinople, who was in desperate need of funds to defend his city. The chapel was therefore designed to have the light, lacy aspect of a reliquary. The result was stunningly beyond expectation. It took its architect (Pierre de Montreuil or, perhaps, Jean de Chelles) barely five years to build a masterpiece of harmonious proportions, delicate grace and equilibrium never attained before.

Although the silver and gold reliquary containing the crown of thorns was dispatched to the Mint during the Revolution, its contents (whether genuine or not) have miraculously survived and are now kept at Notre-Dame. Is it that even the standard-bearers of the Revolutionary ideal did not dare to tamper with the most holy of Christian symbols? The chapel was not shown the same consideration and was used first to store flour, then as a depot for the court house archives; by which time it was so dilapidated that it was put on the market for sale and demolition. In 1847 it still bore an inscription which read: 'National property, for sale'. Fortunately, some enlightened souls, aware of the disastrous crime about to be committed against both art and history, called upon Viollet-le-Duc, Lassus and other artists to restore the church to its ancient beauty. In 1853 Lassus erected a new spire preserving the style of its 17th-century predecessor, demolished by a fire. This is the fifth spire of the Sainte-Chapelle. The stained-glass windows were likewise restored in the last century, 720 of the 1,134 original scenes having been preserved: the result is magical, all the more to be cherished when one realizes that on 24 May 1871, barely four years after the completion of the restoration, the *Communards* had poured petrol over the Sainte-Chapelle, and only failed to set it on fire for lack of time. Today the magical beauty of the Sainte-Chapelle is enhanced at night, when chamber music concerts are held by candlelight.

Retrace your steps and turn left into the quai de l'Horloge, named after its clock tower. The clock was ordered by Charles V around the year 1371 and is the oldest clock in the capital. It was restored by Henri III, as may be deduced from its Latin inscription, 'He who already gave him two crowns will give him a third one' (Henri III was King of France and Poland; the third crown refers to heaven) and from the King's monogram.

At n° 1 quai de l'Horloge is the entrance to the Conciergerie. Originally the seat of the governor of the King's palace - hence its name - it became a prison in 1391 and remained so until 1914. Not unlike the modern *concierge* who supplements his income at New Year and many other such occasions, the Palace *concierge* supplemented his thanks to the vendors who leased the many shops then located within the Palace walls. In the 15th century the passer-by could still hear the screams of tortured prisoners in the *Tour Bonbec* (the most westerly one). During its restoration in 1828, two oubliettes, communicating with the river and spiked with iron points, were found in its basement: needless to dwell on the fate of the prisoners. The name *bon-bec* ('prate' in the Middle Ages) probably alluded to the interrogations that took place on the ground floor: a varied spectrum of torture methods was devised to make the victim confess and denounce his accomplices.

Among the notorious prisoners of the Conciergerie in later years were Ravaillac, the assassin of Henri IV; the mass poisoner La Marquise de Brinvilliers (1630-1676), who had eliminated the better part of her numerous household; and

Cartouche (1693-1721), the most notorious bandit of his age, the terror of Paris. In order to be admitted into his prestigious gang one had to be proved an expert cutpurse. Candidates were made to practise on dummies covered with little bells, until they could strip them without the slightest tinkling. All three prisoners awaited execution at the Conciergerie.

During the Revolution the Conciergerie boasted an impressive list of illustrious prisoners awaiting their deaths: Madame Roland, who had supported the Revolution but sided with the *Girondins* at the wrong time; Marie-Antoinette, who occupied a dreary cell from 2 August to 16 October 1793, when she was taken to the guillotine on Place de la Révolution (Concorde); later Danton, Robespierre and Saint-Just were detained here in their turn, Danton and Robespierre occupying the cells adjacent to the queen's. Today one visits the Conciergerie for the sake of French history, but the impressive Gothic halls and kitchen fire-places deserve to be visited for their architectural merit.

North of these halls was located a section of the prison leading to the dark prison cells, known as *'rue de Paris'*, so named after the Great Executioner, Monsieur de Paris. This post was held by seven successive generations of the Sanson family, from 1688 to 1847, transmitted from father to son. Shortly before the Revolution Louis XVI had set his heart on improving their plight and granted Charles-Henri Sanson an annual fee of 16,000 pounds plus 2,000 crowns for the upkeep of the scaffold and pillory, undoubting he would become his own executioner! Being a royalist, Charles-Henri had no desire to carry out that deed. On 15 August 1792 he had been arrested as 'the despot's employee'; with each execution he would be dispatched to Place du Carrousel, where the guillotine was then erected, and afterwards would be taken back to his cell. At first, executions were few, but when the guillotine began to work at full swing and his expert hand could not be dispensed with, he was released. However, he retired soon after he had executed his sovereign. His son Henri held the position during the Terror, and throughout the following precarious regimes, until 1840, well into the reign of Louis-Philippe. It seemed extraordinary to the film-maker Jean Renoir, that his own grandfather (the painter's father) should have known Henri's chief assistant during the Terror, a man who had lived at the time of periwigs and breeches and who "may have passed Voltaire and Benjamin Franklin in the street, heard Mozart play the harpsichord, and attended performances of Monsieur Beaumarchais!" Old Renoir met the chief assistant in 1845, the year the family had moved up to Paris from Limoges, and when the last Sanson held the position. The two men befriended each other – as a tailor, Renoir's father shared with the latter the pleasure of doing a good job. "After all, they were two good workmen: one cut out cloth, the other cut off heads just as consciously."

As you come out, continue along quai de l'Horloge and take the first turn to the left, rue de Harlay. You will reach the triangular Place Dauphine, one of Paris's romantic gems. Created by Henri IV in 1607 in honour of his son the Dauphin and future Louis XIII, it was enclosed on all sides by arcaded brick-and-stone houses, similarly to its contemporary Place des Vosges in the Marais. Bankers and tradesmen could carry on their negotiations undisturbed, on a site conveniently located only a few steps away from the Louvre. In the 18th century talented young artists, unable as yet to exhibit in the official *Salons*, were given an opportunity to hold an annual exhibition here. Today both business transactions and the art trade have moved to other parts and Place Dauphine is a haven of peace surrounded by small boutiques and pretty eating-places, a provincial nest in the heart of Paris. The restaurant *Paul* perpetuates this atmosphere, both on its terrace in fine weather and indoors otherwise. Its food is succulent, though not inexpensive. From Place Dauphine, do not omit to cross the Pont-Neuf for a glimpse of the lovely garden at the tip of the island, le Square du Vert-Galant, just below the Vert-Galant's equestrian statue. On warm days the garden is popular with romantic lovers, on hot days it is invaded by too many sunbathers. In any kind of weather the view of the Hôtel de la Monnaie (the Mint) and the dome of the Institut de France on the left, the Louvre on the right, and the Pont-des-Arts ahead, is unforgettable. By night it is an enchantment, like Place Dauphine itself, lit up by its lamp-posts like a shining diamond. No wonder such Parisians as Simone Signoret and Yves Montand chose to make it their home.

FROM THE SAMARITAINE TO THE PALAIS-ROYAL

The exploration of the central part of the arrondissement will begin at the Samaritaine department store, opposite the Pont-Neuf. To many greying Parisians the store is associated with its deliberately eccentric commercials, notably the one starring King Kong storming the shop through its top-floor windows. Its celebrated catch-phrase *On trouve tout à la Samaritaine* ('One can find everything at the Samaritaine') has recently been changed into *On trouve Tout-Paris à la Samaritaine*, aiming to add a 'showbiz' touch to a store whose shoppers are notoriously provincial and outdated. But the Samaritaine is well worth a visit for the spectacular view from its terrace and restaurant, as well as for its Art Nouveau and Art Deco decorations.

When Ernest Cognacq, a former draper's assistant at La Rochelle, first set up shop on rue du Pont-Neuf in 1867, he called it *La Samaritaine* in memory of the old water pump situated at the Pont-Neuf till the early 19th century. Thirty years later he commissioned Frantz Jourdain to put up a building to house a full-size department store, a structure of steel and glass in keeping with the progressive spirit of the time. In 1926 Franz Jourdain and Henri Sauvage built the façade on the quai du Louvre, one of the best examples of Art Deco in Paris. In 1930 a new building was added on the corner of rue de Rivoli and rue Boucher, boasting an interesting frieze around it and an impressive staircase inside. All these bear witness to the golden age of department stores, which enabled modest men of genius to build small empires within a few decades. With the help of his dynamic wife, Louise Jay, also a draper's assistant, from rue Rambuteau, Cognacq used his meteoric success to build up a fabulous art collection, now housed in the Musée Cognacq-Jay in the Marais.

Walk along quai du Louvre and turn right into Place du Louvre. On your right are the church of Saint-Germain-l'Auxerrois and the Mairie of the 1st arrondissement. On 24 August 1572, at the stroke of midnight, began one of the bloodiest pages in French history: the massacre of Saint-Bartholomew, ordered by Charles IX but instigated by his mother Catherine de Medici, during which 3,000 Protestants perished. Of the three bells that had signalled the onset of the carnage - Marie, Germain and Vincent, only Marie has survived. It dates from 1527 and is one of the oldest bells in Paris.

Saint-Germain-l'Auxerrois was the royal parish church, just opposite the Louvre, and the royal pew can still be seen inside. When Catherine de Medici was told by her astrologer, Ruggieri, that she would die 'by Saint-Germain', she moved out of the Palais des Tuileries, her newly built residence west of the Louvre, so as to attend mass elsewhere. She settled in the Hôtel de Soissons, on the site of the present Bourse de Commerce, the round building on the western edge of the Forum des Halles, adjoining the column from where Ruggieri scrutinized the stars, which still stands. The queen never returned to her residence at Saint-Germain-en-Laye either, but there is no escaping one's destiny: while in Blois in the Loire Valley, some 16 years later, she took ill, never to recover. A young priest was called to her bedside on 15 January 1589 to give her the last sacrament. The Queen asked his name: "Julien de Saint-Germain," replied the holy stranger.

The original Saint Germain, the Bishop of Auxerre in Burgundy in the 6th century, is said to have journeyed all the way to England to combat heresy. At the end of the 7th century a primitive church was in all likelihood erected on this site, where the Saint had allegedly performed some extraordinary deed. It was probably demolished during the Norman invasions of the 9th century, like all the other churches of Paris. A Merovingian cemetery discovered near by in the 19th century, supports this assumption. The present church was built in the 12th and 13th centuries and the Saint's supposedly preserved relics were laid within. Little is left of this church, greatly altered over the years, particularly in the 18th century. During the Revolution, it became the Temple de la Reconnaissance and after the Revolution was used for storing fodder!

Napoleon's arrival threatened to be more fatal than the Revolution: among his

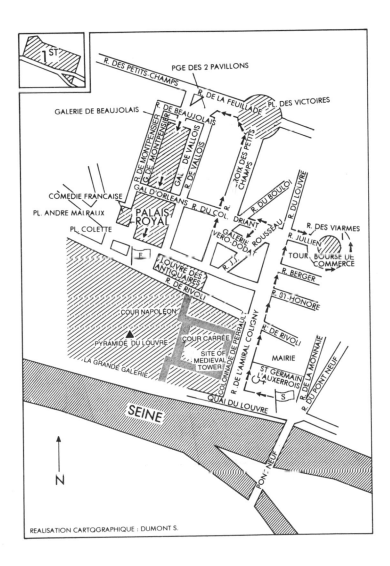

REALISATION CARTOGRAPHIQUE : DUMONT S.

spectacular projects was a regal thoroughfare from the Louvre to Place de la Bastille and on to Place de la Nation. This would have opened a new vista from the Louvre with an impregnable view of the Elephant of the Bastille, an extravagant, colossal statue he had intended for Place de la Bastille, the model of which actually stood on the site of the present Opera House until 1847. Napoleon's project would have entailed the demolition of the church, which fortunately he did not have the time to do, but in 1831 there was question once more of demolishing it and only the relentless efforts of the outraged writer Chateaubriand prevented this disastrous outcome. Lassus and Baltard were called upon to undertake its restoration and give it its present aspect. Inside can still be seen the 14th-century chapel, the 15th-century wooden polychrome triptych and stained-glass windows, the early 16th-century Flemish retable, the 17th-century organ case (brought over from the Sainte-Chapelle) and the 18th-century wrought iron grille around the choir. In front of it are two 15th-century polychrome statues of Saint Germain and Saint Vincent, while a 13th-century statue of Saint Germain can be seen in the chapel.

The adjacent Mairie of the 1st arrondissement is a mere pastiche, dating from the Second Empire, designed to maintain the architectural unity of the place. The flamboyant belfry tower, the work of Ballu (1860), had no other object than to fill up the unsightly gap between the two edifices.

Continue along rue du Louvre beyond rue de Rivoli. On your right is the Bourse de Commerce first built by Louis XVI for the trade of corn, flour and sugar and known as La Halle au Blé. The present rotunda dates only from 1889. The elegant buildings that line the northern curve of the circular rue des Viarmes deserve special mention. The tower of Catherine de Medici's residence was sculpted with exquisite grace, as you can surmise from what has survived. Ruggieri used the tower until the end of his life, and despite his unfavourable predictions, he never fell into disgrace. Before bringing the Queen unpleasant news about her own fate, he had already predicted her husband's mortal injury in single combat. Indeed, Henri II was mortally injured by Montgomery during a friendly tournament.

Cross Place des Ecus on your left and turn left into rue J.J. Rousseau. The famous philosopher lived on the site of today's n°s 52-54. N° 19 opens on to a picturesque outdated arcade, overlooked by most contemporaries: la Galerie Véro-Dodat which will carry you nearly two centuries back. Its beautiful glass ceiling, its black-and-white chequered floor, its mahogany panelling, its brass framings and handles served as backdrop to the promenade of fair ladies in crinolines and gentlemen in tail-coats and top hats, all the fashionable set who hastened to see this new attraction when it opened in 1826. The arcade's gas lights created quite a sensation and prices of property rocketed. But somehow,

Messieurs Verot and Dodat, the two *charcutiers* (pork butchers) who had built the arcade, went bankrupt. In 1836 the celebrated actress Rachel moved to the 3rd floor of n° 38. The ground floor of the house was occupied by the famous satirical paper *Charivari*, to which Daumier contributed his cartoons. It was in the *Charivari* that the word 'Impressionist' was first coined by a journalist called Leroy. He had borrowed it from Monet's painting *Impression, soleil levant* and applied it derogatorily to the entire group of painters who were striving in vain to gain recognition from a stuffy, conformist public that considered them mentally deranged. With the age of the stagecoach, the Messageries Générales opened premises on rue du Bouloi, on the other side of the arcade. From then on, the place became a convenient shortcut for travellers and its magical spell was broken. The *beau-monde* migrated elsewhere. What is left is an oasis of nostalgia, charmingly antiquated shops, among them Robert Capia at n° 26, a world-renowned dealer in antique dolls.

Turn right into rue Croix-des-Petits-Champs with the colossal building of the Banque de France on your left. Founded in 1800 by a group of bankers on Napoleon's initiative, in 1812 the bank moved to the premises of the sumptuous Hôtel de la Vrillière, the home Mansart had built in 1635 for the Marquis de la Vrillière. In 1713 the Comte de Toulouse, the legitimized son of Louis XIV and of Madame de Montespan, bought it and totally transformed it, meanwhile adding the stunning 50-metre long Galerie Dorée, which many prefer to the one in Versailles. Unfortunately, this magnificent example of French early 18th-century interior decoration is rarely open to the public. The premises were largely restored between 1870 and 1875 and only the original façade at n°s 1-3 rue Vrillière has survived. The bank also owns a fabulous collection of 18th-century paintings, highlighted by Fragonard's famous *La Fête à Saint-Cloud*, but these too are usually closed to the public.

Ahead is the Place des Victoires, more famous today for its designer shops than for the victories of the Sun King it commemorates. François d'Aubusson, Maréchal and Duc de La Feuillade, idolized his King and decided to put up a statue in his honour on his own property and at his own expense. The statue was all covered with gold and adorned with His Majesty's court cloak. Its head was disproportionately large, overpowering the rest of the body and decorated with a laurel wreath. On the pedestal, at his feet, four chained women embodied dramatically the King's trampled enemies – Spain, Holland, Germany and Franche-Comté. This done, the preposterous Maréchal proceeded to create a setting worthy of the object of his worship, to which end he called upon the genius of Jules Hardouin-Mansart. The result was the elegant Place des Victoires, whose graceful and harmonious architecture has only partly been preserved. La Feuillade, by then the laughing stock of Paris, is said to have relieved the King when he finally gave up the ghost! The statue was naturally melted down during the Revolution, but was replaced by another one during the Restoration. This time the sculptor Bosio seated the Sun King on a caracoling horse, dressed him up as a Roman emperor, but kept his wig! This is the statue now standing in the centre of Place des Victoires. During Napoleon's Consulate a statue to the memory of General Desaix stood in its place, representing the hero of the battle of Marengo in his natural attire, emulating the heroes of ancient times. But the population of Paris was shocked by such indecent exposure and a fence was soon set up around the General to keep him out of view.

Although designer Kenzo was not the first in his trade to have taken up residence here, his migration in 1976 signalled the rejuvenation of the area, its transformation into the stronghold of contemporary-minded *créateurs*, as opposed to the traditional *couturiers*. A new age was inaugurated, when a Westernized Japanese look was to meet with San Franciscan ecological freedom expressed by *Esprit*; when Chevignon betrayed his native French origins and imprinted Wild West designs on his celebrated bombers; and when Thierry Mugler created his "destructured" glamorous designs, determinedly contemporary, yet French nonetheless. Castelbajac, Ventilo… a fresh breeze was blowing from across the Atlantic which resulted in spacious, airy, luminous premises, lined with wooden parquets and wall panelling, discarding the muffled, cramped, padded atmosphere of the old continent.

Rue La Feuillade, west of Place des Victoires, continues into rue des Petits-Champs. It will take you to rue de Beaujolais, by way of Passage des Pavillons on your left, a charming spot. Turn left on rue de Beaujolais and left again to the Galerie de Beaujolais, leading to the gardens of Palais-Royal. You will enter a world of exquisite tranquillity where time has come to a standstill, a sleepy arcaded enclosure, shut off from the noisy streets around and graced with a Venetian touch. Despite the playful children and the chatty diners of an outdoor restaurant, a quiet secluded atmosphere prevails. Even Buren's striped columns, which jar with the surrounding architecture and stone, and draw here weekend crowds, do not awaken it from its provincial drowsiness.

And yet, between 1784 and 1830 this was the bustling centre of both intellectual and dissolute Paris, lined with cafés and restaurants as well as game-houses and brothels. The Mecca of prostitution, to which whores and courtesans came from all over Paris *'faire le Palais'*, as the saying went. Witness Casanova, who rushed here on his arrival in Paris.

When the palace was built for Richelieu it was known as le Palais-Cardinal. Richelieu bequeathed it to Louis XIII and after the latter's death the royal family moved in. It was conveniently situated close to Mazarin's home on the neigh-bouring rue Neuve-des-Petits-Champs. To facilitate his rendezvous with Anne of Austria, a door was fitted into the wall that surrounded the palace. It proved handy in 1650, during the princely revolt of the *Fronde*, when the Queen and her two sons, the future Louis XIV and Philippe d'Orléans, escaped to Saint-Germain-en-Laye. Later Henrietta of France, the widow of Charles I of England, came to live here with her daughter, Henrietta of England, who later married Philippe d'Orléans. She died in 1661 and Philippe d'Orléans married the princess Palatine by whom he had one son, another Philippe Duc d'Orléans, who would become the celebrated *Régent* after the death of Louis XIV in 1715. He ruled over Paris till 1723, when Louis XV, aged 13 began to rule in effect. It was during the Regent's light-hearted reign that the Palais-Royal became notorious for its *'soupers'* - veritable bacchanalia. His grandson Philippe, the Fifth Duc d'Orléans and father of the future King Louis-Philippe, was in deep debt when he took over the Palais-Royal. He therefore built the arcades and their shops which he rented out, turning the establishment into a profitable business. Gambling houses and brothels opened up too, to ensure substantial profits. The Duke's new line of activities was not to the taste of Louis XVI: "Cousin," he said disdainfully, "you have turned shop-keeper and no doubt we shall see you only on Sundays." Philippe d'Orléans would have his revenge: in 1793, having sided with the Revo-lution, he became member of the Convention under the name of Philippe Egalité and voted for the death of his royal cousin (whom some claim he had hoped to replace). The guillotine, however, took charge of him too, only a few months later.

The newly converted Palais-Royal was opened in 1784 to the satisfaction of all. Among its shops was a cutlery establishment at n° 177 Galerie de Valois, which belonged to Monsieur Badin. Here on 13 July 1793 Charlotte Corday bought the knife with which she stabbed Marat in his bathtub the same day.

But the Palais-Royal was also the intellectual centre of the capital, studded with cafés where such prominent figures as Diderot used to sup and where dangerous new ideas were in progress. Diderot's fictitious, beggarly, parasitical, yet so worldly *Neveu de Rameau* tells us that the celebrated café La Régence (on the site of the present n° 161 rue Saint-Honoré) was the Mecca of chess players. On wet days, when he could not meditate on one of the benches in the garden, the musi-cian Rameau's nephew would step into La Régence and watch a good game of chess. The chessboards were rented by the hour and cost more at night when a candle had to be fixed on either side. "Paris is the place in the world, and the Café de la Régence the place in Paris where the game is best played," he tells us. Now this was no fiction. In fact, François André Danican-Philidor, composer and co-founder of the Opéra-Comique, and also world chess champion, would take on the world's best chess players simultaneously at La Régence, and beat them one by one mercilessly. His *Analyse du jeu des échecs* that he published in London when aged only 22, remains a classic. Diderot's preference, however, went to Légal 'the deep', as he expressed it via his hero. Philidor 'the subtle' annoyed him with his chess activities. He thought he should develop his musical talent rather than devote his time to simultaneous blind games, out of vainglory, "pushing little wooden pieces on a chessboard," as he told him bluntly. In 1794 Napoleon, an excellent chess player too, shared a wretched existence between a dump of a hotel in today's rue d'Aboukir (in the 2nd arr.), and Café de La Régence where he spent hours moving pieces on a chessboard, rehearsing for the strategic showdown soon to come.

During the Restoration of the monarchy that followed Napoleon's downfall, the Palais-Royal became the scene of bellicose duels. Having fought the rest of Europe, the French now set about killing each other off wholeheartedly. The Monarchists assembled in the Café de Valois, the Bonapartists and the Liberals in the Café Lemblin. The slightest provocation ended up with a fatal confrontation. An inhabitant of rue de Montpensier related how between the years 1815 and 1820 he had been woken up over 20 times by the groaning victims of these political clashes. In Paris it needn't be only politics that triggers passionate, violent arguments. At Le Caveau the heated conversations and verbal sparring centred around music and gave way to impetuous confrontations between the partisans of the Italian Piccini and those of the German Gluck!

However quarrelsome a Frenchman may be, his palate and stomach will always bring him back to line, and good fare was to be found in plenty at the Palais-Royal. Le Café de Chartres, at 79/82 Galerie de Beaujolais, another Monarchist stronghold, served a set menu of *vermicelle et poitrine de mouton aux haricots.* Today, its descendant Le Grand Véfour has abandoned homely fare: with its wealth of decorations and choice dishes it is one of the best restaurants in the capital, and as such was targeted by Leftists to be blown up in December 1983. At n° 83 Le Véry created a sensation when it first opened, being the first Parisian establishment to offer meals at fixed prices, high enough nonetheless to ensure a select clientele. Among them was the illustrious painter Fragonard, who actually expired here while savouring a sorbet.

In 1830 the 'bourgeois' king Louis-Philippe ascended the throne. A 'middle-class' puritan, he decided to close down this seat of vice (and of political threat: after all, the French Revolution had also been plotted here). Some Parisians held on to the place for another generation, and at the time of Balzac it was still a popular promenade where art and vice mingled. The more fashionable Parisians had migrated to the new axis of pleasure, les Grands Boulevards, further north; some frequented both. By the time Colette was living at 9 rue de Beaujolais, and Jean

Cocteau at 36 rue de Montpensier, the Palais-Royal had become a closed world and assumed its present aspect of outdated serenity, as described by Colette: "In the mornings we went out for a breath of fresh air - cat, bulldog and me - on the garden chairs, uncomfortable armchairs of venerable age [...] I like to think that a magic spell preserves, at Palais-Royal, everything that collapses and lasts, everything that crumbles and doesn't alter." She goes on to describe its nameless, silent citizens who followed a code of mysterious mutual courtesy: the elderly lady leaning on her stick, the gentleman cultivating little cacti on his window sill, the other gentleman in straw slippers on his early morning walk, or the earnest little boy who might one day lay a marble in the palm of your hand. There was also a venerable lady who might one day read out to you the ode she had written to Victor Hugo. Jean Cocteau was more than just a neighbour, even though he dropped in on Colette *'en voisin'*. He was a friend and admirer who called her 'an ink fountain'. Today's arcades are as peaceful as then, lined with ravishing outdated shops, and the lovely gardens are still an oasis in the heart of a congested city, *"La campagne en plein centre de Paris,"* to quote Cocteau once more.

Leave the gardens through the Cour d'Honneur on its southern edge. On your right is the home of the prestigious Comédie-Française, built between 1786 and 1790 by Victor Louis, the architect of the famous theatre of Bordeaux. Originally destined to accommodate the opera, various other troupes followed before the Comédiens-Français took over in 1799. Their inauguration performance on 30 May 1799 was a double bill of *Le Cid* and *L'Ecole des Maris*, starring the great Talma and the adulated Mlle Mars. At present the Comédie-Française has lost much of its glory and few productions merit your attendance (even if susceptible locals claim to the contrary), except for the experience of being seated in these magnificent historic premises where some traditions have been kept alive – the baton beats announcing the curtain rise, the declamation of the *Marseillaise* on Bastille Day, and the celebration of Molière's death every February. Despite its conservative inclinations, the Comédie-Française has of late followed modern trends and opened a shop in the entrance hall where reference books and attractive gifts are to be found.

In the 17th century, another theatre stood on the corner of rue de Valois and rue Saint-Honoré, built by Richelieu for his palace and named Le Petit Cardinal. It was here that at 10 pm on 17 February 1673 Molière was acting the part of Argan, *le Malade Imaginaire*, when he collapsed on the stage and died of a heart attack.

You will have now reached Place Colette and the adjacent Place André Malraux, a horrendously congested spot during the day, a blissful enchantment by night, when the elegant square is highlighted by its romantic street lamps and its sparkling fountain. In the distance, at the other end of the Avenue de l'Opéra, Charles Garnier's floodlit Opera House scintillates in all its splendour, beguiling you into forgetting that its golden age has long vanished.

Before winding up, we wish to point out that at n° 2 Place du Palais-Royal, east of Place Colette now stands a compound of expensive antique shops known as Le Louvre des Antiquaires. It has replaced the outdated Louvre department store, a flourishing business in the last century, a model for Emile Zola's novel *Au Bonheur des Dames*. When the Louvre des Antiquaires opened in 1978, at a time of economic optimism, its rash, sanguine promoters meant it to become the world's largest such centre. The 250 dealers who opened up shop at this prestigious spot had anticipated bustling business, not reckoning on the recession in years to come: the smoked glass, lacquered painting and parquets diffuse a muffled atmosphere of luxury, but strollers are few and far between.

FROM THE LOUVRE WESTWARDS

The Louvre is an exploration in itself, beyond the scope of this walk. Head for Pei's world-renowned Pyramid in the centre of Cour Napoléon, today's main entrance to the museum. The fact that this hypercontemporary, airy structure is the gateway to what used to be nearly a millennium ago a massive stronghold exemplifies the eternal continuity of Paris throughout ceaseless change.

The original Louvre was just the keep of the stronghold built by Philippe-Auguste in 1190, on the site of the present Cour Carrée. The name 'Louvre' is believed to have derived from *Lupara* or *Lupera*, because packs of wolves lurked here. The kings of France kept their treasures in this tower, as specified in Louis VIII's will, who left to his son, Louis IX, all the gold and silver kept 'in our tower in Paris near Saint-Thomas'.

When the Kings of France came to live here, they each left their stamp on the palace. Whereas Charles V embellished the defensive Gothic construction, François I, the enlightened Renaissance King, razed it to the ground and started out its transformation into a Renaissance palace, on the south west corner of the Cour Carrée. Henri II and III added the two lateral wings and Catherine de Medici, finding it small and lacking in comfort, commissioned the great architect, Philibert Delorme, to build her a new palace further west, perpendicularly to the Seine. It was named the Palais des Tuileries after the two tile factories (*tuile*, 'tile') on the site of today's gardens. Henri IV completed it and joined it to the Louvre by way of the 470-metre-long Galerie du Bord de l'Eau along the river. The Pavillon de Flore joined the two. (The Pavillon Marsant on its northern edge dates from Louis XIV.) The colossal monument expanded further in 1673, when Claude Perrault, the brother of the story-teller Charles (*Sleeping Beauty*) built the

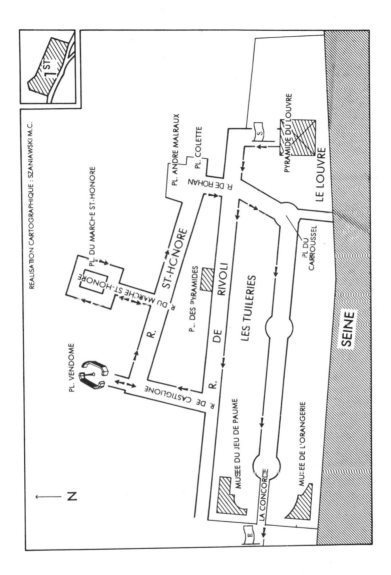

Galerie d'Apollon and its spectacular grand colonnade. But with the departure of Louis XIV for Versailles in 1682 works came to a halt and only picked up again when Napoleon settled at the Tuileries and built a new wing, l'aile de Rohan, north of the Carrousel Gardens.

It was Napoléon III who, at last, completed this gigantic, unsurpassable monument, by extending his uncle's northern wing to the east (l'aile Richelieu) and joining the Louvre and the Palais des Tuileries. But barely was the feat carried out than Napoleon III was ousted. Soon Paris would be ignited by the bloody fury of the *Commune*: a year after the completion of the ultimate Grand Louvre, the Palais des Tuileries was aflame, and a three-century-old project had vanished into thin air never to be undertaken again.

Parallel to its residential function, the artistic role of the Louvre goes back to the Middle Ages, and its transformation into a museum is no mere historical coincidence. It was in the Louvre that Charles V's library was situated, the first attempt in France at building up a collection of man's works. It was shortlived, being dispersed during the Hundred Years' War, but it had created a need for cultural preservation and a love of art which would flourish with the advent of the Renaissance kings, particularly François I and Henri IV, followed later by Louis XIII and Louis XIV. By opening the Galerie du Bord de l'Eau to artists, Henri IV strengthened the ties between the Louvre and the arts, a tradition kept up by Louis XIV, who opened the Louvre to an increasing number of artists. it was a great honour to live in the Louvre, although many who were granted this privilege were no more than flattering parasites.

On 10 August 1793 the Revolutionary authorities converted the Louvre into a national museum. The monarchy had been abolished, Louis XVI had been dispatched to another world and his wife awaited the same fate at the Conciergerie. Short of demolishing it, it seemed the only solution. The Louvre had been a 'white elephant' since the departure of the court to Versailles, and already in 1750 the Cardinal Dubois had suggested its demolition in order to fill the coffers of a spendthrift state. The new museum profited amply from Napoleon's campaigns, the Emperor having filled it with the cultural heritage he had plundered from his conquered bleeding lands, meanwhile renaming it le Musée Napoléon, a name which did not outlive his ephemeral reign. In 1848, in keeping with the new revolutionary spirit, the museum was renamed Le Palais du Peuple.

For all its artistic wealth, the Louvre was ageing, the more so because of its colossal dimensions. The exquisite *Mona Lisa*, the highlight of many an organized tour to Paris in the 1950s and 1960s, could not compete with the pop-art brightly coloured pipes of the Centre Georges Pompidou when it opened in 1976 in the 4th arrondissement. It was quite different on the eve of World War I, when her robbery constituted a national catastrophe, overshadowing all the debates about the imminent declaration of war. On her return journey to Paris from Italy, where she had been concealed by her Italian abductor, she was greeted with the honours of a head of state: at every station a guard of honour was formed to salute her.

The Louvre craved a face-lift and for new blood. Urged initially by the dynamic Minister of Culture, André Malraux, the archaeological excavation of the medieval Louvre began in 1983 as the first step of a vast enterprise. President François Mitterand, a lover of *'grands projets'* (read building projects), continued with the scheme wholeheartedly. Undoubtedly, the Grand Louvre has been his most successful enterprise, the most prestigious and the least disputed. Overall reconstruction was imperative, if its number of visitors was to be substantially increased. Its new underground entrance in the centre of the Cour Napoléon provided an ingenious solution, allowing for ample space. Pei's glass Pyramid was to top it, perfect in proportions (21m high by 34 wide), a scintillating diamond by night. Not everyone hails it: some dismiss it as too avant-garde; others, while not condemning the Pyramid, object to its location, arguing that the historic site should not have been tampered with. Its supporters, on the other hand, contend that it blends harmoniously into the old environment, thanks to its geometrical starkness and transparency. However, there is no denying the metal framework that supports it inevitably obstructs the view of the façades of the Cour Napoléon.

The inauguration of the new Louvre was enthusiastically acclaimed and 5 million visitors swarmed into it within the first six months of its opening, in April 1989, beating all records. Apart from the sensational Pyramid, they could now see - for the first time since the reign of François I - vestiges of the medieval Louvre, which only the 14th-century illuminated manuscript, the Duc de Berry's Book of Hours, *Très Riches Heures du duc de Berry*, had brought to our attention occasionally. In order to expand its exhibition space further, the Ministry of Finance, hitherto located in the Richelieu wing, was transferred to new premises at Bercy (in the 12th arr.), and feverish work began to have it ready in time for for the bicentennial of the Museum, in 1993. When the Richelieu wing opened its doors to the astounded public and officials of France in November 1993, the ambitious project of the Grand Louvre had been completed to everyone's satisfaction. To celebrate the event the museum opened to the public free of charge the following Sunday (the kings of yore on such occasions filled the fountains of Paris with wine). The people of Paris bit at the bait and spent the afternoon queueing up in the bitter cold air of a November day. Those near the end of the queue were refused admission and a mild riot - French-style - ensued. But this was no time for squabbling and free admission was conceded them again the next Sunday.

Today's Louvre is also a business venture as we found out some time later. Making our way underground, the transparent pyramid above our head displaying an ever-changing silver-grey sky, we proceeded in the direction of the Carrousel with enthusiastic anticipation to see Pei's more recent reversed Pyramid, when we discovered that just beyond it lay yet another shopping arcade! This had been cautiously played down during the inaugurational publicity campaign. That the world of *haute couture* should transfer its fashion shows here from the makeshift structures on Cour Napoléon only seemed right, the area having been the birthplace of *haute couture* in the last century. But a shopping arcade that communicates directly with the Louvre is a different matter. "One day a MacDonald's will open under Notre-Dame," someone next to me remarked.

Leave the Louvre through the Pyramid, turn right, then left into rue de Rivoli, the second longest street in Paris. At n° 107/9 the Musée d'Arts Décoratifs and the Musée de la Mode often organize interesting exhibitions. Of late the Musée de l'Affiche has moved here from the 10th arrondissement. Its exciting collection of old posters delights nostalgic enthusiasts. Walk on to Place des Pyramides, named after Napoleon's 1798 victorious campaign in Egypt. Fremiet's statue of Jeanne d'Arc stands in its centre, although historically it should have been a little further east: at 161 rue Saint-Honoré stood Charles V's Porte Saint-Honoré, where the Maiden arrived on 8 September 1429 from the village of Monceaulx (Monceau now in the 17th arr.), at the head of 12,000 men, hoping to take the city. Injured in action, she had to retreat. Her statue on Place des Pyramides became a shrine for all endowed with patriotic fervour and has been singled out too by today's French extreme-right movements - royalists, ultra-traditionalists, ultra-Catholics and ultra-nationalists, Le Pen's heterogeneous followers, including ex-communists and ex-socialists, who under the name of Front National, have determined to keep France 'clean and French'; for which aim they gather here every 1st of May, while dwindling numbers of 'Reds' march up between the République, the Bastille and Nation in eastern, proletarian Paris.

The famous arcades of rue de Rivoli were designed by Napoleon's prominent architects, Percier and Fontaine. Elegant shops followed to cater predominantly to the wealthy British clientele of the neighbouring hotels, in the vicinity of the fashionable Tuileries Gardens. A few have managed to hold out and to resist the massive invasion of the usual tourist paraphernalia: at 224 the celebrated Galignani bookshop; at n° 226 the fashionable *salon de thé* Angelina invites beautiful people to try its *Mont Blanc* pudding, among other delicacies, in a refined 1900 setting. At n° 228 is the discreet entrance to the celebrated Meurice where Thackeray and Dickens once stayed and where penniless Orwell was worked to the bone as a *plongeur*, "the slave of the slave", as we learn in *Down and Out in London and Paris*. The hotel, which he omits to name, is "a vast, grandiose place with a classical façade, and at one side a little, dark doorway like a rat hole, which was the service entrance." The kitchens are the kingdom of hell: "stifling low-ceilinged inferno of a cellar, red-lit from the fires, and deafening with oaths and clanging of pots and pans." Only a double door separated the squalid scullery from the posh dining-room. "There sat the customers in all their splendour and spotless table-cloths, bowls of flowers, mirrors and gilt cornices and painted cherubims; and here, just a few feet away we in our disgusting filth." We wonder whether the German High Command of the Paris garrison who, during the last war, took up residence at the lavish Meurice had ever read George Orwell.

In 1720 a manège was built for young Louis XV on the site of n° 230, then the edge of the Tuileries Gardens (rue de Rivoli being opened only in 1808). With his departure for Versailles it became a riding school for upper class youths, who were meanwhile trained in fencing, dancing and mathematics as befitted the gentlemanly ideal of the time. In the early stages of the Revolution the National Assembly sat here, followed by the Convention. Thus it was here that the first Republic was proclaimed on 21 September 1792 by Danton and that Louis XVI was brought to trial and sentenced to death. At n° 248 WH Smith and at n° 252 the British shirt-makers Hilditch and Key are a remnant of English omnipresence here a century ago. The house standing at n° 258 is crying out for repair, but was once the home of the great statesman Talleyrand, the only one to have wormed his way through all the shaky regimes of the time, and who died here of old age on 17 May 1838, aged 86. His home is believed to have been the most sumptuous palatial mansion in the capital, overlooking the Tuileries.

Retrace your steps and turn left into rue de Castiglione, reminiscent of the glorious past of this neighbourhood. It leads to the fabulous Place Vendôme and the legendary Ritz, the headquarters of the golden couple the Fitzgeralds in the 1920s. They made it their home, but moved about Paris for the fun. Hemingway, quite the reverse, could only afford to come for a drink at its bar, still a worthwhile experience. The Ritz has adjusted to modern demands and opened a *cordon bleu* school, and a health club in its basement. When it opened in 1898, it was the first hotel to install private bathtubs. The shirt-maker Charvet, another old-timer still holds its own at n° 28 and in recent times Giorgio Armani has settled at n° 6, a suitable setting for his refined designs of understated, impeccable good taste.

Place Vendôme is a work of art in its own right, a masterpiece of French classical architecture. It also sums up in a nutshell the switchback history of 19th century France: Girardon's original equestrian statue of the Sun King having been disposed of during the Revolution, Napoleon's Colonne d'Austerlitz came to replace it in 1810. With the Restoration of the monarchy, it was replaced in its turn by the equestrian statue of Henri IV, le Vert Galant; but soon the bourgeois Orléanais Louis-Philippe was put on the throne of France, ousting definitively the Bourbon branch of the dynasty – the Vert Galant was dispatched to the Pont-Neuf and a bourgeois Napoleon in a frock coat and low hat was set up in its stead, to which his nephew Napoleon III substituted an imperial Napoleon in the guise of a Roman Caesar. But in 1871 the *Commune*, temporarily victorious on Place Vendôme and led by the enthusiastic painter Courbet, would have none of it - thousands of patriots struck up the *Marsaillaise* and *le Chant de la Patrie*, to the sound of the triumphant fanfare, as the monument came tumbling down. The Emperor, however, regained his lofty position the following year, when the victorious bourgeois National Assembly of the *Versaillais* sent him back to the top of the column. He has been dominating this mecca of luxury ever since.

Turn left into rue Saint-Honoré. On this western luxurious section of the street can still be seen some *hôtels particuliers* (townhouses), reminders of its aristocratic past, close to the Louvre, then conveniently situated on the road to Versailles. Among its illustrious inhabitants at the time was Madame Geoffrin, who held her famous literary salon at n° 374. The greatest artists and writers frequented her *salon* - Boucher, La Tour, Vernet and the *Encyclopédistes*, as well as renowned foreigners such as Horace Walpole.

Turn left into rue du Marché-Saint-Honoré and continue to the square by the same name. Lined with eating-places, it makes for a charming stopping-place, in somewhat of a resort atmosphere. A hideous concrete garage, several storeys high, used to stand in the middle of the square, but the square had charm and an unpretentious atmosphere, much appreciated by old-timers. Now, yet another shopping centre has been entrusted to the Spanish architect Ricardo Bofill, who has planned to replace the garage with a glass structure, the latest fad. Once more a genuine corner of Paris is in danger of losing its soul.

Back on rue Saint-Honoré, at n° 286 the church of Saint-Roch commemorates the man from Montpellier who dedicated his life to the victims of the plague in Italy and ended by contracting the disease himself. But the unseen hand of God cured him, and subsequently all around him recovered. There was great need for his assistance in these pestilence-ridden parts during the 16th century, when the original church was built and dedicated to him, and also in previous centuries, as confirmed by the existence on this site of an earlier chapel dedicated to Saint Roch. The present church was begun at the time of Louis XIV but took nearly a century to complete for lack of funds. It would have taken much longer if the financier Law had not donated 100,000 pounds towards its completion, not for any spiritual motivation, but so as to be appointed *contrôleur général*. To that end he also converted to Catholicism, and it was at Saint-Roch that he received his first Holy Communion.

Saint-Roch being the fashionable church of Paris, many illustrious Parisians were buried here - Pierre Corneille, Diderot, d'Holbach, Madame Geoffrin (who had also married here), André Le Nôtre, as well as Marie-Anne de Bourbon, the daughter of Louis XIV and of his first mistress, Louise de la Vallière. The funeral celebration of the great Bossuet, the Bishop of Meaux, was also celebrated here, from where he was carried for burial to Meaux, east of Paris. The Dauphin's tutor and the King's right arm in religious matters, Bossuet was also an eloquent writer, famous, among others, for the heart-heaving, somewhat pompous *Oraisons funèbres* he had written for the great figures of his time, notably the Prince de Condé and Henrietta of England.

The church was deprived of its dilapidated bell tower in 1875, when, rather than undertake its costly restoration, the authorities decided to demolish it so as to give access to rue des Pyramides. Its bell was donated to the Sacre-Coeur then under construction. At the beginning of the Revolution the entire church was threatened by the suggestion to open a street through its nave and convert the side aisles into shops! But the church still stands and has among its treasures an 18th-century organ, one of the most beautiful in France. The Christ of the Sacristy was deposited here during the 1848 Revolution by students from the Ecole Polytechnique, who had rescued it from the Palais des Tuileries. It has remained at Saint-Roch ever since.

Back at the junction of Palais-Royal turn right into rue de Rohan towards the Seine, across rue de Rivoli to the Arc du Carrousel. In the 19th century this spacious esplanade was cluttered with an unsightly maze of alleys. "...These houses are wrapped in the eternal shadow projected by the high galleries of the Louvre, blackened on this side by the northern wind [...] One wonders who can live here, what must happen here at night, when this alley turns into a haven for cutthroats, and when the vices of Paris, wrapped in the mantle of night, are given free rein," Balzac wrote in *La Cousine Bette* in 1838.

Balzac's contemporaries - Gérard de Nerval, Théophile Gauthier, Gavarni - liked the place and gathered in one of its tatty houses for their revelry. Yet originally these were sumptuous *hôtels*, erected in the immediate vicinity of the Louvre. The most famous was the Hôtel de Rambouillet, an elegant mansion of red brick and white stone, still in the style of Henri IV and Louis XIII. It stood on rue Saint-Thomas-du-Louvre, which ran parallel to the Tuileries Palace, level with the entrance to the Palais-Royal. Its fame was due to its landlady, la Marquise de Rambouillet, who in the 17th century held her prestigious *salon littéraire* in her *chambre bleue*. All the literary set attended her gatherings - Descartes, Scarron, Corneille, Madame de Sévigné, Madame de La Fayette, Mlle de Scudéry - and also the greatest aristocrats and statesmen, including Richelieu and Condé. This is where the French language, hitherto as crude as the manners of the uncouth society that spoke it, was purified and polished, where conversation developed into an art, even an affectation, in short, where French society finally shed its medieval remnants and was initiated into an urbane lifestyle which was to dominate the next two centuries.

The enclave having deteriorated over the years, Napoleon III had it cleared and replaced by a garden *à la française*, enhancing the beauty of the *arc de triomphe du Carrousel*. The original Carrousel and Tuileries Gardens were laid out for Catherine de Medici in 1564 by Pierre Le Nôtre and were Italian in style, to suit her native tastes. Lying to the east was Le Petit-Jardin, today's Jardin du Carrousel. To its north, the royal stables (now rue de Rivoli) stretched as far as rue des Pyramides. (the northern wings of the Louvre did not exist at the time.) Charles V's rampart walled off the garden to the east, 5 metres east of today's Arc du Carrousel. Le Grand-Jardin west of the Palace (now the Tuileries Gardens) was out of the way and seldom used. In order to secure the Queen's privacy in the Petit-Jardin, access to the rampart was forbidden. The wars of religion left the gardens in a pitiful state and Henri IV had them restored by Jean Le Nôtre, the son of Pierre. This done, the King spent many a leisurely moment in their midst. Driven also by economic considerations, he planted mulberry trees for the cultivation of silkworms, hoping to develop his own silk industry so as not to depend on expensive imports from Milan.

The birth of Louis XIV's first son in 1662 was no small event and Louis XIV meant to celebrate it with all the appropriate dazzling pomp, which included sumptuous equestrian evolutions known as carousel. 15,000 spectators gathered on the grandstand built for the occasion, to watch this brilliantly colourful spectacle on 2 and 3 June 1662. Dressed as a Roman Emperor, the Sun King took part in all the games of dexterity, caracoling and strutting about in order to impress his recent object of desire and future favourite, Louise de la Vallière. The impact of the carousel was such that the garden has been known as Le Jardin du Carrousel ever since. And yet, today's visitor associates the name with Napoleon, who, in several other places too, has dethroned his predecessor in our consciousness. The Arc de Triomphe du Carrousel is responsible for the confusion, since it commemorates Napoleon's 1805 victories. Emulating the Septimus Severus Arch of Rome, Percier and Fontaine erected it in 1806-1808, as a magnificent main entrance to the Palais des Tuileries.

In 1664 André Le Nôtre, the grandson of Pierre, was commissioned by Louis XIV's Minister, Colbert, to redesign the gardens lying west of the palace. Le Nôtre had already distinguished himself at Vaux-le-Vicomte, the splendid home of Nicolas Fouquet, the King's treasurer, which had aroused the envy of the monarch and eventually brought about the downfall of Fouquet. Following the example of Vaux-le-Vicomte, Le Nôtre reshaped the gardens into a perfect model of a *jardin à la française*, in strict geometrical order, gaining full control over nature. In order to remedy the drawback of an uneven surface sloping down to the river, Le Nôtre framed the gardens by two long terraces, La Terrasse des Feuillants to the north and, La Terrasse du Bord de l'Eau along the river, where the royal princes used to play. A monumental gate, la Porte de la Conférence, stood there by the river, part of the city walls Louis XIII had built further out of the centre as the city expanded, a section of which ran through the gardens. It was demolished at the time of Louis XV.

Beyond the gardens, Le Nôtre began the conquest of the rural countryside by way of a long straight alley in the axis of the central alley of the gardens, climbing westwards up the hill of Chaillot and vanishing into the infinite horizon, the future Champs-Elysées. But these belong to the 8th arrondissement.

The Tuileries Gardens were opened to the public in the 17th century, at the happy instigation of Charles Perrault; lackeys, soldiers and paupers, however, were not admitted. In 1780 public toilets were installed - a total novelty!

The central pool was the departure point of the revolutionary ceremony for 'the Supreme Being', orchestrated by a thickly powdered Robespierre dressed in blue, a bouquet of flowers in one hand, a torch in the other, haranguing the crowds. The master of ceremony, the painter David, fretted about at the head of a red-painted float drawn by eight oxen, surmounted by a Liberty figure. 2,400 singers and 1,000 musicians accompanied the huge procession into the Place de la Révolution (Concorde), where they skirted the guillotine before heading for the Champs-de-Mars, in today's 7th arrondissement, for more celebration. Meanwhile a monster emerged from the pool in the shape of a pyramid (!), representing atheism, egoism, false modesty, discord and ambition. Once set on fire, the monster was reduced to ashes and Wisdom appeared in all her splendour. All that is now left of this inflamed idealism are some marble benches disposed in a semicircle on either side of the entrance to the central alley: they had been placed by the well-intentioned Robespierre to accommodate the aged participants. On 10 October 1794, the remains of J.J. Rousseau, wrapped in a gold-studded azure flag, were deposited by the central pool, on their way from Ermenonville (where he had died in 1778) to the new sanctuary of the nation's heroes, the Pantheon, in the 5th arrondissement. This time Robespierre was not present: the guillotine had disposed of him too, a couple of months before.

Intent on preserving both head and throne, Louis-Philippe decided to live 'bourgeoisement' and not to rub his subjects up the wrong way. He nonetheless fenced off the part of the gardens that lay east of the central pool for his own private use. With the downfall of the Second Empire the Palais des Tuileries was gone and the gardens belonged to the people and were open to all and sundry. Since then the Arc du Carrousel has been standing in the middle of a spacious esplanade, its stone of delicate pink hue glowing against the backdrop of the most famous urban vista in the world.

Make your way through the Tuileries Gardens, which were redesigned and spruced up in 1994, after two decades of neglect. You will delight in their position overlooking the Musée d'Orsay and the National Assembly across the river. On either side of the exit, overlooking Place de la Concorde, are the Musée de l' Orangerie by the river and the Musée du Jeu de Paume by rue de Rivoli. Built in 1853, both museums now exhibit interesting works of art of the more recent schools. At the Orangerie these span from the Impressionists well into the 20th (1930), at the Jeu de Paume they are even more recent. The inadequate premises of the latter, where the Impressionists were housed prior to their transfer to the Musée d'Orsay, have been redesigned by Antoine Stinco into a spacious, luminous museum, a perfect setting for contemporary art. Thanks to their new large windows, they become one with a most glorious cityscape, as can be appreciated from the cafeteria.

THE 2nd ARRONDISSEMENT

For nearly two centuries, the Paris stock exchange, La Bourse, has stood imposingly in the heart of the 2nd arrondissement, marking it as the financial centre of the capital. To honour the nascent capitalist era, Napoleon commissioned his architect Brongniart to endow the city with a new temple of finance, emulating those of ancient Greece. Napoleon, however, was not to see the completed monument, which was inaugurated only in 1825, 10 years after his downfall. Originally, the Tribunal of Trade was also located here, but it was transferred to Boulevard du Palais on Ile de la Cité during the Second Empire. The stock exchange remained on the site and drew to the arrondissement a wide spectrum of financial establishments, both French and foreign, thus confirming the position the 2nd had long held as the centre of financial transactions and other communications.

Lying on the northern periphery of Paris, the 2nd was always an intermediary territory between the capital and the outside world. Originally lying outside the city walls, it was incorporated by successive stages into the growing city. Thus, the rue Tiquetonne on its south-eastern edge runs along the site bounded by the first city walls, *l'enceinte* Philippe-Auguste (1190); the diagonal rue d'Aboukir runs along the site of the second one, bounding *l'enceinte* Charles V (1383); rue des Jeûneurs and rue Feydeau run along the routes of the inner and outer roads of the *enceinte* Louis XIII (1636). In 1676 Louis XIV, fortified by his military victories, did away with the walls and laid out a tree-lined promenade instead, emulating the Cour-la-Reine (now the 8th arr.), the promenade planted by his grandmother Marie de Medici along the Seine. These Grands Boulevards (the word comes from the German *Bollwerk*, meaning the top surface of a rampart) ran in a circular arc from the Madeleine to the Bastille, a long stretch that took a hundred years to complete and marked the northern boundary of Paris (and consequently of the present 2nd arrondissement).

On the eastern edge of the arrondissement bustling traffic had, since Roman days, been going in and out of the capital by way of rue Saint-Denis, which led to the villages of Saint-Denis and Pontoise, and on to Rouen. Saint Geneviève, the venerated patron of Paris, gave it a further boost in the 5th century by promoting it as a pilgrimage route to the shrine of Saint-Denis, hence its name rue de Monsieur Saint-Denis. From the 8th century on it became the royal highway through which the kings and queens of France entered solemnly 'the good city of Paris' on their way to the cathedral of Notre-Dame - notably after their coronation in Reims - a tradition maintained for over a thousand years, right up to the coronation of Charles X on 27 September 1827. Such occasions were celebrated by lavish festivities against the backdrop of triumphant arches, of rich silks draped from the house fronts and of fountains flowing with milk and wine. The royal procession with its sumptuous canopy, the colourful attire of its participants provided a splendid spectacle which thrilled the crowds. Royal funerals also went past rue Saint-Denis, departing from Notre-Dame and heading north to the burial site of the basilica of Saint-Denis.

Being the main thoroughfare of the capital, rue Saint-Denis attracted religious institutions, hostels and inns, where kings, pilgrims and other travellers found hospitality, notably in the Hôpital Saint-Jacques on the site of the present n°s 129-135, which was opened by the brotherhood of Saint-Jacques in the early 14th century for the benefit of pilgrims heading for Compostela. The Hôpital de la Trinité had opened a century earlier (at the present n°s 142-164) to offer shelter to latecomers who found the city gates locked after nightfall. Even those travelling to their deaths found solace here on their way to the gallows of Montfaucon (now's 10th arr.). The tumbril carrying them from the prison of the Grand-Châtelet would pause to allow them to kiss the wooden cross of the convent of the Filles-Dieu (n°s 223-239). The convent's inmates, reformed prostitutes, would welcome them to a share of holy water, three morsels of bread and a glass of wine, and could even save their necks by consenting to marry them. It is said that one prisoner, who was offered rescue by a generous yet hideously ugly 'daughter of God', urged the hangman to proceed with his task and deliver him from a still worse fate. This may be the origin of the expression *passer la corde au cou* – 'to put someone's head in the noose', or to trap a man into marriage.

Parallel to rue Saint-Denis to its west, the medieval rue Poissonnière calls to mind the fresh catch from the Pas-de-Calais that was carried through here to the central market of Les Halles. Files of donkeys used to be seen plodding along the street carrying their load and the salty smell of the sea. When the new royal road to the north was completed in 1730, the donkeys were replaced by faster horse-drawn carts. In 1850 the railway replaced these in its turn.

A third route cut across these rural, outlying parts, the diagonal rue Montmartre, opened in the early 13th century to connect Paris with the abbey of Montmartre. When, in the early 19th century, France's prosperity called for a better public transport system, the newly created Messageries, the nationwide network of mail-coach service, set up its central station in the cul-de-sac Saint-Pierre (between the present 115 rue Montmartre and 28 rue Notre-Dame des Victoires). This radiating network perpetuated the calling of the arrondissement as the capital's centre of communications.

Because of its geographical situation, the 2nd arrondissement drew in the most destitute segment of society, particularly between the 15th and 17th centuries. The Hundred Years' War and the Black Plague had left one sixth of the population of France homeless and starving. Deserting the desolate countryside, they made their way into the capital and huddled within Charles V's city walls. They were hardly likely to be disturbed in this tangle of narrow streets and blind alleys next to the city walls, reeking of the open-air sewer, a perilous no man's land, a long way from the city, as some street names testify - rue du Temps Perdu ('vanished times'; now rue Saint-Joseph) and rue du Bout du Monde ('world's end'; now Léopold Bellan), for example. The newcomers became the terror of the town, organized into fearsome bands with their own language and laws. At the time of François I their head was known as 'le Ragot', a word later distorted into *argot* (slang). By day they spilled out into the streets of Paris, metamorphosed into 'blind' or 'maimed' beggars, and preyed upon passers-by. By night they vanished into the neighbourhood's dead-end alleys, where they laid aside their crutches and 'miraculously' recovered their eyesight and missing limbs. Thus these alleys came to be known as 'Cours des Miracles', the most notorious one being situated on rue Neuve-Saint-Sauveur (roughly on the site of the rue du Nil, rue des Forges and rue de Damiette), and ran conveniently along the city walls, the gaps of which provided exits in case of emergency.

Victor Hugo's novel *Notre-Dame de Paris* brought worldwide notoriety to the Cour des Miracles of rue Neuve-Saint-Sauveur, "a gutter of vice and beggary, of vagrancy that spills over into the streets of the capital [...] immense changing-room of all the actors of this comedy that robbery, prostitution and murder play on the cobbled streets of Paris." Hugo, however, took the liberty of tampering with history by transposing this den of thieves from the 17th century to the late Middle Ages, to suit contemporary Romantic fancy. The rabble of the 'Cour des Miracles' made the streets of Paris so unsafe that in 1667 Louis XIV ordered his police lieutenant Nicolas de La Reynie to clean up this hotbed of banditry. This was no easy task, for its occupants put up a heroic resistance. Once defeated, many ended up in the galleys of the king's growing fleet; this was one way of tackling the problem of homelessness, which afflicted one tenth of the population of Paris or 40,000 souls.

As Victor Hugo observed, the proximity of the city walls had brought an influx of prostitutes to the neighbourhood. They took up residence in the south-eastern section of the arrondissement, close to the abundant reservoir of clientele provided by the central market of Les Halles, and left the mark of their trade by way of street names: rue Tire-Boudin ('sausage-jack'; now Marie-Stuart), rue Gratte-Cul ('bum-scraper'; now Gaston Dussoubs)... Attempts to do away with prostitution were made once in a while, but these were usually half-hearted and ineffectual and largely dependent on the inclinations of the individual monarch. Thus, at the time of Louis XV, who was by no means averse to the pleasures of the flesh, the neighbourhood flourished into a breeding-ground of courtesans for the upper classes. It was in Madame Gourdan's glamorous establishment on rue de la Comtesse d'Artois (now rue Montorgueil), that the notorious pimp Jean du Barry discovered the enticing Jeanne Bécu, Mademoiselle Lange by her trade name. Having set her up as procuress in the bordello Dupressoir on rue de Damiette, he threw her into the arms of the Duc de Richelieu, the Cardinal's great-nephew, who, hoping to promote his own interests, threw her into those of the King. A true professional, Jeanne introduced the licentious monarch to a realm of unsuspected pleasures, all the more appreciated since her predecessor, the Pompadour, had long lost her sexual appetite. In order to make her socially acceptable, Jean du Barry married her off to his brother, Comte Guillaume du Barry, who was compensated substantially for the deal and left for Toulouse, while the new Comtesse du Barry became the last of France's royal favourites to the outrage of the scandalized court. In his Lent sermon the abbot of Beauvais bluntly censored the depraved Louis XV, using the transparent disguise of King Solomon, who, having had "his fill of voluptuous pleasures [...] ended by seeking new ones in the base remains of public licence." Outside the court, the people of France were infuriated by the Comtesse's prodigal spending, squandering the country's revenue on finery and on her sumptuous new mansion at Louveciennes. When the time came for revenge, a vindictive nation sent for her in her retreat at Louveciennes and dispatched her to the guillotine.

By the time Emile Zola was born in 1840, at 10 rue Saint-Joseph, this had long ceased to be a no-man's-land but had become a working-class neighbourhood at the heart of the capital, dominated by the teeming bustle and din of the press industry, which had first settled here during the Revolution, when Père Duchesne published a lewd, anarchical paper on rue de Damiette. It was in the tiny area enclosed by rue Saint-Joseph, rue du Croissant and rue des Jeûneurs that the political destiny of France was largely determined. Thus, it was Adolphe Thiers and the journalists of his newly founded *Le National*, together with the representatives of eleven other papers, who brought about the fall of the Bourbon dynasty. After the freedom of the press was abolished on 26 July 1830, Thiers launched a protest movement, which culminated in the three-day July Revolution, known as '*Les Trois Glorieuses*', and in the abdication of Charles X. Similarly, the conflict between the authorities and the progressive press over a banned reformist banquet scheduled for 22 February 1848 triggered off the 1848 Revolution that led to the definitive overthrow of the French monarchy.

On 31 July 1914, the eve of the Great War, Jean Jaurès, the founder of the socialist paper *l'Humanité*, was shot dead through the window of La Chope du Croissant, a hang-out of papermen on the corner of rue du Croissant and rue Montmartre, by Raoul Villain, a 24-year-old nationalist. Jaurès who had tried desperately to prevent the outbreak of the war, ironically, became its first French victim. His assassin benefited from the 'confusion of the time', in other words, from the prevailing nationalist hysteria, and was acquitted.

The neighbourhood with its abundant cheap labour provided an ideal location for the booming press industry of the 19th century; it was also close to the Grands Boulevards, virtually the 'high street' of Paris up to World War I, to which everyone flocked – the rich to the west of rue Montmartre, the poor to the east. Every afternoon hordes of hawkers stormed into the Boulevards shouting out the tantalizing, freshly printed news that would replenish the boulevard-goers with enough gossip to fill up the rest of their day, while they in their turn became the subject of scandal sheets and ferocious cartoons.

While the men were busy nightly at the printing presses, helping unwittingly to unsettle the establishment, the women were worked to the bone for a wretched wage by the burgeoning *haute couture* houses that had settled in the western section of the 1st and 2nd arrondissements. Crammed into tiny rooms where daylight never penetrated, these anaemic seamstresses produced finery to adorn their social betters, which was nonetheless preferable to prostitution which, in 19th-century Paris, was the lot of one tenth of the female population.

Meanwhile the privileged few were enjoying themselves on the Grands Boulevards, west of rue Montmartre, to which the centre of entertainment had shifted from Palais-Royal after the puritanical Louis-Philippe had shut down its shady establishments. They were already present west of rue Montmartre in the 17th century, for when Richelieu took up residence in the Palais-Royal, opposite the Louvre, they in their turn, built themselves homes as close as possible to his. Thus France's leading figures - from the King's ministers Colbert and Louvois to his physician Thévenin and, above all, Richelieu's successor Mazarin - moved to magnificent palatial homes, built for them by such great architects as Mansart or Le Vau. Whereas Richelieu had acquired the vacant site north of the Louvre, and had pulled down the city walls to make room for his gardens, Mazarin built his palace on the extensive grounds lying north of Richelieu's. However, with the rapid growth of the city, the area soon became crammed and was abandoned for the more airy Faubourg Saint-Honoré and Faubourg Saint-Germain. The mansions were torn down, giving way to a new network of streets, and few vestiges have survived to testify to their short life. Even the National Library, which occupies part of its founder Mazarin's palace, was reconstructed in the 19th century beyond recognition.

With the aristocracy gone, the area became home to the rising bourgeoisie, whose fortunes were largely made on the stock exchange, "a hazardous ladder", as Dickens put it, affording dizzying climbs and equally brutal falls, which could end with a desperate jump into the Seine. Zola referred to "the mysterious turn of the wheel of fortune" and both writers marveled at the spectacle of the greedy "all howling and haggard with speculation", according to Dickens again. The successful ones were now on the town, enjoying the fun on the Grands Boulevards, the playground of the new privileged classes and the heart of the modern capital, as symbolized by the first omnibus line, which plied along them between the Madeleine and the Bastille.

This was the golden age of the theatre and 14 houses were scattered around the 2nd arrondissement, rightly claimed to be the birthplace of the theatre. For in the Hôpital de la Trinité on rue Saint-Denis the first mysteries had been staged for the religious edification of the spectators. The glamorous audience of the 19th century had other priorities: they went to the theatre to see and to be seen, equipped with opera-glasses and posted in the strategic vantage-point of their private boxes. The theatre punctuated the life of society; everyone went to the theatre, including all Balzac's and Stendhal's heroes. On Tuesdays, Thursdays and Saturdays one went to see the Italian troupe, the rage from 1841 to 1870, after whom the Boulevard des Italiens was named. One went to applaud the legendary sopranos, la Pasta, la Malibran, la Grisi, the legendary tenors Rubini and Mario and to have one's heart-strings tugged by Rossini, Bellini, Donizetti and Verdi.

Different emotions were aroused at the winter Bouffes Parisiens (the summer Bouffes Parisiens were on the Champs-Elysées), where Jacques Offenbach's works were performed, later at the Variétés. In 1864 *La Belle Hélène* created an unprecedented wave of adulation for the composer and for the leading lady, Hortense Schneider, who scored an even greater triumph in 1867, as *La Grande Duchesse de Gérolstein*. The greats from all over the world, who were all in Paris to visit the Universal Exhibition, came to admire her at the Variétés. After the show William I of Prussia, Alexander II and Alexander Tzarevitch of Russia and Bismarck went to dine at the Grand Seize, the private restaurant of the prestigious Café Anglais on the Boulevard des Italiens. The menu of that celebrated dinner can still be seen in the museum of the restaurant La Tour d'Argent (in the 5th arr.).

Obviously the celebration of the palate was part of the entertainment and the Café Anglais, so called because it was frequented by English officers when it first opened during the Amiens Peace in 1802, was considered the best gastronomic establishment in the capital during the Second Empire, but was already known during the Restoration when Balzac in *Le Père Goriot* set the first *tête-à-tête* between Rastignac and Delphine de Nucingen at the Café Anglais.

Artists were also present on the Boulevards, including those rejected by the established order. In 1874 the first Impressionist exhibition took place at 35 Boulevard des Capucines within the framework of the Salon des Indépendants. The photographer Nadar lent his painter friends his studio for the occasion. The press, however, was less sympathetic and described their works as 'black dribbles', 'slip-bang, swish-swash', done by 'hoaxers' or 'lunatics', the result of 'mental derangement'. It was all too much for the bourgeoisie of the nascent Third Republic.

World War I tolled the bell for Belle Epoque Paris and for the Grands Boulevards. Eventually the elegant fashion houses on rue de la Paix disappeared, as did the setters and polishers on rue Vivienne and rue du Mail who worked for the prestigious jewellers on rue de la Paix and Place Vendôme. Little is left of that glorious past, just a few theatres, such as the Opéra-Comique, also known as Salle Favart (once the renowned Théâtre des Italiens), and the restaurant Drouant on Place Gaillon, where, every third Monday of November, the prestigious Goncourt literary prize is awarded, to the accompaniment of a gastronomic dinner. The venerable Bibliothèque Nationale, the arrondissement's only cultural institution of international note, is scheduled to move to its new controversial home in the 13th arrondissement in 1996, leaving behind only its art section. Fortunately, the pretty Place de Louvois opposite the library is there to stay. This was the site of the Opera House of Paris during the Restoration and the scene of the assassination of the Duc de Berry, heir to the throne, on 13 February 1820, during a performance of the *Carnival of Venice*. The King ordered the theatre to be razed to the ground so as to eradicate the memory of the evil deed, which provided the congested arrondissement with its only open-air garden.

Most of the press has now also migrated elsewhere, leaving the neighbourhood to the cheap clothing industry and to sex. The 'Sentier' quarter is first and foremost a gigantic traffic jam, a chaotic jumble of wheeled carts loaded with huge rolls of fabric, pushed by members of the destitute international community, delivery vans and, at times, a wayward bus. This is the stronghold of the Paris rag trade, much of it in the hands of cheerful, self-confident North African Jews, who make no bones about their spiralling success and their enjoyment of it. Thanks to hard work, astuteness and inexhaustible energy, the 'Sentier' dresses the better part of France, and even beyond, unintimidated by fearsome competition from Taiwan and elsewhere. Currently, however, there is talk of transferring the entire trade to the suburbs, thus putting an end to the havoc, and turning the area into a pedestrian precinct, a further step towards making the 2nd a more salubrious yet soulless and less picturesque arrondissement.

On the other hand, the streetwalkers on rue Saint-Denis are still pacing the same beat as their predecessors of hundreds of years ago, motivated, like them, by hunger and poverty. The only difference is that today the street is lined with glaring neon lights and sex shops and, on weekend nights, jammed with customers, lined up in their cars, bumper to bumper. The 2nd arrondissement has also preserved its role as the capital's link with the outside world, being the site of dozens of travel agents and airline offices. Facing each other on Place de la Bourse, significantly, are the head office of the Club Med, the most famous recreation club in the world, and the stock exchange, two institutions that reflect the values and answer the needs of the middle classes of contemporary France.

WHERE TO WALK

EAST OF RUE MONTMARTRE

A walk into the plebeian eastern section of the 2nd arrondissement is not aesthetically gratifying or spiritually uplifting, but it can be exciting and of historical interest. Avoid coming here on Sunday when, deprived of its teeming bustle, it tends to resemble a ghost town.

We shall start from the northern end of rue Saint-Denis and follow in the footsteps of travellers of yore, who entered the city along this route. Honoured by royalty, it was also selected for the celebrations on 30 June 1878 of the young Third Republic, as depicted in Monet's painting *Rue Saint-Denis* (now in the Musée des Beaux-Arts in Rouen), bursting with a riot of tricolours. The Republic needed a ritual to enforce its legitimacy but was careful to avoid celebrating Bastille Day so as not to arouse revolutionary feelings only seven years after the civil war of the *Commune*. A national holiday was proclaimed to coincide with the Universal Exhibition, which was bound to draw large crowds.

On normal days, rue Saints-Denis was just the bustling high street of Paris, leading from the city gate to the market of Les Halles and to the Châtelet provostship and prison. With so much coming and going, prostitution could not be far off, and today still is as conspicuous as it ever was. Don't let this deter you from venturing here, for rue Saint-Denis is essentially a colourful slice of old Paris.

The Porte Saint-Denis at its northern end had been the gateway to the city since the reign of Charles V. In 1672, Louis XIV, confident that the city no longer needed to be defended after his spectacular victories, had Blondel replace the 14th-century gate, a crenellated construction complete with towers and drawbridge, with the present one for the sole purpose of glorifying his person. At n°s 224-226 on your left stood a religious institution, Les Filles de l'Union-Chrétienne, which provided an education for poor orphan girls and also a home for wives on the brink of marital separation. The wealthier ones occupied the 18th-century house in the courtyard. Despite the additional storeys, which somewhat

2nd ARRONDISSEMENT

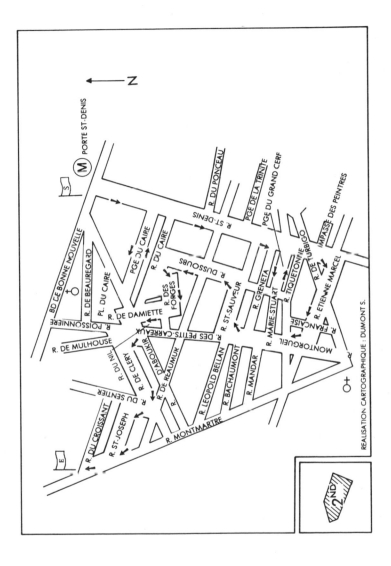

spoil it, the original building retains its elegant proportions, but the lovely gardens in which it stood are gone. A workshop was opened here in the 17th century, providing work for 200 lacemakers, the first of its kind in Paris. After the Revolution the premises found different commercial uses and at one point became a printing house belonging to Monsieur Michelet, the father of the great historian Michelet who was born on this site. The present building was put up in the first half of the 20th century. At n° 237 stood the wooden cross of the convent of the Filles-Dieu, where the tumbril would stop on its way from the Grand-Châtelet prison to the gallows of Montfaucon, to let the prisoner kiss the cross. The convent, which extended all the way to the present n° 223, disappeared in the wake of the Revolution and was replaced a few years later by the Passage du Caire, now strongly redolent of an exotic oriental Bazaar and worth a detour.

Rue du Ponceau on the left (n° 188) replaced the famous medieval fontaine de Ponceau, then supplied with the pure waters of Saint-Gervais (in today's 19th arr.) by way of an aqueduct. On special occasions milk and wine replaced the water to the joy of the merrymaking populace.

N°s 174 and 176, on your right, have gables facing the street, rare examples of a characteristic feature of medieval Paris. As a hygienic measure, these were done away with from the 15th century on, to prevent rainwater from stagnating between roofs, as a result of which Paris was altered beyond recognition, as can be seen from old engravings. The houses stand on the site of the medieval cemetery of the Hôpital de la Trinité, which is a couple of yards ahead. During the Hundred Years' War, which opposed the Bourguignons and their English allies to the Armagnacs, a number of butchered bodies of the latter were dumped here, as well as those of victims of the Black Plague. The Hôpital de la Trinité extended between the present n°s 164 and 142, to which bears witness today the Passage de la Trinité at n° 164. It was set up originally to provide for belated travellers, unable to enter the city after curfew. In 1402 the Confrères de la Passion were let a hall here and began to produce religious 'mysteries', telling the life and feats of Jesus, probably to amplify the stories from the Old Testament that were enacted on the street during royal processions. So popular were these that the Hôpital de la Trinité became the capital's centre of entertainment and the birthplace of its theatre. In the 16th century it became a girls' orphanage known as Les Enfants Bleus because of the blue uniforms of its inmates. The girls were taught a craft from a very young age, an initiative which generated a flourishing arts and crafts tradition in the area up to the Revolution. The fountain at n° 142, called Fontaine Greneta or de la Reine was also supplied by the aqueduct of Saint-Gervais but has long been dried up. Built in 1502, it is one of the oldest fountains of Paris.

Ahead of you to the right (n° 145) is yet another arcade, le Passage du Grand-Cerf where a famous hostelry by the same name ('the big hart') was situated before the Revolution. This was also the Paris terminal of the royal mail-coach service to the north and east. The arcade has been recently renovated and now reflects the elegance of a newly gentrified Paris.

N° 135, a pedestrian stretch between rue de Turbigo and rue Etienne Marcel, marks the site of the first gate of Saint-Denis, the one built by Philippe-Auguste at the end of the 12th century. It was surmounted by a Holy Virgin to suit the religious fervour of the times. François I, a man of the Renaissance, had the gate demolished, but spared the Virgin who was put on a pedestal and moved to the façade of the corner house of the Impasse des Peintres on your left, where it can still be seen. The Impasse des Peintres, probably named for its resident painters who lived here, skirted the old city walls and still has a 16th-century house at n° 4. In the Middle Ages, this was the site of the Hôpital Saint-Jacques where pilgrims stopped on their way to Compostela. It soon became notorious, however, for the misbehaviour of its brothers, and a royal edict of 1388 banned them from "playing cards and dice, going to the tavern in their choir gown, leaving the church during mass in order to converse outside", and from indulging in "indecent laughs, facetious stories and their quarrels." Worse was to come: in the 15th century the institution's chaplains were forbidden to employ young chambermaids.

Rue de Turbigo, which you have just crossed, and rue Etienne-Marcel to your right, bear the mark of Baron Haussmann, who carved them through the neighbourhood's tangle of medieval alleys. Rue Turbigo was opened in order to speed up the transfer of troops to Place de la République, in case of insurrection among the working-classes, in the eastern part of Paris. Rue Etienne-Marcel was opened just south of the site of Philippe-Auguste's rampart. On the other side of the rampart, level with the present n° 20, Robert d'Artois, the nephew of Saint Louis built himself a *hôtel* in 1270. Some 50 years later it passed over to the house of Bourgogne, when the two houses were allied through marriage. A century later Charles V moved the city walls further north, which enabled the Duc de Bourgogne to extend the property to the south and make it appealing enough to become his Parisian home. In early 1408 Jean sans Peur, Duc de Bourgogne, was back in Paris after a year's absence following the assassination by his men of his cousin, Philippe Duc d'Orléans. Knowing he had many foes, he built himself a defence tower within the walls of his property and slept on the fourth and topmost floor, sandwiched between his squire, who slept on the third, and a squad of crossbowmen on the look-out on the crenellated roof. The tower still stands at n° 20, but cannot normally be visited, the only vestige of the Hôtel de Bourgogne and Paris's only military medieval tower to have survived in its entirety (except for the roof, which dates from the 18th century). The Spanish Ambassador persuaded Henri III to spare the tower, while the rest of the property had been parcelled up by François I (hence the neighbouring rue Française, originally named

Françoise). Jean sans Peur's room can be reached by a spiral staircase, of which the first section is in a square turret adjoining the tower and is protected by an iron gate. At its top the proliferating branches of an oak tree are carved into the stone, symbolizing the power of the House of Bourgogne. A second iron gate once protected the last and narrower section of the staircase in a corbelled turret. In spite of these precautions, destiny caught up with Jean sans Peur, even though it took his assassin eleven years to get him. He was killed on the bridge of Montereau, south-east of Paris, at the confluence of the Seine and the Yonne. The murderer - in a perfectly balanced Shakespearean conclusion - was Tanguy du Châtel, head of the Armagnacs, the supporters of his murdered cousin Philippe d'Orléans.

Further down and across the street, at n° 29, was the Théâtre de l'Hôtel de Bourgogne, the first theatre of Paris. The site is in the present 1st arrondissement, but for the convenience of sightseers and for historical coherence it is mentioned here. In 1548 the Confrères de la Passion were expelled from the Hôpital de la Trinité and took possession of this site, vacated by François I. Hard times forced them to let the premises to different troupes, two of which went on to make history. The first one was the Comédiens du Roi who, through wily lobbying, enjoyed the patronage of Louis XIV, to the detriment of the rivalling Théâtre du Marais, which staged Corneille's plays, and Molière's Théâtre Illustre. The Hôtel de Bourgogne produced Racine's work. In 1680 Louis XIV, increasingly bent on imposing his authority, ordered the three troupes to merge into one and to settle on the Left Bank. The only other troupe he tolerated was the Italian one, which was allowed to take over the Hôtel de Bourgogne, delighting Parisians with the adventures of Harlequin, Colombine and Scaramouche. But when in 1697 the troupe derided Madame de Maintenon, thinly disguised as *La Fausse Prude*, she had the theatre closed down. When the fun-loving Regent, Philippe Duc d'Orléans succeeded Louis XIV in 1715, he put an end to the oppressive austerity that shrouded the last years of his reign and swept Paris back into the ring of pleasure. The Italian troupe was invited again to the Hôtel de Bourgogne, where they entertained the audience with Marivaux's light-hearted comedies, the mirror of their own society.

With the growing popularity of the Italian opera, in 1762 the troupe obtained from the Opéra the privilege of creating a new genre in the same vein as the Italian Opera Buffa, the Opéra-Comique - less noble a genre and therefore of little threat to the Opéra. Presiding over the new entertainment were Charles Simon Favart, the playwright and director of the theatre (the Opéra-Comique is often still referred to as Salle Favart), and his wife, née Justine Duronceray, the leading singer. The Italian troupe stayed here till 1783, when they moved to new premises just off the up-and-coming Boulevard des Italiens, named after them. The Hôtel de Bourgogne was replaced by a new leather market, more in keeping with the economic activities of the area.

Turn right into rue Montorgueil, a picturesque pedestrian artery lined with colourful food stalls (closed between 1 and 4 pm and on Monday all day). Since the fresh sea catch from the north used to arrive here, this became the fish section of the market of Les Halles and also the central oyster market of Paris until 1866. The sales office of the *Société des huitres [oysters] d'Etretat et de Dieppe* was located at n° 61/63 from 1780 until the middle of the 19th century and was called Au Rocher d'Etretat, after the famous coastal landmark in Normandy. The town of Fécamp had its sales office further south on rue Tiquetonne. Rue de Montorgueil was also a gourmet's mecca in the last century, famous for such restaurants as Philippe at n° 54 and Le Rocher de Cancal at n° 59 until 1845, then across the street, at n° 78. Balzac considered Le Rocher de Cancale "the meeting place of the best society of Paris and the establishment which best honours French cuisine." All the heroes of *La Comédie Humaine* dined there, but also Balzac's contemporaries - Dumas Père, Eugène Sue and Théophile Gautier among others. The building still stands with the name of the restaurant engraved on the shabby façade. If only it were restored to its glorious past.

Turn right into rue Saint-Sauveur. The 17th-century corner house at n° 12 and n° 23 rue Dussoubs was La Gourdan's notorious brothel, where she settled in 1774. It was on her earlier premises on rue Montorgueil that Jeanne Bécu had first met the notorious pimp Jean du Barry, through whom she became the royal mistress, the Comtesse du Barry. La Gourdan catered to a select clientele from both court and town and moved to this corner house because it offered more discretion. Madame Gourdan even devised a secret exit so as to prevent unnecessary embarrassment: having chosen from among the wealth of costumes in the first-floor changing-room to cloak their identity, clients could leave through a door hidden in a cupboard, which opened on to a staircase ending in the ground-floor antique shop at n° 14 rue Saint-Sauveur. The main entrance of the brothel was on rue Dussoubs till 1865, when it was walled up, but its portal was preserved and moved to rue Saint-Sauveur, where it still stands. Inside, the elegant architecture of the hall and the wrought iron staircase have also been preserved.

Continue along rue Dussoubs, turn left into rue du Caire and left again into rue des Forges and rue de Damiettes. You will have entered the one-time realm of the underworld, the notorious Cour des Miracles, a safe refuge for its population of cutpurses and cutthroats who could vanish like shadows in these narrow streets. But today one is struck rather by the oriental atmosphere enhanced by some of the street names that commemorate Napoleon's Egyptian campaigns and the fervent Egyptomania that ensued - rue d'Aboukir, d'Alexandrie, du Caire, du Nil....

Hence also the astonishing imitation Egyptian sculptures on the picturesque Place du Caire adjoining the old Cour des Miracles.

Rue de Cléry, across the Place du Caire, runs on the site of the counterscarp of Charles V's city walls. It is named after a splendid 16th-century mansion, home of elegant people, indifferent to the proximity of the rabble at its doorstep and heedless of the stench that emanated from the nearby open sewers and from the rubbish dump, roughly in the triangle formed by rue de Cléry, Boulevard de Bonne-Nouvelle and rue Poissonnière. These putrid exhalations *(mofettes)* gave this section of the street the name Mouffetard (like the famous rue Mouffetard in the 5th arrondissement). Similarly, rue du Beauregard, which branches off rue de Cléry, is reminiscent of the rubbish heap that offered a commanding view of the city. This insalubrious environment did not deter members of the upper class from settling here and some elegant dwellings have survived, albeit sorely in need of a face-lift. The corner of Boulevard Bonne-Nouvelle is the spot where, on 21 January 1793, the Baron de Batz and some of his supporters waited for the royal tumbril on its way from the Temple, where Louis XVI had been sequestrated, to the guillotine on Place de la Révolution (Concorde), by way of the Grands Boulevards. Batz had hoped to kidnap the King and save his head, but his plot failed and two of his accomplices were massacred on the spot. Batz managed to escape and devised a scheme to save Marie-Antoinette, then detained at the Conciergerie.

Towards the end of his life, Pierre Corneille lived in the rue de Cléry. After the death of his patron, the Duc de Guise, Corneille had to vacate the apartment given him in his patron's palace in the Marais and consequently solicited his sovereign to allow him to move to the artists' quarters in the Louvre. Although he took the trouble to couch his request in rhyme and pepper it with all the customary florid flattery, the King turned a deaf ear, a deplorable attitude as most of those granted accommodation in the Louvre were base courtiers and parasites. Corneille's star was in the decline and his plays had become outmoded: of all those he wrote on rue de Cléry, *Psyché* alone proved a success. Written to the music of Lully, in collaboration with Quinault and Molière, it sealed Corneille's friendship with the latter and offered him some comfort. Meanwhile, however, Louis XIV had paired with the bigoted Madame de Maintenon and was losing interest in the theatre. Moreover, the resumption of the Spanish wars meant that he was in need of substantial funds. He cut off altogether the pension of the playwright who had given him so much pleasure in his younger days. On 1 October 1684 Pierre Corneille died a pauper on rue d'Argenteuil (now between Avenue de l'Opéra and rue Saint-Honoré), to which he had moved from rue de Cléry two years before. Six days later, *Psyché* was taken up again at the Opéra, so great was its success.

Several arty and intellectual members of society lived on rue de Cléry in the

18th century. André Chénier, the greatest French poet of his time, lived at n° 97. Although few read his poems, he has gone down in history as one of the most tragic figures of the Revolution, having been guillotined only two days before the downfall of Robespierre. A friend of the Revolution at the start, he later condemned its excesses, notably the death sentence of Louis XVI. Siding with Charlotte Corday after her murder of Marat also got him into trouble. Of all the street's inhabitants Jeanne Poisson was unquestionably the one destined to the most glorious future. Born to an unknown father, roughly on the site of the present n° 29, she was educated by the Farmer General (the King's tax collector) Le Norman de Tournehem. When she was 24 she won the heart of Louis XV and became the celebrated Marquise de Pompadour, to the indignation of the court and of its scandalized ladies. At n° 23 lived the poet Ducis, now an obscure figure, yet in the 18th century he cut a figure in intellectual Paris. It was he who introduced Greek drama and Shakespeare's plays to France, and after Voltaire's death he was appointed to his seat at the Académie Française. Louis XV's private secretary Gabriel Herbault, lived at n° 44 across the street. In the 17th century Robert Poquelin, a priest and doctor from the Sorbonne, and also brother of Molière, lived in a modest house at n° 19/21. A century later a sumptuous property replaced it, stretching all the way to today's rue du Sentier. It belonged to the famous couple Lebrun-Vigée, both painters and art lovers, who were the first to allow young artists to exhibit their works alongside those of established artists: previously young artists had been able to exhibit their works only once a year in the open-air Place Dauphine (in the 1st arr.). Thanks to the unflagging enthusiasm of the Lebrun-Vigée many great works of art were discovered and are now hanging in the nation's museums. After her husband's death in 1813, Madame Lebrun-Vigée remained one of the most sought after ladies in Paris, until her own death in 1842, at the age of 87. These days it is hard, in this congested commercial neighbourhood, to picture the 'Greek' *soupers* to which Madame Lebrun-Vigée invited the upper crust of finance, politics and the arts. Dressed as Athenians, they would loll around the table drinking Cypriot wine that was passed round to the sound of lyres. Madame Lebrun-Vigée would preside over the *soupers* dressed as Aspasia, the influential mistress of Pericles.

Turn right at a sharp angle into rue du Sentier, which has given its name to both this rag-trade neighbourhood and to the mentality of its occupiers *(l'esprit Sentier)*. It leads to rue Saint-Joseph on the left, where Emile Zola was born in 1840, at n° 10. At that time, this was the stronghold of the press, where most of the major newspapers were printed - *Le Siècle*, *La Patrie*, among others. Turn right into rue Montmartre, the medieval road that led to the abbey of Montmartre. At n° 140/144 on the right, between rue Saint-Joseph and rue du Croissant, was the cemetery of Saint-Joseph, where Molière was buried on 21 February 1672. It took four days of tough negotiations and the intervention of the King to persuade the recalcitrant clergy of Saint-Eustache, in Les Halles, who regarded the theatrical profession as an insult to the church, to agree to the burial. For a long time it was erroneously thought that the fable writer La Fontaine was also buried here. There was also confusion as to the exact site of Molière's grave. Consequently, when the Revolutionary authorities ordered the remains of the two illustrious writers to be exhumed and honoured elsewhere, other remains were dug up in their stead and eventually found their way to the cemetery of Père Lachaise (now in the 20th arr.), where they still receive undue homage. The cemetery was replaced by a market in 1806, and that in turn in 1882 by a building where, until 1914, several major newspapers were published - *La Patrie*, *Le Radical*, *La Presse* and *L'Aurore*. You can still see the building with the names of *Le Journal du Soir* and *La France* engraved on its façade, supported by four female sculptures. On 13 January 1898 *L'Aurore* ran on its front page the dramatic headline *J'accuse!*, followed by Emile Zola's historic open letter to the President of the Republic, Félix Faure, in defence of Alfred Dreyfus, of truth and justice and a direct accusation against members of the General Staff. 300,000 copies were hawked that day on the streets of Paris and France at large. Tried for libel and sentenced to one year's imprisonment and a heavy fine, Zola fled to England, like other members of France's intelligentsia, before and after, who voiced unacceptable opinions (Voltaire, Victor Hugo, Charles de Gaulle...) But Zola's manifesto polarized French opinion on the Dreyfus case. There were mass riots and street duels fought with swords and pistols. Ten years later the fury against Zola had not abated and his enemies had not disarmed. On the occasion of his pantheonization in June 1908 - the greatest posthumous honour bestowed on the Republic's heroes - they marched through the streets shouting "Spit on Zola ! Death to Zola !", while Dreyfus himself was shot in the arm in an attempt on his life. On 30 September 1902 Zola's body was found suffocated in his house, officially an accidental death, although many, including Zola's son, have always believed it was murder.

By 1914 the nationalist fever was channelled entirely against the *boches* (Germans). On 31 July 1914, at around 9.30 pm, Jean Jaurès was having an animated dinner with fellow journalists from his paper *L'Humanité*, seated by an open window at the the café *La Chope du Croissant* on the corner of rue du Croissant on your right. Raoul Villain, standing outside, drew the curtain, aimed at Jaurès and fired twice: Jaurès was dead for having opposed the war. Inside the café is displayed a copy of the next morning's front page of *L'Humanité* announcing the death of Jaurès, along with cuttings from other papers. Jean Jaures's table is there too, with a blood stain that never came off. Periodically, faithful disciples of Jean Jaurès gather here for dinner and even strike up the Internationale before breaking up. Although the place has been refurbished beyond recognition, you may consider stopping in this historic restaurant for a basic French meal in a genuine neighbourhood atmosphere.

WEST OF RUE MONTMARTRE

Rue Montmartre was the social divide of the arrondissement. West of it lay the pleasure quarters of the privileged. You enter the area by turning left into rue Saint-Marc. To your right lies a maze of arcades - Galerie Montmartre, Galerie Saint-Marc, Galerie des Variétés, Passage des Panoramas, Galerie Feydeau - all reminiscent of that past. Passage des Panoramas was one of the highlights of Paris in the last century, the first place in the city to be gaslit, in 1817. The fashionable set frequented the elegant Café Véron, the pastry shop Félix and, above all, the circular Panoramas, the *dernier cri*. Invented by the English painter Joseph Barker in 1787, they transported the spectator to bloody battlefields or peaceful foreign lands. Passage des Panoramas leads to Boulevard Montmartre. The Café des Variétés, a stronghold of literati till 1870, was at n° 9 to your right. Next door, at n° 7, Le Théâtre des Variétés, where Hortense Schneider created a sensation with Offenbach's *La Grande Duchesse* in 1867, still stands.

Retrace your steps and continue along Boulevard Montmartre. Turn left into rue Vivienne, the backbone of opulence in the 18th century, described by the famous contemporary chronicler Louis-Sébastien Mercier as having "more money in this single street than in the rest of the entire city. This is the purse of the capital." The area still abounds in banking establishments, not to mention the Paris Stock Exchange further down rue Vivienne. Turn right into rue Feydeau and left into rue des Colonnes, which once led to Théâtre Feydeau. Its elegant architecture provided a pleasing backdrop to the scintillating spectators, who would stream into the street during intervals, enjoying the fresh air in summer or taking shelter under the arcades on rainy nights.

Turn left into rue du Quatre Septembre and proceed to Place de la Bourse. The Paris Stock Exchange stands in its centre, on the site of the convent of Les Filles de Saint-Thomas, which was closed down during the Revolution. At a time of nascent capitalism, Napoleon had it razed to the ground and replaced it with this more useful shrine, emulating a Greek temple in style. The Stock Exchange is open to the public, although women were not admitted until 1967 ! Tours (conducted in French) start at 11, 11.30, 12 and 12.30 daily, except Saturdays and Sundays.

At n° 2 Place de la Bourse is the head office of the Club Med, the leisure club famous for its essentially French *savoir faire*, one of the successful French economic ventures. Every year 1.2 million GM (*Gentils Membres*) are looked after by 24,000 young, beautiful, suntanned GO (*Gentils Organisateurs*) in 90 sunny 'villages' throughout the world.

Turn right into rue de la Banque, right again into Passage des Petits-Pères and continue to Place des Petits-Pères, a picturesque nook, away from the din of the city. The welcoming Republican Mairie, decked with a tricolour, and the serene aspect of the basilica of Notre-Dame-des-Victoires create an unexpectedly provincial touch. The illustrious architect of the Invalides, Libéral Bruant, collaborated in the construction of this church, an important pilgrimage shrine. The painting above the high altar shows the Holy Virgin seated on a cloud: at her feet is Louis XIII presenting her with a plan of the church in humble gratitude for having helped him defeat his enemies - hence the man on his right surrendering the keys of the defeated town of La Rochelle, which can be seen in the background. The King's right-hand man, Richelieu, whose initiative it was to eliminate the Huguenots and who in 1628 obtained their surrender at La Rochelle, can be seen to his left. Among famous Parisians who were buried here was Louis XIV's musician Lully. The church was looted and wrecked during the Revolution, then found use as the Paris stock exchange between 1796 and 1809.

Continue along rue des Petits-Pères, rue des Petits-Champs and turn right into rue de Richelieu, on which is the entrance to the Bibliothèque Nationale. This monumental institution was initiated by Charles V in the 14th century, when he concentrated his ancestors' manuscripts in the tower of the Louvre. The collection was scattered around during the Hundred Years' War but was gathered again in the 16th century by Louis XII and especially by the humanistic François I. In 1643 Mazarin rented a property at 8 rue des Petits-Champs, the Hôtel Tubeuf, close to Richelieu's Palais-Royal, so as to keep up with his predecessor. Two years later he owned all the area extending north as far as the present rue Colbert, including a second mansion, the Hôtel de Chivry (later known as Nevers), on rue de Richelieu, a vast domain nearly as large as the Palais-Royal. In 1645 François Mansart was commissioned to build a two-storeyed gallery between the two mansions, to house Mazarin's art collection. Further construction was undertaken along rue de Richelieu in 1649, this time to house his library of 40,000 volumes, the most impressive library in Europe. Mazarin had sent his emissaries to all the courts and kingdoms with instructions systematically to buy all the books that were unavailable in Paris. As a result, between 30,000 and 35,000 volumes were purchased in less than ten years!

After Mazarin's death the property was divided between his two nephews and subsequently changed hands and was greatly altered. Colbert transferred the library to rue Vivienne in 1666, and several financial establishments took up residence here instead, including the stock exchange, which used the premises of the Hôtel Tubeuf from 1724 until the Revolution. In 1721 the Regent bought the

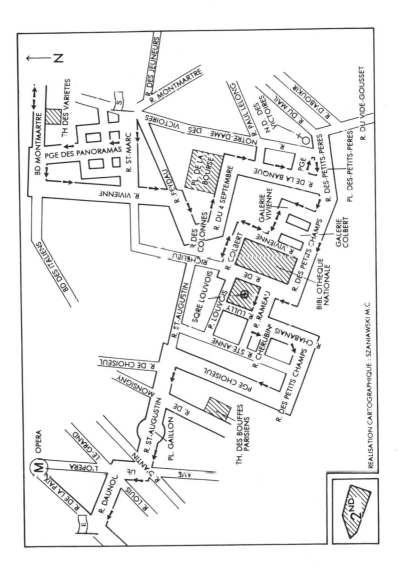

REALISATION CARTOGRAPHIQUE : SZANIAWSKI M.C.

Hôtel de Nevers, where he permanently established the royal library, the Bibliothèque du Roi. The premises underwent major alterations in the 18th and 19th centuries, to cope with the overwhelming expansion of the library, caused first by the Revolution, when a prodigious flow of books confiscated from the aristocracy and religious institutions were transferred here, and then, in the 19th century, by the explosion of printing. the present buildings, designed by Labrouste during the Second Empire, replaced the Hôtel Tubeuf on the corner of rue de Richelieu and rue des Petits-Champs, and the Hôtel de Nevers, on the corner of rue de Richelieu and rue Colbert. This most venerable institution of the 2nd arrondissement has over the years acquired 12 million books, 6 million engravings, 800,000 coins and medals, 400,000 records and an annual intake of about a million magazines and newspapers. A victim of its own success, it is to be replaced by La Très Grande Bibliothèque, due to open in 1996 in the 13th arrondissement. Only the art section, to be renamed La Bibliothèque Internationale d'Art, will remain on rue de Richelieu.

Before crossing into Square Louvois, continue along rue de Richelieu, turn right into rue Colbert and right again into rue Vivienne. On your left are two delightful hidden arcades - the highlight of the 2nd arrondissement - Galeries

Galerie Vivienne

Vivienne and Colbert, an ideal spot for a pause, especially on a wet day. While the Galerie Vivienne, with its tasteful, arty boutiques and good bookshops has a charming, antiquated feel, the Galerie Colbert has been renovated into a more formal, classical compound in true French style, enhanced by its pale pink stone.

Retrace your steps to Square Louvois which stands on the site of Paris's ninth opera house (there have been another four since). Most of them had been destroyed by fire, but not this one. On 13 February 1820, the Duc de Berry, eldest son of the future Charles X, was assassinated at the royal doorway of the theatre (level with n° 5 rue Rameau) by a certain Louvel, as a first step in his scheme to rid France of the entire House of Bourbon. Louvel, however, was caught and guillotined before he had time to do more harm and the opera house was razed to the ground by order of the King, so as to obliterate the scene of the crime. The only reminders of the lyrical past of the neighbourhood are its street names, Cherubini, Rameau and Lully. Lully actually lived near by, in the corner house at n°s 45 rue des Petits-Champs and 47 rue Sainte-Anne. You will notice its listed façade, decorated with musical instruments and masks of Bacchantes and satyrs. At the beginning of the 19th century, the idolized tenor Adolphe Nourrit, who premiered all the masterpieces of the time, lived at n° 6 rue Rameau. During a performance of Halévy's *La Juive* in Marseille, he suddenly lost his voice and could never sing again. In 1839 he threw himself out of a window in Naples. He was only 27. Square Louvois provides the only green patch in this busy arrondissement, and a pleasant one indeed, enhanced by Visconti's graceful fountain and its allegorical figures of the four biggest rivers of France that bear feminine names – which explains why the Rhone is not among them.

Both the square and rue de Louvois commemorate Louis XIV's minister, the Marquis de Louvois, whose sumptuous home extended all the way from rue Sainte-Anne to rue de Richelieu. After it was demolished in 1784, rue de Louvois was opened across its site, the second street in Paris to be bordered with pavements, rue de l'Odéon (in the 6th arr.) being the first one. On the other side of the square, the Hôtel Mirosmenil, built by Mansart and decorated by Le Brun, matched it in splendour. It was demolished during the Revolution and rue Rameau now runs on its site. Walk along rue Rameau and turn left into rue Chabanais, opened in 1776. Its 18th-century mansions with their wrought-iron decorations and broad carriage entrances, constitute a fine example of the architecture of the time. But rue Chabanais was famous first and foremost for its internationally renowned brothel at n° 12, which from 1878 to 1946 catered to the exclusive clientele of the celebrated Jockey Club on Boulevard des Italiens. Most of the crowned heads of Europe, frequented this impeccably tasteful establishment, as did ministers and government leaders of the Third Republic. It is said that their visits were described on their official timetable as 'visit to the President of the Sénat'. An absent-minded official is rumoured on one occasion to have entered a visit to the brothel on the schedule of a queen of Spain, which created no small scandal! The splendid furniture of the house was dispersed at an auction held at Drouot (the Paris auction house in the 9th arr.) on 8 May 1951.

Turn right into rue des Petits-Champs and left into Passage de Choiseul, now a noisy, uninspiring arcade, yet imbued with a cultural past. It was built in 1825 by Tavernier and its architecture bears witness to travellers' accounts of the orient and its exotic bazaars. Until 1965 n° 23 was the site of a publishing house which published the works of the Parnasse poets - Sully Prudomme, Leconte de Lisle, Heredia and François Coppée, followed from 1864 onwards by Paul Verlaine. A few years later Anatole France worked here as editor for roughly ten years. The stage door to the winter Bouffes Parisiens still stands at n° 73. During the winter seasons of 1855 to 1863, Jacques Offenbach, then director of this theatre, could be seen walking through this door. The theatre was pulled down in 1863 and replaced by the present one, which has undergone several face-lifts over the years. The main entrance is on rue Monsigny. By the 1930s the arcade was taken over by commerce and had forgotten about its writers and poets. People flocked to Barlett at Passage Choiseul, where shoes were for sale at the fixed price of 69 francs, whatever the shape, colour or size.

Turn left into rue Saint-Augustin, then on to Place Gaillon, an attractive, peaceful nook, adorned with another of Visconti's fountains, a major Parisian landmark. In the celebrated Drouant restaurant on the corner of 18 rue Gaillon, the Goncourt Prize, the most prestigious of French literary prizes, is awarded every third Monday of November. Monsieur Charles Drouant came up to Paris from Alsace in 1880, as did many of his compatriots torn by the loss of their region to the Germans. Like other Alsatians he began by opening a modest café-restaurant, which soon acquired a reputation for solid quality at low prices. Artists and writers came to sample the deliciously fresh oysters and seafood he brought over from Britanny, and before long the restaurant numbered Alphonse and Léon Daudet, Rodin, Renoir, and Edmond de Goncourt among its regulars.

When the Goncourt Academy was founded in 1894 to administer the Prize, however, it did the rounds of various restaurants in the Opéra area and settled at Drouant's only in 1914, when it had been enlarged and suitably refurbished. The celebrated Ruhlmann created a sumptuous Belle Epoque setting, complete with a majestic staircase and wrought-iron railing, glittering mirrors and a painted ceiling. The ten prize-winners were invited to a gastronomic meal once a month in a private salon, with oak panelling and an impressive chandelier. On their plated silver forks were engraved the names of their succussive predecessors. In *Paris Vecu*, Léon Daudet informs us that the prize money was 5,000 francs - a substantial sum for those days. Above all, it helped to launch the career of deserving authors, unlike the elections to the Académie Française, behind which there was a lot of wheeling and dealing. At the time the Academy Goncourt sat in December, and Léon Daudet was elated on 10 December 1919, when he brought Proust the letter informing him he had been awarded the prize for *A l'ombre des Jeunes Filles en fleurs*. It was not such a triumph, though, Proust having received the narrow margin of six votes. Four went to Dorgelès for his war novel *Les Croix de Bois*, which, obviously, was much more topical. Nevertheless, Léon Daudet claimed that Proust "owed his just renown to the Goncourt prize".

Continue along rue Saint-Augustin to the Avenue de l'Opéra, an enchanting vista by night when the old opera house, the Palais Garnier, is illuminated and the avenue is lit up. Cross the avenue and continue into rue Daunou, a stronghold of the American 'expatriates' in the 1920s, only a couple of blocks away from the American Express on rue Scribe. At n° 5 the red neon sign of Harry's Bar still stands out in the night in the otherwise dark, deserted street, beckoning the passer-by in. This was a favourite hang-out of Hemingway, whose photograph hangs on the wall. His friend Fitzgerald was also a regular and dropped in from the Ritz, just round the corner. Still warm and cosy bar, thanks to its wood panelling, Harry's New York Bar was also the birthplace of the Bloody Mary!

Turn left into rue de la Paix, also to be seen by night, for the sake of the illuminated Place Vendôme ahead. This was the most glamorous shopping street in Paris in the 19th century and well into the 20th, once the site of the church of the beautiful convent of the Capucines. The convent was closed down during the Revolution and converted into a theatre. A popular funfair was held in its gardens and the famous Franconi moved his circus there. In 1806 Napoleon razed the buildings to the ground to make room for a glorious new thoroughfare to honour his name and entrusted the project to his prestigious architects Percier and Fontaine. After his defeat in 1814, however, the street was renamed rue de la Paix to commemorate the signing of the Peace of Amiens. Members of the court and the new Napoleonic aristocracy, and later their Republican heirs, were the chief customers of the elegant shops and *haute couture* houses of rue de la Paix. The establishment of Jacques Doucet, who was to train and shape Paul Poiret, was at n° 23. A discerning art collector and a progressive mind, as well as a celebrated *couturier*, Doucet collected such revolutionary works as Picasso's *Demoiselles d'Avignon* and other works rejected by most of his contemporaries. The milliner Caroline Reboux, who had been launched by the Princesse de Metternich, was also established at n° 23.

The head office of the jeweller Cartier is still at n° 13 rue de la Paix. The house was founded in 1847 by Louis Ferdinand Cartier, who till then had been working for another famous jeweller, Adolphe Picard. He first set up shop near the Palais-Royal, on rue Neuve-des-Petits-Champs (now rue des Petits-Champs), and then moved to the fashionable Boulevard des Italiens, where his customers included the Empress Eugénie and Napoleon III's cousin, la Princesse Mathilde, the 'queen' of fashion. In 1899 his grandson Louis moved to rue de la Paix, by then the centre of luxury of the capital. Cartier's international clientele included Edward VII of England, Alphonso XIII of Spain and the Duchess of Winsor. Cartier also created such national symbols as the baton of Maréchal Foch and the ceremonial swords of some of the members of the Institut de France, the venerable *Académiciens*.

Mellerio, another venerable jeweller's, stood until recently at n° 9. Since he was purveyor to the court, Queen Marie-Amélie allowed him to inscribe on the shop front *'Bijoutier de la Reine des Français'*. At n° 7 was the house of Charles Worth, rightly claimed to be the first *haute couture* designer, who raised the status of dressmaking from craft to art. When Charles Frederick Worth arrived from England in 1845, aged 20, he had the meagre sum of 117 francs in his pocket and knew not a word of French! He had, however, been apprenticed for seven years to the drapers Swan and Edgar, and had a short stay with the renowned silk purveyors Lewis and Allenby. After 12 years of hard constructive work, he opened his own house on rue de la Paix in 1858. The timing was perfect, for this was the heyday of the glamorous Second Empire, ruled by the fashion-conscious Empress Eugénie. Multitudes of social upstarts, ready to squander unlimited sums of money, rotated around the court, emulating its members. These provided an ideal clientele who accepted Worth's tyranny because they could not claim to be his social betters. The reign of the *haute couture* designer thus began.

In 1892 the prosperous banker Paquin set up his wife at n° 5. If we exclude Marie-Antoinette's dressmaker, Rose Berin, Madame Paquin was the first woman designer and also the first woman to be awarded the *Légion d'honneur* in 1913. A prominent public figure, Madame Paquin chaired the 1900 Universal Exhibition. 2,700 employees worked for her establishment, which was located above Robert's chemist shop, opened in 1820 by Dr Roberts, chemist and surgeon to the British Embassy. Now still standing among the travel agencies that line rue de la Paix, the shop is the sole reminder of former glories.

THE 3rd ARRONDISSEMENT

A few street names are all that is left of the mighty fortress of the Knights Templars, the founding fathers of the 3rd arrondissement. They were first organized into a fighting order in the Holy Land in 1118 to protect Christian pilgrims from Moslem attacks. Having accumulated great wealth through gifts bestowed on them by appreciative Christians, they soon owned estates throughout Europe, including one on the eastern edge of Paris on the site of the present rue de Lobau (next to the Hôtel de Ville in the 4th arr.), where a group of Templars settled around 1139, on their return from the Holy Land.

To the north east lay stretches of marshland, remnants of the ancient branch of the Seine that had once flowed down from the heights of Belleville, east of Paris. It took the hardy Templars barely a century to turn it into the market garden (*marais*) of the capital, emulating the monks of Saint-Martin-des-Champs, who had dried up the swamps in the western part of the arrondissement. Having redeemed the land, they moved to its north-eastern edge, where they built a fortified compound, l'Enclos du Temple, complete with watch-towers and crenellated walls, roughly on the site of the present rue du Temple, rue de Bretagne, rue de Picardie and rue Béranger, south of Place de la République. A drawbridge led to its only gate (now corner of rue des Fontaines-du-Temple and rue du Temple).

Using their geographical dispersion to advantage, the Templars founded a kind of international deposit bank, thus continually increasing their wealth, while at the same time preserving their independence behind their crenellated walls - a situation readily accepted by the throne till the end of the 13th century. Philippe-Auguste even entrusted some treasures to them when he left on the Third Crusade in 1190, and Saint Louis did not take offence when in 1254 Henry III of England stayed at the Temple rather than in his own palace. But Philippe le Bel, an ambitious King who had even stood up to the church of Rome, could not tolerate this wealthy state within his state, the less so as he himself was in chronic financial straits. During a mass rising in 1306, ignited by the fifth consecutive devaluation of the kingdom's currency, he accepted the Templars' offer of shelter and took the measure of their stupendous wealth. Eaten up with envy, he set out to contrive their downfall by spreading treacherous rumours and slanders against them. After hideous trials, false accusations, humiliations, torture and the burning of 54 Templars on l'Ile aux Juifs (now the southern edge of Place Dauphine), the French branch of the Order was disbanded in 1313. On 12 March 1314, Jacques de Molay, Grand Master of the Temple, was brought to the stake on l'Ile aux Juifs, where, in the presence of the King, he thundered out prophecies about the King's

71

and the Pope's impending encounter with God. Both Philippe le Bel and Pope Clement V were to die that year – whether by the hand of God or of man has never been established.

Meanwhile the Templars' possessions had been seized by the throne and, to add insult to injury, the Enclos du Temple was given over to their deadly enemies, the Hospitallers. They too had started out in the Holy Land, as early as 1050, initially to welcome pilgrims to Jerusalem, a role complementary to that of the Templars; but by the following century they too had become a fighting order, which gave rise to rivalry and long-lasting enmity. The Hospitallers prospered at the Temple until the Revolution and were disbanded only by Napoleon in the early 19th century.

With prosperity came the inevitable loosening of monastic life and, by the time of the Renaissance, stylish apartments replaced austere cells. In the second half of the 17th century the Palais du Grand Prieur, built by Mansart, matched the splendour and brilliance of the mansions in the heart of the Marais to the south.

Outside the Enclos du Temple Henri IV in particular contributed to the development of this area. Long before the Baron Haussmann, and largely thanks to the wisdom gained from the Wars of Religion, he understood that wide vistas and broad radiating avenues were not only elegant but also helped to keep the population in check and quell street riots. Thus, a monumental Place de France was planned to replace the medieval gate of Saint-Antoine as the new regal gateway to the capital from the east. Majestic avenues celebrating the kingdom's provinces were to fan out of it, while a grand canal running north from the Seine was to grace it with a Venetian touch. The concept was nipped in the bud on 14 May 1610, with the assassination of the King. Now the shabby rue de Poitou, Bretagne and Normandie, and the curved rue Debelleyme that links them are the only trace of that magnificent project.

Henri IV's plan for the first open-air square in Paris, on the other hand, was carried through to completion, albeit after his death. This is the jewel-like Place des Vosges, on the border of the 4th arrondissement, the gem of Henri IV's architectural style. Inaugurated on the occasion of the double wedding of Louis XIII to Anne of Austria, and of his sister Elizabeth to the future Philip IV of Spain, it was named appropriately Place Royale. The festivities began on 5 April 1612 and went on for three days: a motley carousel of extraordinary splendour made its rounds to the sound of trumpets, oboes and violins, while the guns of the Bastille roared in the distance. At night a torchlight procession left the Place Royale and paraded through the streets of Paris to the sound of music, while a magnificent display of fireworks illuminated the sky at the Bastille.

These events elevated the Marais to the position of the undisputed aristocratic centre of 17th-century Paris. Both royalty and the old nobility - *la noblesse d'épée* - had already spotted the Marais in the 14th century: Charles V had moved to the Hôtel de Saint-Pol in search of a safe haven after the traumatic experience of Etienne Marcel's revolt (see chapter on the 1st arr.), but the nobility had sought elbow-room, outside the walls of the congested city. The religious orders, living off its fertile market gardens, were eager to increase their revenue and yielded their possessions readily. By the late 15th century such prominent families as the Guise and the Montmorency were firmly established in the Marais. In the 16th century they were joined by the newly ennobled financial and intellectual bourgeoisie - the Guénégauds, Lamoignons, Ormessons - known as the *noblesse de robe*, who counterbalanced the old nobility by helping the throne to consolidate its growing power, while supplying it with much-needed currency, the purchase of titles being a costly transaction.

During the English occupation in the 15th century, the Duke of Bedford and governor of Paris took up residence in the sumptuous Hôtel des Tournelles, bordering today's Place des Vosges to the north. Later it became the Parisian residence of the royal family, who preferred it to the insalubrious Hôtel de Saint-Pol, in the vicinity of the fetid moat of the Bastille.

The presence of royalty in the Marais, however, ended brutally on 30 June 1559 with the accidental death of Henri II during a friendly tournament in the gardens of the Hôtel des Tournelles (now Place des Vosges), against the Comte de Montgomery, captain of the Scottish guard. His bereaved wife Catherine de Medici left at once the accursed place to settle temporarily in the antiquated Louvre, while awaiting the construction of a more comfortable residence, namely the Palais des Tuileries, to which she moved in 1564. The following year she ordered the Hôtel des Tournelles to be razed to the ground, so as to blot it out of her memory.

But the aristocracy stayed on: with peace restored after the War of Religions, the Marais became the site of feverish building. Fabulous new *hôtels particuliers* were built and older ones sumptuously renovated for the *"gens d'esprit, gens de cour et de la ville, et tout ce qu'il y avait de meilleur et de plus distingué "*("men of learning, courtiers and town dwellers, the finest and the most distinguished"), according to the contemporary eyewitness, the Duc de Saint-Simon. Not until the court was transferred to Versailles in 1682 did the Marais begin to decline, being then too far east.

For the time being its inhabitants displayed their wit and attire in gatherings known as *salons littéraires*, presided over by high-powered women of letters - Madame de Sévigné at Hôtel Carnavalet, Mademoiselle de Scudéry on rue de Beauce. The gatherings around Ninon Lenclos were of a different nature: at a time of rigid, social conventions, she transformed what in others was regarded as scandalous prostitution into a socially acceptable way of life – *"le triomphe du vice conduit avec esprit"* (*"the triumph of vice conducted with wit"*), as Saint-

Simon put it. Her wit and musical talent, allied with her sexual appeal, made her irresistible to the greats of France - the Maréchal d'Estrées, Gondi, Condé, Richelieu, the Sévigné (both father and son) - no one disdained her company and she welcomed them all into her generous bed. The puritanical Anne of Austria was impervious to her charms and eventually had her locked up at the the Madelonnettes, a convent turned prison for repentant whores, despite her protestations that she was "neither a whore nor repentant"! It was a crowded place, for streetwalking abounded in this western part of the 3rd, close to the central market of Les Halles, as reflected in such street names as Transnonain ('Transnovice'), Vertus ('virtues'), Trace-Putain ('Whore's-Trail') and Troussevache ('Jade-Mounting'). Undaunted, Ninon ate ostentatiously during Lent and threw her meat bone out of the window, a brave act in an age of bigotry, when impiety was punishable by death, as her contemporary Claude Le Petit found out when he paid with his life for his licentious *Chronique Scandaleuse ou Paris Ridicule.*

Ninon had however gained the friendship of Queen Christina of Sweden and of Françoise d'Aubigné, wife of the satirical poet Scarron and later to be Madame de Maintenon, whose home was "the meeting-place of the most polished members of the court and of all the great minds of Paris". Molière, Boileau, La Fontaine, Mignard, Lully, the Duc d'Orléans (the future Regent), all went to the modest house at 36 rue des Tournelles, bringing their own food in recognition of their hosts' slender means.

Gaining access to the Temple was also easy for somebody of Ninon's calibre, for the Palais du Grand Prieur was the court of the illegitimate sons of royalty who, like Philippe Duc de Vendôme, the grandson of Henri IV and Gabrielle d'Estrées, led a life of debauchery, but also of literary and artistic brilliance. The Grand Prior, for example, granted La Fontaine an annual pension of 600 francs. After the court's transfer to Versailles it became an alternative court where "gathered those who had nothing to hope for from the King", we are told by Horace Walpole. Louis XVI (who had called his cousin Philippe d'Orléans, the landlord of the Palais-Royal, a shopkeeper) was equally contemptuous of the Grand Prior, the Prince de Conti, his "cousin the lawyer". Horace Walpole, on the other hand, described him as "handsome, of royal port and amiable" but also as arrogant, dissolute and prodigal. The Grand Prior reputedly kept 4,000 rings in one of his drawers, a farewell token from each repudiated mistress; but some claimed he had added many himself. His favourite, the Comtesse de Boufflers, *'l'Idole du Temple'*, reigned supreme over his scintillating court, to which the 10-year-old Mozart was introduced on his second visit to the capital. Ollivier's famous painting of him in the drawing-room playing the harpsichord to an inattentive audience is evidence of the Temple's lack of deep artistic commitment.

On 13 August 1792, a sumptuous dinner was served in the same room. The guests on this occasion were the Royal family and their retenue, virtually the prisoners of the Commune of Paris. The King was addressed as Monsieur and everyone was treated courteously during the sham celebration; but as soon as dinner was over the royal couple, their two children and the King's sister were locked up in the Tower of the Temple, while the other women were transferred to the prison of *La Force* (now in the 4th arr.), unknown to the people of Paris. This was the beginning of the tragic extinction of the Royal family. On 21 September 1792, at the foot of the small tower of the Temple, Superintendent Lubin reiterated the proclamation abolishing the monarchy, announced earlier in the day by Danton before the Convention. The King was kept in the main tower of the Temple till his execution on 21 January 1793 and the Queen till the next summer, when she was transferred to the Conciergerie. The 14-year-old Princess was exchanged with the Austrian authorities for five Republican prisoners and the seven-year-old Dauphin was torn away from his family and left to vegetate in a dark cell in total isolation, till his presumed death on 8 June 1795. He was carried to the cemetery of Sainte-Marguerite (now in the 11th arr.) for burial, but rumours persisted that somebody else's body had been laid there in his stead. When in 1894 it was decided to dig up the remains and examine the bones, they proved indeed to have belonged to an 18-year-old youth. Nevertheless, the mystery of the Temple child has never been resolved, which explains how 43 characters could pretend to the throne of France! It was Napoleon who got hold of the throne instead, whereupon he prudently razed the Temple Tower to the ground, the Royalists having made it their shrine. The original Romanesque church of the Temple and its churchyard soon met the same fate. Only the Grand Prior's Palace was still standing when the Princess Royal returned to the tragic site during the Restoration, there to pray and plant a weeping willow. Used by the Ministry of religion at the time of Napoleon, as a convent during the Restoration and as a military barracks during the Second Republic, it was torn down by Napoleon III in 1853.

By then the Temple area had become a working-class neighbourhood revolving around its thriving clothing market, which had started within the walls of the Temple. For the Enclos du Temple had been a free zone, and thus home to tax-exempted tradesmen and franchised craftsmen, as well as insolvent debtors - a population of 4,000 in all. Charlatan doctors and others could practise here with impunity and Parisians flocked to the Temple to buy its local herb-tea against constipation. In the 17th century Sieur Darce started to manufacture imitation jewellery, an enterprise forbidden elsewhere in the kingdom. A century later the Temple's woollen wigs were the rage and its lipstick was sought after by the ladies of the court.

In short, the Temple was the birthplace of fancy goods and fashion accessories, for the first time available to the masses. Its inhabitants could clear their surplus goods at its annual fair, which Napoleon turned into a permanent market, consisting of four wooden pavilions bearing derisively pompous names: Flore for beddings, Forêt Noire for shoes, Le Pou Volant ('the flying louse') for scrap. To the fourth, Le Palais-Royal, actresses came from all over Paris in search of a piece of velvet riband or a hat, trinkets and baubles, silk and lace, whatever they might need for the stage. A vivid, metaphorical jargon was born here, reflecting the spirit of working-class Paris in the first half of the 19th century, and some of the words, such as *chineur* ('secondhand dealer'), *gonzesse* ('chick'), eventually found their way into French dictionaries.

After work, it was only a short step to the perpetual funfair on Boulevard du Temple, a world immortalized in Marcel Carné's film *Les Enfants du Paradis*, with its theatres, street entertainment, passion and crime. Most of the theatres were on the north-eastern side of the Boulevard, in the 11th arrondissement, whereas the famous eating-places were concentrated in the 3rd as were the criminals. The most notorious was Lacernaire, an aloof, cynical dandy, irresistible to women. Aroused by the *Mémoires* he had written in his prison cell, fascinated by his impeccable attire and his polished French - after all, he had written decent poetry in his day - they flocked to his trial, unmindful of the fact that it was their own society he had challenged: "My duel with society [...] It was the social edifice that I wanted to attack in its foundations, its wealthy members, harsh and selfish, who throw to their dogs the bread they refuse to their fellow man." Writers and artists too were fascinated by Lacernaire and his portrait was recreated by Victor Hugo, André Breton, Marcel Carné (in *Les Enfants du Paradis*), and others since.

On 10 January 1836, at 6 a.m., a priest entered Lacernaire's cell. "Your visit is useless," was all the prisoner said before donning his morning coat and walking out of his cell stoically, headed for the guillotine. He was 33 years of age.

The market-place too was a nest of villains and vagabonds. Their canteen was Chez la Mère Maillard whose *plat garni* consisted of left-overs from the glittering Café Turc and the Cadran Bleu, on opposite corners of rue Charlot and Boulevard du Temple. The Boulevard was also known as Boulevard du Crime because of the endless bloody melodramas enacted in its theatres, but it might equally have been so nicknamed because of the real-life dramas played out on it. In this area, the borders between fiction and reality were blurred.

Throughout the 19th century small trades and workshops gnawed their way into the once aristocratic Marais: elegant courtyards and gardens vanished, 17th-century façades were hidden by artificial facing, majestic halls were partitioned, ceilings lowered, harmonious proportions wrecked. The workers' First International, founded in London in 1864 with the support of Karl Marx, set up its Parisian headquarters at 14 rue de Turennes, an appropriately working-class area. Place de la République, on the north-eastern edge of the arrondissement, became the departure point of working-class protest marches heading for the Bastille, a tradition still sometimes followed, even in these days of ideological confusion.

Waves of poor immigrants settled here too, many of them German Jews taking advantage of the emancipation granted them by the French Revolution. They took up residence on the northern edge of the arrondissement, where the clothing, jewellery and silverware trades flourished. By the middle of the century the synagogue they had built on rue Notre-Dame-de-Nazareth could no longer contain their increasing numbers. Jews from Alsace and eastern Europe came to swell their ranks in the latter part of the 19th century, pushing their way further south, as far as the medieval Jewish Quarter, in the 4th arrondissement. During World War I, mainland China also disgorged her poor, often to work in the arms industry. They too settled in the proletarian 3rd arrondissement, making it the home of the oldest Chinese community in Paris, (a little known fact, as locals are more familiar with the two recent Chinatowns of the 13th and 19th arrondissements). There are many Anglicans among them, from families converted by the English missionaries, and they are served by three churches in Paris, where the same hymns are sung as in England, only in Mandarin. Besides working diligently in the usual Chinese restaurants and food shops, they have taken over the traditional trades of the Temple (leather, fancy goods and imitation jewellery) and thus have, unwittingly, helped to perpetuate French traditions.

On 4 August 1962 the National Assembly passed *La loi Malraux* (initiated by Charles de Gaulle's Minister of Culture, André Malraux), for the rehabilitation of the Marais. Since then, old mansions have been turned into museums and cultural institutions, while stylish boutiques, art galleries and eating-places have little by little replaced traditional trades. However, with the departure of a good part of the original population, the Marais is in danger of losing its authenticity. Time alone will tell whether it will retain its soul or become a tourist showcase.

WHERE TO WALK...

THE MARAIS DU TEMPLE

The Temple Métro station stands in a run-down neighbourhood, melancholy and stale. Even the Temple market (open all mornings, except Mondays) cannot shake off this obsolete atmosphere. Yet this is the site of the one-time Enclos du Temple, and as such deserves your attention. On your way there, step into the church of Sainte-Elisabeth at 195 rue du Temple, the only 17th-century church in the arrondissement to have survived the havoc of the Revolution. Also dating from the 17th century is its fabulous Flemish wood panelling, with its hundred sculpted scenes from the Old and New Testaments. It was bought from the Abbey of Saint-Vaast in the town of Arras in 1945, and has been tucked away since in the dark ambulatory of the church.

Walk along rue Dupetit-Thouars to the corner of rue Gabriel-Vicaire, where a plan affixed to the wall will help you visualize the Enclos du Temple in the different stages of its evolution. Square du Temple, at the end of rue Gabriel-Vicaire, and the Mairie of the arrondissement that overlooks it, to your left, occupy part of its site. No trace is left of the 50-metre tower where the royal family was locked up; only a faded blue line in front of the Mairie marks its limits; this is a pity, for even in the 18th century, when medieval architecture had gone out of favour, the Tower of the Temple was admired and regarded as the most beautiful in France. Across the Square du Temple, on the corner of rue du Temple and rue de Bretagne, stood the Palace of the Grand Prior, where the 10-year-old Mozart played the harpsichord for the Prince de Conti in 1766. The Palace, a sumptuous mansion built by Mansart in 1667, was the enlightened centre of free-thinking Paris. In order to provide l'abbé Prévost (the author of *Manon Lescaut*) with a substantial livelihood, the Prince appointed him chaplain of the Temple, little bothered by the fact that the clergyman never celebrated mass. When the abbot, somewhat embarrassed, pointed this out to him, Conti retorted, "It is of little consequence - I never listen to it." On the other hand, the Prince was much more of a stickler for pedigree and would not marry his charismatic mistress, the Comtesse de Boufflers, although he held her in great respect.

The Square du Temple is one of several gardens opened by Napoleon III, emulating those he had admired during his exile in London. Designed on a miniature scale, it contains, nonetheless, a lake and a waterfall (the rocks come from the forest of Fontainebleau), and provides a rare, refreshing spot of beauty in this passé neighbourhood.

Little is left of the Marché du Temple (erroneously called the Carreau du Temple: the Carreau was the space between the Temple and the market, where pedlars traded with the Temple's inhabitants), just one iron structure north of the Mairie. Following the example of Les Halles, Napoleon III replaced the four wooden pavilions with six iron ones, all the way to rue du Temple. In 1904 they housed the first Paris Fair, but the following year four of them were dismantled, along with the attractive 18th-century Rotunda, once the home of debtors entitled to the protection of the Temple. The present iron pavilion stands on its site, devoid, however, of the picturesque bustle of yore: gone are the ribands, lace and feathers, the *râleuses* ('Mrs Grumpy') who pestered one into buying a *décrochez-moi ça!* ('get this off the hook'! , i.e. a woman's hat) or a pair of *dix-huit* ('eighteen', i.e. shoes), a pun on *deux fois neuf* ('twice nine' and 'twice new'), reflecting the

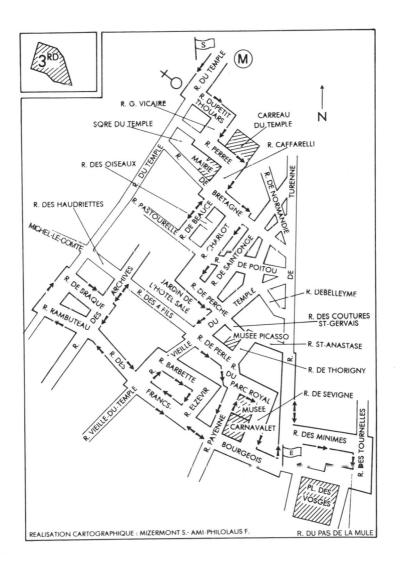

fact that worn out soles were turned over to make a new pair of shoes! Today, by contrast, the market is standardized, transactions are conventional and men's shirts are neatly folded up in hygienic cellophane wrappings...

Walk along rue Caffarelli south of the market, turn left into rue de Bretagne and right into rue de Beauce, now a narrow, shabby alley but a prestigious landmark in the second half of the 17th century. On the corner of rue de Beauce and rue des Oiseaux (first on your left) the enlightened Mademoiselle de Scudéry held one of the most sought after *salons* of her century, her '*ruelle*'. Despite the modesty of the premises, every Saturday a distinguished society would climb up the dark staircase leading to her muffled, obscure sanctuary, men in their long, cascading wigs surmounted by feathered hats, women with pyramid-like headdresses, their white-powdered faces marked by one inevitable black beauty spot. Here, refined conversation and lofty emotions were cultivated to excess, especially by the ladies, in reaction to the brutish coarse manners pervailing since the reign of Henri IV.

Whereas Madeleine de Scudéry's home lacked the magnificence of the wealthier *hôtels*, her garden was a gem. Its acacias and fruit trees emitted exquisite fragrances, which counteracted the fetid stench of the street, where rubbish accumulated in the central ditch, until the rain washed it away. A warbler, a wren and a parrot lived in the garden, adding song to the ravishing sight (hence the name rue des Oiseaux), a source of inspiration to the Scudéry's friends. Thus, in all earnest, the great philosopher Leibniz addressed her parrot in one of his verses. This literary affectation compensated for the fact that the members of the circle were not particularly alluring and that their hostess was by then an ageing woman in her forties. Her favourite suitor, Pellisson, was described by the writer Furetière as short and having "a hump which he carried on his shoulders [...] His two legs were of unequal length; he was blind in one eye and could not see with the other..." And Ninon Lenclos, having skimmed through Mlle de Scudéry's preposterous *Carte du Tendre* - a verbal map of a land of platonic love - called the members of her salon, *les Jansénistes* de *l'Amour*, "because they speak a lot about it but never make it." The female members, the *bas bleus* ('bluestockings'), were targeted by Molière in his immensely popular farce *Les Précieuses Ridicules*. Likewise, Tallemant des Réaux, a keen contemporary eyewitness, took to his heals after a few sessions because their activities were "beginning seriously to bore people".

Yet Madeleine de Scudéry was a woman of great intellect and remained so into her nineties. Madame de Maintenon counted her among her friends and the highly cultured Queen Christina of Sweden visited her when in Paris, as did all foreign

---

*Austere followers of the Dutch theologian Jansen Cornelis (1585 - 1638) who believed in predestination and denied free will.

travellers of note. It must also be said to her credit that she was a loyal friend, for when Pellisson was arrested with Nicolas Fouquet she disavowed neither. As for Pellisson, he may have been unprepossessing, but he was also a distinguished Academician, a leading orator and the King's official historiographer. He also took the initiative in collecting the literary output of those Saturday gatherings and noting down their happenings in *Chronique du Samedi*, which he bound into a blue velvet volume, alas now lost.

Turn right into rue de Bretagne. At the time of writing, the picturesque market of Les Enfants Rouges ('the little boys in red') on the corner of rue Charlot, the oldest market of Paris, has been earmarked for demolition and replacement by a modern block and a car park. The eponymous little boys in red were the inmates of the orphanage at 90 rue des Archives, and were part of the landscape of the Marais. Their female counterparts, dressed in blue,were known as '*les enfants bleus*'. Rue Charlot comemmorates Heni IV's prominent developer who was commissioned to lay out the proposed monumental Place de France. Rue de Bretagne, rue de Poitou further down rue Charlot, to your left, and rue de Normandie, north of rue de Bretagne, were part of this aborted project. After Henri IV's assassination in 1610, Charlot was able to devote his time to making profits and set out to build up the area as speedily as he could. Rue Charlot, an elegant street in the 17th and 18th centuries, dilapidated thereafter, is now in the process of gentrification. Some of its houses deserve attention: n° 38 where a sewing workshop and a metalworks still subsist on either side of a countrified courtyard; n° 33 has already been restored and boasts a magnificent staircase; n° 31 and n° 29 still house vestiges of the neighbourhood's once-flourishing silver trade. The 18th-century *hôtel* at n° 28, the former home of the Marquise de Polignac, is of unquestionable architectural distinction despite its present sorry state. An attractive 17th-century *hôtel* at n° 24 houses an art gallery, one of several in the street. The corner of rue Pastourelle, with its old-fashioned street lamp affixed to the wall and its picturesque café, Le Baromètre, is a rare slice of old Paris straight from an old movie – take it in before it is gone! The house at n° 11 rue Pastourelle boasts a charming courtyard and a beautiful Louis XV wrought-iron staircase.

Back on rue Charlot, continue to the corner of rue du Perche on your left. The old Armenian Catholic church, shaded by two chestnut trees, is the only vestige of the convent of the Capucin monks, who were the fire brigade of Paris, rushing about as best they could in their gowns, each carrying two buckets of water. This is how they were seen at 10 pm on 15 January 1644, dashing down rue du Perche to the Théâtre de Marais round the corner, all aflame. "I saw it burn with horror", reported the President d'Ormesson who lived close by. "So big was the fire, it could be seen throughout Paris. People rushed from everywhere and it was as clear as daylight." With only two buckets of water each, there was little they could do to stop the conflagration.

The church has some relics that belonged to Saint Elizabeth, the sister of Saint Louis, and also the chasuble of the Irish abbot Edgeworth, the last confessor of Louis XVI. In the early morning of 21 January 1793 he was dispatched from here with all the liturgical accessories to the Temple to celebrate the King's last mass. Clearly the Revolution had not sorted out its attitude to religion. Inside the church is a 19th-century Cavaillé-Coll organ, which was played by such musicians as César Franck, Massenet and Léo Delibes. Unfortunately, the church is kept locked except on Sunday mornings during mass.

Walk up to n° 7 bis rue du Perche, known as Hôtel Scarron because Scarron's widow, the future Madame de Maintenon, lived here for a while in 1664. An ordinary-looking house, it has beautiful 17th-century paintings on its ceilings. Retrace your steps and turn right into rue de Saintonge, lined with some 17th- and 18th-century houses. A bronze-fitter and a wrought-iron craftsman still work at n° 4. In 1651 Blaise Pascal was living at n° 13 and working on the problem of vacuum, when his father died, which caused the family the grief of having to move out on Christmas Day. Retrace your steps and turn left into rue de Poitou. The corner *boulangerie* has typical Belle Epoque window panelling, decorated with harvest scenes. Such panels were commonplace at the time but regrettably many have been removed by antique dealers and collectors.

Turn right into rue Debelleyme (like rue de Poitou, a remnant of the Place de France scheme) and cross over to rue Vieille-du-Temple. The Hôtel d'Epinay at n° 110 now houses an art gallery. Its 18th-century door is therefore likely to be open during the day, revealing the architectural splendour of the entrance hall. The framework of the building dates from the early 17th century, maybe in part from before (François d'Epinay was one of Henri III's *'mignons'*), but the gorgeous staircase with its rich, curving, wrought-iron railing, is Rocaille, a style in vogue during the reign of Louis XV. An elegant orangery can be seen inside the garden, surmounted by a typical Henri IV and Louis XIII façade of brick and stone. The Hôtel d'Epernon at n° 106, also has a brick-and-stone façade, except that here the bricks are painted on the wall, a common device at a time when brick was costly. The *hôtel's* frontage is ornamented with a superb sculpted head and two lions couchant on its pediment. The garden at n° 90 lies on the site of an old real-tennis court (*jeu de paume*), which was taken over by the Théâtre du Marais in the 17th century, when the game was going out of fashion. Behind the garden can be seen the back of the Hôtel Salé or Aubert de Fontenay (now Musée Picasso). Throughout its life the Théâtre du Marais had to contend with the jealous manoeuvring of the King's troupe, les Comédiens du Roi, which was established at the Hôtel de Bourgogne on rue Mauconseil, north of the church of

Saint-Eustache. Time and again the Théâtre du Marais was forced to yield its lead actors to their rivals, notably Jodelet, one of the most famous actors of the 17th century. The tremendous success of the Théâtre du Marais was due to the quality of its actors, of course, but also to the collaboration of Pierre Corneille, whose early comedies created a sensation: indeed, in a written petition, the inhabitants of rue Michel-le-Comte (where the theatre was located for a short while) complained about the obstruction caused by the presence of so many carriages and horses, because of which they had to wait until late into the night before they could return home. The theatre's stunning collection of costumes also testifies to the fact that it was a highly lucrative business.

The premiere in December 1636 of Corneille's play *Le Cid*, with the idolized Mondory in the lead role of Rodrigue, electrified the audience. As the writer Boileau reported, *"Tout Paris pour Chimène a les yeux de Rodrigue "* ("All Paris gazes at Chimène with the eyes of Rodrigue"). Today's generations, having plodded through the dilemma of choice between love and honour in tedious French classes, will find it hard to imagine the momentum of the event. The soaring success of the troupe was clouded by a tragic event the following August, when Mondory, was struck by a fit of apoplexy on the stage, which left his arm and tongue permanently paralysed and ended his career.

Nevertheless, Corneille's great tragedies took the theatre from success to success, not dented either by the opening of Molière's Théâtre Illustre in 1643 on the Left Bank or by the devastating fire in 1644. On the contrary, its new leader, Floridor, reconstructed and enlarged the premises, turning them into the most beautiful ones in the kingdom - if hot and poorly ventilated. The theatre was invariably filled to its capacity of 1,500. But once more lobbying by the King's troupe secured Floridor's transfer, which, it was predicted, would be a fatal blow, for he was considered by Corneille himself as the indispensable interpreter of his plays. Nevertheless, the theatre's new director, Philibert Robin, emerged from the wreckage and carried the theatre to even greater heights. Using the first special effects, he created enchanting extravaganzas, the embryonic form of the opera. Never before had Paris marvelled at Mercury descended from a gloriously starstudded sky, at Jupiter appearing in mid-air, darting formidable flashes of lightning, while thunder rumbled in the background. *La Toison d'Or* (*'The Golden Fleece'*) in 1661 was the theatrical event of the century: twice Louis XIV travelled with his entire court from the Louvre to rue Vieille-du-Temple to attend the show. This time the King's musician, Lully, was alarmed at the competition. In 1672 he prevailed upon the King to grant him the monopoly in opera productions and in 1673, after Molière's death, the Théâtre du Marais was closed down and the troupe ordered to join the late Molière's Théâtre Illustre on the Left Bank. The King's official troupe survived into the 1680s, producing Racine's plays, but soon they too were ordered to join the newly merged troupe on the Left Bank. With the increasing centralization of the state, there was room for one troupe only. In 1728, the premises of the Théâtre du Marais were turned into horse stables by the new owner of the Hôtel Salé, Nicolas Le Camus.

Turn left into rue de la Perle. At n° 1 the locksmith museum is located in the Hôtel Bruant (1685), formerly the home of Libéral Bruant, the famous architect of the Invalides. Having bought from the Order of the Fusées the last uninhabited domain in the Marais du Temple (the area between the Temple and rue des Francs-Bourgeois), he replaced the Order's kitchen gardens with magnificent *hôtels particuliers*, thus completing the urbanization of the Marais. Somehow, only the one he has built for himself has survived.

Turn left into rue de Thorigny. At n° 5 stands the Hôtel Aubert de Fontenay or Salé, now the Musée Picasso. Aubert de Fontenay was one of the King's *partisans* who, from the 16th century on, were in charge of collecting his taxes and were later known as *fermiers généraux*. This privileged post enabled its holder to amass a fabulous fortune, but also placed him in a fragile position, between the devil and the deep blue sea, between a jealous despot (cf Louis XIV and Nicolas Fouquet) and a discontented populace. The people of Paris nicknamed Aubert de Fontenay's showy mansion *'l'hôtel salé'* ('the salty hotel'), because he had made his fortune largely through collecting the salt tax, but also because *salé* in colloquial French means expensive: Aubert, who was said to have started out as a lackey, went all out to impress his neighbours. However, like many others, he lost his fortune in the wake of Fouquet's downfall and died before the *hôtel* had been completed. Other *parvenus* were more fortunate and it was not unusual to see them climb from the bottom all the way up the social ladder, as we are told by Molière in *L'Ecole des Femmes:* "I know a country fellow called Gros Pierre, who, not having any other property than a single piece of land, had a muddy ditch dug round it, and pompously called himself Monsieur de l'Isle." Or, as the great observer of the human animal, La Bruyère, summed it up succinctly in his *Caractères*: "Certain people go to bed as commoners and rise noble." Which was precisely what the maternal great-grandfather of the very noble Marquise de Sévigné did, a wealthy tax-collector by the name of Philippe de Coulanges, who had married his daughter into the very old feudal family of the Rabutins. The bridegroom, the Baron de Chantal, being ridden with debts, found the match to his interest, but the rest of the family did not appear at the wedding. Commenting on such *mésalliances* a few decades later, Madame de Sévigné said: "*Il faut bien fumer ses terres* ("One does have to manure one's land").

After Aubert's death the Embassy of Venice rented the dazzling mansion with its richly decorated pediment and its imposing staircase, surrounded by Corinthian pillars, medallions and sculpted eagles - no effort was spared to dazzle all and sundry. Its fabulous wrought-iron balustrade is marked with the letters A for Aubert and C for Mademoiselle Chastelain, his wealthy wife, who had helped him rise in the world but also made him a cuckold. When, a century later, the *hôtel* became the property of Leclerc de Juigné, the Archbishop of Paris, he laid a crimson carpet on the gorgeous staircase and covered up the nude sculptures on the walls. The Revolution left the mansion disfigured beyond recognition. André Malraux's bill of August 1962 for the restoration of the Marais saved it from demolition, and in the same year the City of Paris bought it and leased it to the state. After Picasso's death in 1973, it received the donations of his heirs, including paintings by Renoir, Cézanne, Douanier Rousseau, Matisse and Braque from his private collection, along with some of his own works.

North of the Hôtel Salé, the names of rue des Coutures-Saint-Gervais and rue Sainte-Anastase are still engraved in the ancient stone, a relic of the medieval Marais, when it was shared by different orders who lived off its kitchen gardens (*couture*, as distinct from *culture*, 'extensive farming'). The words 'Saint' and 'Sainte' were blotted out during the anti-clerical days of the Revolution. Retrace your steps and turn left into rue du Parc-Royal, which once led to the gardens of the Maison Royale des Tournelles (now Place des Vosges). To its south, Square Léopold-Achille and Square Gaston-Cain provide a charming spot of greenery, enhanced by an elegant orangery, which once belonged to the Hôtel Le Peletier de Saint-Fargeau, soon to be reached. Square Léopold-Achille was opened in 1931 and honours the then deputy mayor of the 3rd arrondissement. Square Gaston-Cain, opened in 1913, honours the curator of Musée Carnavalet between 1897 and 1914. It serves as an attractive depository for the museum's stones.

Hôtel Boneval at n° 16 rue Parc-Royal, has a charming pavilion hidden in the courtyard. At n° 10, the Hôtel de Vigny (no connection with the illustrious poet) has a magnificent wrought-iron staircase and exquisitely painted beams dating from the time of Louis XIII on several of the ground-floor ceilings. A beautifully painted ceiling on the first floor, ornamented with allegorical figures of the four seasons and the elements, is a fine example of the splendour of a 17th-century interior. The Ministry of Education was planning to pull down the building and replace it with a school but was successfully opposed by the Monuments Historiques after a fierce campaign. Likewise, now that the *hôtel* at n° 8 has been bought by a German cultural body, its renovation and upkeep are secure. The lovely (fake) brick-and-stone house at n° 4 has preserved its period, carved wooden balustrade, a precious rarity.

Turn right into rue de Sévigné, named after the most illustrious inhabitant of the Marais, the Marquise de Sévigné. The Hôtel Le Peletier de Saint-Fargeau at n° 29 was inhabited successively by four generations of the Le Peletier family, who also owned the domain of Saint-Fargeau in Sologne. The last one, Louis-Michel, turned Republican during the Revolution, joined the Convention and voted for the death of the King. On 20 January 1793, on the eve of the King's execution, he was himself murdered by the King's bodyguard in Café Février, in the Galerie Valois of the Palais-Royal, to avenge his sovereign. The Hôtel is now an annexe of the Musée Carnavalet. The historical library of Paris was located here until 1968, when it moved to the neighbouring Hôtel Lamoignon on rue Pavée (in the 4th arr.).

Hôtel Carnavalet undoubtedly is one of the landmarks of the 3rd arrondissement, both as the museum of the history of Paris and as the most famous and most permanent of Madame de Sévigné's nine dwellings in the Marais, the one where she lived the last 20 years of her life. It was built in 1545 for the President of Parliament, Jacques de Lingeris, who was much in favour with François I, which accounts for the contribution of Jean Goujon, the King's official sculptor:

Hôtel Carnavalet

the gorgeous bas-relief of the Seasons in the courtyard is his work. Coysevox's statue of the Sun King is obviously a later addition; having been miraculously rescued during the Revolution, it was transferred here from the Hôtel de Ville. The architecture, a blend of ornate Italian Renaissance and French formality, is characteristic of the reign of François I, who, in the wake of his Italian campaigns, sought to bridge the two cultures. These features are best seen from rue des Francs-Bourgeois, round the corner to the right (see below). In 1572, the *hôtel* became the property of Madame de Kernevenoy, when its name was distorted into Carnavalet. The Hôtel Carnavalet is also, it should be noted, the third oldest non-religious monument in Paris, after the Hôtel de Sens (1475), and the Hôtel de Cluny (1485), respectively in the 4th and 5th arrondissements. The Renaissance Louvre was started only two years later.

Madame de Sévigné, born in 1626 in her grandparents' *hôtel* on Place Royale (now Place des Vosges), lost her father in early childhood and both her mother and grandparents by the age of 10. From then on she was constantly on the move but, except for her numerous long stays in the provinces, she remained within the perimeter of the Marais. Though she occasionally visited Madame de Rambouillet by the Louvre and Madame de La Fayette in Faubourg Saint-Germain across the river, most of her friends - Lamoignon, Ormesson, Scudéry - were near neighbours, and most of her social life rotated around the area of Place Royale, referred to simply as the 'Place'. This peripatetic lifestyle using rented premises was not uncommon among members of the nobility, who tended to be short of cash, their wealth often lying solely in their country estates. Besides, they came up to Paris to have fun and preferred to spend what money they had collecting fabulous pieces of furniture, tapestries and other works of art, which they would take with them from one rented place to the next. They often ran into heavy debt and were sometimes even evicted for unpaid rents.

Madame de Sévigné took a long time finding a home that would suit both herself and her daughter's family. On 7 October 1677 she informed her beloved daughter Madame de Grignan that, at long last, "Thank God, we have the [lease of the] Hôtel Carnavalet. It is an admirable affair; there will be room for all of us and we shall have good air. As one cannot have everything, we shall have to do without parquet floors and without the small fireplaces that are so in vogue; but we have at least a beautiful courtyard, a beautiful garden, a beautiful neighbourhood and good little 'blue girls' who are very well behaved [at the time the 'enfants bleus' occupied the convent of the Annonciades Célestes in the Hôtel Danville next door]." A beautiful neighbourhood indeed, of graceful buildings of religious institutions and of palatial private homes. Come spring their fragrant gardens filled the air with the scent of orange blossom. Above all, Hôtel Carnavalet was just a few steps from the Place Royale, the hub of social life. After endless shilly-shallying, Madame de Sévigné and her daughter took over the first noble floor, while the grandaughters and their governess lived on the second. The imposing staircase (the present one is a later addition brought over from the Hôtel de Luynes in Faubourg Saint-Germain) led to the living-room. Madame de Grignard occupied the second room and Madame de Sévigné the third. It may have been partitioned, since she refers to her *petite chambre*. Although the inventory compiled after Madame de Sévigné's death provides a complete list of her possessions, we do not know how they were arranged. Among them were eight pieces of tapestry relating the life of Noah and seven relating the life of Psyche. Gorgeous silk fabrics covered the furniture, which was proportionately of little value, since in those days both workmanship and wood were cheap. The only paintings Madame de Sévigné owned were family portraits. To celebrate Madame de Grignan's return to Carnavalet in 1680, after a year's absence, the doting Madame de Sévigné arranged for her to have a new room on the ground floor and asked Libéral Bruant to update it and install a parquet floor and a new small fireplace.

Hordes of lackeys, cooks, butlers, tutors and governesses waited on the members of the family during the endless bustle of their comings and goings. And yet, despite a whirling timetable, Madame de Sévigné found the time to devour books, to observe the world around her and to indulge in a substantial correspondence with her daughter, which is an invaluable testimony of 17th-century Paris.

The City of Paris purchased the Hôtel Carnavalet in 1866 and turned it into a museum in 1880. Besides its permanent exhibits, which range from prehistoric days to the French Revolution, temporary thematic exhibitions, connected with the history of Paris, are held periodically.

Turn right into rue des Francs-Bourgeois, from where you will have a good view of the courtyard of the Hôtel Carnavalet and its architecture. The street forms part of the borderline between the 3rd and 4th arrondissements and runs along the site of the northern section of the walls built by Philippe-Auguste. Vestiges of one of its towers can be seen in the basement of n° 7 (in the 4th arr.). The street is named after the inhabitants of an almshouse situated further west, who were exempt from paying taxes because of their extreme destitution. Today this is the tourists' main artery, leading to Place des Vosges, behind you, and is consequently lined with attractive boutiques. Avoid weekend afternoons, when heavy traffic rather mars the pleasure of window-shopping.

A charming *salon de thé* at the corner of rue Payenne is a good stopping-place. Once restored, turn right into rue Payenne. The house at n° 7 is nothing much to look at, but it was the home of the great architect Mansart, the founder of the greatest dynasty of architects of the *Ancien Régime*, among them his great-nephew, the architect of Versailles, and the famous Gabriel family, to whom they were linked by marriage. The Hôtel de Marle at n° 11 has been beautifully restored and now houses the Swedish cultural centre. Originally built for Hector de Marle in the 16th century, it was renovated extensively in the 17th and 18th centuries. Among its residents was Madame de Polignac, much befriended by Marie-Antoinette who entrusted her children to her care.

Retrace your steps, continue on rue des Francs-Bourgeois and turn right into rue Elzévir. The Hôtel Donon at n° 8 now houses the Musée Cognacq-Jay, set up by the founders of La Samaritaine department store, Ernest Cognacq and Nelly Jay, to avoid the dispersal of their private collection of 18th-century paintings, among them works by Fragonard, Greuze, Boucher, Tiepolo. When they bequeathed the collection to the City of Paris in 1928, they stipulated that it was to remain in their 18th-century *hôtel* on Boulevard des Capucines, because it belonged architecturally to the same period as the paintings. Despite these instructions, the collection was transferred in 1990 from the Boulevard des Capucines, where, admittedly, hardly anyone visited it, to the Hôtel Donon, where, it was hoped, it would benefit from the popularity of the Marais. It was also a way of saving the dilapidated Hôtel Donon, parts of which date from the 16th century. Further down the street, on your right, are the lovely gardens of the Swedish cultural centre - a charming sight.

Rue Barbette, on your left, recalls the Hôtel Barbette, the site of the prologue to the Hundred Years' War. An earlier country dwelling had been built here at the end of the 13th century by the provost of merchants, Etienne Barbette. It was known as La Courtille Barbette, which indicates that the spacious grounds, extending from rue Vieille-du-Temple to rue Elzévir, were walled. Barbette provided the capital with the first of its *quais*, the quai des Grands-Augustins (now in the 6th arr.) to thwart the devastating flooding caused by the capricious Seine. He also originated the law that binds landlord and tenant to three months' notice to vacate; this law is still in force. His contemporaries viewed him in a less favourable light, begrudging his collaboration with Philippe le Bel, who lived beyond his means at their expense. When the people of Paris rose against the King at Christmas 1306, the Courtille was not spared. By 1390 it had been totally rebuilt, renamed Hôtel Barbette and was under the proprietorship of Jean de Montagu, Charles VI's superintendent of finance, who sold it to Queen Isabelle of Bavaria a decade later. Jean de Montagu himself met with a tragic end later: jealousy engendered false accusations against him and in 1409 he was decapitated and hanged by the feet at the gallows of Montfaucon (in today's 10th arr.), where his body was left dangling in the wind for three years, before he was rehabilitated.

When the fair, black-eyed Isabelle retired to her newly acquired mansion, her husband Charles VI had partly lost his reason. Officially she moved there to escape his fits of dementia; in fact she was now free to lead her own life, notably in the company of her husband's brother Louis, Duc d'Orléans, who was also the cousin of Jean sans Peur, Duc de Bourgogne. Trouble was brooding: for beyond the eternal struggle for power, the unavoidable consequence of the political vacuum created by the King's mental impotence, there was male rivalry, jealousy and passion between two blood cousins, all the ingredients of a Shakespearean tragedy. Louis, Duc d'Orléans was handsome, gallant and licentious. Jean, Duc de Bourgogne, was short and puny. Louis was the King's brother, Jean, only his cousin. Not only was Louis the Queen's lover, but he also exerted a seductive power over Jean's own wife, Marguerite of Bavaria, a fact of which Jean was not unaware. On Wednesday, 23 November 1407, the Duc d'Orléans was paying a visit to Queen Isabeau who had just delivered a stillborn child, when a King's equerry entered their presence to inform the Duke that His Majesty demanded to speak to him. The Duke left at once for the royal residence at the Hôtel de Saint-Pol (now in the 4th arr.), riding his mule, preceded by three torch carriers, while two pages shared another mule behind him. It remains unclear whether he used the discreet exit into the Allée des Arbalétiers, at 38 rue des Francs-Bourgeois, or the main entrance at 64 rue Vieille-du-Temple. Whichever way, his route went past the Hôtel de Rieux (47 rue Vieille-du-Temple), where 18 hired killers, equipped with hatchets and pointed mallets, lay in wait, led by Raoul d'Ocquetonville whose wife had also been sensitive to the Duke's charm. As the Duke reached the door, the assassins emerged and hurled themselves upon him. "I am the Duke of Orléans!" he exclaimed, believing this to be a mistake. "Precisely so. You are the man we want." Watching from her top-floor window, Jacqueline Griffart, a shoemaker's wife, burst out screaming, "Murder! Murder! ", which caused enough commotion to enable the assassins to flee into the dark. Too late: the butchered, lifeless body of the slain Duke lay in a puddle of blood in the street; close by lay one of the two pages who had been killed in the scuffle.

At the funeral service the following day the Duc de Bourgogne declared, "Never was such evil, such treacherous murder in this kingdom perpetrated." Yet two days later he admitted his crime and fled temporarily to Burgundy, soon to return to the capital and unleash a civil war of unspeakable horror, which opposed the Bourguignons, his supporters, to the partisans of the late Duc d'Orléans in the person of his brother-in-law, Bernard VII, the Comte d'Armagnac. In 1419 Jean sans Peur was assassinated in his turn, but not before having opened the gates of France to invasion by England. Meanwhile, Isabeau had rallied the camp of the Bourguignons, and turning her back on her own son and legitimate heir, the future Charles VII (1403-61), surrendered her daughter Catherine to Henry V of England, making him heir to the throne of France, as we are told both by history and by Shakespeare. Not until 1422 was the Monarchy restored to its lawful king, Charles VII.

The great enlightened Duc de Berry, the uncle of both Louis d'Orléans and Jean sans Peur, had not underestimated the danger inherent in his nephews' feud and hoped desperately to reconcile them. On the Sunday before the assassination of Louis d'Orléans, he had united them in the chapel of the Grands-Augustins next to his palace, the Hôtel de Nesle (now in the 6th arr.), where they received communion and shared the host. He then had them sup and sleep in the same room, the ultimate proof of mutual trust - so soon alas to be betrayed.

Some 150 years later the Hôtel de Barbette belonged to the seneschal of Normandy, Louis de Brézé. The ageing man was remarried to a 13-year-old girl, Diane. While riding one day through rue Vieille-du-Temple, François I noticed her and brought her to the court, but their liaison was cut short by the King's official mistress, the Duchesse d'Etampes. Undeterred, Diane set out to win the heart of the Dauphin and waited for her day, which happened some 20 years later, in 1547, when the Dauphin acceded to the throne of France as Henri II. This time it was the turn of the Duchesse d'Etampes to pack up.

Rue Barbette will lead you to the magnificent 18th-century Hôtel de Rohan, at 87 rue Vieille du Temple, built by Delamair at the same time as the Hôtel de Soubise. The Rohan and the Soubise were members of the same family and shared the same garden. Today both *hôtels* belong to the National Archives and can be visited during temporary exhibitions. The elegant simplicity of the façade overlooking the garden of the Hôtel de Rohan, contrasts with the sumptuous decorations inside, as was the rule in the 17th and 18th centuries. In order to recreate its period setting, some decorations were brought over from other mansions, notably the celebrated *cabinet des singes*, a masterpiece of Louis XV Rocaille style, flamboyant, overladen with tortuous gilt borders, yet somehow delicately graceful, a reflection of the mannered society of the time.

Turn left into rue Vieille-du-Temple. On the corner of rue des Francs-Bourgeois an early 16th-century turret with lace-like carvings is affixed to the corner wall of a house straight out of a fairytale. This was the home of Jehan Hérouet, Louis XII's treasurer. It was damaged by German bombing in 1944 but was later in even greater danger when a French deputy in the National Assembly suggested it being torn down, saying that it obstructed the traffic.

Turn right into rue des Francs-Bourgeois. On the corner of rue des Archives stands the Hôtel de Soubise, some say the most superb *hôtel* in the Marais. In the 18th century it replaced the mansion of the Guise family, the greatest family of the Marais, second only to the King's. At the height of his popularity, Corneille was lodged by the Guise (1662-1664) in one of their apartments. The *hôtel* now houses both the National Archives and the museum of the history of France, offering the visitor a rare opportunity to see an 18th-century interior.

The first Duc de Guise to settle here was François de Lorraine, who in 1553 bought the Hôtel du connétable de Clisson, a Gothic-style mansion (as witness the two turrets on rue des Archives) built by Olivier de Clisson in 1371 on grounds bought from the Templars. A close friend of Charles V and Charles VI, de Clisson personally set out to hunt down Pierre de Craon, who had tried to assassinate Charles VI. It was during that chase that Charles VI had his first fit of dementia in the forest of Le Mans.

The mansion must have been outstanding for it was requisitioned during the English occupation of Paris for the Duke of Clarence, the King's brother, and later for the Duke of Bedford, the Regent of France (1420-35). When François de Lorraine settled here a century later he called on the greatest artists of the day to redecorate the palace in Renaissance style, notably the Italian Nicolò dell'Abbate who executed the drawings of Francesco Primaticcio, the most famous Italian artist of the time, and turned the chapel into the most beautiful private chapel in Paris. A gorgeous frieze ran along its walls above the windows, depicting the procession of the Magi. Contemporaries could recognise the features of the lord of the house in the guise of one of the three kings, which was one way of satisfying one's vanity in those days. In the 19th century, in an extraordinary act of philistinism, the walls were whitewashed. Some of Primaticcio's original drawings are now in the Louvre and in Chantilly, and some copies are kept in the Staedelsches Kunstinstitut in Frankfurt am Main. In 1556 François gave the *hôtel* to his brother Charles, who had opted for a religious career and who, five years later, crowned Charles IX in the cathedral of Reims.

Charles de Guise extended his property as far as rue des Quatre-Fils to the north and rue Vieille-du-Temple to the east and turned the *hôtel* into a palatial mansion, fit for the next landlord, Henri I, le Balafré ('Scarface'), his nephew and son of François. A man of overriding ambition and cunning, he hoped to seize the throne. He started out by respectfully greeting the humblest of Parisians, 'down to picklocks and fishwives', who, in their turn, a sign of loyalty, sported green scarves, the emblematic colour of the House of Guise. He then instigated the massacre of Saint-Bartholomew (August 1572) against the Protestants, before plotting the overthrow of Henri III, which would have cleared the road to power. Henri III pre-empted him, however, and had him assassinated in Blois on 12 May 1588.

It is probably the belligerent life he had engaged in, rather than a taste for Gothic art, that accounts for the survival of the medieval defence turrets of the Hôtel de Clisson, to the delight of today's visitor. Henri de Guise was not a man to beat about the bush. Happening one day to walk into the apartment of his wife, Catherine de Clèves, and catch her in the company of one of Henri III's *mignons*, he had her immediately thrown out of the window (on the corner of rue des Archives and rue des Quatre-Fils) and finished off in the street.

Henri II de Lorraine, Duc de Guise, was the contemporary of Louis XIV. By then the wealth of treasures inside the palace was stupendous. His red velvet bed, embroidered in gold and silver thread and studded with pearls, was one of the highlights. All the arms of the House of Guise were displayed on the base, and an embroidery of Godefroy Le Bouillon, the ancestral hero of the family, decorated the back. Silver and gold, precious and semi-precious stones, provided a glittering backdrop to the House of Guise, along with an abundance of works of art, notably, the series of tapestries in the great hall, *Les Belles Chasses de Guise*, now in the Louvre.

The royal authorities, anxious to appease the Guise, showered them with ecclesiastical offices, which enabled them to accumulate fabulous wealth. Henri II, for example, was the owner of nine abbeys by the time he was 11, and at 15 was appointed Archbishop of Reims! But harbouring ideas about deposing the king became impracticable after Richelieu, chief minister to Louis XIII, had laid the foundations for the reign of absolutism, and Louis XIV had added to his reign the unequivocal emblem of the sun, eliminating those who tried to outshine him (cf Nicolas Fouquet). Louis XIV never forgot the princely revolt - *la Fronde* - that had shaken the early days of his reign, and ruled with a rod of iron. He did, however, give the Guise a free hand, within the limits of the Marais, to lead a licentious and prodigal life and lavish on society scintillating balls as an outlet for their ambitions. Madame de Sévigné left an account of one of the balls held by the Guise, at which "all the courtyards of the Hôtel de Guise were lit up with two thousand lanterns." The King honoured the place with his presence and with a couple of *courante*s but did not stay long "and returned to the Louvre to sup with his usual company." An astute monarch indeed!

Henri II vented his energies in a complicated love-life, marrying and having his marriages annulled, despite the fact that he was both archbishop and nine times abbot, which got him into trouble with the royal authorities. In 1638, Richelieu's opposition to his marriage, regarded as incompatible with his ecclesiastical status, led him to leave Paris and rally a coalition against the authorities, which involved even Spain. He was sentenced to death in his absence, executed in effigy as was the custom and his house was sealed and confiscated. When he returned to Paris in 1643, after the accession of Louis XIV, he at once resumed his amorous pursuits. In 1646 he went as far as visiting Rome, in the hope of obtaining the annulment of his second marriage, so as to marry a third time. The Pope refused categorically but the Duke used the opportunity to travel to Naples and get himself involved in an insurrection against Spain - to which, in the end, he was taken as prisoner. Blood ran quick in the veins of this Guise who also fought a duel over the lovely Comtesse de Montbazon with the Marquis de Coligny (Madame de Sévigné's father), who died of his wounds several months later. When his mother and brothers refused him access to the family jewellery, which he meant to bestow upon a new fiancée, the calculating, go-getting Mademoiselle Pons, he kicked them out of the house. His conduct, which contemporaries attributed to insanity, was the talk of the town and the subject of mockery. Designated great chamberlain and master of ceremonies by Louis XIV, he could now strut about with a permanent troop of 36 pages and 12 Moors and indulge his luxurious tastes, surrounded by the most beautiful women in the land. On the occasion of the birth of Louis XIV's first son in 1662, he led the *quadrille* of the *carrousel*, wallowing in his vanity, not unlike his ancestor, who had led the procession of the Magi in Nicolo dell'Abbatte's frieze, on the walls of the family's chapel.

The death in 1696 of the last Guise and the dispersal of their treasures marked the extinction of the dynasty and also the beginning of the decline of the Marais. It is significant that while a new buyer was being sought, the house was let to the Portuguese Embassy who used it as a gambling dive! Nevertheless, the lustre of the Marais subsisted until the Revolution, for example in the form of the splendid Hôtel de Soubise that rose out of the ruins of the Hôtel de Guise. It was built by Delamair in 1705 for the illustrious House of Rohan-Soubise. Its first proprietress, Anne de Rohan, was the wife and cousin of Charles de Rohan, the Prince and Maréchal de Soubise, and the sister of Armand de Rohan, landlord of the Hôtel de Rohan. Having yielded her charms to Louis XIV, he offered to finance the construction of the new *hôtel*, a situation to which the cuckolded husband chose to turn a blind eye. Wagging tongues said that, while "Louis XIV had supplied the wood [*bois* also means 'antler', hence a pun on the cuckold's horns, as is the case in French], his friends threw in the stones (i.e. were hard on him)".

Charles de Rohan was in great favour with Louis XV who described him as "very good and very excellent prince", and equally with Madame de Pompadour, who obtained several high commands for him during the Seven Years' War. Madame du Barry, Pompadour's successor, also offered him her friendship. When Louis XV died in 1774, de Rohan was the only member of the nobility to follow him to the basilica in Saint-Denis, while on either side of the road the crowds cheered at the passing of the unlamented King. The Prince died three years later and was thus spared from seeing his house being confiscated and looted, its spacious halls used for storing gunpowder and the courtyard cluttered up with booths for the sale of lottery tickets. The lovely garden that lay between the two *hôtels* was wrecked. After the Revolution, it was turned into a public garden and in 1808 Napoleon conceived the idea of keeping the nation's archives here. Today the entire history of France is packed into 200 km of shelves, while the wall paintings, the works of Boucher, Van Loo and others, give the visitor an idea of aristocratic taste in the first half of the 18th century. The apartment of the Prince on the ground floor and that of the Princess on the first provide a rare example of a Parisian interior of the time. The present Hôtel de Soubise is a masterpiece of elegant harmony. Its courtyard with its spectacular colonnade is unique and all those who love architecture should be grateful to Delamair for having preserved the two Gothic turrets at a time when medieval art was regarded with contempt.

Continue into rue Rambuteau and turn right into rue du Temple. At n° 71, the Hôtel d'Avaux, also known as Saint-Aignan, is one of the noteworthy mansions in the Marais, as befits its first two illustrious proprietors: the Comte d'Avaux, Louis XIV's ambassador to Holland, Venice, England and Sweden; and Paul de Beauvilliers, Duc de Saint-Aignan and son-in-law of the great statesman Colbert. Unfortunately, the premises are usually closed to the public. Turn right into rue de Braque, a lovely, quiet street. The elegant 18th-century *hôtel* at n° 4/6, has a splendid wrought-iron staircase. Seen from this angle, the Gothic turret of the Hôtel Clisson ahead of you is sheer delight.

Turn left into rue des Archives and continue to the corner of rue des Haudriettes, at which is the charming Haudriettes fountain and the exquisite sculpture of the sleeping naiad, innocently unaware of her loveliness. Across the street, at n° 60, the Hôtel Guénégaud, is a 17th-century masterpiece of elegant simplicity and perfect proportions, supposed to be the work of François Mansart. The property of the City of Paris, it houses the hunting museum.

Retrace your steps and turn back into rue des Francs-Bourgeois. The old Allée des Arbalétiers at n° 38, so called because it led south to the training field of the crossbow-archers (*les arbalétiers*) served as the side exit of the Hôtel Barbette. This may be the spot where the Duc d'Orléans was assassinated (the alternative is the main entrance at 64 rue Vieille-du-Temple). This dark alley, with the crooked profiles of its houses jutting out, still has a medieval feel. Plaques on each side of the alley used to remind the passer-by of the night of the terrible crime that plunged France into the longest disaster of her history:

> Dans ce passage
> En sortant de l'hôtel Barbette
> le Duc Louis d'Orléans
> Frère du roi Charles VI
> a été assassiné
> par Jean sans Peur
> Duc de Bourgogne
> Dans la nuit du 23
> au 24 Novembre 1407.

(In this passage, on leaving the Hôtel Barbette, the Duke Louis of Orléans, brother of King Charles VI, was murdered by Fearless Jean, Duke of Burgundy, in the night of 23 to 24 November 1407).

The plaques were removed in 1908, and never put back again, thus wiping out the memory of an essential landmark in French history.

N° 36 and 34 are on the site of the alms-house where 48 of the above mentioned *francs bourgeois* (tax-exempted paupers) were given shelter in the 14th century but reviled by their neighbours. At n° 30 the Hôtel d'Alméras or Hôtel de Fourcy, dates back to the reign of Henri IV and an impressive period staircase can still be seen inside. The delicately sculpted door, however, is early 18th-century Regency. The façades of the *hôtel* at n° 26 belong to different periods and are representative of their styles, pointing to the different phases of its extension: the street façade is late 18th century, the courtyard façade is early 17th and the garden façade is late 16th.

Continue past Musée Carnavalet and turn left into rue de Turenne. Henri de la Tour d'Auvergne, Vicomte and Maréchal de Turenne, lived at n° 66, but only vestiges of his home have survived. Having led the royal troops against the rebellious Conti during the *Fronde*, he was praised by Bossuet in his famous *Oraison funèbre*, a classic of 17th-century French epic literature. Today this is a functional street, lined with wholesale clothing shops, on the whole devoid of charm. However, a beautiful façade can be seen at n° 23, the home of Edouard Colbert de Villacerf, the Queen's chief butler at the time of Louis XIV, later the King's superintendent of construction. The *hôtel's* exquisite boudoir, all painted and gilded, can now be seen at Musée Carnavalet.

N° 54 (and the portal of n° 52) was the home of Montrésor, a staunch enemy of Richelieu and Mazarin and a hero of the *Fronde*. But it is n° 56 - a plain house with a modest statue of the Virgin tucked in a niche, on the corner of rue de Villehardouin - that has gone down in history as the home of the burlesque writer and poet Scarron and of Françoise d'Aubigné, an ill-matched couple indeed. Scarron was deformed and crippled and 26 years older than the 15-year-old Françoise, but an impoverished orphan like herself had only two choices in life: marriage or a nunnery. At 15 Françoise was already a practical, clear-sighted woman. Once widowed, she rose from the role of governess of Louis XIV's children to that of his official mistress, then to become his wife, Madame de Maintenon - the only such case in French history. The King's nickname for her, '*ma solidité*', encapsulates the contrast between her and the schemers at court, and the secret of her success.

Scarron signed the lease on 27 February 1654 for the modest annual rent of 350 pounds (Mlle de Scudéry paid roughly the same rent on rue de Beauce). Though relatively poor (he did keep five servants), Scarron was much sought after because, as his contemporary Tallemant des Réaux put it, "It is perhaps one of the marvels of our century that a man in that state and so poor can make others laugh the way he does." His wife reported that at night he screamed out in pain, which even strong doses of opium could not relieve. By day, however, he hid his pain under the cover of laughs and sallies. Writers and noblemen climbed to his spacious room on the second floor to enjoy his company (Françoise probably lived in a two-room apartment on the first). Although he was relatively poor, his four-poster bed was covered with yellow damask, as were the four armchairs and the twelve chairs disposed around it. A Venetian mirror hung on one of the walls, a rich tapestry on another. A painting by Nicolas Poussin, *Le Ravissement de Saint Paul* (now in the Louvre) probably hung there too, Scarron having nagged the recalcitrant painter into giving it to him.

The guests would draw the twelve chairs to a long table and eat the food they had themselves brought. Nobody minded for great fun was guaranteed in return and, at times, the presence of the poet's fair wife, though more often she withdrew, offended by the coarse behaviour of her husband's companions. Scarron died in this house in 1660 aged 50, leaving debts and a new literary genre, the burlesque, the literature of a cripple, who used his biting pen as a weapon of revenge.

The Hôtel du Grand-Veneur at n° 60 is a magnificent late 17th-century mansion. Its hunting motifs were added in the 18th century, when the mansion belonged to the master of the royal hounds *(Grand-Veneur)* It now belongs to a commercial company which has restored it beautifully and turned it into a showroom, where visitors may wander freely.

Retrace your steps. Rue des Minimes, on your left, evokes the third Franciscan monastery of Paris (the first two being in Chaillot and Vincennes), so called as a mark of humility. Turn right into rue des Tournelles, and on to rue du Pas-de-la-Mule. A famous cabaret, La Fosse aux Lions, was situated here in the 17th century, a gathering-place where literati such as Tallemant des Réaux, Voiture and Saint-Amant gathered for a hearty drink in merry company between visits to the great families of Place Royale. The proprietress, La Coiffier, had the clever idea of introducing meals at set prices: some claim she was the first to do so in Paris. Nowadays dining around Place des Vosges is less basic, the atmosphere more polished and prices considerably higher. There are several eating-places under the arcades; or you may wish simply to relax in the lovely gardens. Place des Vosges lies mostly in the 4th arrondissement, and is covered in that chapter.

SAINT-MARTIN-DES-CHAMPS

Those with extra energy and time, and who like authenticity with little glamour and no fuss, might visit the western part of the arrondissement, where few fellow tourists are likely to cross their path.

Starting off from the Temple Métro station once more, make your way west through rue Notre-Dame-de-Nazareth, the main artery of this small Jewish enclave. Is it because of its pre-destined name that the street has a Middle Eastern feel to it, with its cheap, wholesale clothing and fabric shops and its nonchalant bustle? Its population now is made up predominantly of North African Jews, but when its synagogue was built in the early 19th century, at n° 15, it was to accommodate the Ashkenazi, not the Sephardi community. Only about 500 Jews were living in the capital when the Revolution broke out; in 1394 Charles VI had banished them, a ruling reiterated by Louis XIII in 1615 (which suggests that some had meanwhile returned). In the early 19th century, however, after their laborious emancipation, they were given equal rights and consequently allowed back into the capital. Over 2,000 moved in during the First Empire. By 1840 8,000 Jews were living in Paris; by 1853 there were 20,000. There were only two Ashkenazi synagogues in Paris at the time - on rue du Temple and rue des Archives - which could barely accommodate the influx. Moreover, the one on rue du Temple closed down in 1818, when the landlord sold the building that housed it. Sandrié de Jouy was commissioned to build a synagogue on rue Notre-Dame-de-Nazareth, which was inaugurated in 1822. Its construction, however, proved faulty and 30 years later it was replaced, with financial aid of James de Rothschild, by the present synagogue. With the ever-increasing number of Jews in Paris, it soon became necessary to build an additional synagogue; this was built at rue de la Victoire (in the 9th arr.) and became the main synagogue of Paris. By the end of the Second Empire (c. 1870) there were 30,000 Jews in Paris and by the end of the century 40,000.

Turn right into Passage du Pont-aux-Biches; the trickling water of a lovely Wallace fountain - so called after Sir Richard Wallace, who offered about 100 such fountains to the city of Paris - will encourage you up its steep flight of steps. In rue Meslay, ahead of you, a charming 18th-century façade has survived at n° 42 but at n° 46 an ordinary building replaces the house where the writer George Sand (Aurore Dupin by her real name) is presumed to have been born on 1 July 1804. Retrace your steps and continue into rue Volta straight on, then turn right into rue Vertbois, evocative of the green woods of days of yore. In August 1814 the English poet Shelley is supposed to have stayed at the Hôtel de Vienne at n° 76 on his way to Switzerland. A kosher fast-food restaurant now stands on the site.

Across the street you can see a section of the 13th-century crenellated wall of

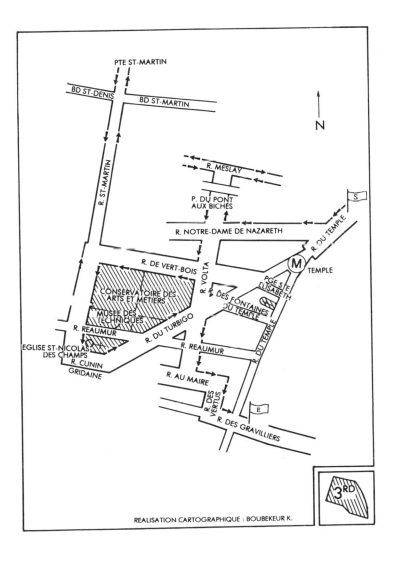

REALISATION CARTOGRAPHIQUE : BOUBEKEUR K.

the medieval priory of Saint-Martin-des-Champs and its watch-tower, now surmounted by a 'pepper-box' slate roof. The tower owes its miraculous survival to the determination of Victor Hugo who, in 1882, wrote a letter of protest that began, "Demolish the tower – no; the architect – yes! " The tower was restored the very year, along with the pretty 18th-century fountain next to it.

Like other early Christian shrines of Paris, the priory of Saint-Martin-des-Champs originated in the 6th century, with a primitive oratory on the Ile de la Cité. Like the others it too commemorated the site of a miracle performed by its patron saint - in this case the healing of a leper by a kiss - in a distant past, and therefore had more to do with legend than with historical accuracy. In the 8th century a chapel replaced it north of the island, but this was torn down by the Normans a century later, together with the rest of Paris. The priory was not built until the 12th century. Situated some distance from the city, it was secured with a rampart, four corner watch-towers and 18 turrets. It also had a gaol, the scene of a savage massacre of the Armagnacs by the Bourguignons during the Hundred Years' War. At the time of Louis XIV prostitutes captured on the neighbouring streets were kept here to await deportation to New Orleans. In September 1719, 180 male prisoners were brought here from the prison of Bicêtre in the 13th arrondissement, to be married to 180 women. The couples were then chained to one another and marched to La Rochelle on the Atlantic shores, from where they embarked for Louisiana.

The monks of Saint-Martin played a major role in the development of this part of the arrondissement and also gave the kingdom some renowned churchmen, notably the Cardinal de Richelieu; but all this came to an end with the Revolution and in 1798 the Conservatoire des Arts et Métiers, which had been founded in 1794 like several other majour schools, was granted the premises (enter from n° 292 rue Saint-Martin).

Rue Saint-Martin lies on the ancient Roman road from Lutetia to the north and is a continuation of the Roman *cardo* (main urban street), rue Saint-Jacques south of the Seine. To the north is the Porte Saint-Martin, the triumphal arch built by Louis XIV to celebrate his victories over the Franche-Comté, the Germans, the Spanish and the Dutch. If you walk up close, you will see the sculpted figure of the Sun King in the nude as the invincible, muscular Hercules, but bewigged as always. Louis XV passed under this emblematic monument on his return from Flanders, Napoleon on his return from Austerlitz and the Allies after the battle of Waterloo... When the focal point of the city shifted to the west, the Arc de Triomphe on the Champs-Elysées replaced it as the symbolic ceremonial arch.

The priory church is one of the rare medieval churches still in existence in Paris. Dating largely from the 12th and 13th centuries, it boasts the first example of Gothic rib vaults in the capital, although the windows of its chapels, with their semi-circular vaults, are Romanesque. The church tower is gone, except for its Romanesque base, which can be seen from rue Réaumur. The highlight of the building is the Gothic dining hall, now the library of the Conservatoire. This masterpiece of ethereal lightness is mercifully - unlike so many other treasures - not officially closed to the public, but should be entered discreetly, as it is a reading room. In the wall opposite the pulpit is the 13th-century door that used to lead to its fine cloister, shamefully demolished in the early 18th century. On the premises (n° 270) is also the Musée National des Techniques, part of which is located in the old church of Saint-Martin. An impressive and enlightening display of inventions will enable the visitor to follow man's technological adventure through the centuries – from the sun dial to satellites from the first standard units for measures and weights to the early recordings and early cinema, from steam engines to Blériot's aircraft with which he was the first to cross the English Channel in 1909 – it is all there in neat, methodical order, yet exciting nonetheless.

At n° 254 the parish church of the borough of Saint-Martin, Saint-Nicolas-des-Champs, provides a fine example of the evolution from the Gothic to the Renaissance style. It has preserved, notably, its Renaissance portal on the south side, and most of its picturesque tower dates back to the early 15th century. Among the parishioners buried here should be mentioned Mlle de Scudéry, who died in 1701 aged 94, Guillaume de Budé, the founder of the Collège de France who died in 1540, the father and uncle of La Bruyère, the author of the indispensable *Caractères* and some members of the Ormesson family. The renowned 18th-century actor, Talma, was baptized here.

Turn left into rue Réaumur and left into rue Turbigo for a view of the back of the church. Continue along rue Turbigo to the junction of rue Volta and rue des Fontaines-du-Temple. The area between rue Vertbois, rue Volta and rue des Fontaines-de-Temple (up to n° 6) was the vast domain of the convent of the Madelonnettes, of which the only surviving vestige is a section of the walls, visible at n° 6. The convent was built in 1618 for the purpose of saving the souls of fallen women who, it was hoped, would follow the example of Mary Magdalen after whom they were named. Women of all kinds were locked up here for various shades of misdemeanour, or for none. Madame de Lescalopier, for example, was caught while riding on horseback to elope with her lover and was dispatched to this *"fatal tombeau des amourettes"* ("fatal tomb of passing love affairs") - as reported by the contemporary poet, Loret. Ninon Lenclos, its most notorious inmate, was locked up by Anne of Austria to put an end to the commotion she created among the greats of the court and of the capital, despite protestations that she was "neither a whore nor repented". When it was rumoured that her suitors, languishing outside the walls, were planning to burn the place down, a patrol went the rounds every night, until the authorities deemed it more prudent to remove her from Paris, to a convent in Lagny, further east. Whereas ladies of quality had their own private, heated rooms, plenty of food and the company of visitors, life at the Madelonnettes for the lower orders was no picnic. When the premises (a women's prison since the Revolution) were being demolished in 1868, a number of skeletons were found under a trap-door behind one of the church pillars, suggesting that some rebellious detainees had been kept there to die.

Retrace your steps and turn left into rue Volta across rue Réaumur. The street now narrows and passes through an area where the Chinese predominantly hold sway, particularly on the right-hand side of the street; on the left-hand side the North African Mustapha holds his own and serves couscous. An astonishing anachronistic sight awaits you at n° 3 : a Chinese restaurant and a Chinese hair-stylist share a medieval half-timbered house, some say the oldest house in Paris, built several centuries before the reign of Louis XIV, when the first Chinaman was introduced into France. At the end of the 13th century the house may have belonged to the bailiff of the borough of Saint-Martin. This Chinese community is the oldest in Paris, descended from immigrants who arrived during World War I, and now as then are generally small traders, as you will notice on rues Le Maire and Gravilliers. Most Parisians have never heard of this tiny Chinatown in the 13th-century borough of Saint-Martin (rue au Maire, incidentally, refers to the Mayor of the borough and rue des Vertus to its prostitution). The inhabitants cater to their own people, in the way of food and Chinese video tapes, but also to out-siders, selling inexpensive leather goods and imitation jewellery, thereby perpetu-ating the traditional trades of the Temple. To finish your walk you could join them for a no-nonsense meal in one of the Chinese restaurants.

THE 4th ARRONDISSEMENT

Rising out of the silver waters of the Seine, like some regal vessel, haloed by the glowing rays of a rising or a setting sun, Notre-Dame, "the old queen of our cathedrals", diffuses her splendour all around, a spellbinding vision between water and sky. Between 1163 and 1330, man's yearnings for the divine were carved into her stone by hosts of anonymous artisans, who, by some intuitive grace, slipped imperceptibly from the Romanesque to the Gothic style, yet managed to sustain her architectural unity and create a homogeneous masterpiece out of an infinite profusion of diversity and detail.

For centuries the people of Paris had found spiritual nourishment in the eastern part of the Ile de la Cité. As many as 23 church steeples pierced its medieval sky, and even a synagogue found a place in this tiny area, until Philippe-Auguste had it converted into the church of Sainte-Madeleine; at the same time he confiscated the Jews' possessions, using the proceeds partly to finance the construction of the market of Les Halles, before expelling them altogether from the kingdom of France in 1182. Thus ended their centuries-old presence on rue de la Juiverie, the central axis of the Ile de la Cité, once the ancient Roman *cardo* (main urban street), now the very heart of Christiandom. (When 16 years later, Philippe-Auguste invited the Jews back, so as to squeeze them dry once more, they did not return to the island; some settled on the left bank, where Jews had lived before, but most concentrated on the right bank, where the new Paris was developing, on rue Saint-Bon, south of the present church of Saint-Merri, from where they eventually spread to the neighbourhood of rue des Rosiers, further east).

The site of Notre-Dame had already been the foremost shrine of the heathens, as is confirmed by vestiges of a pillar-shaped monument dedicated to Jupiter, found in 1711 under the cathedral's chancel and now on display in the Musée National du Moyen Age at the Hôtel de Cluny (in the 5th arr.). The shrine was erected by the corporation of water merchants, the *Nautae Parisiaci*, (hence its name, Le Pilier des Nautes), who engraved the names of their own gods alongside those of Rome. One of the inscriptions dates it to the reign of Emperor Tiberius, (AD 17-34), which makes it the oldest sculpted monument found in the capital. Its central position on the intersection of the east-west water course and the north-south *cardo* made it a privileged site for the cult of the chief god in the Roman pantheon and a pivotal point for trade. Incidentally, because of the way in which Paris has expanded homogeneously and in a spiral, Notre-Dame has never lost its central position and after 2,000 years still marks the point from which the distance to any other place in France is measured.

The mosaics of the Roman temple came in handy some 300 years later, when, as diggings under the chancel confirm, the early Christians replaced it with a church dedicated to Saint Etienne. By the next century, such was the speed of expansion of Christianity that another church was built just west of it, dedicated to Notre Dame (Our Lady). The church of Saint-Etienne was spared by the Norsemen against a huge ransom, but Notre-Dame was destroyed and replaced later by another church. Both were in a sorry condition by the 12th century, when the Bishop of Paris, Maurice de Sully, decided to replace them with a glorious monument transcending every other in the kingdom, an ambitious goal, condemned by some as contrary to the Christian ideal of humility. Every craftsman was harnessed to this great project and imprinted into the vertical stone his imagination, thoughts, knowledge and faith.

Notre-Dame became the parish church of the kingdom and as such host to all its major celebrations: royal weddings, funerals, victories; but only two coronations, both controversial: that of Henry VI of England who had conquered France and that of the Emperor Napoleon. The legitimate dynasties stuck to the cathedral of Reims throughout. It was in Notre-Dame that the conversion of Henri IV to Catholicism was celebrated in 1593, and in 1687 Louis XIV came all the way from Versailles to thank the Lord for restoring his health. In modern times (1970), the funeral mass of Charles de Gaulle was celebrated here.

Notre-Dame equally offered sanctuary to the poor and distressed. Its square (*le parvis*) - a sixth the size of the present square - was the social centre of the city, providing entertainment, spiritual comfort and commerce, by way of annual fairs, edifying mystery plays with stories taken from the Holy Scriptures and religious processions when the reliquaries of saints were carried here from their respective churches. Geneviève, the patron saint of Paris, was consistently a favourite. In times of crisis her reliquary was brought here from its home on the Left Bank, and the people would implore her on their knees to intercede on their behalf.

Rabelais's hero Gargantua naturally went to Notre-Dame during his visit to Paris. Followed and gawked at for being a stranger and a giant, he found the Parisians an irresistible target for a practical joke. Having climbed the church tower, he "unfastened his codpiece and, lugging out his pleasure-rod, he so fiercely bepissed [on them] that he drowned two hundred and sixty thousand four hundred and eighteen, exclusive of women and children." In Rabelais's version of the story, the city of Lutetia (meaning 'white'), so called because of the white thighs of its maidens, henceforth became known as Paris, (from *par rie*, 'for a laugh', in recognition of Gargantua's jest).

At a time when intellectual activities were restricted to theology Notre-Dame was also the seat of learning of the capital. In the early 12th century, however, the philosopher Guillaume de Champeaux, followed by a throng of disciples, crossed the Seine and settled south of the river, turning the left bank into the academic and intellectual centre of Paris for centuries to come.

The Romans had preceded him, having spilled over from the island to the firm soil of the hilly left bank, the site of Gallo-Roman Lutetia. The new Paris that grew out of the ashes of the Norman devastation, on the other hand, sprang up on the right bank because its strand (*grève*, hence Place de Grève, now Place de l'Hôtel-de-Ville) was an invaluable asset to the corporation of water merchants (*les marchands de l'eau*) who were the backbone of the new city's economy and remote descendants of the early *Nautae Parisiaci*. Having bought the strand from Louis VII in the 12th century, they made it their new harbour instead of the rudimentary Saint-Landry, on the northern bank of the island, then moved to the natural plateau that rose above the strand, the only site on the right bank that escaped the flooding of the Seine. From then on medieval Paris was made up of three entities: the right bank, its economic sinew, called La Ville; the left bank, its intellectual mind, L'Université, and the island, its original city, La Cité. The little island lying to its east was covered with meadows, reeds and willows and totally uninhabited. During the troubled times of the 14th century, a defence tower was built on its eastern tip with a moat to its west, which divided it into two: l'Ile Notre-Dame, serving as the cathedral's recreational grounds, and l'Ile aux Vaches, the domain of grazing cows (and also of laundresses and lovers). In the first half of the 17th century, when these two bucolic havens could no longer resist the encroachment of the city, the moat was filled in and the two islands were united once more into the Ile Saint-Louis.

Philippe-Auguste was the natural ally of the water merchants, whose prosperity ensured his own. Before leaving on the Third Crusade, he therefore decided to have the right bank belted by a rampart but, being a seasoned businessman, he made the merchants finance it themselves: after all, they could afford to pay and he in return was offering them protection, which seemed a fair deal.

With economic growth there was soon need for an administrative structure and by the next century a kind of corporation or tribunal of commerce was set up on Place de Grève, la Maison de la Marchandise, later known as le Parloir aux Bourgeois. This was the embryo of the municipality of Paris, as is illustrated by the fact that the city's aldermen were elected among its members and the provost of Paris was the head of the corporation. Likewise, the municipality adopted the corporation's seal, the same one used by the *Nautae Parisiaci a* thousand years earlier: with only minor changes, this remains the coat of arms of Paris. The provostship lasted until the French Revolution, although by then it had long lost its independence and played an insignificant role. In the early days, when its members represented the prosperous merchants of Paris, it could be as much of a threat to the throne as were its princely subjects, as in the case of the bloody

revolt led by the provost Etienne Marcel in the 14th century. As the throne con-
solidated its authority, it learnt to keep them under check by abolishing the free
election of members and appointing them to their posts instead. Etienne Marcel
was the first provost to settle in a town hall on Place de Grève, a two-storeyed
house he had bought from the king on behalf of the city in 1357. It was known as
La Maison des Piliers because it stood on a row of arcades. A magnificent
Renaissance building replaced it in the 16th century, begun at the time of
François I but completed only during the reign of Louis XIII. At a time of commercial expansion, François I encouraged the prosperity of the bourgeoisie and
therefore entrusted the famous Italian architect, Boccador, with the prestigious
project.

The festive Renaissance-style Hôtel de Ville now stands as a reminder that the
4th arrondissement is the birthplace of the Paris we know, the stronghold of the
city's authorities since its beginning, the home of the only governing institution in
Paris still on its original site. Even during the Revolution it was left in peace, for
being a bourgeois institution it was not contested. The anti-bourgeois proletarian
Commune, on the other hand, burnt it down in 1871, but the victorious bourgeois
government of the Third Republic rebuilt it at once in its old style, so as to brush
off this unfortunate incident and demonstrate that its possession was irrevocable.

The Place de Grève was also a focal site in the life of the city, where people
would gather in the early hours of the morning in search of work: this was known
as *faire la grève*, an expression still in use but nowadays meaning 'to go on
strike'. The square was also used for festivities, in particular for the *fête de la
Saint-Jean* on 24 June, when a 10-metre-high bonfire, accompanied by fireworks
and firecrackers, celebrated the birth of John the Baptist. Occasionally the King
would come over to light the fire, heralded by the sound of trumpets. But the
Place de Grève is remembered above all as the main place of public executions
and the gallows were a permanent fixture. Not that all the victims were hanged:
some were dispatched promptly by the sword or the axe, others were quartered,
others still - mainly witches and heretics - were burnt at the stake. The type of
crime and the social rank of the victim also determined the category of punish-
ment: decapitation for a nobleman, hanging for a menial... Many notorious criminals were executed here, for example Cartouche, the terror of Paris in the early
18th century, Ravaillac, the assassin of Henri IV, and the Marquise de Brinvilliers, a mass poisoner. These occasions provided entertainment to Parisians of all
social ranks who thronged into the square and crammed on to rooftops. A fee was
sometimes charged for places at the windows.

On Friday 17 July 1676, Madame de Sévigné, posted on the bridge of Notre-
Dame, watched the Marquise de Brinvilliers, in a shift and a cornet, being pushed

on to the tumbril that was to carry her to Place de Grève, "a doctor [confessor] by her side, the executioner on the other. To tell the truth, this made me shudder." The bare-footed prisoner had a rope around her neck, which Madame de Sévigné could not see because of the huge crowds. "Never was there seen such a crowd, nor was Paris ever so astir, nor so attentive." After all, the Marquise de Brinvilliers was one of the most sensational serial killers in the history of France.

After prolific sexual activity that began when she was seven, Madame de Brinvilliers was married off but soon took a lover, the slender, blue-eyed cavalry officer Godin. Her principled, honest father had him locked up at the Bastille with a sealed letter from the King, but Godin used his time there to make the acquaintance of an Italian named Exili, an expert on poisons. Once released the two went on experimenting in Exili's laboratory and sharing their findings with Madame de Brinvilliers, who, having squandered the generous dowry provided by her father, now plotted the elimination of her family, so as to receive the entire inheritance. She became a benevolent member of the staff at the Hôtel-Dieu hospital, next to Notre-Dame, the better to experiment first on patients. Having got the proportions right, she applied them to her father, who must have been of a more robust constitution than the patients of the Hôtel-Dieu, for it took her ten attempts to finish him off. Her two brothers soon met with the same fate, but her attempt to poison her sister and sister-in-law failed; nor could she eliminate her husband, for Godin, not being very anxious to marry her, removed the poison secretly at each attempt. When Godin died (naturally) before the venture was over, he left behind a casket with 34 compromising letters, 27 'recipes' headed 'curious secrets' and some samples of poisons. The Marquise fled to a convent in Belgium, which granted her right of sanctuary, but the French authorities got her out by subterfuge. Meanwhile they also got hold of her memoirs, an edifying autobiographical confession of a life peppered with adultery, incest, attempted abortions and successive murders. The sensitive Madame de Sévigné found her execution rather harrowing, writing to her daughter later that day, "At last, it is all over, the Brinvilliers is in the air: her poor little body was thrown after the execution into a very big fire, and the ashes to the wind…"

The French Revolution did not retain Place de Grève for its executions, other than for the guillotining of the odd common criminal. On the other hand, it was on Place de Grève that the remains of Geneviève, the patron saint of Paris, were burnt by an ideologically confused and brainless populace, indifferent to the fact that she had dedicated her life to the welfare of the people. Public executions continued here until the advent of Louis-Philippe in 1830, who ruled them out because "the generous citizens had so gloriously spilled their blood (on Place de Grève) for the national cause", during the July Revolution. In 1832 the guillotine was transferred to the remote Place Saint-Jacques in the 13th arrondissement.

Like most people of their class, both the Marquise de Sévigné and the Marquise de Brinvilliers had their homes in the nearby Marais, which by then extended east of Place de Grève, all the way to the Grands Boulevards, a much vaster area than the initial historical Marais du Temple, roughly today's 3rd arrondissement. This was the golden age of the Marais, all spruced up and shining new, studded with magnificent *hôtels*, each with an elegant courtyard in front and an exquisite garden at the back - *entre cour et jardin*. The streets had no pavements and, with the cobbles extending right up to the façades of the buildings, looked like beautiful courtyards. On this stage a fascinating variety of people acted out their lives - monks in the mantles of their respective orders, orphan girls in blue and orphan boys in red, gentlemen dressed in all their splendour, escorted by a train of servants in rich bright liveries. The ladies, however, moved about only in carriages, the streets being frequented by cutpurses, cutthroats and streetwalkers, who would come over from the seedy west to try their luck.

A few pioneering families had already moved to the southern part of the Marais (now the 4th arr.) in the 13th century, but the real boost to the area was given by the Dauphin and future Charles V, when he settled in the Hôtel de Saint-Pol in 1365, following Etienne Marcel's rebellion. The house had been the Paris pied-à-terre of the archbishops of Sens, and was protected on one side by the Seine and on the other by the fortified gate of Saint-Antoine, soon to be reinforced by a veritable fortress, the Bastille, and by a new rampart around the right bank of the city. Having purchased it in 1361 and three neighbouring dwellings by 1365, the Dauphin merged them into the Hôtel de Saint-Pol, a vast estate now bounded by rues Saint-Paul, Saint-Antoine and Petit-Musc and the Seine, with lovely gardens, a fruit orchard and even a menagerie. He intended this to be his permanent home and when he came to the throne in 1364 as Charles V, he signed a deed stipulating that "the Hôtel de Saint-Pol was irrevocably united to the domain of the crown." But in time the smells emanating from the rampart's moat and from the open sewers on rue Saint-Antoine became too much and he deserted it for the Louvre and the Hôtel des Tournelles (in the 3rd arr.). Charles VI, who succeeded him to the throne, was too deranged to be affected by such discomfort and remained there until his death in 1422, but his wife Isabelle (Isabeau) of Bavaria moved to the Hôtel de Barbette (also in the 3rd arr.). François I found it "a large *hôtel* most vague and ruinous and of very little value", and had it replaced by a convent which he gave to the Order of the Celestins.

A forward-looking king, François I encouraged the development of the Marais and the sale of land by the religious orders to the wealthy newcomers in search of space. In the 16th century the Marais was already a neighbourhood of superb elegance of which only traces remain, because in the 17th century its architectural masterpieces were swept away and replaced by more fashionable buildings. One such dwelling belonged to the Italian Jaquetti di Diaceto, a contemporary of Catherine de Medici, whose palace, on the site of the present Marché Saint-Gervais, had paintings by Raphael and Michelangelo hanging on its walls.

The opening of Place Royale (now Place des Vosges) was a determining factor in promoting the Marais. This was the first open-air square in Paris, and a magnificent one. Surrounded on all four sides by exquisite bright pink brick and white stone pavilions in neat order, these served in 1612 as an enchanting backdrop of the most dazzling celebration recalled by Parisians, that is, the double wedding of Louis XIII and his sister Elisabeth, respectively to the Infanta of Spain and her brother,which was fixed to coincide with the inauguration of the square. The square became the most prestigious address in the most desirable neighbourhood of Paris, as claimed by the abbé d'Aubignac: "The most beautiful quarter in the town of stylishness [i.e. Paris] is the big square which can verily be said to be royal." His contemporary Scarron, in *Adieux aux Maretz et à la Place Royale*, described

> Ses dedans somptueux, ses superbes lambris
> Ses riches ornements, ses peintures sans prix,
> Ses rares cabinets, ses dais et ses balustres.
> (Its sumptuous interiors, its superb panelling/Its rich ornaments, its priceless paintings,/Its rare cabinets, its canopies and its balustrades).

At a time when Versailles was no more than a hunting lodge, great architects such as Mansart and Le Vau and painters such as Le Brun, Mignard and Vouet dazzled Paris with their talent. Polychrome cupids, lyres and garlands of flowers against a background of gold decked the halls of splendid apartments, while gilded foliage and grotesques or scenes from Greek mythology adorned their ceilings. Tapestries and damask hangings, mirrors and carpets, silk and velvet upholstery, silver and gold embroideries added further splendour to those interiors, not to mention the collections of paintings and furniture of some of their occupants, notably those of the Duc de Richelieu, the prodigal great-nephew of the Cardinal. Many of the paintings he owned, in particular ten works by Nicolas Poussin, now hang in the Louvre, the Duke having sold them to Louis XIV in order to buy some 20 paintings by Rubens, the largest series of that painter's works ever to be brought together by a private person. (Most of them are now in the Arte Pinakotech in Munich).

Place Royal was also a stopping-place of foreign ambassadors arriving in Paris. Having been met at the Porte Saint-Antoine by the municipal troops and the Royal Swiss Guards, they would use rue Saint-Antoine as their route to the Louvre because it was the broadest artery in the city. On the way they would stop at

Place Royale to parade their dazzling attire, their carriages and the livery of their train - all for the prestige of their country. Vying with them, the natives strutted in all their splendour on the balconies of Place Royale, spectators and actors at once, and also judges, distributing points to each delegation of this international contest. Needless to say, those ambassadors of exotic, far-away lands often came out on top. Christina of Sweden, who had abdicated and was an enlightened feminist long before the term was coined, also drew large crowds to Place Royale on her official entry into Paris, and the balconies of the square were filled with the most distinguished members of society, among them Henrietta of England and the Princesses of Orange and of Conti.

Place Royale was also a favourite choice for duels, watched from the balconies by the ladies whose favours were being sought: some of these could boast of several suitors who had given up the ghost for their sake. Louis XIII's minister, the Cardinal Richelieu, was determined to put an end to this raging epidemic and in 1626 took drastic measures to enforce a ban on them. Accordingly, when Boutteville contravened his ruling, believing that his glorious pedigree would put him above the law (he was said to have descended from the first Baron of France), Richelieu had him decapitated on Place de Grève, together with his witness Des Chapelles, and had their bodies and heads exposed as an example on a table in the main hall of the Hôtel Angoulême (now the historical library of Paris). Madame de Sévigné's grandfather, the Baron de Chantal, was also involved in the duel and sentenced to death, but he and the two members of the opposing party managed to run for their lives and were therefore replaced on the rope by dangling paintings. As an ultimate act of defiance, the three had their lackeys return to Place de Grève during the night and remove the paintings. In 1643 Richelieu died and the duels resumed as never before.

With the transfer of the court to Versailles in 1682, the centre of gravity of Paris shifted west, entailing the decline of the Marais, while the French Revolution dealt it its final blow. With the development of industry in the 19th century, once-beautiful mansions were converted into collections of workshops, which proliferated like cancerous growths on rooftops, on neglected house-fronts and inside courtyards. It became a lugubrious environment, inhabited by the poor. Many of them were Jews who made their way back to the area around rue des Rosiers, where, in the 13th and 14th centuries, they had led a precarious existence, punctuated by successive expulsions and returns according to the whims or economic calculations of respective monarchs, which ended in 1394 with their definitive expulsion from France. Some took advantage of loopholes to return, and there were always some Jews living in Paris, which explains why in 1615 Louis XIII reiterated the ban. It ended only with the emancipation of the Jews on 27 September 1791. Their presence was perpetuated through the name of rue des

Juifs, which became rue Ferdinand Duval only in 1900. The Jewish newcomers of modern times tended not to stay long: as they improved their lot they moved elsewhere, to be replaced successively by new arrivals, the most recent significant group being the North African Jews of the early 1960s.

In 1962, André Malraux's bill calling for the rehabilitation of the Marais was passed in the National Assembly, and in 1965 the area was declared a 'protected zone'. One by one parasitical appendages were removed from historical buildings, which underwent thorough restoration before being turned into museums or cultural centres. An annual festival helped promote the resurrected Marais among tourists and Parisians alike, while expensive boutiques were substituted for the old neighbourhood shops and workshops. When the high-flying clothes designer Chevignon took up residence on the premises of the antiquated Turkish baths in rue des Rosiers, there was an outcry among nostalgic sentimentalists, and the word 'assassin!' was scrawled on the pale pink walls of the building.

West of the Marais lay an infested neighbourhood of damp, dark, narrow alleys. An enclave now limited by rue Saint-Merri, rue du Grenier Saint-Lazare, rue Saint-Martin and rue du Temple (in the 3rd arr.) became the rubbish dump of the market of Les Halles and was derisively named Beaubourg (*Beau Bourg*). In the 1970s, however, the name became associated with avant-garde pop culture, when the seedy streets on the *plateau Beaubourg* were cleared to make room for a gigantic community arts centre, the Centre Georges Pompidou, which commemorates its originator, the President of the Republic, a lover of contemporary art. Pompidou did not live to see the project completed, having died in 1974, three years before its inauguration. Richard Rogers and Renzo Piano sought to express the spirit of the time in their bright blue building with bright red and blue piping, which, when seen from an elevated viewpoint, stands out in the silver-grey cityscape. Most Parisians were scandalized that two 'hippy' architects should have been allowed to build a 'refinery' in the historic heart of the city. Nearly twenty years later the building still ranks first among the city's monuments they wish to see wiped out! And yet it is visited *en masse*, beating all records: 28,000 visitors per day, 8 million per year (as against 2.5 million visitors for the Eiffel Tower), and over 400 million since it first opened in 1977. These figures, however, mask the fact that visitors often come here because access to most of the building is free of charge, notably to the library, which is heavily used by default, the University of Paris being unable to accommodate all its students. The result is an interminable queue on the second floor, made up of a daily average of 11,000 readers waiting to occupy the 1,800 available seats.

The homeless and winos too take advantage of free admission and sometimes take shelter in the library, especially in winter. A recorded announcement in the library warns readers to beware of pickpockets, and the occasional syringe is to be found in the toilets. In short, the Centre Georges Pompidou has become Paris's mecca of mass culture, although a different atmosphere prevails in the Museum of Modern Art on the 4th floor, which charges admission and is free of queues. Of the museum's collection of 35,000 works, space permits only 850 to be exhibited at any one time. A fee is also payable for admission to temporary exhibitions, on the 5th floor, which attract queues, if they are on a popular theme.

The quality of the exhibitions has fallen off somewhat, as have the premises and the environment. By early 1993 the fact had to be faced that the Centre Georges Pompidou was sorely in need of repair. Measures are now being taken to have it renovated by 1997, in time for its twentieth anniversary. Its 'piazza' is also to be renovated. Since the opening of the Centre, this has been a focal point in the street life of Paris. Buskers, acrobats, mime artists, jugglers, fire-eaters, portrait painters and pickpockets share this spacious square, spontaneously recreating the medieval atmosphere of the *parvis* of Notre-Dame. Today's performers, however, have come from the four corners of the earth and give expression to the multi-cultural nature of Parisian society, in which the African component indisputably predominates, at least in the field of music. This street culture reflects the inexorable march of the city towards a multi-racial society in the face of the extreme right-wing Jean-Marie Le Pen and his followers. Just as Parisians' ancestors carved their emotions meticulously into the stone of Notre-Dame, today's residents identify with the slapdash, brightly-coloured Centre Georges Pompidou and with the bright-coloured mobile sculptures that play in the water of the Stravinsky fountain by its side. As if by some predetermined design, Notre-Dame and the Centre Pompidou, the two shrines of the people of Paris, stand guard at the borders of the arrondissement from which the city emanated, Notre-Dame rising out of the waters where a tribe of navigators once plied, the Centre Pompidou rising out of the asphalt that supports a mass population of city dwellers. Both reach up to the heavens, Notre-Dame by way of its towers, the Centre Pompidou by way of an escalator. Half-way between, the Hôtel de Ville takes care of the terrestrial needs of the people.

WHERE TO WALK...

THE ARSENAL

On the eastern edge of the 4th arrondissement lies an attractive area, bypassed by most pedestrians. If you wish to discover it, do so on a Wednesday afternoon, when the Arsenal Library and the apartments of the Grand Master of Artilleries, on the corner of Boulevard Morland and Boulevard Henri IV, are open to the public (2 to 4 pm, except 1st to 15th September). Sully-Morland Métro station is where you get off.

Built in the 14th century for the manufacture of ammunition, the royal Arsenal lay along an arm of the Seine (now Boulevard Morland), which made the small stretch of land lying to the south into an island, the island of Louviers. In 1563 a gigantic explosion - which could be heard as far as Melun, 46 km south-east of Paris - blew most of it up, after which it was used only as an arms depot, while the rest of the site was turned into a dwelling for the Grand Master. At the time of Henri IV the post was held by his minister, the Duc de Sully, who commissioned Philippe Delorme, the great architect of the day, to build him a palatial home, befitting the glamorous figure he cut and splendid enough to entice his King to visit him there. It was in fact while Henri IV was on his way to the Arsenal from the Louvre, on 10 May 1610, that Ravaillac jumped onto his coach and stabbed him to death. Sully's apartments were surrounded by beautiful courtyards and gardens, where he organized spectacular jousts and cavalcades, notably a magnificent carousel in 1606 in honour of Henri IV who had made him Duke: led by four representatives of the great noble families, it embodied the four elements, in keeping with the spirit of the Renaissance. The apartment now in existence, however, was not Sully's but belonged to the wife of La Meilleraye, Louis XIII's Grand Master.

Louis XIII did away with the foundry as well and a court of justice was set up in its stead by Richelieu, of sorry memory, for this was where the scandalous trial of Nicolas Foucquet, Louis XIV's treasurer, was held in 1664. Officially tried for embezzlement, Fouquet's real crime was having built the sumptuous palace of Vaux-le-Vicomte for himself and having challenged the blazon of the Sun King. Louis XIV's minister, Colbert, convened a band of magistrates in his pay, yet the courageous d'Ormesson stood up to the King who wished to see Fouquet sentenced to death and sentenced him to banishment only. For his pains, d'Ormesson was exiled to his estate south-east of Paris, but the intellectual élite of the time - Boileau, Racine, Bossuet, Bourdaloue, Madame de Sévigné - sided with him and came to visit him there. La Voisin's trial in 1680 was another memorable event. Women of distinction, taking the Marquise de Brinvilliers as a model, set out to eliminate those they found cumbersome. La Voisin was one such, evidently among many: when she was questioned, so many names of high-ranking ladies began to leak out that the procedures were hastened so as to silence her before too much embarrassing information was divulged.

By then France had entered a peaceful lull and Louis XIV could divert his attention from bellicose activities to the construction of the palace of Versailles. The old abandoned foundry, where the army's cannon had once been cast, now came in handy for the casting of the numerous bronze statues that were to decorate the gardens of the new palace that was meant to dazzle all the courts of

Europe. At the same time the King's megalomania was fed by having his entire grand armoury displayed at the Arsenal, to demonstrate France's invincibility; all foreign dignitaries visiting France were taken to see this magnificent array - a subtle reminder as to who was top dog!

In the second half of the 18th century the tenant of the Arsenal was the Minister of War, the Marquis Paulmy d'Argenson, who set up in his apartments a library of over 100,000 volumes, among them illuminated medieval manuscripts. Louis XVI's brother, the Comte d'Artois and future Charles X, bought the library in 1785 and enriched its collections. The revolutionary authorities flooded it with the confiscated treasures of the neighbouring convents and also transferred here the Bastille's archives. Thus, the prison register is still kept here, as well as the death certificate of the legendary Man in the Iron Mask. In 1797 the library was opened to the public under its new name, Bibliothèque Nationale de l'Arsenal. Charles Nodier, the head of the library from 1824 to 1844, gathered here the Romantic writers Victor Hugo, Lamartine, Alfred de Musset, Alexandre Dumas, Sainte-Beuve and others, perpetuating a 200-year-old Parisian tradition of *salons littéraires*. Towards the end of the 19th century, when Heredia was curator of the library, his *Parnassien* poet friends gathered here. At present the library owns 1.5 million volumes with a substantial department on the performing arts. Its theatre section is of particular interest and includes the archives of such great stagemen as Louis Jouvet.

The library was set up in the Arsenal's extension that was built by the famous Boffrand for the Duc du Maine, the legitimized son of Louis XIV and Madame de Montespan, who moved here in the early 18th century. This was a luxurious town dwelling, to suit the polished, frolicsome society of the time, but as a tribute to its initial military vocation, Boffrand enhanced its façade with sculptures of smoking mortar and cannon. The main entrance to the library, however, is set in the old façade. On either side of the vestibule, the busts of Henri IV and Sully are reminders of the heyday of the Arsenal. A majestic staircase leads to the reading rooms and to the private apartments on the first floor. The apartment of Madame de Meilleraye provides a unique example of a Louis XIII interior. The Maréchal de Meilleraye had just married the young Mlle Cossé-Brissac and commissioned Simon Vouet to create for her a dwelling of great splendour, as can be appreciated from the magnificence of every detail. The Duc du Maine's apartment next to it has several lavish reception rooms, above all, a fabulous music room, exquisitely decorated to please a light-hearted society.

Across the street is the Pavillon de l'Arsenal, a glass and steel structure dating from the 19th century, which served as an art gallery and later as a warehouse of the Samaritaine department store. Since 1988 it has been home to temporary exhibitions dealing with different aspects of town planning in Paris, which have been increasingly visited by Parisians. To wind up, walk along quai Henri IV and turn left into Boulevard Bourdon, along the marina of the Bassin de l' Arsenal, a blissful haven reminiscent of sunny holidays. Boulevard Bourdon will take you to Place de la Bastille where our exploration of the Marais will begin.

FROM THE BASTILLE TO THE HEART OF THE MARAIS

As you enter the Marais from the corner of Place de la Bastille and rue Saint-Antoine, you are following the route taken by the foreign ambassadors and their trains, when entering Paris during the *Ancien Régime*, and even by the King when repairing to the Louvre from his palace in Vincennes. This was also the itinerary of Louis XIV's wedding procession, on its way from Place du Trône (now Place de la Nation) to the Louvre. No doubt it is hard to picture the formidable, eight-towered fortress of the Bastille that was built here in the 14th century to fend off an English assault from the east. The corner café, with its clinical-looking designer furniture and succulent pastry display in its window, is hardly suggestive of the medieval gate that stood here, complete with a moat, drawbridge and crenellated walls. The pink cobbles on the ground outline the exact location of the Bastille, but nobody pays any attention to them. If anything, it is the golden statue of the Spirit (*Génie*) of Liberty on top of the Bastille column that catches the eye as it glitters in the sun, bringing to mind the heroic destruction of this symbol of oppression.

By the time it was stormed, however, the Bastille had long ceased to conform to its image of merciless brutality. In fact, in the 17th century and especially in the 18th it had become a sort of luxury prison, often used for members of the aristocracy sent here, with a sealed letter from the King, for a period not exceeding a few months. Thus, when the Man in the Iron Mask was brought here, since no-one could see his face, rumour had it that he was the twin brother of Louis XIV!

Within reasonable limits the prisoners could maintain their previous lifestyle, bringing over their own furniture and servants, entertaining visitors and even keeping amorous rendezvous. Voltaire used his time to complete his play *Oedipe*; the Marquis de Sade draped his cell walls and brought over his own wine from Provence; while the Cardinal de Rohan once hosted a lavish dinner party on 20 guests. Although this lifestyle was financed by the prisoners' families, the upkeep of the Bastille was a costly business, owing to the high fees paid to its highly qualified staff of doctors, priests, chemists and surgeons, not to mention the highly paid governor. When Voltaire was released in 1717, the Regent granted him a pension of a thousand crowns; Voltaire thanked him graciously, with particular reference to the food received at His Highness's expense, but suggested that in future he need not trouble to provide him with lodgings!

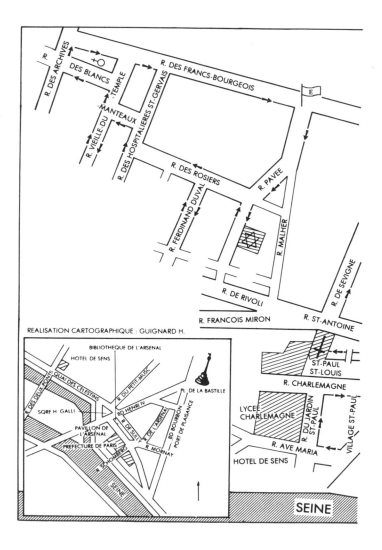

REALISATION CARTOGRAPHIQUE : GUIGNARD H.

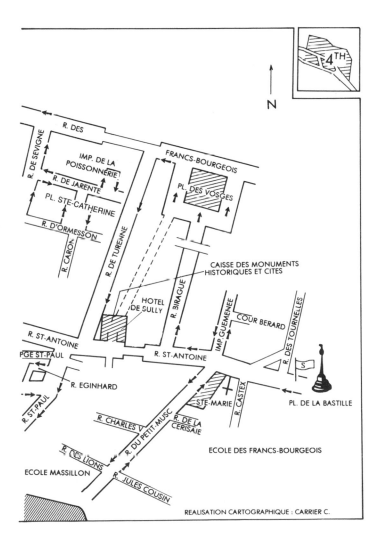

In order to cut down on state expenditure the Minister of Finance, Necker, had shut down the prison of Vincennes in 1784 and was planning likewise to demolish the Bastille. A square named Place Louis XVI was to replace it, but one battered tower of the fortress of the prison was to be preserved as historical testimony. A statue of Louis XVI stretching out a liberating hand in the direction of the demolished gaol was to surmount a pyramid made up of chains, bars and locks retrieved from the Bastille. But the patriotic *sans-culottes* got there first. Their heroic assault against tyranny and the deliverance of the victims of oppression turned out to be much less glorious than the uplifting myth history has since created, for all they found in the Bastille were seven prisoners: four forgers, one accomplice to an attempted murder, who had been locked up in the Bastille for over 30 years, a count who had committed incest and was sent there at his family's request with a sealed letter, and one feeble-minded wretch, also kept here at the request of the family, whom the liberating forces transferred to the celebrated asylum at Charenton. An eighth prisoner had been sent to Charenton ten days earlier - the notorious Marquis de Sade, who had been transferred here from Vincennes when it was demolished in 1784. He too had been arrested at the request of his family, anxious to remove a cumbersome relative whose sexual perversion was not limited to the written word. It was in Vincennes that he wrote *Justine* and *Gomorrah*. In June 1789 the governor stopped the prisoners' daily walks on the towers because of the growing unrest in the neighbourhood. This enraged the Marquis who made himself a sort of megaphone and yelled through it that the prisoners were being slaughtered inside. On 3 July 1789 he created such a commotion that he had to be removed from the sight of the restless crowds and at 1 in the morning he was transferred to the prison section of Charenton. When that prison was closed down in 1803, he was locked up in the asylum for 'licentious dementia'.

Rue Saint-Antoine, which has preserved its medieval, winding route, is enhanced by the domes of the churches of the Visitandines and Saint-Paul-Saint-Louis on the left-hand side. On the right-hand side the street opens into a tiny, pleasant square in which stands a statue of the 18th-century playwright Caron de Beaumarchais, a local inhabitant. N° 5 across the street is an old, countrified little house, a remnant of past times. At n° 17 is the reformed church of Sainte-Marie, once the church of the Visitandines; this was one of the historic sites of the Marais but it is unfortunately open only during Sunday service at 10.30 am. In the 15th century an aristocratic mansion stood here, which belonged successively to illustrious figures such as Louis d'Orléans, the brother of Charles VI and the archbishop of York during the English occupation. Eventually it became the property of the Comtesse d'Etampes, the widowed sister of Charles d'Orléans, and was known as the Hôtel d'Etampes, later to be bought by François I. Diane de

Poitiers, Henri II's all-powerful favourite, resided here in 1554, followed two years later by Philippe Delorme, the architect of the Tuileries and of Sully's dwelling in the Arsenal.

It was only in 1628 that the building became a religious institution, when the Order of Sainte-Marie-de-la-Visitation (or Les Visitandines) bought it. Founded by Saint François de Sales, the Bishop of Geneva, the order was dedicated to the education of girls and to the relief of the sick. A first convent was opened for that purpose across the Swiss-French border from Geneva, in the town of Annecy. It was headed by an enthusiastic supporter of the Bishop's charitable ideals, Jeanne Frémiot from Dijon, the wife of the Baron de Chantal and the grandmother of the Marquise de Sévigné. In 1619 she arrived in Paris and opened a convent in the southern suburb of Faubourg Saint-Marcel (now in the 13th arr.), before moving to the more central position of the Marais two years later, to the Hôtel de Cosse on the present site of n° 26-30 rue du Petit-Musc, first to your left. Its gardens communicated with the Hôtel d'Etampes, which she purchased in 1628 to allow for further expansion.

The Visitandines chose to settle in the Marais because it offered them both the moral and the financial support of the high nobility, and before long they were able to expand east all the way to the Bastille and as far as rue de la Cerisaie to the south. Such was their prestige that in 1628 the illustrious François Mansart was happy to build their chapel, a rotunda surmounted by a 35-metre dome, which was inspired by Santa Maria Rotondo in Rome and served as a model for several other Parisian churches, notably the Val-de-Grâce and the Invalides. Its crypt was also an architectural feat, its vault being supported by a single pillar.

The chapel was known as Notre-Dame-des-Anges, while its mother superior, the Baronne de Chantal, took on the name of Mère Angélique. The prestige of this institution is also underlined by the fact that Vincent de Paul, the most prominent churchman of the 17th century, who was later beatified for his altruistic life and charitable work, was appointed its first chaplain in 1632, the year the cornerstone of the church was laid, and held the position for 28 years. A century later, the founder of the order, 'la Bienheureuse Mère', became the only married woman to be beatified.

The place also served as a retreat for members of society. Madame de La Fayette, author of La Princesse de Clèves, retired here under the name of Soeur Angélique, possibly to avoid Louis XIII's overtures, in parallel with the heroine of her novel. Her relationship with the King remained platonic throughout, although he kept coming to visit her. Mazarin's niece, Hortense Mancini, on the other hand, was locked up here against her will, for hers was a less exemplary life. As an act of revenge she is said to have filled the stoup with black ink and gloated at the sight of the nuns' smeared faces. Several members of society were brought for burial to the chapel crypt, notably Madame de Sévigné's great-uncle, the archbishop Frémiot and brother of Jeanne; her mother, Marie de Coulanges; and her hot-headed husband, Henri de Sévigné, who died in a duel. The disgraced Minister of Finance, Nicolas Fouquet, a close friend of the family, was also buried here. The order was abolished during the Revolution and the buildings demolished, except for the chapel, which was thereafter used as a revolutionary club, hence the famous Phrygian cap of the *sans-culottes* sculpted above the side door. The club was led by the inflammable, rabidly feminist Théroigne de Méricourt, who later became demented and was locked up in the horrific institution *La Salpêtrière* (in the 13th arr.). In 1803, Napoleon decided to put all religions on an equal footing and gave the church to the Protestants. It has remained in their hands ever since.

Next to the church, at n° 21-23 stands one of the beautiful *hôtels* of the Marais, the Hôtel de Mayenne, best appreciated from across the street. At the time of writing it is a striking example of the way a monument looks before and after a face-lift. N° 21 is a school and being presumably short of funds is in a sorry state, while n° 23 has been stunningly renovated, revealing its Louis XIII architecture, with its characteristic brick-and-stone façade and its imposing slate roof (a style also known as *bleu, blanc, rouge* – *bleu* for the slate, *blanc* for the stone, *rouge* for the brick).

Charles VI owned an earlier *hôtel* on the site, which he gave a present to his brother, Louis d'Orléans. After his assassination, it went to his son, Charles D'Orléans, a great poet. In 1578, Quélus, Henri III's *mignon*, was brought here after a duel motivated, in this case, by politics: he, Maugiron and Livarot were Henri III's *mignons* and were fighting his cause against d'Entragues, Ribrac and Schomberg, members of the Catholic League, headed by Henri le Balafré, Duc de Guise. It was a duel of unspeakable savagery after which all the participants lay dead or seriously injured. Quélus, who had been stabbed 18 times, took 33 days to die, during which time Henri III ordered the busy street of Saint-Antoine to be strewn with straw so as to stop all the traffic. It is believed that Henri III's assassination was plotted in this *hôtel* by the Duchesse de Montpensier, the Balafré's sister, in revenge for her brother's assassination in 1588. On 1 August 1589, Henri III was sitting on the latrine in his tent in the camp of Saint-Cloud, wearing only his dressing-gown, when Jacques Clément broke into his tent and pierced him through the heart.

The present mansion was built in 1613 by Henri de Lorraine, son of the Duc de Mayenne, one of the greatest families in France of the *Ancien Régime*. In 1812 it became the boarding section of the neighbouring Lycée Charlemagne and the premises consequently deteriorated dramatically. In 1870 it was leased by the brothers of the Christian School of rue des Francs-Bourgeois, which is why it is now called Ecole des Francs-Bourgeois. The Hôtel de Mayenne stands on the corner of rue du Petit-Musc, which is lined with charming old houses. The corner house of rue Charles V was the home of the notorious poisoner, La Brinvilliers. If you stroll through the street all the way to the *quai*, you will see the impressive façade of the Hôtel Fieubet at n° 1, richly sculpted in a Spanish Baroque style.

Retrace your steps, cross rue Saint-Antoine and walk into Impasse Guénémée, a picturesque, narrow, dead-end alley, lined with old, crooked houses, which once led to the royal palace of the Tournelles and later to the Hôtel Rohan-Guénémée on Place Royale (now Place des Vosges). Its back entrance was at n° 12 of this alley. Turn round for a superb view of the Hôtel de Mayenne. As you retrace your steps, notice the unusual pediment at n° 6 on your left, with its pile of thick books sculpted into the stone. This may have been the entrance to the convent of Les Filles de la Croix, another religious institution dedicated to the education of girls, whose head was the sister of the mother superior of the Visitandines. At present a lovely courtyard lies behind the thick wall, hidden from the public eye. In the 1950s Impasse Guénémée was a favourite of Simenon's Commaissaire Maigret, who appreciated a good, no-nonsense French meal at the modest café-restaurant that until recently stood on the corner of rue Saint-Antoine.

Back on rue Saint-Antoine, turn right into rue de Birague. Ahead of you is the impressive brick-and-stone arcaded Pavillon du Roi, a foretaste of the gorgeous Place des Vosges on the other side. This is the most spectacular approach to the square, through which the prestigious foreign guests of the kingdom entered it, notably Christina of Sweden, on the evening of 8 September 1656, preceded by four cavaliers seated on horses with coats embroidered in gold and silver and gem-studded harnesses. After her came the city guards, archers, Swiss Guards, the fanfare and the city aldermen carrying the gold-and-silver brocade canopy of

Place des Vosges

the abdicating queen, but with no-one underneath: free-spirited Christina refused to take her place there. When night fell the glittering procession was magically illuminated by torch lights. The Place Royale was equally illuminated and its gorgeous wrought-iron balconies crowded with France's nobility in their most fabulous garb. Trumpets sounded and the guns of the Bastille could be heard in the distance.

The Pavillon du Roi was built as the keystone of Place Royale. Reflecting the King's supreme position in the social hierarchy, it is taller than all the other buildings of the square except for the Pavillon de la Reine which matches it on the northern side of the square (in the 3rd arr.). Thirty-six houses, nine on each side, surround the square giving the illusion of perfect symmetry. The architects, probably Androuet du Cerceau and Claude Chastillon, created a ravishing harmony of red brick, white stone and grey slate, "a certain shade of colour so pleasing to the eye", according to Sauval, whose *histoire et recherches des Antiquités de la Ville de Paris* is an irreplaceable contemporary testimony.

The equestrian statue of Louis XIII was substituted in 1829 for the early statue erected in 1639 to commemorate the double wedding of the two royal couples on 5,6 and 7 April 1612. Originally Henri IV had the idea of setting up a silk-and-silver weaving mill (*'une manufacture de soye et argent fillé à la façon de Milan'*) along the northern side of the square, a venture intended to reduce French dependence on Italian imports. To this end he had mulberry trees planted in the Tuileries Gardens for the breeding of silkworms and 200 workers were brought over from Italy to work in the mills. But somehow the venture failed, the buildings were pulled down and the Place Royale became instead the living quarters of the most prestigious families of the nobility. The mansions were much larger than the narrow façades overlooking the square would suggest; in fact they extended a long way back. Besides, some of the families owned more than one house. Their splendid furnishings and fittings are all gone, as are the wall paintings, plastered over without compunction when new tastes came into vogue. Nevertheless, the Place des Vosges remains a place of beauty and harmony, enhanced by the serene atmosphere of its arcades, by the old street-lamps and by the geometric layout of the square and its four fountains. However, some neat flowerbeds would do the garden justice.

Turn right on Place des Vosges and continue to Musée Victor Hugo at n° 6 (even numbers are right of the Pavillon du Roi, odd numbers are to the left). Built in 1604, this was the largest and one of the famous mansions in the square, the home of the great Rohan-Guénémée family. It extended along rue Birague towards rue Saint-Antoine and had the largest alcove in Paris, according to Sauval, "all gilded and painted by Cotelle". A sketchbook of Cotelle's drawings for the mansion, now kept at the Ashmolean Library in Oxford, preserves the memory of his magnificent monochrome paintings against a background of gold, for which the Prince de Guénémée paid him more than 17,000 pounds. Sauval also reports that the large casement windows of the mansion "overlooked the largest garden of Place Royale". The landlady, Anne de Montbazon, Princesse de Guénémée, was a cultivated person who even learnt Hebrew. She was also a desirable person over whom the Duc de Guise fought a duel with Coligny, or rather murdered Coligny, when, against all chivalrous etiquette, he grabbed the latter's sword and stabbed him to death.

When Victor Hugo came to live here in 1832, aged 30, he occupied the second floor apartment, which now houses the museum. By then the square was known as Place des Vosges, in honour of the mountainous eastern *département* (district), which was the first to pay off its taxes to the young Republic in 1800. The years Victor Hugo spent on Place des Vosges were very creative, resulting in such works as *Les Chants du crépuscule, Ruy Blas, Les Rayons et les ombres*. It was here that he sketched out two of his major works, *La Légende des siècles* and *Les Misérables*. This was also a time of intensive exchange of ideas and merry gatherings of the Romantic circle. The poet Théodore de Banville described how in summer "the big door of the apartment remained open and the smell of flowers and leaves entered through the windows." The young guests would go out for a stroll and a smoke in the square's alleys, then "come up again, intoxicated by the night and the azure, into the dazzling atmosphere of torches and dancing." (Incidentally, Theodore de Banville still referred to the square as 'Place Royale' - traditions die hard...) On the personal front, however, this was a painful time: Hugo's wife Adèle became the mistress of writer and critic Sainte-Beuve in 1831 or 1832, while his own liaison with Juliette Drouet began in 1833. A back staircase in his study allowed him to leave the apartment unnoticed and repair to his rendezvous with the *boulangère* in rue du Petit-Musc, by way of Impasse Guénémée.

By 1902 the city of Paris owned the building and decided to turn it into a museum and thus honour one of the most venerated figures of the Third Republic. Victor Hugo's environment was recreated, including fragments of his later life, between 1848 and 1885, when he was no longer living here. Thus the room, including the Louis XIII four-poster bed, in which he died on 22 May 1885, in a building now demolished at 22 Avenue d'Eylau (in the 16th arr.), was put together in Place des Vosges in what used to be his study. His exile on the island of Guernsey is also recaptured on Place des Vosges. Hugo had taken Juliette Drouet along and set her up in a little cottage within sight of his own home; the decorations of her dining-room in Guernsey are now in what used to be the original lounge of the apartment.

Retrace your steps and continue as far as the Hôtel de Sully, at n° 7, originally built in 1624 by the great Androuet du Cerceau for Monsieur Gallet, a money speculator, who indulged in this extravagance after he had won 1,200,000 pounds at La Blondeau, the gambling house in Place Royale, where one played 'for high stakes'. However, he lost his fortune as suddenly as he had made it and had to yield the house to his creditor. When Henri IV's former minister Maximilien de Béthune, Marquis de Rosny and Duc de Sully, bought this place ten years later, he was 75 years old, a fulfilled old man, laden with titles and pensions, who liked to strut under the arcades or dance the pavan with young women of doubtful reputation, unaware of the outdated figure he cut in his Renaissance garb. At the same time, he apparently did not mind being cuckolded by his young wife and went so far as to provide generously for the upkeep of her lovers. But he did not wish to bump into them on the main staircase, and had a separate one installed, leading to his wife's apartments.

The next generations at the Hôtel de Sully continued in the same vein. Sully's daughter, the Duchesse de Rohan, had an illegitimate son and since her own daughter, Marguerite de Rohan, seemed set fair to follow in her footsteps, it was decided to remove her from her mother's influence and send her to live with her aunt on the other side of the square. Widowed in 1655, the Duchesse moved to the present n° 26 from where she was evicted in 1672 for refusing to pay her rent (despite her colossal wealth). All her furniture was seized and piled into the square to await removal, in view of all – not that anyone was particularly shocked. Living beyond one's means and getting into debt was an accepted way of life among the nobility.

Voltaire too was involved in the long history of the Hôtel de Sully, its landlord, the Prince de Rohan, having picked a quarrel with him at the Comédie-Française on the occasion of the performance of his play *Oedipe*. When the Prince had Voltaire beaten up, both for the fun of it and to mark his social superiority, Voltaire invited him to a duel, but was spurned and instead he was locked up at the Bastille. As a child of the bourgeoisie he would never forget the humiliation inflicted on him by a representative of the nobility. On his release he went into exile in England, where he learnt about social liberty, a notion he later brought back to France, sowing the seeds of revolution.

Today the Hôtel de Sully belongs to the Caisse Nationale des Monuments Historiques et des Sites, dedicated to the preservation of the historical and cultural heritage of France. It could not have fallen into better hands, and indeed has been beautifully restored in its original aspect, down to the box borders of the garden, as can be seen from an old engraving by Israël Silvestre. The main entrance to the *hôtel*, then as now, is on rue Saint-Antoine (n° 62), and it was built like most mansions of the time '*entre cour et jardin*' ('between courtyard and garden'), the courtyard standing in front of the main building, the garden at the back. In the main building is a bookshop specializing in the heritage of France, enhanced by a painted, Louis XIII wooden ceiling. The sculptures of the Seasons and the Elements in the courtyard probably date from the time of Sully. An ancient olive tree graces the garden. It is sheer delight to sit in its shade on a serene summer day. Like us, you may even be lulled by a flautist.

The famous 19th-century actress of the Comedie-Française, Rachel, lived for a while at n° 9, although by then she was ailing and had ceased to work. A gastronomic restaurant, l'Ambroisie, is here now, noticed only by those who know. N° 11 was the home of a notorious courtesan, Marion Delorme, who was ten years older than the even more notorious Ninon Lenclos. Her lovers included the Cardinal de Richelieu, whom she visited twice, once dressed as a man. The second time the Cardinal gave her a present a basket of 60 pistols, we are told by Tallement des Réaux, a notorious gossip. The Cardinal's great nephew, the Duc de Richelieu, lived at n° 21 and was also known for his sexual appetite. He claimed to have been the lover of all the females in Place Royale.

Retrace your steps to rue Saint-Antoine and cross over into rue Saint-Paul, named after a 7th-century church, which disappeared with the rest of Paris during the Norse raids of the 9th century. A new church replaced it in 1107 and was enlarged substantially in the 14th century to accommodate its growing number of parishioners. A small vestige of its tower can still be seen at the corner of n° 32. The street led to the bustling harbour of Saint-Paul, where passengers embarked for a three-day journey to Auxerre in Burgundy. Horses were also washed there, which added to the filth of the Seine, by then as polluted as it is today. Undaunted by such trifles, Henri IV used to bathe there in the nude on a hot summer's evening, soon to be followed by his subjects. Every evening in August 1608 as many as 4,000 of them frisked about in the water, between Charenton, east of Paris and the Ile de la Cité. The women were hidden by a 'tent', but their keenness to get a look at the men, who bathed in the nude like their king, even inspired a verse:

> On y accourt pour voir l'homme en son naturel
> Et tel qu'il est sorti des mains de l'Eternel.
> (One rushes over to see man in nature's garb
> And such as he came out of the Eternal's hands.)

At n° 31 turn right under the archway and on to rue Eginhardt, a tiny Jewish enclave in the 17th century, even though officially no Jews were living in Paris at the time. However discreet, it is mentioned by Alphonse Daudet in *Les Rois en Exile*. On the right is a shady courtyard with pretty trellises, an old well and a charmingly useless old stone bench on which nobody ever sits. Rising above, bathed in sunshine, is a rustic, old tiled roof complete with picturesque attic windows and a stocky chimney-stack. As you turn left and reach the corner of rue Charlemagne, you will notice an old street name engraved in the stone of the corner house on your right, rue Neuve Sainte-Anastase, after a religious order once established here. Back on rue Saint-Paul, you will now reach a succession of charming courtyards, zigzagging from one to the next, up and down pretty steps, unfolding new surprises at each angle. This is a compound of antique dealers and secondhand shops known as 'le village Saint-Paul' whose setting is as pleasing as the contents of its shops.

Continue in the direction of the Seine and turn right into rue Ave Maria for a spectacular view of the Hôtel de Sens, a magical sight by night. This is the oldest civilian monument in Paris, the only example of the transitional period between the Gothic and the Renaissance. Although its exquisite turrets were true watch-towers, as was appropriate in feudal times, great attention was already devoted to their ornamentation, and it is this combination of austerity and grace that makes them such a splendid work of art. The mansion was originally built by the Archbishop of Sens, Tristan de Salazar, the highly cultivated son of a Spanish Captain who had saved the life of Louis XI in 1465, in the battle of Montlhéry, which strengthened the bond between the throne and the archbishopric of Sens. Tristan de Salazar commissioned Martin Chambiges to build this new palace on the site of the archbishopric's previous pied-à-terre, which he did not like, but he never had the time to enjoy it. He died aged 87 in 1519, just before the *hôtel* was completed.

At that time the archbishopric of Sens was much more important than that of Paris and had seven dioceses under its rule. Their Parisian dwelling, therefore, was often left vacant, especially during the civil wars of the 15th and 16th centuries. Some claim that this is what preserved its original architecture: if it had been occupied permanently, it would have been altered according to changing fashions. The fact that it was intermittently occupied also enabled Henri IV to borrow it for his repudiated wife, Queen Margot, when she was allowed back to Paris, in 1605 (see chapter on 6th arr.). Although she was by then 52 and had lost her figure, her hair and her fresh complexion (and therefore introduced the use of face powder!), her sexual appetite had not been assuaged. Her lover at the time was the 20-year-old Comte de Vermond, whom she soon discarded for an 18-year-old lackey, Julien Date, or, as she romantically renamed him, Date de Saint-Julien. Their liaison was short-lived, for on 5 April 1606 the Comte de Vermond, consumed by jealousy, killed his rival on the threshold of the Hôtel de Sens. The next day he had his head removed on the same site by order of the vengeful Margot, who watched the execution from her window. No sooner was this done than she left the site, crossed the Seine and settled in her magnificent new palace, still under construction. Like other historic monuments of the Marais, the Hôtel de

Sens was later converted into various commercial businesses, such as a jam factory, a laundry, a glassworks and a warehouse. Little has therefore survived inside, except for one majestic fireplace and a beautiful spiral staircase in the tower. The city of Paris bought it in 1911 and its restoration began in 1929. In 1961 it was handed over to the Forney library of decorative and fine arts, a venture begun by Aidé-Samuel Forney, a Parisian manufacturer of the 19th century, and continued with his legacy. The beautiful reading room is open to the public and well worth a visit.

Retrace your steps through 'le village Saint-Paul' as far as rue Charlemagne. Beyond the pretty green fountain across the street rises the back of the church of Saint-Paul-Saint-Louis, the Jesuits' stronghold in the 17th century and much of the 18th. Adjoining it to the left is the Lycée Charlemagne, a well-known school. Turn right into rue Charlemagne and left into rue Saint-Paul. A narrow alley on your left, the Passage Saint-Paul, will take you to the side door of the church (its main entrance is on rue Saint-Antoine).

The Jesuits arrived in the Marais in 1580, 46 years after Ignatius of Loyola had founded the order in Montmartre. In order to impede the expansion of Protestantism, Charles de Bourbon, the abbot of Saint-Germain-des-Prés, whom the Catholic League had appointed King, bought a *hôtel* on this site and gave it to the Jesuits, who replaced it with a modest chapel dedicated to Saint Louis. Louis XIII's right-hand man, Richelieu, granted them his full support, determined to create a centralized, all-powerful State and to eliminate anything that got in its way (e.g. the Huguenots, whom he crushed at La Rochelle). The present church was built during his joint rule with Louis XIII and it was the King himself who came over to lay its cornerstone on 7 March 1627. In order to demonstrate where the State's allegiance lay, Richelieu celebrated its inaugurational mass on Ascension Day, 9 May 1641, in the presence of the King. A fabulous royal procession left the Louvre at 8.30 am and half an hour later reached the church, illuminated by hundreds of candles. The Cardinal, in vermilion satin and gold lace, officiated against a backdrop of shining black marble, gilded wrought-iron decorations and paintings specially commissioned from renowned artists such as Vouet, Philippe de Champaigne and Vignon. The highlight of the church was the sumptuous retable of gilded bronze, and in front of it a glittering tabernacle of massive silver, overladen with sculptures and decorations, some would say to excess. "There is no altar in the kingdom that is more richly decorated and where there are more reliquaries, vessels, more candelabras, more girandoles, more lamps and other such things unknown to our ancestors, who liked simplicity in the house of God, and that the new orders have invented so as to arouse the declining devotion of the last few centuries", wrote Germain Brice in his *Guide de Paris* in 1685. But to the Jesuits, this display of luxury did not seem offensive. On the contrary, they believed it inspired awe among the poor, who are more inclined "to pray to God in a spacious, well-decorated church than in a dirty, poor, neglected place." In the afternoon of that Ascension Day 100 Jesuits, bearing a candle each, went to the old church of Saint-Paul round the corner to fetch the relics of Saint Louis and Saint Ignatius and deposited them in the new church, which enjoyed the favour both of the court and of Condé, who descended from Saint Louis. It is needless to describe the resentment and frustration of the clergy of Saint-Paul.

Throughout the 17th century the most magnificent religious ceremonies were celebrated here. Music played an indispensable part in the staging of devotion. The most prestigious musicians were called upon to play on its organ - Nicolas Métru, who had been Lully's master, Michel-Richard Delalande, and, above all, Marc-Antoine Charpentier, whose famous *Miserere* was composed for this church. Its orators were equally talented: when Bourdaloue came to preach, the entire neighbourhood was cluttered up with carriages. He became a household name, rather like some modern entertainers, and there was even a type of hat named after him. Madame de Sévigné, a regular of the church, reported Bourdalou's archetypal Jesuit evasiveness in his funerary oration for the great Condé, who had betrayed his King, believed neither in God nor in the Devil, been cruel in battle and maintained a scandalous private life: "The heart of the great Condé," Bourdalou said, "was solid, honest and Christian."

But the wheel of fortune turned and after a century and a half of being in favour, during which time the head of the church was also the King's confessor, the Jesuits lost all credibility under Louis XV and in 1762 were expelled from France. The chapel of Saint-François-Xavier was now dedicated to the Holy Virgin, and the chapel of Saint-Ignatius became the chapel of the Holy Heart. The Revolution did away with the lot and in 1804 the newly opened Lycée Charlemagne was given a substantial part of the order's premises. Vestiges of their presence there remain, such as Gherardini's mural which decorated the Jesuits' library. The older parish church of Saint-Paul was demolished but its name was transferred to the former Jesuit church, so as to perpetuate at least its memory. The church now commemorates both Saint Paul and Saint Louis, but most Parisians are unaware of its Jesuit past and know it only as Saint-Paul.

Even though the church has been stripped of its past glitter, the walls with their overwrought sculptures create an atmosphere that is dizzying and oppressive, and it is a relief to leave through the main door and be out on rue Saint-Antoine, the site of the first gate of Saint-Antoine at the time of Philippe-Auguste. After the gate was demolished the street widened at this point and was used for special celebrations. On 26 August 1660 the wedding procession of Louis XIV and Marie-Thérèse stopped here on its way from Place du Trône (now Place de la Nation) to the Louvre, drawing additional attention to the church of Saint-Louis, which served as a glorious backdrop to the events in front of the façade. Today this is a busy street junction, crowded with traffic and pedestrians, overflowing with colourful food shops, an excellent place to buy the best food and drink produce of France.

Cross over and walk into rue de Sévigné, which celebrates the most illustrious lady of the Marais. In 1791 the playwright Beaumarchais opened a theatre at n° 11, largely built of material retrieved from the demolished Bastille. Like its glorious predecessor from the time of Corneille, it was known as the Théâtre du Marais. However, its career was short lived, as in 1807 Napoleon decided to shut down most of the theatres in Paris. The façade overlooking the street has survived, though, complete with elaborate pilasters and wrought-iron decorations. The wall at the back of the courtyard is a vestige of the horrific prison of La Force, of which more later.

Turn right into the charming and quiet rue de Jarente. N° 6 on your left opens into a lovely, cobbled, elongated courtyard, lined with countrified houses and their rambling vegetation. The silence is broken only by bird-song and, occasionally, the sound of a flute or a piano. There is a similar but more modest courtyard at n° 4. Some workshops - very numerous at one time in the Marais - have subsisted on the ground floor. Rue Caron to your right, a picturesque, cobbled street for pedestrians only, has a pleasant open-air café terrace and leads to the exquisitely italianate Place Sainte-Catherine, an enchanting spot on a warm summer night, when you may wish to dine on one of its terraces. If you continue along rue de Jarente beyond rue Caron, you will come to a tiny dead-end alley on your left, Impasse de la Poissonnerie, with a charming fountain. This whole enclave stands on the grounds that once belonged to the order of Sainte-Catherine.

Retrace your steps to rue de Sévigné. Ahead of you, at n° 13, is a spectacular example of the social, and therefore architectural, evolution of the Marais. The archway and magnificently sculpted wooden door indicate that this was the home of a person of note. Through the archway, however, is an extraordinary jumble of parasitical constructions, climbing on top of one another to house various workshops. Even a chalet has found its way into this eccentric compilation. Another indicator of the evolution of the Marais is the shop on the left-hand corner of rue des Francs-Bourgeois, now a fashionable clothes shop but formerly a neighbourhood *boulangerie*, as can be seen from its Belle Epoque window panelling. Turn left into rue des Francs-Bourgeois. At n° 23/25 lie the pretty back gardens of the Hôtel Lamoignon, the entrance to which is on rue Pavée to your left. Before turning into it, notice the corner building on your left, with its medieval-looking corbelled turret, a picture from a fairy-tale book.

The Hôtel Lamoignon is one of the oldest mansions in the Marais, built on land bought from the Order of Sainte-Catherine. It belonged to Diane de France, Duchesse d'Angoulême, the legitimized daughter of Henri II, and was therefore known as the Hôtel Angoulême. In 1658 it was rented by President Lamoignon, hence its present name. Lamoignon was the most senior magistrate of France, a highly respected person, "the wise, the learned, the first Lamoignon", according to the churchman Bossuet. The writer Boileau added his own praise: "Ariste (Lamoignon) whom Louis and Heaven have chosen to regulate their scales and dispense their laws." Indeed Lamoignon presided over the most sensational trial of the time, the trial of la Brinvilliers, whom he sentenced to death after 26 court sessions. A person of great learning, Lamoignon took pride in his library, and the intellectuals of the day - Bourdaloue, Racine, Boileau, La Rochefoucauld, Madame de Sévigné - gathered at his home. Moreover, every Monday from 5 to 7 in the afternoon, a 'literary academy' made up of 18 scholars met here for serious discussions and lectures on matters such as classical literature or ancient history – an Academie Française in the making.

His great grandson, Lamoignon de Malesherbes (now remembered mainly in the name of a major Paris boulevard), was born here in 1721 and later became a minister of Louis XVI. During the Revolution he attempted in vain to save the King from his death sentence. After the Revolution the *hôtel* was divided up into apartments, one of which was occupied, from 1867 to 1876, by Alphonse Daudet and his family. His son Léon wrote in *Paris Vécu.* about his happy, luminous childhood here, stimulated by the presence of his father's friends, Zola, Turgenev, and the 'giants' Goncourt and Flaubert, so called because they were so tall. Léon Daudet also noted that "behind our Hôtel Lamoignon was a chemical factory. They proliferated in those days in the Marais…". The mansion was earmarked for demolition and was saved *in extremis* when the City of Paris bought it in 1928. In 1968 the historical library of Paris was set up here. It has one of the most pleasant reading rooms in the capital, with a beautiful Louis XIII ceiling and overlooking the lovely back gardens. Some departments of the library, however, are now based in an unsightly building recently adjoined to the Hôtel Lamoignon, which would have been better served by a garden on the site.

At n° 10 rue Pavée is a well-known synagogue, the work of the Art Nouveau architect and decorator Hector Guimard, famous for the green vegetal archways he made for the Paris Métro stations. Hector Guimard had married the Jewish American Miss Oppenheimer and with the rise of Nazism left for the States, where he died forgotten. The synagogue stands on the edge of the Jewish enclave of the Marais, which starts on rue des Rosiers ahead. Before entering it, proceed to the corner of rue Pavée and rue Malher to give a thought to a gentle, fair-haired princess whose life came to a tragic end here. During the French Revolution the prison of La Force, which extended along the site of the present n° 14-22 rue

Malher, was used to detain political enemies of the nation. Although the Princesse de Lamballe was totally apolitical, she had sinned a) by being a princess, and b) by being Marie-Antoinette's friend, for whose sake she left her safe refuge in England and returned to the lion's jaws, hoping to join her at the Temple. Instead, the Revolutionary authorities sent her to La Force. On 2 September 1792, a three-day outburst of fury broke out in the city when several prisons, among them La Force, were attacked by the blood-thirsty mob, an episode known as *le massacre de Septembre*. After a mockery of a trial, during which the Princess refused to speak against the Queen, she was sentenced to be transferred to the Conciergerie, the antechamber of the guillotine, but the delirious mob seized her on the way out and dragged her to the corner of rue Pavée and rue Malher where she was literally torn apart. Two wild processions now parted ways: one carried her mutilated body to the Faubourg Saint-Antoine, the stronghold of the *sans-culottes* east of the Bastille; the other, bearing her impaled head with its dishevelled long blonde hair through the streets of the Marais, headed north for the Temple, where they displayed it in front of the window of the Queen's cell.

Retrace your steps and turn left into rue des Rosiers, a wide artery at this end, which has gradually been taken over by fashionable boutiques. However, beyond rue Ferdinand Duval it narrows to medieval proportions and has maintained its picturesque Jewish character. This is the backbone of the Jewish *pletzel*, where bookshops alternate with enticing eating places and food-stands, and abundant posters announce coming Jewish events. Goldenberg, on the corner of rue Ferdinand Duval, and Finkelztajn, on the corner of rue des Ecouffes, are two shrines to which people flock for (comparatively expensive) traditional Jewish savouries. On the whole, however, it is the North African community that has taken over most of the food shops, selling their own variety of Jewish cuisine, and at lower prices. Rue Ferdinand Duval was known as rue des Juifs until 1900. In the back of the courtyard of n° 20 stands a house that may have belonged to a Jew, since it was known as the Hôtel des Juifs. It is believed to date from the 18th century, which supports the assumption that Jews, albeit few in number, continued to maintain a presence in these parts, even though officially banned. With or without Jews, rue des Rosiers never lost its commercial flavour, and even in the golden age of the residential Marais it was lined with shops and maintained a plebeian atmosphere. The Jewish enclave continues into rue des Hospitalières-Saint-Gervais to your right. At n° 6 is an old Jewish boys' school, an easy target for hounding down Jews during the last war: 165 pupils were deported from here, despite the headmaster's efforts to save as many as he could. The words N'OUBLIEZ PAS (DO NOT FORGET) are engraved on the wall, a desperate gesture against indifference. Before the Revolution the site was covered with the lovely gardens of the convent of Sainte-Anastase, which was built in the 17th century, next to the

Order of Saint-Gervais. Across the street, the attractive vaulted architecture of the former market of Saint-Gervais adds a picturesque touch of antiquity to this spot. It now houses temporary exhibitions and fairs.

To your left is rue des Blancs-Manteaux, celebrated during the Liberation by Jean-Paul Sartre in a poem made famous by the singer Juliette Gréco. The white gowns in question were those worn by the religious order of beggars that Saint Louis brought up to Paris from Marseilles in 1258. Twenty years later they were replaced by the Order of Saint-Guillaume, les Guillemites, who wore black gowns, but the name stuck. The church of Notre-Dame-des-Blancs-Manteaux stands beyond a children's playground, but first turn left into rue Vieille-du-Temple for a glimpse of the magnificent wooden door at n° 47, behind which stands one of the most glorious *hôtels* in the Marais, the Hôtel Amelot de Bisseuil, unfortunately closed to the public. It is also known as the Hôtel des Ambassadeurs de Hollande, after the Ambassador of Holland, who reputedly lived here in the early 18th century. Some fifty years later, from 1766 to 1768, the playwright Beaumarchais lived here and wrote his most famous work *Le Mariage de Figaro*. Beaumarchais was in fact first and foremost an arms dealer, and a major supplier of the Americans in their fight for independence from the English. Here he set up his company, *Societé Roderigue Hortalez & Cie*, for this purpose, which was secretly financed by the French and Spanish governments. When the American Revolution finally broke out, a sumptuous ball was given here in its honour.

The mansion dated from the 17th century and disposed of a relatively small area, compensated for by its indescribably lavish decorations. Unusually in those days, one of the rooms was allocated specifically for dining. The house also had 'an Italian chamber', a two-storeyed room, usually surmounted by a dome, with a gallery and balustrade half-way up, where musicians could perform. Only the most luxurious mansions had such rooms and this is the only one to have survived. The garden, on the other hand, seems to have been quite ordinary. According to an English observer, Martin Lister, there were only a few wilted orange trees in the orangery and he did not like the green trellis, although he did admire the Roman statue that stood in a niche in the centre of the trellis, and the fig trees, daffodils and tulips. The *hôtel* has been beautifully restored by the Caisse des Monuments Historiques, but the public is not allowed in. Whether or not you will gain entry to the courtyard when you ring the doorbell, depends on luck.

Retrace your steps, turn left into rue des Blancs-Manteaux and proceed to the church. Although originally built at the end of the 17th century, it was altered and enlarged in the 19th century by Victor Baltard. The contrast with the church of Saint-Paul-Saint-Louis is striking. In an overall stark setting the figure of Jesus stands out above the high altar against the central window. Above the altar, the glory of God unfolds in a man-made golden sun, while the rays of nature's sun shine through the window, crowning the Saviour in divine splendour.

Beyond the church, at n° 22, is a financial establishment called Le Crédit Municipal de Paris, which also opens onto 55/57 rue des Francs-Bourgeois. This establishment, originally known as le Mont de Pieté, was founded as a pawnshop by Louis XVI. Napoleon transferred it to this location. Ordinary financial transactions, such as loans, are now carried out here, but also operations connected with the arts, such as auctions. At times the premises on this side are used for temporary exhibitions, while those on rue des Francs-Bourgeois have been turned into an up-market, plush restaurant, where you can dine to the accompaniment of music performed by a crystal-voiced singer. You will reach rue des Francs-Bourgeois by turning right on rue des Archives and right once more.

The 17th-century Hôtel de Coulanges at n° 35 was meant to be replaced by a block of flats in 1961. The press raised the alarm and managed to save it and Malraux's bill in 1962 did the rest. The 17th-century Hôtel d'Albret at n° 31, possibly built by François Mansart, is unquestionably one of the most beautiful mansions in the Marais and houses the city's cultural services. César Phoebus d'Albret was exiled from Paris by Richelieu, following a duel, but later Anne of Austria allowed him back. Because he was devoted to Richelieu's successor, Mazarin, he was appointed Maréchal de France in 1654. He loved luxury, knew how to mingle with the right people and make his way through society into high spheres. It was here that Madame de Montespan (his cousin's wife and Louis XIV's mistress) made the acquaintance of Scarron's widow, née Françoise d'Aubigné. The Montespan picked her out, believing that her discreet conduct would make her an ideal governess for her eight illegitimate royal children, hidden on the site of the present n° 108 rue de Vaugirard. A fatal misjudgment! After the children had been legitimized, the self-effaced Françoise penetrated into Versailles, where she was provided with her own apartment as governess of the court. Equipped with the title of Marquise de Maintenon (Madame de Montespan had incautiously given her the domain of Maintenon as a gift), she bided her time patiently and when the Queen died in 1683, she began to manoeuvre herself into the King's heart and supplant her unwary rival. Madame de Montespan retired to the convent of Saint-Joseph in the Faubourg Saint-Germain, where she died in 1707 at the age of 66, while Madame de Maintenon married the King secretly in 1684, the only mistress to have married a French king. She died in 1719, aged 84, having outlived His Majesty by four years.

A well-known *salon de thé* at the corner of rue des Francs-Bourgeois and rue Payenne may be a good place to finish your walk. It boasts a wide variety of succulent pastries and also sells some interesting knick-knacks and toys. Another *salon de thé*, a place with many devoted regulars, is *Le Loir dans la Theière* ('The dormouse in the teapot'), commemorating Alice and her tea party at n° 3 rue des

Rosiers, in the section between rue Malher and rue Pavée. It has a wonderfully cosy clutter of unmatching old furniture, including weary leather armchairs, and sells delicious pies, salads and pastry - but then so do many other places in the Marais.

FROM THE CENTRE GEORGES POMPIDOU
TO THE HÔTELS DE SENS ET D'AUMONT

The western part of the 4th arrondissement, lying on the edge of the central market of Les Halles, was seldom graced by the distinguished members of society. The Centre Georges Pompidou was never meant to be an elitist preserve but a cultural centre for the people, and thus is appropriately situated here. Deliberately open to the street, its transparent architecture abolishes all barriers between the street and the Centre. People on the esplanade therefore enjoy an exciting X-ray panorama of the escalator swarming with visitors, while those on the escalator can see the receding and approaching crowds at their feet. Inside, too, barriers have been abolished and partitions reduced to a minimum, so that an atmosphere of a bustling but spacious street prevails. Admission to most of this space is free of charge and in the Salle d'Actualité you will find all the current papers and magazines.

Just outside the building, on the northern edge of the esplanade, is a small building, at present looking like a slum and covered with graffiti. This is the recreated studio of the Romanian sculptor Brancusi, which well-meaning planners believed they could bring to the street, but they have since had second thoughts. Now that the Centre is to be renovated, the studio is to be transferred indoors. The American photographer Man Ray, a pivotal figure in Paris's artistic circles in the first half of the 20th century, was not offered this privilege, although his widow, Juliette, fought tooth and nail for his studio to be reconstructed here. When France refused to help raise the money, the Smithsonian Institute came forward with an offer to recreate Man Ray's studio - but in Washington DC! Before you visit the Centre Pompidou, it is a good idea to check on current events; once there, just be guided by your instincts.

South of the Pompidou Centre, Tingley and Nicky de Sainte-Phalle have created a cheerful pop-art fountain with colourful, mobile sculptures that are nudged about playfully by the water. Children love it and have integrated it into their world of play, and adults, with or without reservations, have learnt to live with it.

Continue south into rue Saint-Martin, once the old Roman road on the north-south axis of the *cardo* of ancient Lutetia, which led to the towns of Louvres and Senlis. Since the road had to cross the marshy right bank, the Romans raised its causeway so as to prevent it from being flooded. This stretch of rue Saint-Martin is enlivened by shops selling an eclectic array of goods, from genteel traditional

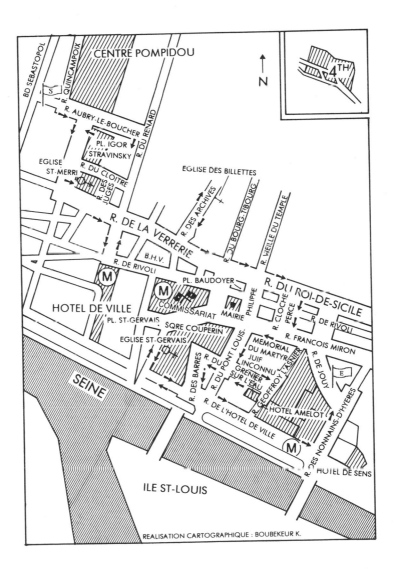

needlework to brilliant ceramics from Britanny. The church of Saint-Merri, at n° 78, dates from 1520, which accounts for its flamboyant Gothic style. Over the years, however, it has undergone many alterations and lost many of its Gothic elements, including its Gothic pillars and vaults and its beautiful stained-glass windows. (Its entrance façade was added in the 19th century.) Still, the fact that it stands is a miracle in itself, since it served as a gunpowder factory during the Revolution. The church has preserved a bell dating from the 14th century and in the crypt is kept one of the oldest stoups in Paris, bearing the arms of Anne of Austria. The crypt is situated on the probable site of a chapel built in the 6th century, Saint-Pierre-des-Bois, where the Abbot of Saint-Martin-d'Autan, Merry or Médéric, was buried on 29 August 700. Like all holy men of early Christian times, he was said to have performed miracles, even after his death. On 29 August 884 the Bishop of Paris, Gozlin, honoured his precious remains with a marvellous reliquary. Legend has it that when the remains were brought out they scintillated like gems, which determined Eude le Fauconnier, the priest of Saint-Merri, to replace the modest chapel with an imposing church. Someone, however, got the dates muddled up, since Eude le Fauconnier actually lived some two centuries later.

Turn left into rue de la Verrerie, a major street of old Paris on its east-west axis, where a glassworks was located. Its presence attracted the guild of stained-glass and enamel craftsmen who made it their stronghold between the 13th and 18th centuries, when their art went out of fashion. Among the craftsmen of the 13th century was a certain Jacquemin Grigonneur, who lived roughly on the site of n° 28. Having come across the game of cards which had just been introduced from India via the Arabs, he set about painting three packs of cards, *"à or et à diverses couleurs pour l'esbattement du roy"* ("in gold and various colours for the distraction of the king"). The King in question was Charles VI, who, having partially lost his sanity, was in need of various occupations to replace that of government, and it was he who served as a model to Jacquemin Grigonneur for his King of Hearts. Later, the wife of Charles VII, Marie d'Anjou, served as a model for the Queen of Clubs and his favourite, Agnès Sorel, for the Queen of Diamonds. Jeanne d'Arc joined the pack as the Queen of Spades. Whether the game pleased His Majesty is not on record, but it became the rage, so much so that by 1397 it was banned on workdays and by 1409 was forbidden to churchmen.

At n° 76 stands an 18th-century façade with two charming cupids, the entrance to the presbytery. A small courtyard on the right leads to two turrets on either side of the southern portal, through which the covered way of the church is reached (not open to the public). Notice also the beautiful wrought-iron decorations at n° 74. Turn left into rue des Juges Consuls, an old alley, too narrow to have a pavement. Le Tribunal des Juges Consuls, the nucleus of our Tribunal de Commerce, had its back entrance in this street (at n° 2-4), and gave it its name. N° 3 boasts a lovely 17th-century façade. Behind its door (when it can be opened) are the apse and the flying buttress of the church. A pretty view of the northern side of the church can be had from rue du Cloître-Saint-Merri.

Back on rue de la Verrerie, walk up to rue du Renard for a good view of the eastern façade of the Centre Pompidou, which some witty journalist has nicknamed *Notre-Dame-des-Tuyaux* for its bright pop-art pipeworks. To the south are Notre-Dame and the Hôtel de Ville, majestic and beautiful from this angle. The magnificent reception halls of the Hôtel de Ville and the main staircase designed by Philippe Delorme can be visited only during temporary exhibitions or on guided tours (Mondays at 10.30 am). Rodin's bust of the Republic, the painted scenes of Paris life by Willette and the murals by the official painter of the Republic, Puvis de Chavannes, all testify to the determination of the bourgeois Third Republic to demonstrate its victory over the proletarian *Commune* that had burnt down the Renaissance town hall.

Opposite the Hôtel de Ville the BHV (Bazar de l'Hôtel de Ville) department store is the Paris stronghold of do-it-yourself *(bricolage)* and as such is crammed with suburbanites every Saturday afternoon, when it becomes a bedlam. During the Second Empire, Xavier Ruel, a small shopkeeper, set up shop here, which he called Bazar Napoléon and was the first to launch what today would be termed as market survey: before choosing the site, he scattered pedlars in different areas of Paris, supplying them with screws, nails and other trifles to sell, and watched to see where they would be most successful. It turned out that screws and nails sold best at the corner of rue des Archives and rue de Rivoli. When Napoleon III fell, the shop became the Bazar de l'Hotel de Ville, shortened into BHV in the last 30 years, to suit a new generation pressed for time. Retrace your steps and continue along rue de la Verrerie, where 17th-century façades have survived at n°s 48, 50 and 52, which belonged to prominent figures; n° 52 was the home in 1682 of the Président des enquêtes, the presiding judge of investigations.

Turn left into rue des Archives and cross over. At n° 22-24 stands the church of Les Billettes, on the site of the house of the Jew Jonathas in the second half of the 13th century. In 1290 a woman to whom he had lent money spread the word that he refused to give her back the clothes she had pawned unless she delivered him the host received during Holy Communion on Easter Day, in the church of Saint-Merri. Once in possession of the host, Jonathas, this enemy of Christianity, hacked it with a knife and a flow of blood gushed forth. He then threw the host into a cauldron of boiling water, which turned instantly red, while the host rose out of the cauldron and hovered above the woman's head. Panic-stricken, the woman rushed out of the house, which was surely possessed by the Devil. She told the entire neighbourhood her story, naturally much embellished, which inevitably meant that Jonathas would die at the stake. The house was seized by Philippe le Bel and soon after a chapel called la Chapelle du Miracle, was built here and given to the Order of the Frères Hospitaliers de la Charité de Notre-Dame, who were replaced in the 17th century by the Carmelite Order of Les Billettes. This church too became Protestant after the Revolution and has remained so. It is normally closed except during chamber music concerts, which are enhanced by its excellent acoustics. The highlight of the church, however, is its monastery cloister, which miraculously survived the French Revolution and is thus the only medieval cloister in Paris. It now houses temporary exhibitions, sometimes of ethnic artefacts, which look wonderful against this background of Gothic architecture.

Retrace your steps into rue de la Verrerie. A lovely house of beautiful pink stone and wrought-iron decoration stands at n° 18, previously the warehouses of the BHV department store and recently taken over by the Tunisian designer Alaïa. If the premises are open, walk inside to admire the impressive metalwork and dream over the murals of faraway, sunny lands. Alaïa grew up in Tunisia in the small and modest *concierge* lodgings of his parents, where he discovered the world of *haute couture* through fashion magazines. Inspired particularly by the Spanish Balenciaga, he taught himself design and eventually ended up in Paris, but in the up-and-coming Marais rather than in the traditional western parts, which made sense for someone of the younger generation. Even now that he is internationally established, Alaïa has remained in the Marais, and while most *couturiers* display their new creations on the catwalk by the Louvre (and since 1994 on their new premises beneath the Carrousel), Alaïa prefers to unveil his collections in the Marais.

Rue Bourg-Tibourg ahead opens into a lovely square to the right, lined with trees and cafés. Beyond, on Place Baudoyer, the two tricolours of the Mairie of the 4th arrondissement and of the police station face each other, respectively to left and right, against the backdrop of the elegant, subdued façades of rue François-Miron. Rising to the right is the charming old bell-tower of the church of Saint-Gervais, surmounted by its slate roof. Rue du Bourg-Tibourg, to the left, is lined with pot-bellied houses that give it an antiquated look, while its vista closes on to a lovely 17th-century façade of French classicism at its best.

Turn left into rue Cloche-Perce, a charming spot with its flight of steps on either side of rue de Rivoli, its old street lamp and the tables and chairs sprinkled on the pavement outside the café. Continue up to rue François-Miron. On its right-hand corner, at n°s 11 and 13, are the only two half-timbered houses of Paris which can be securely dated to the 14th century (the one on rue Volta may have been a restoration). With their slanting, gabled roofs facing the street, and the old street sign Le Relais Saint-Gervais, they provide a tiny sample of medieval Paris, when the gables of houses faced the street (see walks in the 2nd arr.). Beautiful 18th-century dwellings line the other pavement, from n° 2 to n° 14. The Couperin family, of whom more later, lived at n° 4. At n° 30, at the back of a little courtyard, which is reached through a corridor, are the vestiges of a Renaissance mansion, the home of Marie Touchet, Charles IX's favourite. Hers was the only son he ever had, and, had he been legitimate, Henri IV would have never acceded to the throne and the history of France would have taken a different course. After Charles IX's death, Marie Touchet married François de Balzac d'Entragues by whom she had two daughters. The elder, Henriette, Marquise de Verneuil, became the mistress of Henri IV.

A century and a half later the notorious Cateau la Borgnesse lived at n° 68, in the Hôtel de Beauvais. Catherine Bellier by her real name, she became chambermaid to Anne of Austria, who must have confided to her about her love life with Mazarin, and also her concern that her son Louis should not take after his frigid father, Louis XIII. The chambermaid took the matter in her own hands and promptly proceeded to initiate the young king in the facts of life, to the delight of the Queen Mother, who consequently appointed her husband, Pierre Beauvais, hitherto a mere mercer in the shopping arcade of the Grand Palais, Councillor to the King and gave him the title of Baron. The new Baron and Baroness were also granted enough money to build themselves a luxurious mansion and received permission to use the services of the King's first architect, Antoine Lepautre. They were even offered the stones that had been meant for the extension of the Louvre. Mazarin objected, claiming this was going too far, but was overruled. Cateau's social climb was so meteoric that Louis XIV's wedding procession stopped in front of her *hôtel* on its way to the Louvre. All the balconies were decorated with Persian rugs and crowded with members of the court. One was reserved for Anne of Austria, Henrietta of England (Charles I's widow) and her daughter Henrietta of France, scintillating under a red velvet canopy, another for Mazarin and Turenne, the hero who defeated the princely revolt known as *la Fronde*. Cateau was derided by the upper-crust for letting out shops on the ground floor of her *hôtel*, a practice fit for a commoner only, but she was not bothered by the gossip and led a dissolute life, attended by an impressive list of lovers, even though she was said to be ugly and was blind in one eye.

Over a century later, in 1763/4, seven-year-old Mozart stayed at the Hôtel de Beauvais together with his father and sister Nannerl, the guests of the Ambassador of Bavaria, Count Van Eyck, who occupied the *hôtel* at the time. On 1 January 1764, Mozart was introduced to Versailles and acclaimed as a child prodigy. He for his part, was very frustrated because Madame de Pompadour did not kiss him.

Retrace your steps and turn right into rue du Pont-Louis-Philippe. Beautiful people like to gather in the corner Mexican café, La Perla. The street itself has some very beautiful, expensive boutiques. Turn left into rue du Grenier-sur-l'Eau, enhanced by yet another graceful Wallace fountain. The street leads to rue Geoffroy-l'Asnier, a weavers' stronghold in the Middle Ages. Across the street, the 17th-century portal of the Hôtel Chalons de Luxembourg is of exceptional beauty, with its majestic lion's head ensconced in a shell. The knocker with its finely chiselled horses has also survived. In the 19th century the mansion was divided into apartments, one of which was occupied by the writer Gabriele d'Annunzio in 1914. Across the street, at n° 17, stands the Memorial to the unknown Jewish Martyr. Archives about the calamities that befell the Jews throughout history are preserved here and can be consulted, while a flame burns permanently in the crypt, in memory of the 75,000 deportees who never returned from the death camps during the last war.

Retrace your steps and continue along rue du Grenier-sur-l'Eau and up to the back of the church of Saint-Gervais-Saint-Portalis, which stands on top of a mound - a ravishing sight. As you turn left into rue des Barres you will see, to the south, steps leading down to the river and café terraces, so welcoming in warm weather. The mound rising above what was then marshland was picked out as the site for the first church in this area, built in the 6th century to serve a population of fishermen and boatmen. It was named after the twin brothers Gervais and Portalis, who had been martyred by Nero in Milan, but is nowadays commonly referred to as Saint-Gervais. Like all the early churches in Paris, it was probably destroyed by the Norsemen. Only when the new Paris became prosperous and secure on its right bank was there need for a parish church. Construction began in the late 15th century by the famous Chambiges but it was not officially completed until 1657, partly because of the uneven soil, perhaps also for lack of funds. Hence its various styles, from a post-medieval bell-tower to a typical 17th-century façade (on the other side of the church), made up of three storeys, superimposing successively the Ionic, Doric and Corinthian styles. This was the first one of its kind in Paris and elicited Voltaire's remark, "this is a masterpiece, lacking only a square to hold its admirers." Being the only parish church in the area, it also served the population of the Marais. Marie de Rabutin was married here to the Marquis de Sévigné on 4 August 1644, at 2 in the morning as was customary among the nobility, while both the poet Scarron and the painter Philippe de Champaigne were buried here. The Revolution caused the church considerable damage, but worse was to come on 29 March 1918, on Holy Friday, during mass, when one of Big Bertha's shells hit the church, killing 50 and injuring 200.

Above all the church of Saint-Gervais is associated with the great Couperin dynasty, organists from 1656 to 1826. The first Couperin was Louis, an organist and composer, who was succeeded at the organ by his brother Charles. Charles's son, François, was the greatest of them all. Charles devoted a lot of time to the musical education of his only child and took him to the church to listen to the organ. So great was François's precocious talent that, when he was only 11, the clergy of Saint-Gervais made an official pledge, signed before a notary, that he would succeed to his father's chair. His father died unexpectedly the same year, however, and François was deemed too young for the task. Michel-Richard Delalande offered to act as a regent out of sheer admiration for the young Couperin, who for the time being became the organist of Saint-Jacques-la-Boucherie, which stood along the pilgrimage route to Santiago de Compostela, in the butchers' neighbourhood. (Its tower survived the Revolution and still stands on Boulevard de Sébastopol, just north of Place du Châtelet. Pascal made use of its altitude in 1648 for his experiments on gravity.) When six years later, Delalande was called upon for higher functions at La Chapelle Royale, François Couperin was given the chair at Saint-Gervais, although he had to wait to be 21 before he could be officially confirmed in the post. François died in 1733, neglected and ignored by frivolous Paris, indifferent to such music as the *Leçons des Ténèbres*. The present organ of the church was built by Clicquot 25 years later and was played by his son Nicolas, followed by Armand-Louis who was killed accidentally by a bolting horse in 1789. At this crucial moment in French history, his successor, Pierre-Louis, was required to compose variations for the revolutionary song *Oh, ça ira!* which was performed at the time in Notre-Dame and has since been immortalized by the vibrating voice of Edith Piaf. The last member of the Couperin dynasty was Pierre-Louis's daughter Céleste, who died in 1860.

As you walk round to the main entrance of the church, you will notice a shop that sells monastic produce and artefacts, and some other buildings that belong to the Compagnons du Devoir. (Their main office is at 82 rue de l'Hôtel-de-Ville, which runs south of the church.) This guild traces its origin to King Solomon, who, in legend, assisted by his two foremen Soubise and Maître Jacques, built the Temple of Jerusalem. More realistically, Les Compagnons du Devoir are probably descended from the cathedral builders of the Middle Ages. Back in the 16th century they set up a pension and mutual aid scheme, which points to their precocious social awareness. Today, 4,000 youths throughout France are trained in 20 different branches of the building profession, in the spirit of brotherhood and with a strong work ethic. Their workmanship is of the highest standard, worthy of the missions entrusted to them, such as the restoration of France's most prestigious historical monuments.

Retrace your steps along rue de l'Hôtel-de-Ville. Ahead of you is the glorious Hôtel de Sens described earlier, a stunning sight from this angle too. Turn left and walk along rue des Nonnains-d'Hyènes. Ahead, on your left, behind a vast garden *à la française*, is the extraordinary back façade of the Hôtel d'Aumont, which now houses the Tribunal Administratif, at n° 7 rue de Jouy. Designed by the famous Le Vau for Michel-Antoine Scarron, the poet's uncle, it was later transformed by François Mansart for its new proprietor, Antoine d'Aumont, Marquis de Villequier and governor of Paris. Decorated by Simon de Vouet and Charles Le Brun (Le Brun's magnificent ceiling has even survived), it was one of the most superb dwellings in Paris, and housed d'Aumont's fabulous art collection. You simply must return here after dark, when the illuminated Hôtel de Sens on your right and the illuminated Hôtel d'Aumont on your left will afford one of the most magical sights in Paris.

THE ISLANDS

The last walk will take us to the two islands, the Ile de la Cité, at the foot of Notre-Dame, and to the Ile Saint-Louis - the ultimate jewel. Cité Métro station, next to Boulevard du Palais, will be our starting point. Having wandered through the flower market by way of rue de Lutèce, and enjoyed its riot of colours (except on Sundays, when the flowers give way to birds, and on Mondays, when it is closed), turn right into rue de la Cité which leads to the esplanade *(parvis)* of Notre-Dame, enlarged to its present size in the 19th century by the Baron Haussmann and is now named Place du Parvis Notre-Dame. In the Middle Ages, when it was only a sixth this size, the people of Paris were awestruck by the overwhelming height of its towers as they crowded at their feet. The equestrian statue of Charlemagne stands imposingly in front of the cathedral to the right. Of particular interest is the underground museum that displays the finds of archaeological digs undertaken here. These are beautifully illuminated and will enlighten you about ancient Lutetia.

Bordering the esplanade to the north is the Hôtel-Dieu, the oldest hospital in Paris and for centuries its only hospital. When it was built in the 12th century, it was situated on the southern side of the esplanade, from where it expanded gradually to occupy the whole area between the Petit Pont and the Pont au Double. The Bishop of Paris, Maurice de Sully, undertook its construction, at the same time as that of the cathedral of Notre-Dame. This enterprising man was born into a very poor family in Sully-sur-Loire in 1120; in 1165 he baptized the Dauphin, the future Philippe-Auguste. An earlier hospital and a chapel stood here back in the 9th century, both bearing the name of Saint-Christophe. They too must have been swept away by the Norsemen. Maurice de Sully ordered each canon of Notre-Dame to contribute a bed to the hospital when he died, a welcome initiative at a time when five patients shared one bed, as was the case well into the 18th century. It was also only at this relatively recent date that patients were separated according to sex and disease. The hospital enjoyed the protection of the Crown

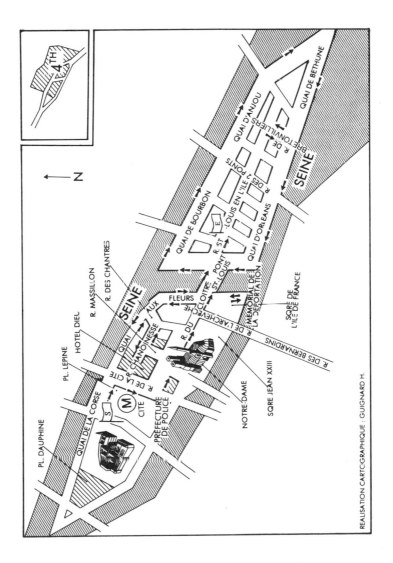

REALISATION CARTOGRAPHIQUE : GUIGNARD H.

and, when Philippe-Auguste left for the Crusade, he magnanimously offered the hospital the straw of the vacated horse stables as extra bedding. Saint Louis, and his mother Blanche de Castille ruled that anyone in need be admitted, regardless of sex, nationality or religion, except those afflicted by contagious diseases. By this time, efforts were also being made to reduce the number of patients per bed to three, hence the sarcastic observation, "each bed is shared by three – the ill, the dying and the dead." In the 17th century, the hospital expanded to the Left Bank, connected by way of the Pont au Double. Bridges were often built on at the time, and the Pont au Double had a glass gallery, which served as a promenade for the patients. A narrow corridor for pedestrians ran along the hospital premises, allowing Parisians to cross the river for the price of a double farthing, hence the name of the bridge. The hospital was moved to its present location during the radical transformation of Paris at the time of the Baron Haussmann.

And now for Notre-Dame. The cathedral is all the more venerated by visitors as they believe it to be one of the oldest standing vestiges of medieval Paris. However, most of what you see is the work of Viollet-le-Duc dating from the 19th century only. Many of the cathedral's treasures were simply done away with because they were no longer in vogue, notably the gorgeous chancel screen, the high altar and the tombs, all of which disappeared in 1699. In the middle of the 18th century the fabulous 13th-century stained-glass windows were replaced by plain glass so as to bring in more light, but some of the original glass of the two rose windows is still there. The one on the western façade was studded with gold stars against an azure background, providing a halo for a statue of Virgin and Child flanked by two angels, each bearing a chandelier. On the night of Sexagesima, the chandeliers would be lighted with candles and all the priests of Notre-Dame in their cassocks would gather on the *parvis* to sing litanies throughout the night.

Whatever was spared over the generations hitherto, was looted and profaned during the French Revolution. The bare, dilapidated edifice that remained standing was dedicated to Reason and the esplanade became known as le Parvis de la Raison. When Napoleon chose this symbolic shrine for his coronation in 1804, the walls had to be draped with hangings to make up for their bareness. That they were standing at all was a miracle, for the cathedral had been earmarked for demolition and put up for sale. A potential buyer had even been found, the 'Citoyen Simon', Claude-Henri de Rouvroi Saint-Simon by his previous name, a member of the same family as the duke and writer of *Memoirs*, and who was later to found the utopian Saint-Simonian sect. Fortunately circumstances prevented the sale of Notre-Dame from proceeding.

By the early 19th century the Romantic movement had aroused a growing interest in medieval values and a revival in taste for the Gothic, which had been spurned only recently. Victor Hugo undoubtedly deserves most of the credit for bringing the plight of Notre-Dame to the attention of the public in 1831 through his novel *The Hunchback of Notre Dame*. At his instigation a temporary restoration committee was set up by the poet Alfred de Vigny, the painter Ingres and the Catholic politician Montalembert. A competition for a contract to restore the cathedral was launched in 1844 and won jointly by Viollet-le-Duc and Lassus, but the latter soon died and Viollet-le-Duc alone remained in charge of the colossal enterprise. A past master in the art of restoration, his conception, however, was that restoring "does not mean maintaining a building. It has to be re-established in a complete state that could never have existed before." Thus the southern side of the cathedral, with the sacristy and guard's house, are typically 19th-century and the dainty steeple, together with its profusion of graceful floral designs, was 'homemade' by Viollet-le-Duc. However, the gargoyles and the other statues on the walls, all have a medieval appearance, as does the 'Gothic' furniture inside, most of it designed after old drawings. Restoration work finished in 1864 and the cathedral was consecrated on 31 May. By May 1871 it was again under threat. 'The bloody week', the climax of the civil war of the *Commune*, began on 24 May: all the benches and barriers were piled up in the centre of the nave and sprayed with petrol. The house doctors of the Hôtel-Dieu were alerted just in time to rush in and extinguish the fire. It seems that Adolf Hitler too intended to destroy Notre-Dame to mark the end of his occupation of the coveted city.

As you approach the western façade, try to picture the polychrome statues of yore, standing out against a background of gold. 28 statues are lined up above the three portals, representing the 28 Kings of Judah. These are reproductions of the original medieval statues, smashed by the Revolutionaries who mistook them for the Kings of France, an understandable confusion shared by the inhabitants of the 15th century. Indeed, an engraving from that time represents two passers-by admiring what they take to be statues of Pépin le Bref and Charlemagne, while a shrewd rogue takes advantage of their absent-mindedness to steal their purse. The Kings of Judah are celebrated because Jesus descended from their dynasty; nevertheless, the church's traditional animosity to the Jews is also evident: engraved on the stone under this row of statues is the defeated Synagogue, characteristically blindfolded, with the triumphant church standing on her right (on our left).

There is no doubt that Notre-Dame was meant to please the ear as well as the eye, and its two medieval towers resounded to the peals of many bells. All the seven bells of the northern tower were melted down during the Revolution. In the southern tower there were two huge bells - Marie, likewise gone, and Jacqueline, which has survived, a gift to the Lord from Jean de Montagu for having blessed his wife Jacqueline with a daughter. When the bell was brought down to be alloyed with bronze, during the reign of Louis XIV, the ladies of the kingdom are said to have brought along their own jewellery to be melted down at the same time: this, according to some, accounts for the purity of Jacqueline's peal. Inside the cathedral a Cavaillé-Coll organ resounds on many occasions and has been played by the greatest of French organists, notably Pierre Cochereau, its regular organist until his death in 1984. Back in the late 15th century and the early 16th, Léonin and Pérotin founded the polyphonic school here.

Running along the northern side of the cathedral, rue du Cloître Notre-Dame is full of tourist paraphernalia, its cafés inevitably commemorating Victor Hugo's heroes Casimodo and Esmeralda. But the street also boasts quaint old houses along the alley at n° 16. At n° 10 is the cathedral's museum, repository of documents, particularly from the 17th century. The cloister of Notre Dame was a veritable town surrounded by walls, inhabited by peaceful canons and canonesses, who waited here serenely and in total seclusion to be called back to God for eternal rest. However, after 1354 no women were allowed in, except for matrons who tended the ill. The canons were allotted 37 houses, as well as a pleasant garden on the eastern tip of the island. When one of them departed, the family would have to clear his belongings within a fortnight, after which the house was put in good repair and sold to another canon. The canons were highly respected, learned churchmen, and many top members of the ecclesiastical hierarchy came from their ranks, including Popes Grégoire IX and X, Adrien V, Boniface VIII, Clement VI, Innocent VI, 29 Cardinals and a great number of Bishops. Opposite the present n° 18 was the church of Saint-Jean-le-Rond, on the threshold of which an abandoned baby was found on 16 November 1717. The baby's mother was Madame Tencin, a one-time canoness, his father a *chevalier* named Destouches. The baby himself grew up to be the illustrious *Encyclopédiste*, d'Alembert. In her younger days Madame Tencin had had numerous lovers including the Regent. As she grew older, she opted for a more spiritual existence and presided over one of the most prestigious literary *salons* in the capital.

Turn left into rue Chanoinesse, a serene and peaceful artery, of which tourists who flock to the cathedral are, mercifully, unaware. Notice in particular the two houses on the opposite sides of rue des Chantres - the countrified house at n° 10 with its picturesque shutters and its top terrace, bursting with green vegetation, and the elegant 17th-century mansion with its beautiful wrought-iron decoration. In the year 1118, the house that stood on the site of the present n° 10 was occupied by the canon Fulbert: it was a substantial property with grounds extending along rue des Chantres, probably as far as the site of 9 quai aux Fleurs along the river. In that fateful year Fulbert welcomed into his home both his niece, the 17-year-old Héloïse, who was related to the great Montmorency family, and Pierre Abélard, then 39 years old. It made sense to the canon that his niece should benefit from the remarkable knowledge and intelligence of this great master of rhetoric and dialectics, a disciple of Guillaume de Champeaux, and he therefore asked Abélard to take charge of her education. He omitted to take into consideration the forces of nature and the fact that Pierre Abélard had great charisma (which is why throngs of students followed him to the Left Bank when he settled there). Pierre was handsome, brilliant, a poet and an accomplished musician. Master and pupil ended up in each other's arms, and before long Héloïse was pregnant and had to be sent to Brittany to have her baby out of society's sight. Fulbert meanwhile awaited his opportunity for vengeance and, when it came, took Abélard unawares and castrated him. From then on the love between Abélard and Héloise became as mythical as that of Tristan and Isolde, an impossible love that was neither accepted by the establishment nor fulfilled and therefore could not even become an act of defiance. Salvation could lie only in death, except that in this case it was a true story:

It so happens that they both died at the age of 63. Just before Héloïse died, she secretly recovered the body of Abélard and brought it over to the oratory of Parclet, which she had founded near Nogent-sur-Seine. On her death, their bodies were laid in the same coffin and remained so for two and a half centuries, until 1497, when the oratory of Parclet was threatened with ruin and the coffin was moved to the church of Petit-Moustiers. Here a prudish nun separated their remains and laid them in two separate tombs. The Revolutionary authorities united them again in a single coffin, in 1792, but fixed a lead partition between them, then sent them back to Nogent-sur-Seine. Meanwhile Alexandre Lenoir was filling his newly created museum of French monuments with whatever he could rescue from the clutches of the Revolution and transferred the famous lovers to it. In 1817 they were deposited in the church of Saint-Germain-des-Prés, though not for long. The new cemetery Le Père Lachaise, on the eastern edge of Paris, was trying to enhance its prestige among the bourgeoisie of western Paris, as yet reluctant to lay its dead in those remote plebeian parts and was looking for illustrious tenants. The monument was therefore transferred to Père Lachaise the same year. At last, the lovers found a permanent abode in what has since become the 7th division of the cemetery, in the unlikely company of Paris's 19th-century bourgeoisie. In 1844 two medallions representing the two lovers were fixed to the door at n° 9 quai aux Fleurs.

Rue des Chantres is a silent, narrow, romantic alley, enchanting by night, when lit up by the street lamps affixed to its houses. The flight of steps at the end of the street, leading up to the river, and the church tower of Saint-Gervais, across the Seine, complete this exquisite picture. Next on your left is rue Massillon, with a beautiful 18th-century house at n° 8, the home of the cathedral's choir school, La Maîtrise de Notre-Dame, first founded here in 1455 and replaced with the present premises in 1740. As you make your way back to rue Chanoinesse, take in the picturesque view of slanting roofs and attic windows rising above a solid wall and nestling among the branches of an old tree, filled with the song of birds. Continue along rue Chanoinesse. N° 22 is an elongated, squat, rustic-looking house and the restaurant La Lieutenance, with its colourful flags, tries to recreate the illusion of medieval times. It is particularly lovely at night.

Retrace your steps on rue Chanoinesse, so pretty from this angle. Beyond rue Massillon the street curves gently to the right and runs parallel to the bend of the river. Beyond the curve, the back of Notre-Dame will appear in all its splendour, framed with trees and enhanced by the brick building at n° 1, decorated with colourful ceramic. Ahead, lying along the river, is the pleasant garden of Notre-Dame, Square Jean XXIII. This breath-taking cityscape is scandalously marred by the lines of tourist coaches that are allowed to park along rue de l'Archevêché, and by the recent constructions that now clutter the skyline. Rue de l'Archevêché is an insult in itself, having been carved into the garden to siphon off traffic. If you can focus solely on rue des Bernardins (the continuation of rue de l'Archevêché that climbs up the hill on the Left Bank), you will comprehend the compact nature of the medieval city, tightly huddled at the foot of Notre-Dame.

The garden continues beyond rue de l'Archevêché under the name Square de l'Ile-de-France. To the west you will see the back of Notre-Dame and its graceful spire, to the east is the timeless scenery of the Ile Saint-Louis with its weeping willow bowing to meet the waters of the Seine. At the very tip of the garden and thus of the island, facing the bejewelled Ile Saint-Louis and the rising sun, is the crypt of the Memorial of the Deportation, washed by the lapping waters of the Seine. It shelters the tomb of the Unknown Deportee. Respectfully austere, the bare, raw stone that covers the walls matches the bare, raw wounds inflicted upon the victims' bodies and souls. Spear-like motifs in the black iron evoke the memory of those whose flesh was lacerated by the Nazi torturers. There is no superfluous pathos in this place, just a few lines engraved into the bare walls to sanctify the innocent, often those of poet Robert Desnos, who died in Theresienstadt (now in the Czech Republic), just when the Allies were liberating the camp.

The pedestrian bridge will take you to the tiny Ile Saint-Louis, our ultimate destination and Paris at its best: colourful food shops and eating places, boutiques in impeccable taste, four gem-like hotels are united into this miniature world, enhanced by an overall 17th-century architectural unity that would put the rest of Paris to shame. Occasional scars and eyesores exist here too, but so much of the old heritage has been preserved that they are not obvious to the untrained eye. In the 17th century the two uninhabited islands were joined into the Ile Saint-Louis and built up. The canons of Notre-Dame, who hitherto relaxed in the western island, fought off development but were defeated by the urbanisation of Paris, which accelerated during the latter peaceful part of the reign of François I and exploded into a fever at the time of Louis XIII and Louis XIV:

> *Toute une ville entière, avec pompe bâtie*
> *Semble d'un vieux fossé par miracle sortie*
> (An entire city, built with pomp, seems miraculously
> to have sprung out of an old ditch),

as Pierre Corneille wrote in *Le Menteur* in 1643, with the l'Ile Saint-Louis in mind. Of course, a stretch of land in such a central location could not continue forever to be a place of recreation, even though the loose soil was unsuitable for construction and costly reclamation was necessary. Moreover, the two islands had to be united and bridges erected. Hence the Pont-Marie, which commemorates the first entrepreneur of the project, Christophe Marie (not Marie de Medici, the Queen Mother, as is often believed, though she was indeed very much involved in the development of the island). The saintly woman represented in the sculpture on the Pont de la Tournelle, in the continuation of Pont-Marie, is not the Holy Virgin either, as others deduce, but Geneviève, patron of Paris.

The construction on the island was largely undertaken by the most prestigious architects of the day, predominantly by Louis Le Vau, to suit the demands of the prominent members of society who settled here. The houses had narrow façades because of shortage of land on the island, but they made up for this by being quite deep, as you can see when occasionally you come upon an unlocked door. The most talented painters decorated these homes, but, unfortunately, little is left of their magnificent work, and what remains is in private hands.

It took less than a century to complete the work and by the end of the 17th century the entire island was covered with *hôtels* of almost austere classical beauty, which brought out the lovely texture of their stone and their graceful wrought-iron decorations. By the end of the 18th century Louis Sébastien Mercier could write: "The island is a quarter hemmed in by the river and separated from the Cité. It seems to have escaped the great corruption of the town, which has not yet penetrated here. No girl of easy virtue can find lodgings here: no sooner is she found out than she is expelled. The bourgeois keep an eye on each other […] It has been said accurately: the inhabitant of the Marais is an outsider 'on the island."

Turn left into quai de Bourbon and walk to the tip of the island – a romantic haven with a ravishing view over the Ile de la Cité. All the houses from n° 53 to n° 41 were built by François Le Vau, brother of the great Louis (n° 53 and n° 43 were actually built by both), hence their homogeneous features. N° 43, built for their sister Anne Le Vau, came to be known as La Maison du Centaure because a bas-relief (now badly eroded) representing Hercules about to strike Nessus was carved on its façade. When the Ile Saint-Louis became popular with literati, Guillaume Apollinaire lived here for a while, and was visited by Marie Laurencin, his companion, and by Francis Carco and Max Jacob among others. His apartment window gave onto a spectacular panorama, encompassing the Louvre on the right and the mound of the Latin Quarter, La Montagne Sainte-Geneviève, on the left. François Le Vau sold n° 51 next door to Jean-Baptiste de Champaigne, nephew of the famous court painter Philippe de Champaigne. An artist in his own right, Jean-Baptiste was in charge of the decoration of the island's church of Saint-Louis-en-l'Ile. The Hôtel de Jassaud at n° 19, on the corner of rue Le Regrattier, was the home of Nicolas de Jassaud, secretary to Louis XIV. Having received a substantial inheritance from his uncle and a no less substantial dowry from his wife, he could afford to build himself this masterpiece of equilibrium and grace, undoubtedly the most beautiful *hôtel* on the quai de Bourbon. The façade needs to be seen from a distance to be fully appreciated, and is also in need of a face-lift to bring out the ochre of its stone and the fine wrought-iron balcony on the first floor. Camille Claudel lived in a ground-floor studio at the back of the courtyard from 1899 to 1913, when she was tragically interned in a mental home. The wrought iron grilles fixed to the ground-floor windows of n° 15 date from the early years when the island was not quite a safe place at night. You can see how far the building has subsided, owing to the unstable quality of the soil. However, the houses on the island are not in danger of collapsing because they are supported by one another. The painter Emile Bernard, the father of symbolism and an important member of the group of Pont-Aven, lived here from the late 19th century until his death in 1941. N° 11 was built for the painter Philippe de Champaigne but, since he was the court portrait painter and Marie de Medici's first valet, he lived most of the time in her palace, the Palais du Luxembourg (now in the 6th arr.).

At the corner of rue des Deux-Ponts, the restaurant Au Franc Pinot prides itself on its fare and on its long history, which began in the 17th century, when it catered to passengers arriving by boat from Melun and to boatmen who dropped in for a pint of red wine. The shop that stood at n° 3 closed down in 1913 and its beautiful wooden panelling was transferred to the Metropolitan Museum in New York, where it serves as a background to the 18th-century French silverware display. Rue des Deux-Ponts runs along the old moat that divided the island into two in the 13th century. When it was filled up in the 17th century, a narrow street was laid out and, as elsewhere, was lined with elegant houses. The street was ruined in 1930 when it was widened, allowing traffic to furrow through the island, and by the late 1960s two drab blocks of flats trespassed on this former architectural shrine.

Cross over and continue along the quai d'Anjou, where you will find the two most prestigious dwellings on the island, the Hôtel de Lauzun at n° 17, with its gilded wrought-iron balcony and gilded fish-scale decorations on its water spouts, and the Hôtel Lambert, at n° 1. The Hôtel de Lauzun is attributed to Louis Le Vau and became the property of the Duc de Lauzun in 1682, although he hardly had time to live here, having fallen from favour along with Nicolas Fouquet and likewise been consigned to the fortress of Vignerol. In the 19th century the mansion was divided up into apartments and often let to artists and bohemians, disrespectful of both premises and neighbours. Charles Baudelaire, Théophile Gautier and other members of the *Club des Haschichins* surrendered here to the artificial paradise of hashish. To one remonstrating neighbour Baudelaire wrote in 1840, "Sir, I chop up wood in my living-room, I drag my mistress about by her hair; this is done in everybody's home and you have no right to interfere." Nevertheless, it was here that Baudelaire wrote the first poems of *Les Fleurs du Mal*. In 1928 the City of Paris purchased the mansion, thereby saving it from demolition, and undertook its restoration, notably the allegorical paintings on the ceiling above the monumental staircase and the dainty friezes above the doors with their chubby, curly-headed cupids, all attributed to Charles Le Brun. True to the style of the reign of Louis XIV, the profusion of luxury is stunning, reaching its peak in the *petit boudoir*, where the judicious use of mirrors triggers off an endless succession of reflections of polychrome exuberance. Unfortunately, the house is open only to the guests of the City of Paris.

The quai d'Anjou was in great demand among artists because of its tranquillity and the beautiful architecture left by Louis Le Vau. The famous landscape painter Daubigny lived at n° 13 from 1837 to 1845, followed later by his friend, the sculptor Geoffroy Deschaume, who was working on the restoration of Notre-Dame with Viollet-le-Duc. Honoré Daumier lived at n° 9 from 1846 to 1863. A century earlier the Marquis de Marigny, brother of the Pompadour, came to live at n° 7, a beautiful, austere building of wonderfully textured stone, the façade of which follows gracefully the bend of the *quai*. The original owner of the building was an ironmonger, which again goes to show that even a rigid hierarchy has occasional lapses. Since 1843 this has been the headquarters of the bakers' union. The mansion at n° 3, which Louis Le Vau reserved for himself, also has a façade that follows the curve of the *quai*, at its sharpest bend, where it adjoins the Hôtel Lambert, his masterpiece and the island's best known landmark. The actress Michèle Morgan once lived here, but it has belonged to the Rothschilds since 1976. Its glorious rotunda-shaped wrought-iron balcony is best admired from the river as all those who have been on a boat ride know. The first Lambert to be connected with the mansion, Jean-Baptiste Lambert de Thorigny, died before it was completed and the house went to his brother Nicolas. The greatest talents of the day - Le Brun, Eustache Le Sueur, Patel - were brought in to create an extraordinary interior, which would have disappeared if Prince Adam Czartorisky had not bought the house by auction in 1842 and maintained it respectfully, as have the Rothschilds since. Unlike most of the mansions in Paris, which now house offices, Hôtel Lambert remains a private residence.

The Hôtel de Bretonvilliers, by contrast, its neighbour on the quai de Béthune, across rue Saint-Louis-en-l'Isle, did not survive at all. It was said by contemporaries to be beautiful beyond words and for 200 years the most splendid mansion on the island. Engravings by shuch artists as Israël Silvestre and Nicolas Raguenet (now at the Musée Carnavalet) confirm Tallement des Réaux's view that "This *hôtel* and its garden enjoyed the best location in the world after the Seraglio of Byzantium." The owner of the *hôtel* was Claude Le Ragois de Bretonvilliers, secretary to the King's Council, and Tallemant des Réaux went on to report, with some glee, that his wife was "very beautiful, cuckolded him, even beat him at times and shrieked a lot, although she had brought him no dowry." During the French Revolution the *hôtel* was confiscated and awarded as first prize in the national lottery organized by the Convention. Soon after it was divided up and the magnificent decorations by Nicolas Poussin, Nicolas Mignard, Simon Vouet and Sébastien Bourdon were dispersed. The garden survived until the 1860s, when Haussmann's bulldozer was working to full capacity and swept it away. A new bridge, the Pont de Sully, the Boulevard Henri IV and the Square Barye, were integrated into the new landscape. Walk into rue de Bretonvilliers. Whereas many streets of Paris were laid out after a property had been chopped up, rue de Bretonvilliers was part of the property, serving the back of the *hôtel* and three of the houses across the street. These communicated with his mansion by way of the three-storeyed house surmounting an arcade, in front of you. A less happy sight will meet your eyes when you retrace your steps and notice that a chunk of the Institut du Monde Arabe now blocks the horizon like some glass rampart. Time and again in contemporary Paris overall aesthetics have been overlooked and vistas wrecked, thus destroying precisely those features that have made Paris one of the most breath-taking cities in the world.

Quai de Béthune perpetuates the name of Maximilien de Béthune, Henri IV's minister, better known as the Duc de Sully. Both the King and his minister are generously commemorated in this neighbourhood, because of its proximity to the Arsenal, where Sully lived. The *quai* was originally known as quai des Balcons because Louis Le Vau wanted a balcony on each façade. Although not everyone followed this precept, there are certainly more balconies here than elsewhere. The elegant n° 16/18 belonged to the gallant Duc de Richelieu or to his widow and later to their descendants. It too was magnificently appointed but eventually partitioned into apartments and for many years its second floor was occupied by the writer Francis Carco, who died here in 1958, leaving behind invaluable accounts of lower-class Paris in the first half of this century.

N°s 20 and 22 are further examples of 17th-century elegance, with grand staircases hidden behind locked doors. N° 20 has a magnificent ceiling, painted by Mignard. More unforgivable damage was wrought in 1935, when Helena Rubinstein bought Louis Le Vau's fabulous mansion at n° 24 and replaced it with the present uninspiring block of flats. The beautiful door by Etienne Le Hongre was retained at the entrance, by way of meagre consolation. President Pompidou lived in one of these flats, where he and his wife amassed an excellent collection of contemporary works of art. He died here in 1974. Between 1912 and 1934 Marie Curie lived at n° 36, on the corner of rue des Deux-Ponts, and later René Cassin, the 1968 Nobel Peace Prize winner. Beyond rue des Deux-Pont lies the fourth and last of the *quais*, the quai d'Orléans, a delightful stretch facing the back of Notre-Dame and its gardens. At n° 6 is the Polish museum named after the exiled poet Adam Mickiewicz and founded by his son Ladislas in 1903. It is dedicated to the Romantic period and houses many documents relating to Chopin. There is also a reading library belonging to the Polish historical and literary society.

Make your way to our starting point and turn right into rue Saint-Louis-en-l'Ile, the main artery of the island, which runs along its central axis from east to west. This is the village high street, where the locals do their shopping, and a delightful place in the first half of the morning, before the trickle of tourists turns, as the day wears on, into a mass invasion. The huge and pre-medieval looking restaurant Nos Ancêtres les Gaulois, at n° 39, is full to capacity every night with tourist parties enjoying a country-style buffet, washed down with red wine from the barrel. Their time, however, is allocated, so as to make room for other fellow-tourists in the latter half of the evening. It is noisy, it is fun, it is kitsch, and everybody seems to enjoy it.

Besides the wonderful shops, which are an attraction in themselves, the street has four exquisite hotels, usually, it must be said, fully booked well in advance. The first three are on your right-hand side and have a countrified feel. The fourth is at n° 54 across the street, but you may first wish to see the island's church, which displays a unique spire with an openwork design and an original clock. The church was designed by Louis Le Vau (yet again!), but, because it took over 50 years to complete, by the time it was finished in 1726, it had been excessively decorated in the Jesuit style. The hotel at n° 54 is called Hôtel du Jeu de Paume because it occupies an old *jeu de paume*, the very popular ancestor of tennis and squash, which gradually went out of fashion at the time of Louis XIV. The hotel owners have preserved the old timber skeleton of the building and added a glass-walled lift, unfolding a panoramic view of the premises as the guests go up to their rooms. Decorations are in impeccably good taste and the surroundings leafy and tranquil. The visitor is guaranteed an unforgettable stay.

Whether you are a visitor or among the privileged few who reside here, the Ile Saint-Louis should be savoured like a glass of good wine and must include a taste of Bertillon's ice-cream from one of its stands, preferably from the one on the western tip of the island that faces the back of Notre-Dame. Here, on a hot summer day, you will join an endless queue of strollers, waiting patiently in the most beautiful spot of Paris for a scoop or two of the city's most delicious ice-cream. Unless you prefer to do so sitting down on the sunny terrace of the Flore-en-l'Ile, next door.

Ile Saint-Louis

THE 5th ARRONDISSEMENT

Romantic myths of Left Bank intelligentsia revolving around the venerable Sorbonne are brutally shattered on the Boulevard Saint-Michel, the main artery of the Latin Quarter, where the 5th and 6th arrondissements meet. The Sorbonne is still there, just off the Boulevard, but the forlorn chime of its chapel bell, which has punctuated the studies of generations of scholars, is drowned out by the din of the traffic and the general hubbub of this age. Nor do the young people who stream past Place de la Sorbonne ever bother to glance at its 17th-century chapel and its graceful dome. The proliferation of junk clothes and junk food outlets along the Boulevard cater more appropriately to their needs, foreshadowing yet another decline in the long history of the 5th arrondissement – the longest in mainland Paris – a history of spectacular achievements and of dramatic setbacks.

It began during the Roman occupation of Gaul, when the growing population of the Ile de la Cité spilled over on to the left bank, the right bank being covered with marshes. Roman villas appeared on the slopes of Mount Leucotitius (now the Montagne Sainte-Geneviève), where the air was purer, soon to be followed by more dwellings along the *cardo* (the north-south axis, now rue Saint-Jacques) that led to Orléans. A secondary *cardo* ran roughly along what is now Boulevard Saint-Michel, while the two *decumani* (east-west axes) ran along what is now rue des Ecoles and rue Cujas.

By the end of the second century – a period of peace *(pax romana)* – this became a desirable neighbourhood of beauty and luxury, as shown by archeological finds (e.g. the marble and polychrome mosaics in rue de la Harpe, the frescoes in rue Amyot), some of which can be seen at Musée Carnavalet. At the foot of the hill, where rue Soufflot now runs, lay the Forum, the political, economic and religious centre. The northern baths were those of Cluny (corner of Boulevard Saint-Michel and Boulevard Saint-Germain); the eastern baths were on the site of the present Collège de France at Place Marcel Berthelot; and the southern baths, also known as the Forum baths as they were located in its vicinity, were on the corner of the present rue Gay-Lussac and rue Le Goff. An aqueduct, which ran all the way from the Rungis basin (near Orly airport) through parts of today's 13th and 14th arr. (the Montsouris neighbourhood, rue de la Tombe Issoire, rue Saint-Jacques, etc.) supplied them with water. Sections of the aqueduct have been discovered on rue Saint-Jacques, between rue Malebranche and rue Royer-Collard. To the west, on rue Racine (now 6th arr.), was the semicircular amphitheatre overlooking the Seine; the imposing arena, the second largest in the whole of

Gaul after that of Nîmes, faced the east so as to take advantage of the natural east-facing slope and the setting sun, which lit up the podium, and, in the background, the pastoral Bièvre meandering through green meadows towards the Seine.

The Germanic invasions of the mid-3rd century pushed the local population back into the safety of the Ile de la Cité, not to return to the ravaged left bank until a century later and never to enjoy its previous luxury. Rural dwellings now clustered around the hill, vineyards grew on its sunny slopes. Outsiders of a new creed, the early Christians, were arriving from the south and contributing to undermine the stability of Rome. (A Christian cemetery has been discovered in the area around the junction of rue Saint-Jacques and Boulevard Port-Royal.) Rome was soon to crumble in any case - the sweeping waves of Goths and Vandals of the early 5th century proved irresistible, and in 451 Attila the Hun was at the gates of Paris with his 700,000 men. Once more the terrified population was ready to flee the left bank, but the sweet and gentle Geneviève bolstered up their courage, prophesying that Paris would be spared.

In the 17th century Geneviève was romanticized as a shepherdess, but the real Geneviève was in fact born in Nanterre to a well-to-do Roman father and a Greek mother, although she did lead an ascetic life devoted to the poor and the sick. As she also performed miracles and as her prophecy concerning Attila came true, she naturally acquired a great following and eventually became the patron saint of Paris. Moreover, since it was under her guidance, as much as through the influence of his wife Clotilde, that King Clovis converted to Chrisianity and made Paris his capital. These were the two decisive factors in bringing about the unity of France, which was to be marked with a Christian temple to God, again under the auspices of Geneviève. The basilica of Saint-Pierre-Saint-Paul, built on top of the hill, on the site of the present parish church of Saint-Etienne-du-Mont, was thus the nucleus of what was to become the abbey and borough of Sainte-Genevieve and, more broadly, of the Latin Quarter and the future arrondissement. It was completed in 510, just in time for its crypt to receive the remains of King Clovis, who died that year, aged 46, and of Geneviève, who died in 512, aged 89. When Queen Clotilde died in 543, aged 70, she was also buried in this crypt. By sheltering the remains of these three figures who had shaped ancient Gaul into the united, Christian kingdom of France, with Paris as its capital, the basilica is also in a sense the most important historic and spiritual shrine in Paris. For generations the kings of France valued this symbol of the legitimacy of their rule and each went to pray at Geneviève's tomb after his coronation.

Geneviève's reliquary, which remained the object of the utmost veneration up to the French Revolution, was fashioned in 630 by the famous Saint Eloi, the patron of goldsmiths and later minister and treasurer to King Dagobert I. Chiselled in gold and studded with gems, it lay in the stone sarcophagus of Geneviève.

In times of invasion it was hidden outside the city; in times of floods, epidemics and other calamities, following a day of penitence and fasting, it would be carried in a procession to Notre-Dame through streets decked with multicoloured drapery and strewn with flowers, to the continuous chiming of all the city's church bells. The story goes that when the reliquary was brought out in 1130 because of a raging epidemic, all were cured but three sceptics who would not prostrate themselves when it passed by and therefore died. By the year 1725 there had been 114 such processions. Needless to say, so much handling of the delicate reliquary was bound to damage it over the centuries. Also, various sovereigns found it flattering to their egos to have it redecorated. Thus, when in 1625 it left its original resting place in the crypt for its present position behind the altar, it was heavily bejewelled, bearing the marks of the reign of Marie de Medici; nothing was left of the artistry of Saint Eloi.

In November 1793 the reliquary was stripped of its precious stones and sent to the Mint to be melted down. Against all logic, the remains of Saint Geneviève were burnt on Place de Grève (4th arr.), and the ashes thrown into the Seine, watched by a mob of gleeful *tricoteuses*. In one fell swoop, the French Revolution outdid the formidable Norsemen and destroyed twelve hundred years of devotion to the virtuous Geneviève, who had fed the poor, restored sight to the blind and even life to a dead man, a national figure who had embodied precisely the same ideals as those of the Revolution, a heroine as patriotic as Jeanne d'Arc! Somehow, the wooden sculptures of the reliquary have survived (now in the Louvre), although they have lost their arms. In 1803 a fragment of the Saint's sarcophagus was discovered in the crypt. It was put into a reliquary and placed, like the original one, above the altar of the church of Saint-Etienne-du-Mont, where it still is.

The Revolution also swept away the great abbey that bore her name, founded in the 7th century by a group of monks who came to settle next to her holy shrine. Only the square church tower on rue Clovis remains *in situ*. The few other surviving vestiges are now part of the Lycée Henri IV: the medieval vaults, kitchens and refectory, the cloister, the grand staircase dating from the 18th century and the dome of the abbey's magnificent library. The abbey was a great place of learning, closely bound up with the University in the Middle Ages. Its abbot therefore also held the post of chancellor and presented the University diplomas to graduates. Fortunately most of the volumes of its library were rescued by the monks at the time of the Revolution and are now preserved at the Bibliothèque Sainte-Geneviève, at 10 Place du Panthéon.

In the 13th century the Latin Quarter became the centre of learning not just of France but of the whole of Western Europe. The Norse attacks of the second half of the 9th century forced the terrified population back to the original cradle of the

Ile de la Cité; when they ventured out again a hundred years later, they headed for the right bank, sealing its destiny as the economic nerve of the city (see chapter on 4th arr.). Philippe-Auguste had wished to see equal development on both banks and in 1210 he financed the extension of the city walls to the left bank in order to attract new settlers, but the bourgeois and merchants who lived near the harbour of Place de Grève refused to move. The religious orders, by contrast, were happy to settle on the left bank, which was rich in fertile land and also carried shrines and memories from early Christian days. Since education was then entirely in the hands of religious institutions, it was on the left bank that learning developed and thrived. By 1115 a renowned centre of learning had been established in the abbey of Saint-Victor (on the site of the present University of Paris VI and VII at Jussieu) by its first abbot, the eminent theologian Gilduin, who had moved here from Notre-Dame and was later succeeded by Pierre Abélard. In Rabelais' story, set three centuries later, the hero, Pantagruel, comes to study in Paris and naturally visits the world-renowned library of Saint-Victor; on the eve of the French Revolution, this contained nearly 40,000 volumes and over 20,000 manuscripts.

The University was established barely a decade after the completion of the left bank section of the city walls. The first official written reference to the *Universitas Magistrorum et Scolarium Parisiensium* dates from 1221. At the beginning it did not have a permanent home and while its headquarters shifted from the church of Saint-Julien-le-Pauvre to the convents of rue Saint-Jacques, the teaching took place in the open air, on Place Maubert, and mainly on rue de Fouarre near by. The teachers stood on wooden trestles, while the students brought along their own fodder to sit on (*fouarre* in old French), hence the name of the street which soon became synonymous with the University as a whole. Brawls, uproar and political and religious agitation were also daily occurrences in rue de Fouarre, to such extent that in 1358 the Regent and future Charles V had the street barred with chains on both sides. The neighbourhood taverns, low dives and brothels supplied this rowdy population with cheap wines fit to 'boil the potted heads of wolves'. This was the Latin Quarter that François Villon roamed a century later and of which Rabelais gave a saucy account. Placing fried turds in graduates' hoods and pinning fox-tails or hare's ears to students' buttocks were favourite pranks. Nor was the rest of the population spared – shop signs would disappear, hysterical dogs would run about with pots and pans tied to their tails, maidservants were pestered or worse... Above all, the church was a special target among these roguish, anticlerical, even heretical youths.

Nonetheless, the Latin Quarter was first and foremost a prestigious seat of knowledge. In order to attract newcomers, Philippe-Auguste granted the left bank considerable autonomy. With the presence of three powerful abbeys – Sainte-

Geneviève, Saint-Victor and Saint-Germain (now in the 6th arr.) – Rome was bound to step in and take over. Thus, the newly founded University, whose teaching, it must be remembered, was strictly limited to theology, was under the direct tutelage of the Pope, who said of Paris that it was the oven where the intellectual bread of the Latin world was baked. Elsewhere one fed newborn babies, here one fed robust minds. The greatest theologians and thinkers came to teach in the Latin Quarter and helped to make it the intellectual centre of the world: the German Albert, on Place Maubert (the name is possibly a contraction of Maître Albert); his Italian disciple Thomas Aquinas, perhaps the most prominent medieval theologian; the Florentine Brunetto Latini and master of Dante Alighieri, on rue de Fouarre. Dante himself came to study in rue de Fouarre in the early 14th century, as his Paris-born countryman Boccaccio tells us.

Little by little permanent colleges superseded the makeshift places of earlier days, first providing accommodation and later teaching. One such college was founded in 1253 on the present rue du Sommerand, by Robert, the chaplain and confessor of Saint Louis. Born to a humble family in the village of Sorbon in the Ardennes, he became so great a scholar that the King had him dine at his table: *"li Roy le faisoit mangier à sa table* ('The king had him eat at his table"). The college became the seat of the faculty of theology and was known as La Sorbonne, after the native village of its founder. Its expansion was so spectacular that it soon overshadowed the other institutions and many foreigners still mistake it for the entire University of Paris.

When the Hundred Years' War broke out, the University, which had gradually lost the privileges granted it earlier by the throne, sided with the English against the King of France and, later, against Jeanne d'Arc. Paris was in ruins, the territory of wolves, and the Montagne Sainte-Geneviève had become an 'annexe of Oxford'. In due course peace was restored and in 1437 the University submitted to the secular authority of Charles VII.

The Italian campaigns of 1515 heralded the advent of the Renaissance, impressing upon François I the artistic and intellectual achievements of Italy as against those of the University of Paris, by then a fossilized body. In 1529, in order to counteract its dogmatic and strictly theological teachings and propagate the humanistic ideal of the Italian Renaissance, he founded the Collège de France, next to the Sorbonne (just off rue des Ecoles). It was first known as Le Collège des Trois Langues, as Hebrew and Greek were taught there besides Latin, but it was soon renamed the Collège du Roi after its founder. Lectures were given in French – a revolution in itself. The French language was given a further boost at the time of Henri II, when the poets Ronsard and Du Bellay and their friends founded the group called *la Pléiade* to crusade in defence of the French language. In their manifesto, *Défense et illustration de la langue françoise*, written by Du

Bellay in 1549, they called for the development of a national literature, like in Italy, to be supported by an enriched French language, and discarded Latin as obsolete.

Over the centuries the number of chairs created at the Collège de France increased from the initial three to over 40 today, but its principles have remained unchanged: it has always been, and still is, independent of the University of Paris and the lectures have always been, and still are, free of charge and open to the public. Among its illustrious professors will be mentioned the historian Michelet; Champollion who had deciphered the Egyptian hieroglyphs; the mathematician and physicist Ampère; the historian and writer Renan; and the philosopher Bergson.

The Collège du Roi was not the only modernistic institution to threaten the retrograde Sorbonne and the other institutions of the Latin Quarter. Le Jardin du Roi (now Jardin des Plantes) opened at the time of Louis XIII further east, on the sunny side of the future 5th arrondissement, was an even greater menace. Back in the 13th century some members of the nobility had magnificent country houses in this pleasant area watered by the Bièvre, notably on the site of the present rue du Fer-à-Moulin, then known appropriately as Bourg-Riche. On its northern side lay the enchanting estate of the Hôtel Clamart, through which flowed the Bièvre, shaped into artificial lakes and reaches, meandering through rocks, caves and waterfalls. Later on, however, the monks of Saint-Victor damaged the Bièvre by repeatedly deviating its course for their agricultural needs, but even in 1640 the area was still sufficiently pleasant for Louis XIII to choose it as a site for a botanic garden for medicinal herbs, as suggested to him by Jean Hérouard, his famous physician. The Jardin Royal des Plantes Médicinales, as it was then called, had a pedagogical funtion too: 1,800 different plants were gathered to be used also by medical students. Once more, the University was deprived of its monopoly of teaching, not this time just by rival ancient languages but by botany, chemistry and, from 1643 on, by anatomy – a very serious threat to its authority. For two centuries, scientists of world renown contributed to the development and propagation of natural science, notably Cuvier (1769-1832), the father of paleontology, and Buffon (1707-1788), the administrator of the Jardin des Plantes and member of the Académie des Sciences, who devoted 40 years of his life to the much popularized, 44-volumed *Histoire Naturelle*. Thouin, Tournefort, Linné, Geoffroy Saint-Hilaire, the Jussieu family, Daubenton and Lacépède, all contributed to the glorious scientific reputation enjoyed by the south-eastern part of the arrondissement, and are now honoured in its street names.

No doubt the withered Sorbonne needed to be revivified. Like the rest of the Latin Quarter, it had suffered from the Hundred Years' War and from the wars of religion in the latter half of the 16th century. The enterprising Richelieu, who had once been a student at the Sorbonne and was now its dean, undertook its renovation, laying the cornerstone of its chapel in 1625. His project, however, was purely architectural and little was done to reform the curriculum, which, until the Revolution, remained restricted to theology. No wonder, therefore, its beautiful compound, the work of Lemercier and Le Brun, was given a rough time by the anti-clerical Revolutionaries: some of its marble was stolen, part of the chapel dome was left to crumble, and weeds to invade the courtyard. In the early 19th century the Sorbonne was used as living quarters by several dozen artists who had formerly lived in the Louvre. During the Restoration a new scheme for the renovation of the Sorbonne was put forth and was carried out step by step throughout the 19th century. The Sorbonne was entirely reconstructed and expanded, to include the faculties of science and of letters as well as the school of librarians, the Ecole des Chartes, and the Ecole Pratique des Hautes Etudes. The extended compound, a rectangle bounded by rue de la Sorbonne and rue Victor-Cousin, rue Cujas, rue Saint-Jacques and rue des Ecoles, surmounted by an observatory tower on rue Saint-Jacques, was inaugurated in 1901 and has retained the same architectural aspect ever since. It has also retained the pompous *pompier** murals painted by Puvis de Chavanne, the official artist of the Third Republic.

It was not just the Sorbonne that was changing. Napoleon, a great reformer in matters of higher education, had already restructured the University and founded the celebrated Grandes Ecoles, for the training of France's future engineers, outside the framework of the university; these still enjoy immeasurable prestige and overshadow the university. The Ecole Polytechnique, the most prestigious of them all, trains France's top mathematicians to become the nation's elite and is still a military school, whose cadets, the celebrated 'X', take part in the military parade down the Champs-Elysées on 14 July. Until 1977 it was located in the heart of the Latin Quarter, in the premises of the medieval Collège de Navarre on rue de la Montagne-Sainte-Geneviève. Its transfer to the southern suburb of Palaiseau, has somewhat deprived the Latin Quarter of some of its festive pomp, for previously, on ceremonial occasions its cadets could be seen passing by in their Napoleonic uniforms, bearing their traditional slender swords. Just as prestigious intellectually is the Ecole Normale Supérieure, founded in 1794 to provide the nation with highly cultivated and competent teachers. The greatest scientists of France, precisely those now commemorated in the streets names of the arrondissement, numbered among its professors. Today the Ecole Normale Supérieure has expanded beyond the Latin Quarter and even to the provinces, but the premises on rue d'Ulm, south of the Place du Panthéon, remain the most prestigious ones.

---

*Uncreative academic painter in the second half of the 19th century

The Revolution had made a clean sweep of the abbeys of Sainte-Geneviève and Saint-Victor and of many of the smaller institutions. The social and economic evolution of 19th-century France completed the transformation of the 5th. Its educational calling meant that it could not become industrialized. Nor could it become residential: a plebeian population of tanners and butchers sprawled since the time of Louis XIV along the Bièvre, while Place Maubert - '*la Maube*' - had been home to rowdy students and other hot-headed ruffians since the Middle Ages, a place of crime, vice and public executions, the 'cesspit of la Maube', as Erasmus called it. In the early 20th century it was frequented by terrifying 'Apaches' and other hoodlums and louts. The neighbourhood around rue Mouffetard was no more inviting. *In Down and Out in Paris and London*, written in 1928, George Orwell gives a frightening account of the neighbouring rue du Pot-de-Fer (Orwell himself lived at n° 6, where no policeman would venture on his own after dusk. He describes his street as "a ravine of tall, leprous houses, lurching towards one another in queer attitudes, as though they had all been frozen in the act of collapse". Amidst a population of destitute Arabs, Poles and Italians, and unhindered by the noise and dirt, "lived the usual respectable French shopkeepers, bakers and laundresses and the like, keeping themselves to themselves and quietly piling up small fortunes." This was the social composition of the area in a nutshell. Haussmann had already endeavoured to keep the plebeian segment of this population in check by bulldozing rue Monge, rue Gay-Lussac and Boulevard Saint-Marcel. However, whereas in other parts of the city, he had created radiating avenues so as to facilitate the circulation of government troops in the case of street riots, his plan in the 5th was to isolate each potential hotbed of social unrest from its neighbour.

Along the newly opened streets rose the usual hygenic, Haussmannian blocks of flats, ready to accommodate the intelligentsia, who, being less prejudiced than the prim and proper bourgeois, did not mind rubbing shoulders with the lower classes who added a touch of local colour to the neighbourhood. The 5th thus became the most characterful and diversified arrondissement, with its share of medieval streets, colourful marketplaces and neighbourhood shops, multitudes of bookshops and Left Bank cabarets... It was also the most youthful arrondissement, with scores of thousands of students blending daily into the picturesque local population.

Then, in 1968, a wind of revolt blew across the planet, from the Latin Quarter to Prague, from Berkeley in California to China. There was no premeditated political motivation on the part of the students when, during the month of May, they transformed the Latin Quarter into a battlefield. Rather it was a vague discontent with an amalgamation of capitalism, imperialism (including the Vietnam War, of course), budding consumerism, the rigidity of bourgeois values and hidebound tradition. *'L'imagination au pouvoir'* ('let imagination rule'), one of their favourite slogans, was scribbled on many a wall. Barricades were erected on all the main arteries to fend off the forces of the riot police, advancing in close order, and cobblestones were dug out of ancient streets and hurled at them. The trees along the boulevards were not spared, and those who had foolishly left their cars in the Latin Quarter overnight retrieved burnt-out wrecks the following day.

By the end of June, the summer holidays had begun, always a period of hibernation in the Latin Quarter, and by the following autumn the students' riots had died out like a flash in the pan. But the State had drawn its lessons from the riots and proceeded to 'dismantle' and decentralize the University. The great actor Jean-Louis Barrault, who had supported the students, was banished from the Odéon theatre (in the 6th arr.). The main victim of the *événements de mai*, however, was the mutilated arrondissement itself, which lost its old cobbled streets (too threatening to an authoritarian state, which replaced them with dull asphalt) and the better part of its student population, exiled and scattered all over the Paris area, packed into ugly, ramshackle premises, often in seedy neighbourhoods. To crown it all, these new rootless compounds were given numbers instead of names - Paris I, Paris II, Paris III... up to XIII, all in the name of modernity. The participants in the *événements* grew either into disillusioned bourgeois known as _ex-soixante-huitards_ or into frustrated misfits known as *soixante-huitards* _attardés_. Fortunately the excellent Lycées Henri IV, Louis-le-Grand and Saint-Louis are still there, as is the Ecole Normale Supérieure on rue d'Ulm. But the University has suffered beyond repair and its students have often become second-class citizens, superseded by the élite who have been creamed off by the Grandes Ecoles.

The arrondissement has meanwhile been 'cleaned up' and gentrified like many other parts of Paris and is not disdained by top academics, writers and politicians. Even President Mitterand has taken up residence on rue de Bièvre off the once-seedy Place Maubert. This bourgeoisie lives in discreet seclusion away from the beaten track of Boulevard Saint-Michel, where a junk bazaar has replaced most of the bookshops that went the way of the students. Today the Boulevard Saint-Michel stands for what the students of spring 1968 vaguely sensed, rejected and desperately resisted – the inexorable triumph of the consumer age.

WHERE TO WALK...

FROM PLACE SAINT-MICHEL TO THE SORBONNE

Energy permitting, the 5th arrondissement can be visited at a push in one intensive day, but a couple of leisurely days would be preferable, if you wish to take in the atmosphere of its different neighbourhoods. Place Saint-Michel by the

Seine is a convenient arrival spot and is at its best in the morning when it is less crowded. As you walk east along the quai Saint-Michel, you will see Notre-Dame across the river in all her stunning beauty, washed by the rays of a morning sun. Turn right into rue Xavier-Privas, part of a medieval enclave but now proliferating with cheap Greek and North African restaurants and catering to tourists predominantly from the northern hemisphere; only the odd French native wanders around here. Most of the houses date from the 17th century, when the street was erroneously named rue Zacharie (street signs indicating the name Zacharie could still be seen recently at n°s 9 and 13), a distortion of its medieval name, Sachalie, from *sacs-à-lie* ('bags of dregs'); dregs of wine were dried up and burnt to cinders here before being used to dress cloth and leather. Turn right into rue de la Huchette, already famous in the 17th century for its roasts and for its cutpurses, as witnesses Berthod in 1652:

> *Vers la rue de la Huchette*
> *Mais prends bien garde à tes pochettes!*
> (Round rue de la Huchette/Watch out for your purse).

The street remained disreputable into the 20th century and in the 1920s boasted three brothels, the most famous of which, Le Panier Fleuri, was on the south-eastern corner of rue Xavier-Privas. A laundry on the opposite corner served as a clandestine annexe, where a client could choose from among the three laundresses without jeopardizing his reputation. Rue de la Huchette also has a famous jazz club, le Caveau de la Huchette, at n° 5. It was once a meeting-place of the Templars of the Rose Croix, then taken over in 1772 by the Freemasons, who turned it into a secret lodge, complete with an underground passage to the Châtelet and another one running under the cloister of Saint-Séverin. During the Revolution the building was requisitioned by the Convention and used as a court of justice and prison. The most prominent players in the Revolution were brought here for trial - Marat, Danton, Robespierre - and their effigies still decorate the walls. In the late 1940s and 50s the Caveau de la Huchette was a mecca of jazz, which, after the Nazi repression, became the musical expression of the avant-garde, with Coleman Hawkins, Art Blakey, Lionel Hampton and Memphis Slim among the performers. The 50s were also a time of literary turmoil and avant-garde theatre productions. In the Théâtre de la Huchette at n° 23, Ionesco's *Cantatrice Chauve* and *La Leçon* have been showing since 1957, the longest run recorded in Paris.

Retrace your steps, turn right and continue along rue Xavier-Privas, then turn right into rue Saint-Séverin and left into rue de la Harpe, an important artery of Roman Lutetia, the secondary route that ran parallel to the *cardo* (now rue Saint-Jacques). In medieval times it continued as far as the city gate, where Boulevard Saint-Michel and rue Monsieur-le-Prince now meet. The Boulevard Saint-

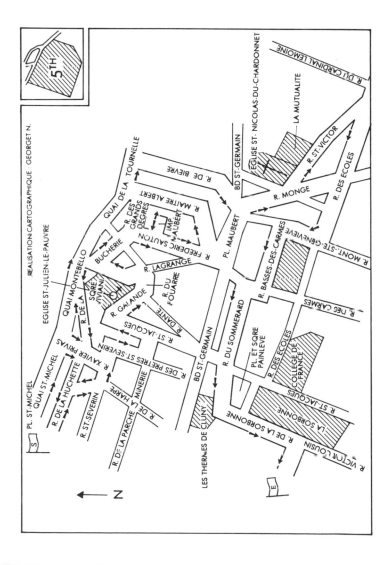

Michel supplanted it at the time of Haussmann, in 1855. The harp of the name is said to come from a 13th-century street sign that showed King David playing the harp; this indeed used to be a Jewish enclave with its own synagogue (on the corner of the present rue Monsieur-le-Prince) and cemetery (round the south-western corner of Boulevard Saint-Michel, in the 6th arr.). In the course of its history rue de la Harpe was named several times after its Jewish population: *Vetus Judearia*, *Vicus Judeorum*, rue de la Juiverie, rue de la Vieille-Juiverie and, indeed, *Vicus Reginaldi dicti le Harpeur*, King David, of course.

Retrace your steps and turn right into rue des Prêtres-Saint-Séverin. On your left is the church of Saint-Séverin, most of which, including the spire, dates from the 15th century, which accounts for its characteristic, flamboyant, Gothic style. However, the first three bays of its nave, the three bays of its southern aisle and its church tower date from the 13th century. It is not quite clear whether the patron saint of the church was the Séverin who had covered the ailing King Clovis with his cloak, or his contemporary, Saint Séverin the Solitary, who had lived in a neighbouring oratory dedicated to Saint Martin, the holy man who had shared his coat with a pauper. The church of Saint-Séverin was in fact connected with Saint Martin, as illustrated by the 19th-century bas-relief of the tympanum above the tower door, which depicts him sharing his coat with a pauper, and a relic of that famous coat was believed to have been kept in the church. Because Saint Martin was the patron saint of travellers, it was the custom to hang horseshoes here on returning home from a journey, as a token of thanks. The church garden with its cloister - a haven of bliss - lies on the site of the parish churchyard, which was reached through the church. In the 17th century the following implacable lines were inscribed at its entrance:

> *Tous ces morts ont vecu, toi qui vis, tu mourras;*
> *L'instant fatal est proche et tu n'y penses pas.*
> (All these dead men once lived, you who live shall die; the
> fatal moment is near at hand and you do not think of it).

Turn into rue de la Parcheminerie, the stonghold of scribes and manuscript copyists in the 13th century, when it was known as rue des Escrivains. In the 14th century it was taken over by the parchment dealers and consequently renamed rue des Parcheminiers. The dealers prospered thanks to the Latin Quarter's abundant population of masters and students, but towards the end of the 15th century were severely hit by the import of paper from China. However, the book trade remained the main calling of the street throughout the 17th century, and it was this that drew the playwright Pierre Corneille here in 1673, even though it was a long way from his home on rue de Cléry (now in the 2nd arr.) and he was then 73 years old, poor and ailing. A relative from Rouen accompanied him on this expedition when Corneille's shoe came unstitched and needed to be repaired. Corneille paid out his last three coins, too proud to accept his friend's assistance. "I cried to see so a great genius in this state of destitution", reported the friend.

Turn left on rue Saint-Jacques, the ancient *cardo* that led to Orléans in Roman days, the pilgrims' route to Santiago de Compostela in Spain in the Middle Ages, when accordingly it was given its present name. Several churches and inns were erected at the time along the road to serve the pilgrims. As a token of their successful journey, the pilgrims would bring back scallop shells from Compostela, which is near the sea. Eventually craftsmen took to carving shell designs on the stones and furniture of the churches, some of which have survived. This is also how the celebrated *Coquille Saint-Jacques*, a prized gourmet dish, found its way into French cuisine.

Cross over and turn left into rue Saint-Julien-le-Pauvre. It will take you to the little church by the same name, one of the three oldest churches in Paris, along with Saint-Germain-des-Prés and Saint-Pierre-de-Montmartre. A 12th-century well in front of the entrance adds to the rusticity of the church, further enhanced by the pretty Square René Viviani. Here is another of those charming fountains known as Wallace fountains in honour of Sir Richard Wallace who donated them to Paris in 1872. At the time, however, passers-by would stop to drink their water from small cups attached to chains. An ancient robinia tree (so called after the botanist Robin who had introduced it from North America in 1601), one of the two oldest trees in Paris (the other is in the Jardin des Plantes), leans wearily against a buttress, unable to support its own weight, adding to the atmosphere of ancientness that prevails.

The story of Saint Julien le Pauvre was narrated in the 13th century by Jacques de Voragine in *La Vie des Saints, La Légende dorée*. However, it is Gustave Flaubert's *Trois Contes* that made it more widely known to modern readers. Julien killed his parents unwittingly, as had been prophesied by a stag whose doe and fawn he had killed in the hunt. Julien went into exile, in the hope of avoiding his fate, but in vain. However, unlike his pagan Greek predecessor Oedipus, our Christian hero was redeemed by Christ, after having devoted his life to the poor. A 14th-century stone carving at n° 42 of the neighbouring rue Galande shows him and his wife helping a pauper cross the river in a barge. The pauper turns out to be Christ, the river is the Seine and the site of Julien's dwelling is, of course, the site of the future church. It so happened that the dwelling was located, most conveniently, at the junction of the road that led to Orléans and Spain and the one leading to Lyons and Italy. An oratory and a hostelry were erected in the 6th century, when France became Christian under the rule of King Clovis and when the first oratory dedicated to Saint Geneviève was also built. Both were swept away by the Norsemen in the 9th century.

The better part of the present church goes back to the 12th and 13th centuries and has retained its rudimentary aspect, devoid of bell-tower and transept, which adds to its charm. Since 1899 it has been a place of worship for the Greek Catholic community, the Melchites, which accounts for the icons hanging in front of the altar. The authorities of the Third Republic, intent like Haussmann on shaping Paris into a modern city and improving the flow of traffic, earmarked the church for demolition in 1877. The practical-minded technocrats of the new age were unperturbed by the destruction of the historical seat of the medieval open-air university in the neighbouring rue de Fouarre, along with the parish church of its illustrious masters - Maître Albert, Thomas Aquinas, Dante and Petrarch: rue Lagrange, opened as an extension to Haussmann's rue Monge, was meant to run through the site of the church and on to rue Saint-Jacques! Fortunately, a general outcry averted the disaster, making Saint-Julien-le-Pauvre the only survivor out of 20 churches that once stood here.

To the right of the church, at 52 rue Galande, is a well-known cabaret, le Caveau des Oubliettes, where you can spend a pleasant evening listening to old French songs in the setting of the medieval oubliettes (in the company of other fellow tourists, which should not necessarily deter you). The next-door horror museum has closed down, but its guillotine, on which J.F. Kennedy inclined his head in 1960, is now on display in the establishment's bar. At n° 42 rue Galande, now a well-known repertoire cinema, is the oldest street sign in Paris, a bas-relief dating from the 14th century, which depicts the miraculous meeting between Saint Julien and his wife with Christ, whom they help across the Seine. A century earlier, when this was still a rural area covered with vineyards, there was a Jewish cemetery here. It was opened in 1198, when the Jews were allowed back to France after their expulsion in 1182 but was closed down by Philippe III, le Hardi in 1270.

Rue Galande will take you to what is left of rue de Fouarre, a tiny chunk of a street, wedged between rue Lagrange and rue Dante, four houses in all. It was already the artery that led from Ile de la Cité to rue de Fouarre in the Middle Ages, as well as to the various colleges of the Latin Quarter and the two abbeys of Sainte-Geneviève and Saint-Victor. Here in the open air, although there is nothing left to remind you, the great minds of Europe, mounted on wooden trestles, dispensed their teaching to rowdy students seated on piles of hay. The students were assembled in four colleges according to their national origins: Normandy at n° 8, France at n° 10 and Picardy and England at n° 17 (hence the neighbouring rue des Anglais further down rue Galande). The school of Picardy was still open at the time of Louis XV and its chapel was pulled down only in 1182.

Continue on rue Lagrange towards the Seine, turn left on quai de Montebello, providing yet another splendid view of Notre-Dame. Beyond Square René-

Viviani is rue de la Bûcherie, called after its medieval harbour where the logs of wood *(bûches)*, which were floated into the capital, were unloaded. At n° 37 the antiquarian bookshop Shakespeare and Company is a wonderfully dusty place, irresistibly inviting. Its owner, the American George Whitman, named his shop after the historic 'Shakespeare and Company' on rue de l'Odéon (in the 6th arr.), which belonged to his friend Sylvia Beach. Like Sylvia, who supported artists and first published James Joyce's *Ulysses*, Whitman too has extended his support to writers and the premises look as much like a home as like a shop. On Sunday you may even be offered a cup of tea and many an expatriate has found here a welcoming roof.

Retrace your steps and continue on rue de la Bûcherie across rue Lagrange. You will have entered a gentrified enclave of picturesque narrow streets, unspoilt as yet by mass tourism. Not so long ago this was still a disreputable area. N° 15, on the corner of rue de l'Hôtel-Colbert, was the site of the first medicine faculty of Paris, established in 1472, before which medicine was taught in the open air, on rue de Fouarre. For centuries knowledge of medicine remained very limited, largely through the fault of the church. Supersition prevailed, bodies for the study of anatomy were unavailable (except when bribe could obtain one of the bodies dangling from the gallows of Montfaucon). On the other hand, instruction in medicine was accompanied by elaborate ceremonial; the ludicrous attire of the faculty was satirized by Molière in his *Malade Imaginaire*. Surviving dissertations that have reached us bear testimony to the gross ignorance of the time, treating such issues as whether a foetus resembles the father or the mother, and the use of sour herring for driving away fleas. The school was reconstructed several times over the generations but remained here until the Revolution. In 1745 it was expanded by the Dane Winslow, who founded the Anatomy Amphitheatre in the elegant *hôtel* that is still standing. In 1775, after the law faculty had moved to new premises on Place du Panthéon, its vacated premises on rue Jean-de-Beauvais were annexed by the growing faculty of medicine. It was only after the Revolution that the medicine faculty moved to its present location in the 6th arrondissement (but has meanwhile expanded elsewhere again).

Ahead is the triangular, tree-planted Place Frédéric-Sauton, at the junction of rue de la Bûcherie, rue des Grands-Degrés, rue Frédéric-Sauton and rue du Haut-Pavé overlooking Notre-Dame – a charming spot where you can stop for a drink or a bite. Turn right on rue Frédéric-Sauton and left into the leafy, placid Impasse Maubert. At n° 4 was Exili's laboratory where, some 350 years ago, Monsieur Godin and his mistress, the notorious Marquise de la Brinvilliers, experimented on various poisons before setting out to eliminate her family (see chapter on 4th arr.). Retrace your steps and turn left on rue Frédéric-Sauton, then left at a sharp angle into rue Maître-Albert, right into quai de Montebello, where another charming tree-shaded junction, albeit less secluded, will welcome you to a café. Turn right again into rue de Bièvre. While the peaceful, almost deserted rue Maître-Albert commemorates the great German master of the Middle Ages, rue de Bièvre is called after the diversion canal of the river Bièvre, which was dug by the monks of the abbey of Saint-Victor in the 12th century to work their mills and water their magnificent gardens (to the outrage of the rivalling abbey of Sainte-Geneviève). The canal flowed alongside the present street, then a country lane, and into the Seine. Some 200 years later, it was incorporated into the moat of Philippe-Auguste's city walls and before long became a putrid sewer. Chroniclers report that rue de Bièvre and rue Maître-Albert were the filthiest streets in the capital, the public latrines of the University; yet they had such prominent residents as the poet Crébillon (1674-1762), Restif de la Bretonne (1734-1806), observer of 18th-century Paris, and possibly Dante who may have begun *The Divine Comedy* here. Today President François Mitterrand resides at n° 22 but the sewer now flows underground.

Both streets lead to Place Maubert, best seen on market days - Tuesday, Thursday or Saturday morning. In the 13th century, Place Maubert, like rue de Fouarre, served as an open-air university. Its most illustrious master was the Maître Albert, hence probably the contracted name Maubert, although some people believe the square was named after Jean Aubert, appointed abbot of Sainte-Geneviève in 1161, when all this area was part of the abbey's domain. In the 15th century, students and masters vanished to the permanent colleges established on the hill and Place Maubert became the gory site of public executions, especially at the time of François I, who relentlessly hunted down the budding sect of Lutherans. The cruelty and savagery with which Lutherans were tortured before being burnt alive were such that even the Pope tried to intercede on their behalf. Until the middle of the 18th century, Place Maubert remained a horrific place of public executions, surrounded by a vast mire, 'the cesspit of Maubert' as Erasmus referred to it, a gathering-place of rowdy youths, beggars, tramps and louts. In 1588, during the student insurrection against Henri de Guise, this was also where the first barricades in Paris were erected.

Cross Place Maubert and turn left into rue Monge and left again into rue Saint-Victor where the church of Saint-Nicolas-du-Chardonnet is situated. Named after the blue thistles *('chardon')* that once grew here, the church is the shrine of the most fundamentalist French Catholics, members of the National Front and others of the extreme right.

Back in the 16th century, at the time of the War of Religions, this was already a centre of Roman Catholic piety and reaction. In the 17th century the reconstructed church was decorated by Charles Le Brun, the master painter of Versailles, who was later supplanted by Mignard. He died a broken man in 1690 and was buried in this, his parish church. Both his tomb and his mother's can be seen inside. Next to the church, at n° 24 rue Saint-Victor, stands the Palais de la Mutualité, the headquarters of the Fédération Mutualiste Parisienne, inaugurated in 1931 by the President of the Republic, Paul Doumer. The building houses a health centre but is known mainly for its large meeting hall, which has hosted performances by France's top singers, including Charles Trenet, Georges Brassens, Juliette Gréco and the Belgian Jacques Brel. Groups from abroad have sung here more recently, Simple Minds, the Pogues, UB 40, among others. Its principal claim to fame, however, has been its progressive political gatherings, led by such historic figures as Pierre Mendès-France and held, ironically, next door to the centre of reactionary activity of Saint-Nicolas-du-Chardonnet. During her visit to Paris in 1981 Indra Ghandi came to the Mutualité to honour the place where her father, Jawaharlal Nehru, had attended the Peace Conference in 1938.

Continue left on rue des Ecoles up to rue du Cardinal-Lemoine. An elegant house, the Hôtel Lebrun, stands at n° 49. It was built in 1700 by the famous Boffrand for Charles Le Brun's nephew (the painter's name is spelt both ways). A succession of prominent residents followed, notably the painter Watteau, in 1718, and Buffon who moved here in 1766, devoting the better part of his time to his monumental 20-volume *Histoire Naturelle*.

Retrace your steps into rue des Ecoles and turn right into rue de la Montagne-Sainte-Geneviève. At n° 4 the police museum is located on the second floor of the police station. It is a very exciting place where the history of Paris is brought to life, thanks also to the wax figures scattered around. Your visit, however, will be more enlightening, if you can come back once you have explored the rest of Paris. A 17th-century map of Paris, for example, even shows the notorious Cour des Miracles (see chapter on the 2nd arr.). There are portraits of notorious criminals such as la Brinvilliers, La Voisin and Ravaillac; a menu seized by the police during the siege of Paris in 1870 is also on display, listing gastronomic dishes of dog and cat meat. The massive door that used to guard the death cell of the prison of La Grande-Roquette in the 11th arrondissement is also on display, just on the way out.

Turn left into rue Basse-des-Carmes, then right into rue des Carmes and left into rue du Sommerand, which leads to the Hôtel de Cluny opposite the Square Paul Painlevé, the Parisian pied-à-terre of the abbey of Cluny in Bourgogne, a gem of a Renaissance mansion and a sole reminder of so much architectural beauty that has been lost. A sundial in the courtyard reads *'Rien Sans Nous'*, referring, not surprisingly, to Louis XIV. The scallop shells *(coquilles Saint-Jacques)* sculpted on the front wall are inspired by the shells the pilgrims used to bring back from Compostela. Today the mansion houses the museum of medieval art whose exquisite selection of *objets d'art* blends harmoniously into the architecture. The jewel in its crown, however, is the set of six gorgeous tapestries of the *Lady and the Unicorn*, undoubtedly among the most splendid and graceful in the world and on no account to be missed.

Adjacent to the museum are the remains of the Roman baths *(les Thermes)*, where fragments of sculpture from Gallo-Roman Lutetia can also be seen, notably the *Pilier des Nautes*, the oldest piece of sculpture discovered in Paris (see chapter on the 4th arr.).

Square Paul Painlevé represents the history of the Latin Quarter in a nutshell, starting with a sculpture of the she-wolf that suckled Romulus and Remus; a replica of the one in the Capitol, it was a gift to Paris from the city of Rome, a homage to Gallo-Roman Lutetia. The sculpture of Montaigne, the Renaissance essayist, embodies the intellectual spirit of the Latin Quarter at a time when it broke down the barriers of theology; while the statues of Nénot, of Puvis de Chavanne and of Octave Gréard (by the same Nénot) commemorate the Sorbonne of the Third Republic that still stands: Nénot was its architect, Puvis de Chavanne its painter and Octave Gréard its rector.

The Sorbonne stands across the street, bounded by rue des Ecoles, rue de la Sorbonne and rue Victor-Cousin, rue Cujas and rue Saint-Jacques. A walk around this monumental mass reveals little of interest but you may wish to know that the observatory on the corner of rue Saint-Jacques and rue des Ecoles was erected on the site of the church of Saint-Benoît, one of the oldest churches in Paris, which disappeared, like so many others, during the Revolution. The church had been nicknamed *'la mal tournée'* ('badly turned') because its altar had been oriented to the west instead of the east, but after this had been put right in the 15th century, it became known as Saint-Benoît-la-Bistournée *('la bien tournée')*. It was here that one of its chaplains at the time, Guillaume Villon, raised his adopted nephew François, the famous poet. When François Villon, the archetypal rowdy student, fell foul of the law, he took refuge here. Visiting the Sorbonne (enter through 17 rue de la Sorbonne) may not prove easy, as much of it is often closed to the public, notably its 2,700-seat Grand Amphithéâtre, which is only opened for special events. The more the pity for it shelters Puvis de Chavanne's mural, *Le Bois Sacré*, so characteristic of the academic style that was in favour during the first decades of the Third Republic and left no room for the Impressionists and that came to be known as *Pompier*.

Despite its appalling acoustics, the amphitheatre is often used for cultural events and concerts. During the socialist era of the 1980s, the authorities used it to covene the international intelligentsia to a four-day conference to meditate upon and discuss the prospects of peace on this planet, watched from the top of their marble pedestals by the ponderous Robert de Sorbon, Richelieu, Descartes,

Pascal and others. In early September 1992, shortly before the French referendum on the Maastricht treaty, President Mitterand also chose the symbolic setting of the Grand Amphitéatre for his historic televized confrontation with the right-wing opponent Philippe Séguin, who objected to the treaty. No detail was spared to arouse pro-European sentiments among viewers - even the carpet under the President's feet was studded with twelve gold stars against a regal blue background, oddly reminiscent of the *Ancien Régime*... More followed in October 1992, in a two-day gathering entitled *Recontres de la Sorbonne*, when such topics as 'art and liberty', 'the spirit of solidarity among the French' and other favourites like 'peace', 'tolerance' and 'rights of man' were discussed by a hotch-potch of celebrities.

Richelieu's chapel also merits a visit. However, it is open only during temporary exhibitions and on special occasions. It houses the Cardinal's tomb, which was designed by Le Brun and executed by Girardon. The pendentives of the dome were painted by Philippe de Champaigne, the court's portrait painter. On the other hand, Lemercier's classical architecture can be appreciated at all times, both from the courtyard of the Sorbonne (enter through n° 12 rue de la Sorbonne) and from the bustling Place de la Sorbonne.

FROM THE PANTHEON EASTWARDS

The second half of the day will be devoted to the exploration of the Montagne-Sainte-Geneviève and its surroundings. Make your way to rue Victor-Cousin, the continuation of rue de la Sorbonne, and turn left into rue Soufflot. Ahead of you is the colossal Panthéon, the sepulchral temple of France's national heroes, standing massively on the razed summit of the hill and overshadowing both the parish church of Saint-Etienne-du-Mont and the Tour Clovis (on the opposite side of rue Clovis), the latter being the only vestige of the medieval abbey church of Sainte-Geneviève. In 1744 Louis XV came down with the pox and vowed to erect a new church for Saint Geneviève should he recover, remembering that back in the 5th century she had restored the health of some of her countrymen. The clergy, who saw in the King's illness a divine retribution for his debauchery, urged him to go further and vow to end his liaison with the Duchesse de Châteauroux, the last of four sisters he had successively led astray. The King's prayer was answered and before long he was up and about, forgetful of his vows. He promptly resumed his amorous liaison with the Duchesse and would just as soon have overlooked his pledge to build a new church, but the residents of the abbey of Sainte-Geneviève, whose personal interests were at stake, proved tenacious and the King had to comply. A grand edifice of gigantic dimensions - 110 metres long, 82 wide and 83 tall - was erected by architect Soufflot, crowning the top of the hill, which had been levelled, and complemented by the new elegant building of the law faculty (its matching town hall on the other side of rue Soufflot was not added until a century later). A broad avenue (now rue Soufflot) ran westwards, opening a new vista on to the gardens of the Palais du Luxembourg, adding a final touch to this regal setting. However, for Soufflot the venture ended tragically: the subsoil having been riddled with pits by the potters of ancient Lutetia who had extracted here their clay, he had difficulty reinforcing the foundations and libellous accusations were showered on him. He died a broken man before the monument was completed. The old abbey church was abandoned without compunction, its Gothic style having long since gone out of fashion; in 1790 it was torn down and a few years later rue Clovis was opened on its site. Only old engravings remind us of its presence next to the parish church of Saint-Etienne-du-Mont.

The monumental new edifice now found better use as the eternal abode of France's recent heroes, to which end some alterations were made, not necessarily for the better. Its 42 lateral windows were walled up, which gave the monument a wholly dismal aspect. The front pediment, overlooking rue Soufflot, however, was enlivened with patriotic fervour by the allegorical figures of *La Patrie* crowning Virtue and Liberty and crushing Despotism, and by the uplifting inscription, 'AUX GRANDS HOMMES LA PATRIE RECONNAISSANTE', shining in gold letters. As contrary forces shook France throughout the 19th century, the destiny of the Panthéon vacillated to accommodate her respective regimes. Napoleon restored it to God, a decision solemnly sealed by the conservative Louis XVIII when he dedicated the church to Saint Geneviève on 3 January (the Saint's holy day) 1822. However, the 'citizen' King, Louis-Philippe, returned the monument to the Nation as soon as he acceded to the throne and had its front pediment decorated with the patriotic allegories that are still there. His successor, Napoleon III, following in the footsteps of his great-uncle, dedicated it once again to the holy Geneviève, while the Third Republic replaced the cult of the holy cross with that of patriotism and national grandeur, but needed an emblematic hero for its consecration. It so happened that Victor Hugo, the embodiment of the Republican ideal, died conveniently in 1885, providing the Republic with the perfect candidate. Even Voltaire's funeral procession had not been as grand as his, starting at the Arc de Triomphe and ending here. The elevating inscription *Aux Grands Hommes...* (which for the past hundred years had been alternately put up or taken down with each change of regime) was restored to its original position on the front pediment, finally there to stay.

The monument's tenants were also shuffled around during that agitated period. When the great orator of the Revolution Mirabeau fell into disgrace in 1794 his naked body was displayed in public before being thrown into a common grave. His vacated place was given to Marat, whose body met with the same fate in

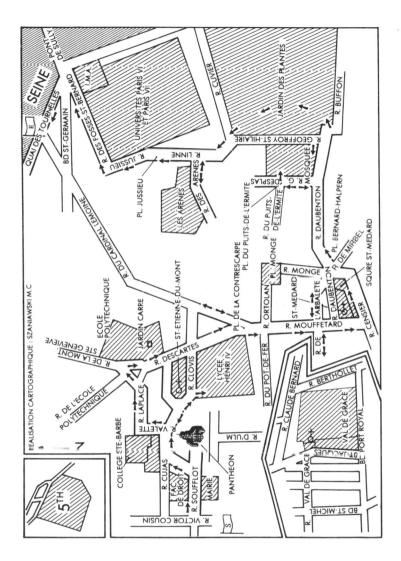

1795. So did Voltaire and Rousseau in 1815 – this time at the hands of the Royalists – who regained their place, however, with the fall of the Bourbon dynasty. They have since been joined by dozens of other glorious figures, among them Emile Zola, Bergson, Saint-Exupéry and Jean Jaurès, occupying the sizable crypt originally intended for the monks of the abbey. Saint Geneviève herself would have fallen into oblivion, had it not been for Puvis de Chavannes's work depicting her as the protector of Paris, and Gros's mural of her apotheosis, which decorates the dome and lightens the otherwise stark interior of this temple.

Following Republican traditions, François Mitterrand also used the Panthéon for a public relations gimmick after he had been elected President in 1981. The monument was after all the resting-place of Jean Jaurès, the spiritual father of socialism. Lured by the petals of the socialist rose and by the sound of Beethoven's *Ode To Joy*, the people of Paris thronged to the Panthéon - unwittingly rehearsing for the Berlin Happening some years later. However, by the time the ashes of Jean Monnet, Europe's founding father, were brought to rest at the Panthéon in 1988, the patriotic surge had died down and they were greeted with indifference by pedestrians and with downright fury by exasperated drivers trapped in gigantic traffic jams. In March 1994, on the occasion of Women's Day, President Mitterrand made the revolutionary suggestion that the remains of Marie Curie should be laid here too, the first woman to be granted this honour.

History and emotions set apart, if you want a breath-taking view, climb to the top of the Panthéon.

At n° 10 Place du Panthéon is the library of Sainte-Geneviève, repository of tens of thousands of volumes and manuscripts rescued from the abbey during the Revolution. It was built at the time of Louis-Philippe, the first iron-frame building in the city, before the railway stations and before Les Halles. The library stands on the site of the famous Collège de Montaigu, founded in 1314 and notorious for its filth and lack of hygiene - even for those days! - and for the harsh discipline inflicted upon its pupils, the '*capettes*'. Rabelais referred to the place as the '*collège de pouillerie*' ('squalor') and claimed that the slaves of the Tatars and the Moors were treated better than its pupils. However, the college was world-renowned for its academic excellence and numbered among its pupils Erasmus, Ignatius of Loyola, Calvin and, in all likelihood, Rabelais himself. When the new church of Sainte-Geneviève was inaugurated by Louis XV, the '*capettes*' were given an exceptional week's holiday so as to make up the numbers for the ceremony, from which the people of Paris, having lost their respect for Louis XV, stayed away.

You now come to the church of Saint-Etienne-du-Mont. A first parish church was built in the 13th century, when the adjacent abbey church became too small for its congregation. By the end of the 15th century the area's population had increased dramatically, necessitating the construction of a new church. The flamboyant style of its architecture was characteristic of the time. The interior is striking for its asymmetrical structure, its magnificent chancel screen - the only one to have survived in Paris - and the highly ornate 17th-century organ. Here lie the remains of Pascal and Racine, and more important still, the remains of Saint Geneviève. These lie in a brass reliquary, a poor 19th-century substitute for the historic, bejewelled one that vanished with the fury of the Revolution in 1793. The stone underneath was rescued from the abbey's crypt and is believed to be part of the Saint's original sarcophagus. On 6 September 1914 the Germans were at the gates of Paris, just as the formidable Huns had been a millennium and a half before. Parisians thronged here to pray that day and once again Paris was spared. When the war was over many came back to thank their patron for having helped them to survive the carnage and left plaques of gratitude affixed to the walls of her chapel. Tucked among them is a plaque from a grateful student who had done well in his examination back in 1890! Before leaving the church, do not overlook the fabulous collection of 16th- and 17th-century stained glass, displayed in the cloister of the Chapelle des Catéchismes.

Across rue Clovis the tower of Clovis is the only remnant of the old abbey church. It lost its spire in 1750 and is now altogether enclosed within the prestigious Lycée Henri IV, which was founded after the Revolution. Among its pupils were Alfred de Musset, Viollet-le-Duc, the Ducs de Chartres, the Duc de Nemours and the Duc d'Aumale, the Prince de Joinville, the Baron Haussmann and all the sons of Louis-Philippe. Unfortunately, French schools are hermetically sealed to outsiders and, unless by prior arrangement, you will not be able to see the remains of the abbey, notably its library, now the dining-room of the school. If you peep through the doorway, however, you will at least catch a glimpse of its lovely courtyard bursting with flowers.

Retrace your steps and continue along rue Valette to your right. Another famous college, the Collège de Fortet, stood at the corner of rue Valette and was also attended by Jean Calvin. Its ramshackle old tower in the courtyard of n° 21 is in fact known as the Tour Calvin because the Swiss rebel, who had defied established theology, is said to have escaped from it when the authorities ordered his arrest. Having climbed down the tower by a rope of knotted sheets, he vanished from the Latin Quarter, never to return. The Collège de Frotet was also where, in 1585, the Duc de Guise assembled La Très Sainte Ligue, which plotted to overthrow Henri III.

At n° 4 the Collège Sainte-Barbe is the only college in the Latin Quarter that dates from the *Ancien Régime*, although the present buildings date from the 19th century. The 16th-century poet and historian Buchanan taught here and Jean

Calvin may have studied here too for a while. In more recent times the aviator Louis Blériot and Gustave Eiffel were among its pupils. Turn right into rue Laplace, an ancient, narrow, quiet street with medieval vaults at n°s 18, 20 and 22 that are said to date from the 12th century. The Collège des Grassins, once a prestigious college, was founded in the 16th century on the site of the present n° 12 and was shut down during the Revolution. At the end of the street, across a picturesque square, is the entrance to the former gardens of the Ecole Polytechnique, which moved to the southern suburb of Palaiseau in 1977. The Ecole Polytechnique was founded in 1794, to meet an urgent need to provide the nascent French Republic, threatened on all sides by monarchical states, with a highly competent scientific élite. Its list of cadets is most impressive: Maréchal Foch and Maréchal Joffre, the heroes of World War I, after whom two pavilions in the gardens are named; the great mathematician Henri Poincaré; Haussmann's landscape gardener Alphand, who designed Paris's loveliest gardens; Fulgence Bienvenüe, the founding father of the Métro; and more recently, the President of the Republic, Valéry Giscard-d'Estaing. Also attributable to the school's alumni are such engineering achievements as the building of the circular road around Paris *(le boulevard périphérique)*, of the Paris airports (both Orly and Roissy-Charles de Gaulle) and of the Concorde aircraft.

The site of the Ecole Polytechnique had previously been occupied by the Collège de Navarre, founded in 1304 by Jeanne de Navarre, the wife of Philippe le Bel. Except for the 100-year span of the Anglo-French war, when the Latin Quarter was in a sorry state, this had for centuries been the most prestigious establishment in the Latin Quarter, enjoying the patronage of the King, who made it a substantial grant - which, however, the school chose to use to buy rods and canes! The highest-ranking nobility, including the royal family and the Guise, sent their children to the Collège de Navarre. For a while it was known as the Collège des Trois Henri, after Henri III, Henri IV and Henri de Guise, who had all attended this establishment, and were said to have had amorous rendezvous here with the same mistress. Richelieu, Bossuet, the Prince de Savoie and Condorcet, among others, were all pupils here. Around Christmas 1456 François Villon and two of his companions supped at the tavern of La Mule, next to the church of Saint-Benoît la Bistournée, mentioned above. They had not gathered to celebrate the Nativity but to organize a burglary. Soon after the three accomplices broke into the Collège de Navarre (which Villon had attended himself) and made off with the takings of the till (the substantial sum of 500 *écus*). An imprisonment (with sessions of questioning and torture) in the Châtelet followed, the first loop in a downhill spiral that ended with the poet's being sentenced to the gallows. All that remains of yet another glorious institution annihilated by the Revolution is the central part of the façade of the Pavillon Foch.

Retrace your steps, turn left into rue Descartes and peep into rue Saint-Etienne-du-Mont on your right, a narrow alley leading back to the church of Saint-Etienne-du-Mont: there is a charming pocket-sized garden on the right, shaded by a clump of birch trees. Continue along rue Descartes. At n° 30 stands an elegant 18th-century *hôtel*, the former home of the Duc d'Orléans, Louis le Pieux, the son of the Regent. A man of virtue and culture, a sincere Jansenist*, knowledgeable in Hebrew as well as in science, Louis was disgusted by the decadence at the court and retired to this house after the death of his young wife, Jeanne de Bade, in 1726, so as to be close to the abbey of Sainte-Geneviève. He remained here all his life and died in his second floor bedroom in 1752, leaving a son, a virtuous captain named Louis-Philippe, the father of the illustrious Philippe Egalité and grandfather of another Louis-Philippe, the future King of France. Before continuing down rue Descartes, take a look at the Tour Clovis standing against the dome of the Panthéon - a beautiful picture from this angle. If you look down rue Clovis to your left, you will see a section of Philippe-Auguste's city walls. A dilapidated room on the third floor of n° 39 rue Descartes was the home of Paul Verlaine. After making an attempt on the life of his former friend, the poet Arthur Rimbaud, he spent some time in jail, then tried to return to the fold of Christianity, but absinth got the better of him and he sank into a life of depravity. Verlaine shared his seedy room with a wretched street girl and died here on 8 January 1896.

Rue Descartes, and its continuation rue Mouffetard, follow the course of the ancient Roman way that led to the south. A city gate was built here in 1200, La Porte Bourdelle, and rue Descartes was known as rue Bourdelle up to 1809. Before continuing into rue Mouffetard, you may like to see where Ernest Hemingway lived. If so, turn left into rue du Cardinal-Lemoine, where in 1922 he and his young bride Hadley occupied a tiny flat on the fourth floor of n° 74: a dingy, dark place with no running water and smelly toilets on the landing. Hemingway also rented a tiny room to work in on the top floor of 39 rue Descartes, claiming it to be the very one in which Verlaine had died. From June to October 1921 James Joyce lived in a third floor flat at n° 71 across the street, which belonged to the literary critic Valéry Larbaud. He was finishing *Ulysses*, a task accompanied by plenty of drink, and often had to be escorted home. Before you walk back, take a look at the countrified hotel at n° 75, Hôtel des Grandes Ecoles, a heavenly patch of provincial France, surrounded by a charming garden, hidden from the din of urban life and very reasonably priced. Retrace your steps and continue into Place de la Contrescarpe, the 'village' square of the neighbourhood, 'Apache' territory in Hemingway's day and since time immemorial the haunt of students, youths and humanity in all its variegated forms. Although the

*Austere followers of the Dutch theologian Jansen Cornelis (1585 - 1638) who believed in predestination and denied free will.

square itself was not created until 1852, this had always been a very busy junction - a jumble of sedan-chair carriers, horses, servants, and others, particularly those on rowdy outings to taverns beyond the city walls, where wine was untaxed and therefore cheaper. The most famous of those taverns was La Pomme de Pin, mentioned by Rabelais and frequented also by the Renaissance poets of *La Pléiade* who had united to promote the French language. The tavern was not at n° 1 as the inscription inaccurately states, but on the corner of the present rue Mouffetard and rue Blainville, where there is now a Häagen-Dasz ice-cream parlour - incongrously perhaps, but in keeping with the times.

Rue Mouffetard is the backbone of a picturesque neighbourhood of narrow streets that criss-cross down the eastern slope of La Montagne Sainte-Geneviève. If you want to see its lush food stalls, do not come between 1 and 4 p.m., nor on Sunday afternoons or at any time on Monday, when they are closed. This is one of the colourful spots of Paris, albeit somewhat marred by an invading rag trade, Balkan restaurants, Latin American night-life and American ice-cream parlours. Unquestionably, this is no longer the genuine 'village' that catered to locals, many of whom prefer to shop at the nearby market of Place Monge (open Wednesday, Friday and Sunday mornings). However, the lower part of rue Mouffetard and such side streets as rue de l'Arbalète have kept their authenticity and are full of charm - a riot of succulent food stalls through which a hotch-potch of humanity elbows its way. Here leeks and potatoes can be bought from a friendly Tunisian, Brazilian food from a native of the Ivory Coast, while three energetic young Jews in their age-old black attire stride across the street for the evening prayers in a nearby synagogue. Yet, despite this rich ethnic mosaic, somehow the neighbourhood has remained essentially Parisian.

Not so long ago this used to be a poor man's district, close to the oozing and malodorous waters of the Bièvre that had long lost their primeval purity. Before the 15th century the borough of Saint-Médard lay by the happy river and took pride in its vineyards and bucolic surroundings. Some of the most prominent Parisians even built splendid country homes in these sunny parts. But when the butchers, dyers and tanners came over, they ravaged the Bièvre, which from then on gave off a nauseating stench, '*mouffettes*' or '*moffettes*', possibly the origin of the name rue Mouffetard. With the pollution of the river came social havoc, and with the presence of hot-tempered butchers and rowdy youths inebriated with cheap wine, brawls and scuffles were the daily and nightly lot of the area. In the early 18th century the authorities sensibly stationed the *gardes françaises* at n° 36, down the street on your right. N° 61, where the *garde républicaine* is now stationed, on the other hand, was a humble convent, built in the middle of the 17th century. By the early 18th century it was threatend with ruin and was rescued by the devout Madame de Maintenon, who responded to the Mother Superior's

rue Mouffetard

appeal by sending the Marquis d'Argenson, the head of the police, to supervise the work. Alas, on one of his visits he met a young novice... The Mother Superior hearing that the lovers were plotting to elope, tried to stop them, but the wrathful d'Argenson refused to give way: if the Mother Superior wished to see her convent restored, she would have to renounce the novice. Having little choice, she complied.

The church of Saint-Médard, down rue Mouffetard on the left, was originally the parish church of the borough of Saint-Médard. Lying prettily on the junction of the road and the Bièvre, it was built on the site of a 7th-century church, which was destroyed by the Norsemen in the 9th century. Its remains were discovered only in 1978, although its existence had been suspected for some time. Saint Médard lived in the 6th century and was councillor to the Merovingian Kings. In the year 545 he crowned a fair and virtuous village girl with a garland of white roses and gave her a dowry of 25 pounds, thus starting the village tradition of the annual *fête des Rosières*, celebrating the chastity of one of the maidens.

Although there is mention of the church in Pope Alexander III's bull, dating from his visit to Paris in 1163, the earliest vestiges, notably its nave and façade, are 15th-century, and typically so in their flamboyant style. The church of Saint-Médard entered history on 1 May 1727 when its virtuous and humble deacon, Pâris, died. Despite his high social rank - his father had been councillor at the Parliament - Pâris refused the priesthood of the church and led an ascetic life of self-renunciation and mortification, which wore him out and caused his premature death at the age of 36. Like many parish priests and members of the Parliament, Pâris had been an ardent Jansenist, and at that time Louis XIV, encouraged by the Jesuits, was persecuting Jansenists. More than any other form of opposition, religious dissension threatened the monarchy because it questioned the very notion of absolutism by divine right. Following the deacon's death a wave of mass hysteria swept through the capital. Convulsive fits, self-flagellation and delirium were the symptoms noted among his friends and worshippers, the *convulsionnaires*, predominantly women. For five years they gathered at his grave, prancing, barking and mewing, as though possessed and were therefore known as *sauteuses*, *aboyeuses* and *miaulantes*. They would be nailed to crosses, trodden on by heavy youths, swallow blazing charcoal, have their tongues pierced... and beg for more. When eventually the alarmed authorities shut down the graveyard in 1732, Pâris's fanatical followers simply moved to private quarters. Only the expulsion of the Jesuits in 1762, the deadly enemies of the Jansenists, put an end to this frenzy which had lasted 35 years and had constituted a much greater political threat to the throne, according to the Marquis d'Argenson (son of the previous one and minister of Louis XV), than "English philosophy which affected at the very most a hundred *philosophes* in France". The graveyard has been replaced by a pleasant public garden, but traces of the graveyard door can still be seen at n° 39 rue Daubenton. As you reach the bottom of rue Mouffetard, turn back for a last picture-postcard view of the festive, colourful slope, with the old church of Saint-Médard framed on the right by shady trees.

Walk alongside the garden of the church on rue Censier, turn left into Place Bernard-Halpern and rue Monge beyond it, and on to rue Daubenton. On your left is the Mosque of Paris, a gem of Moorish architecture, a slice of North Africa or Andalusia. Inaugurated in great pomp by President Doumergues in 1926, when France was anxious to honour her Muslim subjects for their contribution to the war effort, the best Moroccan artists and craftsmen were summoned to decorate it with magnificent tiles and mosaics and drape its walls with rich damask. The ceiling of its arcades was made of cedar from the Lebanon and its Turkish baths were panelled with marble and steamed with the mist of the Orient. Its patio, decked with rose beds and with a marble fountain, is still faintly filled with the scents of Arabia. On Friday, before and after prayer time, swarms of colourfully dressed Muslims gather at the main entrance on rue du Puits-de-l'Ermite. Visitors to the *salon de thé* use the entrance on the corner of rue Geoffroy-Saint-Hilaire and Daubenton, where, on a hot day, it is pleasant to drink mint tea under a shady fig tree, on the small patio with its trickling fountain.

Across the street, on the corner of rue Buffon to your right, is the main entrance to the Jardin des Plantes. Next to it is a spacious 18th century *hôtel*, bought by Buffon in 1772 to serve as residence for the director of the gardens, a post he himself then held. Thomas Jefferson, who was a dinner guest here several times, both admired Buffon, "a man of extraordinary powers in conversation", and was warily deferential to him: "We saw Buffon in the garden but carefully avoided him." Buffon died here, fulfilled and happy, in 1788, aged 85, just in time to avoid the storm of the Revolution. Under his supervision, and with the support of King Louis XVI, himself a lover of nature, geography and science, the gardens had reached their peak. The botanical gardens contain about 10,000 odd species of plants, a tropical glasshouse, the trunk of a 2,000-year-old sequoia tree and a cedar of Lebanon brought over by Jussieu in 1734 (apparently from England), which was the main attraction of the gardens for some time. The Museum of Natural History has a collection of skeletons, shells and stuffed animals and a section on paleontology and mineralogy. The gardens' well-stocked menagerie started out accidentally, when the city authorities decided to rid the streets of animal-tamers and ruled that all animals be brought here. On 9 July 1826 Charles X was offered a giraffe as a present from the Pasha of Egypt. The 'King's animal', the first giraffe to tread French soil, was paraded through the streets of the capital on its way to the Jardin des Plantes, cheered by enthusiastic crowds. Before long Paris was gripped by a craze for giraffe images - on brooches, combs, umbrellas, anything one could lay hands on. In the winter of 1870/71, however, when Paris was besieged by the Prussians, the starving people invaded the menagerie and devoured all its animals. They did the same with the rats and cats of the capital. However, despite the hardships of the times, they took the trouble to cook them first with their innate culinary talent. Turned into succulent dishes, these animals even found their way on to restaurnt menus.

Use the exit on the corner of rue Cuvier and rue Geoffroy-Saint-Hilaire and walk down rue Linné. The junction of rue Linné and rue Jussieu, a tree-studded triangle, once full of charm, is now marred by the presence next to it of the ugly premises of the University of Paris VI and VII, basically the scientific branch of the University of Paris, a disastrous substitute for the magnificent abbey of Saint-Victor that stood here earlier. The abbey was closed down during the Revolution and demolished in 1811 to make room for the wine market of Paris, La Halle au Vin, which in 1812 Napoleon opened here, conveniently across the river from the wine warehouses of Bercy (an earlier wine market was situated on the corner of the quai Saint-Bernard and rue des Fossés-Saint-Bernard). The upsurge of protest against the dismantlement of the market in the late 1950s / early 1960s was of no avail: once again Paris charged recklessly into the future and replaced a chunk of its past with one of its futuristic, jerry-built atrocities. It is a relief to turn left into the steep, meandering rue des Arènes, dipped in greenery, a preserved territory thanks to the presence of the ancient Roman arena. Like in ancient time the semi-circular amphitheatre faces the east; during performances the stage was thus illumintated by the golden rays of the reclining sun against the pastoral backdrop of the Bièvre and its meadows.

Although a place called Les Arènes appears in a deed from 1284, and a late 18th-century map indicates *le clos des Arènes*, and a 13th-century account mentions imposing ancient ruins next to the abbey of Saint-Victor, nobody believed the arena really existed until the 1860s, when some workmen came across it accidentally, while building the rue Monge. Haussmann's remodelling of Paris was not of course to be hindered by such trifles and in 1870 the two thirds of the arena that had thus been unearthed were demolished to make room for new blocks of flats on rue Monge and for the depot and offices of the Compagnie des Omnibus. The last third, which was dug up in 1883, was likewise meant to be destroyed, but Victor Hugo and others intervened and thwarted the designs of technocrats. The Roman arena that you can now see consists of the original section and a reconstruction of the demolished part, which was undertaken in 1918. There is no accounting for man's absurdity! The Arena's tier faces the east as it did in ancient times, when the Bièvre and its meadows served as a pastoral backdrop to the podium, illuminated, like the performers, by the reclining rays of the sun.

Retrace your steps and continue along rue Linné. In the courtyard of n° 4 some lancet arches are the only traces left of the magnificent abbey of Saint-Victor, which was demolished in 1811. Its famous library contained 40,000 volumes, including one of the most ancient books ever printed, *Les Epîtres de Saint Jérome* (1470). Naturally Rabelais's hero Gargantua visited it during his educational journey to Paris. Only *'gens d'étude'* could use this library, and only three times a week, 'three hours in the morning and four hours after dinner'. Today many of France's libraries are still obstinately shut to the layman.

Continue along rue Jussieu and turn right into rue des Fossés-Saint-Bernard, which replaced the moat (*fossé*) dug alongside the city walls during the Hundred Years' War to consolidate the defences of the vulnerable city. Henri IV added to the walls the defensive gate of Saint-Bernard, which was replaced, at the time of Louis XIV, by a triumphal arch (similarly to the Portes Saint-Denis and Saint-Martin that have survived). The gate was pulled down shortly before the Revolution. Turn right along the quai Saint-Bernard for a visit to the Institut du Monde Arabe, designed by Jean Nouvel and inaugurated at the end of 1987 to mark a new era of Franco-Arab cultural collaboration. It was one of those triumphant *'Grands Projets'* trumpeted by the media and which occasioned much rejoicing during Mitterand's first seven-year term of office, not to mention the usual dash to see and experience the novelty – above all the roof restaurant, which has a spectacular view over the Seine. Contrary to the Tour d'Argent, a short way down the river, it offers meals that are within the bounds of affordablility.

Continue along quai des Tournelles, so called after the round defence tower erected by Philippe-Auguste on the easternmost edge of the Left Bank. A small, square-turreted castle, known as the *Château de la Tournelle*, replaced it, probably at the time of Charles VI. The castle was rebuilt by Henri II and at the time of Louis XIII became a depot for convicts awaiting the galleys; it remained so until 1790, by which time it was too dilapidated to be restored and was torn down. Its inmates were then transferred to the neighbouring Collège des Bernardins. On 2 September 1792 the three-day *massacre de Septembre* began, when the bloodthirsty mob unleashed its fury on places of detention and exterminated anyone it could lay hands on. When it was falsely rumoured that the inmates of the Collège des Bernardins were clergymen in disguise, it stormed the depot and assaulted its 73 occupants, who put up a fierce resistance. Robust though they were, they could do little with their bare hands to save themselves and all except three were slaughtered.

The world-famous Tour d'Argent occupies the top floor of n° 15 quai des Tournelles. Guests enjoy both gastronomic cuisine and a spectacular view of the Ile Saint-Louis and Notre-Dame. However, even here some are more privileged than others and the round table that offers the best view is reserved for the most privileged of them all. The first Tour d'Argent, which opened in 1582, was a countrified, one-storeyed inn, yet even then it was a gastronomic establishment, much appreciated by the court of Henri III. It is believed that the fork was used here for the first time in France during the reign of Henri IV, when the restaurant reached its peak. The Revolution destroyed this symbol of lavish decadence, but once the turmoil was over the feast resumed. Naturally, the establishment changed ownership many times in the course of its long life, but since 1913 it has been in the hands of the Terrail family. If you are not among the happy few who can afford a meal, you can nonetheless visit its food shop and museum across the street.

THE VAL-DE-GRÂCE

A visit to the 5th arrondissement is not complete without the Val-de-Grâce, one of the most important religious monuments of 17th-century France and the only one in Paris to have been preserved in its entirety. Situated on the southern end of rue Saint-Jacques, at 1 Place Alphonse-Laveran, it can be reached easily by the n° 38 bus, which runs along Boulevard Saint-Michel. Like the Panthéon, the story of the Val-de-Grâce began with a vow, when the 36-year-old childless Anne of Austria vowed to build a temple to God should she be granted an heir. A year later, in 1638, a first son was born, the future Louis XIV. When in 1645 he reached the age of reason, the Queen brought him over to lay the cornerstone of the future royal abbey. This became one of the finest examples of 17th-century French architecture, designed by François Mansart and Lemercier, who took particular pride in its graceful dome. Inside the dome Mignard painted an astounding mural depicting 200 figures, among them Louis XIII and Anne of Austria, to the glory of God. In 1793 the Convention decided to convert the abbey into a hospital and a medical school for the army, a decision that came into effect in 1796. In 1852 Napoleon III added a medical library to the school which by now owned 130,000 theses and 4,000 other works. Inevitably expansion was necessary and the buildings suffered much damage, but in 1978 a happy initiative was taken to restore the old monument and separate its activities from the rest of the hospital. By 1996, in time for the bicentennial, it will be completed by the addition of a museum of the army's health service. The chapel, cloister and garden à la française have already been restored and if you visit them you will perhaps agree with Guillaume Brice who, in 1685, wrote in the first guidebook to Paris, "Foreigners here must agree that things in France can be made beautiful and regular like those one goes to admire in Italy."

THE 6th ARRONDISSEMENT

In fine weather, the terrace of the Deux Magots, at the foot of the medieval church tower of Saint-Germain-des-Prés, overflows with a medley of locals and tourists from the four corners of the earth. They have gathered here to raise ghosts from a past blessed with an aura of Left Bank intellectual and artistic nonconformity and of postwar scandalous existentialism. Here the intelligentsia spent their days in heated conversation on bustling café terraces and at night plunged into its basements, to be caught up in frenzied sounds of Dixieland or Bebop. The rest of Paris showered insults upon these *'rats de cave'*, ('basement rats')*'troglodytes'*, ('cave-dwellers')*'qui ont du Sartre sur les dents'* (a pun on *'tartre'*- who have tartar/Sartre on their teeth, that is, who talk of nothing but Sartre). Simone de Beauvoir was derided as *La Grande Sartreuse* (a pun on *'Chartreuse'*, a Carthusian nun) or *Notre-Dame de Sartre* (a pun on *'Chartres'*). To her friends she was known fondly as *Castor* because of her methodical diligence. Today's visitors to the Deux Magots look vaguely for Jean-Paul Sartre's chair, not knowing that Sartre's hang-out, during the last war, was not the German-infested Deux Magots but the upstairs of the next-door Flore: a heating stove placed in the middle of the room by the café's owner, Monsieur Paul Boubal, proved a blessing, particularly during the harsh winter of 1943/4. Huddling into these cosy premises, J.P. Sartre, Simone de Beauvoir and others spent their days at separate little tables, absorbed in their writing, Sartre working on *Les Chemins de la liberté*, de Beauvoir on *Tous les hommes sont mortels*. But the spacious, sunny terrace of the Deux Magots on the square is more appealing than the narrow terrace of the Flore, constricted by the traffic-ridden Boulevard Saint-Germain, especially in summer, when it is often livened up by buskers and by the celebrated merry-making band of the Beaux-Arts school. J.P. Sartre and Simone de Beauvoir did not, however, stay long at Saint-Germain – by the time passers-by sought them out after the war, they had migrated elsewhere, notably to the bar of the Pont-Royal hotel on rue du Bac (in the 7th arr.).

Although Sartre's 'band' did not frequent the Deux Magots, others did and the presence of Jacques Prévert and his 'band', of Picasso, André Breton, Mouloudji, Roger Blin, to mention but a few, amply justified the establishment's catch-phrase: *'le rendezvous de l'élite intellectuelle.'* Following Parisian traditions, each coterie took up residence in a given café and, within that café, in a distinctly delineated territory. During the 1920s, for example, Paul Valéry, André Gide, Joseph Kessel, Léon Blum and Gaston Gallimard frequented the terraceless but highly 'atmospheric' Brasserie Lipp; in the 1930s André Breton and his Surrealist friends preferred the Deux Magots, which, however, fell out of favour during the Occupation because it was popular with the Germans. After the war communists and their sympathizers gathered at the Bonaparte on Place Saint-Germain-des-Prés, or in Marguerite Duras's flat on rue Saint-Benoît, while musicians showed preference for the Royal Saint-Germain (now replaced by the Drugstore Publicis). If few connect the Flore with Sartre, fewer still are aware that several decades earlier it had been the haunt of the promoters of political anti-semitism. Here in 1899, when the retrial of Alfred Dreyfus unleashed vehement passions throughout France, the virulent Jew-hater Charles Maurras, Léon Daudet, son of Alphonse, and others founded *l'Action Française*, a movement and a magazine of unspeakable virulence, which prepared the ground for what was to come four decades later. It is not insignificant that, in 1945, on being sentenced to life imprisonment for collaboration and expelled from the Academie Française, Charles Maurras cried out: "It is the revenge of Dreyfus!"

The American 'expatriates' who joined in during the 1920s, came for fun rather than for ideology. Making good use of the favourable dollar exchange rate and breaking loose from the shackles of prohibition at home, they found Paris a place of plenty and of limitless opportunities. The newly-wed Hemingways, freshly arrived in Paris in December 1921, could enjoy a hearty meal at the Pré-aux-Clercs, on the corner of rue Jacob and rue Bonaparte, for the puny sum of 6 francs, with wine at 60 centimes extra. And although many Americans had to content themselves with a dingy hotel room with no running water, up a steep staircase, the sense of freedom, away from puritanical America, the colourful streets overflowing with abundant, cheap food, and the sens of comradeship provided by the smoky cafés largely compensated for those shortcomings. Of course there were also those Americans who were not short of money at all. Natalie Barney's literary salon at 20 rue Jacob, with its charming, shady courtyard overgrown with ivy, was the gathering-place of the beautiful people, where friendship, love, art and literature were celebrated in a mock Greek temple, dubbed *Le Temple de l'Amitié*, in an atmosphere of genteel refinement – Miss Barney disliked the crude atmosphere of café terraces, but had to compromise eventually and allow whisky to be served instead of tea. However, the main occupation of the 'expatriates' was writing, for which encouragement came from two American ladies: Gertrude Stein, who opened her home at 27 ruc dc Fleurus to those in whom she had faith - or who did not threaten her; and Sylvia Beach, who was able to publish and sell their works through her shop, Shakespeare and Company, at 12 rue de l'Odéon. It took a lot of courage on her part to publish James Joyce's *Ulysses* in 1922, but she trusted his genius and was proved right.

Dingy hotel rooms were the order of the day until well after the war - La

Louisiane on rue de Seine (Simone de Beauvoir's quarters), Le Montana on rue Saint-Benoît, Le Madison on Place Jacques-Copeau, Le Taranne on Boulevard Saint-Germain, The Pont-Royal on rue du Bac (in the 7th arr.) - all now respectable three- or even four-star establishments. Meals were taken in cheap 'canteens' such as Le Petit Saint-Benoît, still going strong on rue Saint-Benoît, or Le Catalan on rue des Grands-Augustins, where Picasso ate during the Occupation, conveniently across from his studio at n° 7, and frequented also by Dora Maar, Paul Eluard, Jean Cocteau and Balthus. But the backbone of Saint-Germain were its café terraces, between which the 'Germanopratins' drifted, straying from their 'home' cafés at different times of the day. The Flore and the Deux Magots, for example, were afternoon favourites, while the Rhumerie Martiniquaise, at n° 166 Boulevard Saint-Germain, filled up at night. It took them barely five minutes to cross the 'village', a tiny rectangle bounded by rue Jacob, rue Bonaparte, Boulevard Saint-Germain and rue Saint-Benoît, with some extensions here and there. In its heart stood the church of Saint-Germain and its square; around it lay bustling cafés caught up by the fever of the 1920s, which had spread to here from Montparnasse, only four stations away by Métro from Vavin and easily reached on foot. Though somewhat abated, the fever persisted throughout the war, exemplified by the Zazous, those jolly youngsters, in provocative attire and passionately keen on jazz – it was after all one form of protest against the German occupiers. No sooner was Paris liberated than the entire neighbourhood blazed into freedom. The explosion, which lasted into the early 1950s, this time focused on Saint-Germain-des-Prés, occasionally spreading to Montparnasse.

The blast of trumpets accompanied the blaze through the small hours of the night, as Boris Vian and his friends celebrated the end of oppression at the Tabou, on rue Dauphine. Pushing east Claude Luter brought his unbridled clarinet and Dixieland to the basement of Lorientais on rue des Carmes (in the 5th arr.), in the heart of the Latin Quarter. When the parents of his student audience lost patience with their offspring swinging all night and skipping classes the following morning, the place had to close down and Claude Luther's orchestra ended up at the more expensive Vieux-Colombier, where he was later joined by an American jazz clarinettist called Sydney Bechet; but the audience was no longer the same. The Tabou also had to close down after an ephemeral existence of several months, due to complaints from neighbours. Club Saint-Germain, at 13 rue Saint-Benoît, took up the baton in 1948 with a glorious array of American jazzmen - Charlie Parker, Coleman Hawkins, Max Roach, Duke Ellington Miles Davies - though it never succeeded in recreating the wild, spontaneous atmosphere of the Tabou.

Meanwhile the French natives expressed their new freedom in their own way. At the Rose Rouge on rue de Rennes (before that on rue de la Harpe in the 5th arr.), the Frères Jacques, combined the words of Prévert, Queneau or their own, with music, acrobatics and mime to create a new genre of perfectly lubricated, three-minute songs of sheer joy. Juliette Gréco, more sedate, theatrical, dressed in black, and with her low-pitched, ironical voice, became the spokeswoman of 'existentialist' Saint-Germain as she sang to the lyrics of Sartre, Queneau, Desnos and Prévert and to the music of Kosma, such songs as the unforgettable *Feuilles Mortes*. All-purpose black had first been worn by Saint-Germain because it had come in handy in those days of penury. However, in a city bent on fads, it soon became the trademark of Saint-Germain's youths and of Gréco, their model. Meanwhile, perpetuating French traditions of protest, a new generation of anti-establishment poet-singers - Georges Brassens, Jacques Brel, Léo Ferré, Francis Lemarque - made their appearance in the vaulted cabarets of Saint-Germain, at L'Arlequin, L'Echelle de Jacob, L'Ecluse and Le Quod Libet.

The liberation also released bulimic creativity. Art galleries, such as those of Pierre Loeb on rue des Beaux-Art and René Breteau on rue de Seine, flourished, new ones opened and dozens of exhibitions, displaying the works of artists such as Atlan, Hartung, Henri Michaux, Serge Poliakoff and André Masson, were organized to satisfy a public starved of art and culture. The concept of art itself was questioned and revised. The painter Fautrier, for example, wrote, *"Je rêve d'un tableau mal composé, vilain de couleurs, mal dessiné, mais qui existe"* ("I dream of a badly painted picture, of ugly colours, badly drawn, but which exists"). Dubuffet insisted on the use of raw materials because "painting becomes insipid if it does not return from time to time to its stone age."

Above all, Saint-Germain drew together France's anguished intelligentsia, united in their sense of its helplessness in the face of war's devastation. Jean-Paul Sartre spoke for them in his definition of man's 'existentialist' condition: *"La guerre en mourant, laisse l'homme nu, sans illusion, abandonné à ses propres forces, ayant enfin compris qu'il n'a plus à compter que sur lui "*("War in its agony leaves man naked, disillusioned, abandoned to his own resources, having at last understood that he can rely only on himself"). Albert Camus claimed that it was required of his generation to rise "up to its despair" (*être à la hauteur de son désespoir"*).

People in great numbers took up their pens, hoping out of the ashes of destruction to reconstruct a better world. All of them were anti-fascists and all, whether pro-, anti-, ex- or future communists or just sympathizers, defined themselves in reference to the Communist Party, the party of 'cent *mille fusillés*' (one hundred thousand shot dead), which promised total revolution to purge and redeem the world and which in the 1946 legislative elections, had obtained 28.6% of the votes. Essays, novels, plays, poems flooded the desks of old-established publishers such as Gallimard, who boasted an impressive list of authors - Camus, Queneau, Duras, Ionesco, Genet, Mouloudji - and also the translated works of

Hemingway, Faulkner, Dos Passos and Steinbeck. Small new houses followed suit: Le Point du Jour, which published Paul Eluard, Tristan Tzara... and especially Jacques Prévert; Le Sagittaire, which published Queneau, Adamov and André Breton; Le Scorpion, Boris Vian's publisher; and Minuit which took pride in its underground past during the Occupation. It had been founded by Vercors (real name Jean Bruller) in order to publish his famous *Silence de la Mer*; other members of the Resistance had joined him and under guise of pseudonyms contributed courageously to the war effort: Louis Aragon (François La Colère), Elsa Triolet (Laurent Daniel), François Mauriac (Foriez) and Paul Eluard (Jean du Haut) among them. New reviews and magazines also proliferated. Some were ephemeral but others were to last, such as *Le Temps Moderne*, founded by Sartre, *Combat*, with Camus as chief editor, *Les Lettres Françaises*, one of the numerous mouth-pieces of the Communist Party, with Aragon as chief editor, and *La Table Ronde*, co-founded by Raymond Aron, Albert Camus and André Malraux. Understandably, the desperate absurdity of man's condition was the underlying theme of postwar playwrights as well - Eugène Ionesco, Albert Camus, J.P. Sartre, Adamov and Samuel Beckett. Saint-Germain-des-Prés supported the theatre passionately, welcomed experimentation and followed enthusiastically a new genera tion of actors, among them Suzanne Flon, Loleh Bellon, Maria Casarès and Gérard Philippe.

La Hune, a bookshop-gallery at the very heart of Saint-Germain, just between the Deux Magots and Flore and opposite Lipp, became the focus and meeting-place of the intelligentsia. It had first been set up by a group of young book-and art-lovers, on rue Monsieur-le-Prince, on the fringe of the Latin Quarter. In 1946, Jeanne Bucher, highly regarded as the owner of a famous art gallery on Boulevard du Montparnasse, visited it and exclaimed, "*La Hune sera célèbre!*" At the new site, exhibitions were held upstairs and books sold downstairs, to help promote the works of writers and artists. La Hune also published some written works.

The intellectual and artistic calling of the 6th, however, though stimulated by the war, goes centuries back. Its eastern section is part of the Latin Quarter, whose tradition of scholarship dates from the Middle Ages. To the west, the arrondissement developed around the abbey of Saint-Germain-des-Prés, which started as a basilica in the late 6th century: "I have begun to build a church..." we are told by Childebert, son of Clovis, in a deed dating 6 December 558. It was the Bishop of Paris, Saint Germain, who had urged Childebert to erect a sanctuary for Saint Vincent, the patron of wine-growers and the martyred deacon of Saragossa which Childebert had taken from the Wisigoths. A relic of the Saint's tunic and a gold cross, said to have belonged to King Solomon, which Childebert had brought back from Saragossa were laid in the new basilica. Later Childebert and Saint Germain were also laid there, as was the royal family for the next hundred years.

Saint Germain was determined to bequeath to posterity a monument of splendour, decorated with magnificent mosaics and topped by a gilded roof. Glittering in the sun amidst peaceful meadows, it was deservedly nicknamed *Saint-Germain-le-Doré*. Beyond artistic aspirations, Saint Germain also had in mind political considerations in choosing this site on expansive fertile land, which would secure economic prosperity. Being a clear-sighted politician, he proceeded to extricate the monastery from episcopal jurisdiction, thus paving the way for its future independence as a powerful abbey, and meanwhile gaining popularity among the people whose well-being he had ensured. Before long the brilliant, enterprising Bishop became a legendary miracle-worker superseding even the fabled Saint Vincent.

Thus, it was thanks to Saint Germain's supernatural intervention that the abbey set up a heroic resistance to the Norsemen three centuries after his death, as reported by a contemporary monk called Abbon. One Danish brigand was tied up to a chariot by the Saint, then chased into hell by Death; another one lost his way on one of the turrets and rolled off the steep slope of the roof; a third lost his sight as he turned his eyes towards the Saint's sepulchre, whilst a fourth was snatched away from above, apparently by the invisible hand of the Saint. At a time of boundless imagination, Abbon's testimony increased the prestige of Saint Germain as the patriot who had fought back the invincible Dane and bore significant political consequences on the destiny of the abbey. In 903, while the abbey was still lying in ruins, King Charles le Simple reconfirmed its possessions and soon the abbey was reconstructed and enjoyed greater prosperity than ever before. Less than a century later the church tower that still dominates the Place Saint-Germain-des-Prés pierced the skies of Paris. On 21 April 1163, when the church was at last completed, it was consecrated by Pope Alexander III. The Bishop of Paris Maurice de arrived for the occasion in his ceremonial attire, but the Abbot exerted pressure on the Pope to have him withdraw, a spectacular humiliation intended solely to mark the independence of the abbey. By that time an embryonic borough was germinating here, the nucleus of the arrondissement, which in all logic would have expanded homogeneously to the east, towards the centre of the city, had Philippe-Auguste not decided otherwise.

Having decided to extend the city walls to the Left Bank, he began by erecting the tower of Nesle by the Seine (roughly on the site of the present Institut de France), to secure the control of the Seine to the west and as a pendant to the tower of the Louvre on the Right Bank. The new walls ran from the tower, along the present rue Mazarine, rue de l'Ancienne-Comédie and rue Monsieur-le-

Prince, leaving the abbey and its dependencies outside the city boundaries. With the foundation of the University of Paris and its growing power in the 13th century, the area lying within the city walls naturally fell within the University jurisdiction and by the 14th century was totally beyond the control of the abbey, much to the displeasure of the latter, especially as the University then enjoyed great privileges and prestige. Most of the remaining vacant land of the future arrondissement was taken over by various religious orders, with the encouragement of the throne, in particular the pious Louis IX. Thus, this pastoral expanse was transformed with graceful architecture, neatly cultivated domains and the magnificent, palatial pieds-à-terre of the provincial clergy, of which the Hôtel de Cluny (in the 5th arr.) alone has survived. Unable to use these homes during the Hundred Years' War, the provincial clergy sold them off to prominent families of the *noblesse de robe*, who were pleased to settle in them alongside a couple of already resident old families of the *noblesse d'épée*.

Meanwhile, west of the city walls, life rotated around the abbey, which was fortified in its turn because of the war. Following the usual feudal pattern, a rural population cultivated the land, largely covered with vineyards, while tradesmen and craftsmen were grouped into guilds, earning much less than their counterparts in the city. The annual fair of Saint-Germain boosted the economy of the borough and provided a considerable source of extra income to abbey and royalty alike. Tradesmen, artisans and money-changers flocked here from far and wide, displaying the most gorgeous commodities of the day. Drapers from Flanders, jewellers from Italy, bankers from Lombardy and Jewish pedlars converged here between 3 February and Palm Sunday (and usually beyond), turning the area around the present rue Mabillon into the colourful crossroads of Europe. This was carnival time too, when people of all social classes came to be entertained, even princes and royalty until their move to Versailles. In a letter written on a Wednesday evening of February 1607, Henri IV instructs his minister Sully to withdraw three thousand crowns from his savings account and pay off to a certain Berringhen the gambling debt he had incurred at the Fair. While artists, encouraged by the highly cultivated abbots of Saint-Germain, used the opportunity to exhibit their works and gain recognition, animal-tamers (it was here that the rhinoceros made its first Parisian appearance in the 18th century), street performers and puppeteers offered the area an embryonic form of theatre, all of which contributed to the development of the arrondissement as a place where the performing and fine arts could flourish, unlike the 5th arrondissement, which was above all confined to learning.

However, the theatrical tradition of the arrondissement developed mainly outside the fair. In 1643 Molière established his first theatre, Le Théâtre Illustre, on the site of a a *jeu de paume*, Les Métayers (now rue Mazarine). In 1672 Lully's opera house was inaugurated with his opera *Pomone* in the neighbouring Jeu de Paume de la Bouteille (now on the corner of rue Mazarine and rue Jacques-Callot). The same premises were taken over by the newly-founded Comédie-Française after Molière's death the following year, Lully having moved to yet another *jeu de paume*, L'Etoile, close to the Luxembourg Gardens (now rue de Vaugirard). Molière's troupe and the troupe of the Marais were merged into one company called *Les Comédiens du Roi* and their new premises, situated next to the Hôtel de Guénégaud, were known as Le Théâtre Guénégaud. The theatre was inaugurated on 9 July 1673 with a highly acclaimed performance of Molière's *Tartuffe*. In 1689 they moved to yet another *jeu de paumes* on rue des Fossés-Saint-Germain (now rue de l'Ancienne-Comédie), and opened the season on 17 April with a double bill of Racine's *Phèdre* and Molière's *Médecin Malgré Lui*. In 1782 a new magnificent theatre opened on Place de l'Odéon to accommodate the prestigious troupe which twelve years earlier had to close down its century-old home on rue des Fossés-Saint-Germain because it was on the verge of collapse.

More importantly, the Saint-Germain fair was at the origin of arguably the most essential cultural and social institution in France in these past 300 years. Indeed, when in 1672 two Armenians called Pascal and Maliban began to market a newly introduced exotic beverage from the Orient called coffee, at the price of two and a half sous per cup, they were confident in its future universal popularity. At first, however, it received mixed response: some supported its beneficial medicinal qualities, others claimed it caused impotence. The Princess La Palatine, Louis XIV's sister-in-law and mother of the future Regent, had definite tastes in matters culinary and declared it smelt like the breath of the Archbishop of Paris. A Sicilian nobleman who had been helping the two Armenians, Francesco Procopio dei Coltelli by his Italian name, better known today as François Procope, added to the beverage its cultural dimension when around 1685 he opened the first Parisian café on rue des Fossés-Saint-Germain. By 1723 the chronicler L.S. Mercier counted between 600 and 700 such establishments in the capital. When the Comédie-Française moved across the street in 1689, Le Procope became its antechamber, from where the general public watched the comings and goings around the theatre and could spread gossip around. Critics gathered here too to determine the fate of actors and actresses or of a new play, a practice maintained throughout the next century. Thus it was here that in 1784 Beaumarchais waited anxiously for the verdict on his play *Le Marriage de Figaro*.

The Laurent, on the corner of the present rue Dauphine and rue Christine, followed suit and both became places of intellectual exchange, gradually replacing the literary salons, albeit without the refinement and the polish. Here names were smeared, coarse diatribes and vociferous insults sallied forth, occasionally coming to a head in duels, which were fought in the back yard next door, an atmosphere derided by Voltaire:

Quand Piron, contre l'Olympie
Avait bien vomi son fiel;
Quand Rousseau le misanthrope
Avait bien philosophé
ça, Messieurs, disait Procope,
Prenez donc votre café.
(When Piron against Olympia had vomited all his venom; / When Rousseau the misanthropist / had amply philosophized / Well then, gentlemen, said Procope, / do have your coffee.)

Voltaire himself was no less venomous towards his mortal enemy, Fréron:

L'autre jour, au fond d'un vallon,
Un serpent mordit Jean Fréron.
Que pensez-vous qu'il arriva?
Ce fut le serpent qui creva.
(The other day, at the bottom of a valley,
A snake bit Jean Fréron.
What do you think happened?
The snake it was that died.)

Montesquieu, on the other hand, was struck rather by the pretentiousness of the clientele:

Il y en a une [maison où l'on distribue du café] où l'on apprête le café de telle manière qu'il donne de l'esprit à ceux qui en prennent: au moins, de tous ceux qui en sortent, il n'y a personne qui ne croie qu'il en a quatre fois plus que lorsqu'il y est entré.
(There is one [house where coffee is served] where coffee is prepared in such manner that it bestows wit upon those who drink it: at least, of all those who leave, there is not one who does not think that he now has four times more than when he entered.)

Les Lettres Persanes

But the Procope was also a place of serious intellectual debate, where Diderot and d'Alembert conceived the idea of the *Encyclopédie* and where new ideas germinated that would bring about the fall of the *Ancien Régime*. Already in 1685 the head of police, La Reynie, and the King had been forewarned that "in several places of Paris, where coffee is served, there are gatherings of all sorts of people...". Aware of their potential for subversion, Louis XIV ordered one of his functionaries to write a report on the matter and, although no action was taken against those establishments, they were flooded with spies, to which the *philosophes* responded by inventing a coded terminology. Hence 'liberty' became known as Jeannette, 'religion' as Javotte and God as Monsieur l'Etre. Louis XIV had good reason to worry, for a century later the Procope became the stronghold of the Revolutionary intelligentsia, many of whom were living locally, among them Danton, Camille Desmoulins and Marat. In the 19th century the Procope again became the haunt of literati, such as Musset, George Sand, Théophile Gautier and Balzac and later of Verlaine, Huysmans and Emile Goudeau and others. Obviously the atmosphere of the Institut de France rubbed off on its clientele and the area at large.

The forerunner of the Institut de France on the site was the Collège des Quatre-Nations, which was founded and funded by Mazarin to ensure the education of noble students from the four nations defeated and annexed by France. There was also a project for an academy where young members of the nobility would be initiated into the arts and skills that made up *l'honnête homme* – art, science, riding, dancing and fencing – but the University, having a different notion of education, opposed the project and it therefore never materialized, except for the library. The site of the long disused Hôtel de Nesle, opposite the Louvre, provided a privileged location for the new institution. 24 elegant shops sheltered by an arcade opened next to it, displaying paintings, engravings, beautiful furniture and books, and attracting discerning clients for the next hundred years.

During the Revolution, when the place was used as a prison, the father of the guillotine, Dr Guillotin, was himself detained here. Mazarin's enterprise foundered but the library flourished: tens of thousands of volumes, looted from the closed-down abbeys and convents, filled its shelves, as well as those seized from the King's private collection and from various members of the nobility. In 1805 it was decided to transfer to these disused premises the five academies founded in 1695 and hitherto established in the Louvre: the Académie Française, the Académie Royale des Belles-Lettres, the Académie Royale des Sciences, the Académie Royale de Peinture et Sculpture and the Académie d'Architecture. In 1816 the last two were merged into the Académie des Beaux-Arts while a fifth academy, the Académie des Sciences Morales et Politiques, was founded in 1832. Together they make up the Institut de France. On 1 February 1989 Peter Ustinov, sporting the green costume of an *Académicien* with its splash of gold embroidery of laurel leaves, and its honorific sword, was elected to the Académie des Beaux-Arts, to the *fauteuil* vacated by Orson Welles. On 27 October 1992 a similar honour was bestowed on Vaclav Havel, the President of post-communist

Czechoslovakia which was then on the brink of breaking up, when he was elected to the Académie des Sciences Morales et Politiques, there to join such glorious figures from the past as Alexis de Tocqueville, Albert Schweitzer and Raymond Aron.

Perhaps because it is the oldest of the five academies founded by Richelieu in 1635, the Académie Française outshines the other four and even some locals confuse it with the Institut de France, of which it is only one component, assuming that an *Académicien* is necessarily a member of the Académie Française. The Académie Française is certainly an institution of great prestige and election to it both an honour and a media event. Entrusted with the task of preserving the French language, its 40 venerable members guard against any threat from the 'vulgum', the latest dating from 1991, when the Minister of Culture, Jack Lang, had all but passed through an extravagant spelling reform. A stronghold of conservatism, the Académie waited 350 years before it admitted its first woman, the writer Marguerite Yourcenar, in 1980. A sign of the times is that Captain Jacques-Yves Cousteau is now also an *Académicien*. Throughout its history, the Académie has rejected nonconformist candidates - La Fontaine, Beaumarchais, Balzac (4 times), Emile Zola (24 times!) and, more recently, poet/singer Charles Trenet. There were also those who spurned the proffered honour - Descartes, Pascal, Diderot, André Malraux, de Gaulle - and those who were expelled after the last war - Charles Maurras and Maréchal Pétain - a rare measure, since an *Académicien* is by definition 'immortal'.

The aura of the Académie Française should by no means eclipse that of the Académie des Beaux-Arts, which, in the last century, contributed largely to the promotion of art in the arrondissement. Dominique Ingres, Charles Garnier, Victor Baltard, Hector Berlioz, Charles Gounod and Gabriel Fauré were among its members, and even Delacroix, who was something of a renegade and was rejected seven times before gaining admittance.

In the early 19th century, the premises of the Institut de France were used as temporary studios by David, Horace Vernet, Pradier and others awaiting the completion of the school of Beaux-Arts next door. When the school finally opened on rue Bonaparte and quai Malaquais, throngs of art students invaded this northern section of the arrondissement, enlivening the street scene with a bohemian bustle, recreating some of its medieval atmosphere. Indeed, in the Middle Ages the University owned an enclave on the extensive domain of the abbey, the Pré-aux-Clers, where rowdy youths from the Latin Quarter would come to create havoc and to antagonize the community of the abbey. In the 19th century this was a derelict neighbourhood, just fit for an impoverished population of would-be artists, occupying wretched attics or dingy hotel rooms, where they lived from hand to mouth. In *Scènes de la Vie de Bohème*, better known in Puccini's operatic version, Henri Mürger depicted Rodolphe and Marcel's Christmas Eve, spent by the fire of a hotel room: "... the damp logs of poor drift-wood burnt away without any flame, generating no heat." Rodolphe reminiscences on the three-penny restaurant on rue du Four, "where we were so hungry when we had finished eating." "Bohemia," Henri Mürger wrote, "is the apprenticeship to artistic life: it is the preface to the Academy, to the Hôtel-Dieu [hospital] or to the Morgue."

Without the presence of the aristocracy, the 6th would not have had that extra touch of worldliness that makes it the most sophisticated arrondissement in Paris. Moreover, without the energetic patronage of the aristocracy, artistic creativity could have not flourished here before the Revolution. There were always some noble families established in or visiting the area. In 1718 a contemporary mentions the presence of 12 princes and over 300 barons and counts. No dwelling in medieval times could match in size and beauty the Hôtel de Nesle, standing by the water, facing the Louvre, and adjacent to the defence tower by the same name. It was built in the 13th century by Simon de Clermont, Seigneur de Nesle. Philippe le Bel bought it in 1308 and from then on it remained in the hands of the royal family. When Jean Duc de Berry and brother of Charles V (1340 -1416) lived there, it became a dwelling of exceptional splendour. A great patron of the arts, the Duke assembled the finest artists of his time at the Hôtel de Nesle, notably the Limbourg brothers who produced a beautiful illuminated manuscript known as his Book of Hours *(Les Très Riches Heures du duc de Berry)*, one of the world's masterpieces of medieval art (which inspired the sets of Laurence Olivier's *Henry V*). Among the illuminations is the world-renowned view of the old Louvre as seen from the Hôtel de Nesle. The *hôtel* enjoyed a magnificent position by the water but by the same token suffered periodic flooding. Hence the construction of the first *quai* in Paris, in 1313.

Nearly three centuries later Marguerite de Valois chose to reside opposite the Louvre, her childhood home when, as daughter of Henri II, she was Princess Royal. She built herself a mansion along the Seine, the entrance to which was on the corner of the present rue de Seine and quai Malaquais and moved there in 1606. However, as the repudiated wife of Henri IV she had to bear with the presence of Marie de Medici, Henri IV's new wife, in the royal palace, across the water. Queen Margot, as she came to be known, devoted special attention to the mansion's gardens, which became the joy of the neighbourhood when she opened them to the public. From across the Seine, Marie de Medici eyed her gardens and before long had a promenade laid for the King, the Cours-la-Reine, on the opposite Right Bank. Nor did she stop there. For a while she had had her eye on a 16th-century *hôtel* belonging to François de Luxembourg. In 1611 the widowed Queen bought the *hôtel* and set out to create a dwelling and gardens in the image of the Pitti Palace of her native Florence. The Palais du Luxembourg, as it came to be known, later also contributed to the promotion of art, for in 1750 its east wing was turned into a painting museum, the first of its kind in France. Even during the devastating days of the Revolution the future arrondissement maintained its artistic mission. In 1791 the Chapelle des Louanges, built by Marguerite de Valois on her estate, in praise of the Patriarch Jacob, was converted by the archaeologist Alexandre Lenoir into a museum, le Musée des Monuments Français, where he deposited whatever monuments and sculptures he could rescue from the wreckage. The Chapel (now 14 rue Bonaparte) became the nucleus of the above-mentioned Beaux-Arts school during the Restoration.

The opening of the Drugstore Publicis in the 1960s, a glitzy version of an American drugstore, heralded a new era. Baroque ugly hands, mouths and eyes belonging to members of *Tout-Paris*, from Brigitte Bardot to Jean Cocteau, decorated the flashy premises, creating no small sensation. The Royal Saint-Germain that had stood here before, one of the pillars of the 'village', had had its day. Today's Saint-Germain, like the rest of the arrondissement, is a very expensive district, inhabited by successful artists, writers, professionals and by members of showbiz and of *Tout-Paris*. Its once-dingy hotels have become three- or four-star *hôtels de charme* and a small cup of espresso at the Deux Magots costs as much as 21 francs. Largely taken over by the *prêt-à-porter* industry, usually on the expensive side, its consumers have little in common with the impoverished war generation. This is even truer of the clients of the antique shops and other boutiques located in the north-western section of the arrondissement. With its art galleries around rue de Seine and its scattering of antiquarian bookshops, Saint-Germain has become the glamorous shadow of its past, typified until recently by the Castel night-club, jealously reserved for the glittering few and a world away from the makeshift, free-for-all Tabou.

Nostalgia aside, the 6th arrondissement is in many ways unique. No arrondissement combines so many hues, shades and touches: the discreet charm of old courtyards on rue Jacob, rue des Saints-Pères, rue du Cherche-Midi; artists' studios near Montparnasse; quaint alleys charged with history on the edge of the Latin Quarter; or the sheer beauty of its *quais*, graced with the dome-capped Institut de France and the stunningly classical Hôtel de la Monnaie: all these make the 6th is a treasure trove for the aesthete. This is also where France's leading publishing houses are based - Gallimard, the Presses de la Cité, Hachette, Robert Laffont, Flammarion, Plon, Stock, Seuil - as well as multitudes of bookshops of all kinds and sizes, some specialized, some not, some dusty, some glittering, some downright practical, some fabulous.

Crowning it all, a palette of riotous colours sets ablaze the area around the junction of rue de Seine and rue de Buci, where a ravishing array of flowers, an array of culinary delights and the music of buskers provide the most exquisite appeal to the senses.

WHERE TO WALK...

FROM PLACE SAINT-MICHEL TO THE INSTITUT DE FRANCE

Our first walk will take us to the north-eastern section of the arrondissement, which, despite the artificial border between the 5th and 6th arrondissements created by Haussmann's Boulevard Saint-Michel, is still part of the Latin Quarter. This time we suggest you come in the afternoon, if you want to enjoy the jolly atmosphere enhanced by buskers' music. Place Saint-Michel, our starting-point, is dominated by Davioud's fountain of muscular energy, erected to the glory of the archangel who struck down the dragon; it thereby makes amends for the demolition in 1781 of the 12th-century chapel of Saint-Michel, which stood across the river, next to the Sainte-Chapelle. The monument is, in fact, no more than a facing on the side wall of the first house on the block, a clever device to create a grand gateway to the Boulevard Saint-Michel without taking up any space. Its effect is rather obscured these days by the mobbish atmosphere that prevails in front of the fountain.

Walk along Boulevard Saint-Michel and turn right into rue Francisque-Gay. Ahead is a sea of colourful sun umbrellas at a central café on Place Saint-André-des-Arts; these, along with the picturesque, flowered façade of the brasserie l'Alsace à Paris on your left and the rustic low-roofed café opposite make the place look like a holiday resort. Only the name recalls the medieval church of Saint-André, where Voltaire was baptised in 1694, and which, having been closed down during the Revolution, was razed to the ground in 1808.

Turn right into Place Saint-Michel and left under the archway across the street, to enter a maze of quiet, narrow streets, with its medieval layout preserved intact. Rue de l'Hirondelle, beyond the archway, is an ancient, silent alley, ignored by passers-by, except for some youngsters on a night out, who leave graffiti on old historical houses as an act of defiance, rather as their ancestors did in the days of François Villon and Rabelais. One such historical building, n° 20/22, is now defaced and derelict, but its magnificent entrance door and the wrought-iron decoration of its façade indicate that this was once the home of a person of note. Closer scrutiny reveals a salamander sculpted in the stone and eroded by time, the emblem, you may remember, of François I. Indeed, here stood the splendid love-nest he had built for his favourite, Anne de Pisseleu, Duchesse d'Etampes. Renowned both for her radiant beauty and her wide knowledge - *"la plus belle des savants et la plus savante des belles"* - the Duchess decorated her house with beautiful tapestries and murals, thus also providing work for artists and patroniz-

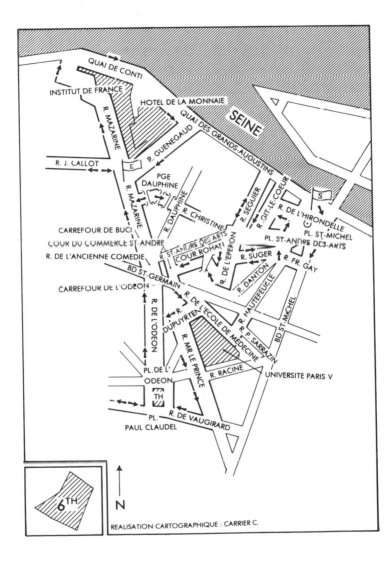

REALISATION CARTOGRAPHIQUE : CARRIER C.

ing the arts. Anne took advantage of her hold over François I to meddle in public affairs. Inevitably she made enemies, particularly among the followers of Diane de Poitiers, her most formidable foe, albeit ten years her senior. When François I introduced Diane to the court, Anne made short shrift of her, unaware that the wheel of fortune would some day turn against her. For Diane found comfort in the arms of the Dauphin, Henri, and bided her time. In 1547, after seven years of open warfare between the two women and their respective clans, François I died and the impatient Henri II came to the throne at last. The ravishing Anne was banished to the provinces, and to add insult to injury, was ordered to hand over her personal jewellery to her rival. The lascivious Venus, the emblem of the Duchesse d'Etampes, was supplanted by Diana, the virtuous goddess of the hunt, the emblem of the new favourite. In the seraglio of France almost every dog had its day: after all, in 1526 Anne had ousted Françoise de Châteaubriant, the King's then mistress, after a merciless struggle. The present house was built only in the 18th century and it is not clear whether the salamander on the façade and the other salamanders on the bas-relief in the courtyard were transferred from the original building or mere copies.

At n° 25 le Caveau de la Bolée is an old-time cabaret, where Charles Baudelaire spent many a night with his mistress Jeanne Duval. Paul Verlaine and Oscar Wilde also liked the place. Its 13th-century cellar hosts a nightly French-style cabaret show and a modern jazz quintet on Sundays, while its ground-floor back room is a stronghold of chess addicts. Turn left into rue Gît-le-Coeur, lined with some elegant old façades, notably the one at n° 12 with its wrought-iron decorations, now a well-known repertoire cinema. Turn right into rue Saint-André-des-Arts. Note the gorgeous façade at n° 27 on the right. An old bookshop at n° 37, founded in 1878, takes pride in its beautiful editions of history books and is fighting a rearguard action to perpetuate the scholarly traditions of the Latin Quarter, in the face of an invasion of T-shirts and modern paraphernalia.

Rue Séguier to your right is a drowsy, pleasant street that leads to the river. It was a stronghold of the Left Bank's nobility, who had bought out the Parisian properties of the provincial clergy. N° 3, for example, belonged to the Bishops of Lodève in the 15th century and to the Bishops of Rodez in the 16th. The Bishops of Autun and subsequently those of Laon owned the *hôtel* on the site of n° 6 in the 14th century. The *hôtel* was sold to a member of the nobility after the Hundred Years' War and in the 16th century belonged to the Duc de Nemours-Savoie. The Hôtel Séguier at n° 16 is named, like the street, after a famous magistrate who lived here in the first half of the 19th century; although between 1588 and 1672 the Séguier family had already produced a dynasty of illustrious magistrates. In the 18th century the *hôtel* had been inhabited by Madame Marigny, widow of the Pompadour's celebrated brother, who had been in charge of all the construction projects in the capital. Notice also the exquisite corner window of the antiquarian bookshop at n° 8.

Back on rue Saint-André-des-Arts, on the corner of rue de l'Eperon, the restaurant Allard is another old-timer and staunchly maintains its tradition of solid, excellent, unpretentious French cuisine. At n° 47/49 rue Saint-André-des-Arts stood the *hôtel* of Jeanne de Navarre, wife of Philippe le Bel. For several generations it remained the property of the crown and home to various members of the royal family. Later, in 1612, it was the home of Jacques de la Guesle who, in 1589, had hired Jacques Clément to assassinate Henri III. The King was sitting on his commode in his tent at the camp of Saint-Cloud, wearing nothing but his dressing-gown, when Clément burst in and stabbed him to death.

Retrace your steps and turn into rue de l'Eperon. N° 45 on the corner is the Lycée Fénelon, the first girls' lycée in Paris, which opened in 1883. Rue de l'Eperon offers charming courtyards, peace and greenery and the extra reward of the pretty vista of rue Suger, at a sharp angle on your left. At n° 1 rue Suger, Saint Louis had established the Order of the Sachettes, who were later supplanted by the Augustins, Philippe le Bel's protégés. At n° 3/5 stood a famous college founded in the 14th century, Le Collège de Doissy. Its chapel was taken over in 1770 by the Portuguese Jewish community who were timidly moving into the neighbourhood at the time and turned it into a synagogue, the first to be put into service in Paris since the Jews were expelled in 1394. Continue along this pretty street, then retrace your steps and walk along rue de l'Eperon. Turn right into rue du Jardinet, a serene and romantic alley, with its overhanging street-lamps. The best is yet to come: three successive courtyards, known as la Cour de Rohan, are perhaps the jewel in the crown of the arrondissement. Like nesting Chinese boxes, each courtyard reveals new surprises as it unfolds before your eyes. The crooked paving, the ancient well at n° 1 on your left, the cascading creepers and the rose bushes are all bound to enchant you. The third courtyard is painter's paradise with its jumble of balconies, terraces and windows of all shapes and sizes. From the centre of the shady courtyard two trees stretch up their endless, slender trunks, reaching out for the sun, then spread open their leafy branches above the roofs to offer them their shade. As you approach the exit allow your eyes to wander up over the extraordinary jumble of terraces, exploding with rose bushes, ivy and honeysuckle that climb above a white cottage with bright blue shutters. A row of rustic garrets, decked with a neat row of geraniums, completes the picture.

As you walk out of the courtyard, you will see on the cottage walls paintings of the enlightened representatives of the *Siècle de Lumière*. The great luminary, Voltaire, cut out of ply wood, has even taken up position on the pavement outside. It is all tourist kitsch but the charm works. For you have landed in the alley of the Cour-du-Commerce-Saint-André, the heart of the 18th-century Enlightenment, the stronghold of its *Philosophes*, who gathered, notably at the Procope, the very cottage in front of you, where they paved the way for the Revolution. Now that this enclave has been given a face-lift it looks rather like a Disneyland re-enactment of history but, taken with a pinch of salt, it is fun, with its colourful flags and shop signs, recreating pre-industrial street life. The cobblestones are hard on the feet but add to the atmosphere. In cold weather you could take refuge and sample the delicious pastry in a cosy British-style *salon de thé*, La Cour de Rohan, to your right. On a warm afternoon or evening, you may prefer the out-door terrace of a turn-of-a-century bistro to your left, cheerfully surrounded by bright geraniums. There is also a 'pub' with a miscellany of 'Revolutionary' ref-erences and a British touch. Here history is celebrated by way of a cocktail drink dubbed 'the guillotine' in a setting evocative of old tavern days. A guillotine, of questionable humour, is displayed on its awning. If you are after history in a big way, then the Procope is your place. It does not serve outstanding fare, but there is an entire history lesson posted in its windows, recording that here Robespierre and the Montagnards met on the eve of the Revolution, Benjamin Franklin draft-ed the alliance between Louis XVI and the new American republic, playwright Piron quarrelled with Voltaire and Voltaire conceived here *Candide*. Few passers-by stop to read the information, as the street is full of other distractions – a crêperie to the right, savouries from Auvergne to the left, Nadaud's splash con-temporary furniture opposite and music-making on rue Saint-André-des-Arts. Who has time to delve into history?

Yet the Cour-du-Commerce-Saint-André is history itself! All the more so, since it was opened in 1776, when the feverish intellectual turmoil in Paris reached its peak. The Boulevard Saint-Germain did not, of course, exist at the time, and the passageway, lined with picturesque stalls and two long lanes for playing *boules*, continued as far as the southern pavement of Boulevard Saint-Germain, now Car-refour de l'Odéon. Most of the houses still date back to that year and will be of particular meaning to the American visitor, whose early history is so tied up with that of France. A century later the famous writer and literary critic Sainte-Beuve occupied two rooms on the first floor at n° 2, then a lodging hotel. On 28 May 1871, following a week of bloody fighting, which ended with the defeat of the *Commune*, one of its famous leaders, Jules Vallès, took refuge in Sainte-Beuve's apartment disguised as a male nurse. A tower of the famous walls of Philippe-Auguste is encompassed within the premises of n° 4, rising all the way up to the roof - a formidable construction indeed! N°s 8 and 9 particularly are connected with the historic days of the Revolution. N° 8 was the printing-shop where Marat published his paper *l'Ami du Peuple*, which, contrary to its benign name, was a vindictive sheet advocating wholesale despoilment and executions and demand-ing the heads of 270,000 enemies of the homeland, above all the *Girondins*.

Marat and his companion Marie-Simone Evrard had sold all their possessions to raise funds for their publication, while the Revolutionary authorities provided them with the premises and secured them with a double gate. N° 9, the workshop of the German carpenter Schmidt, was the place where in April 1792, Dr Louis Guillotin first put into practice his theories about the guillotine by experimenting on live sheep. For a while now he had been cogitating a decapitation device that would speed up executions. In October 1789, at the National Assembly, Dr Guillotin had already suggested a new, more efficient mode of execution, a proposition rejected at the time. "The blade whistles," he had told the Assembly, "the head falls, the blood gushes forth, the man is no more - with my machine I shall make your heads topple off in a flash and you will feel but a light breeze on your necks." His description was greeted by an uproar of laughter. But by 1792 mass executions of the enemies of the *patrie* were envisaged and on 25 March Dr Louis, the permanent secretary of the Academy of Surgery, was commissioned to carry out Guillotin's project. Things moved fast now: after its first experiment on the Cour-du-Commerce-Saint-André, which proved a success, the machine was tried on three dead bodies at the hospital of Bicêtre (in the 13th arr.) on 17 April. By 25 April '*Louison*' or '*Louisette*' (the early name of the machine, which honoured Dr Louis, an injustice soon remedied), was ready for the first public execution on Place de Grève. The victim was Jacques Pelletier, condemned for assault and theft. Meanwhile a mechanic by the name of Guillot was working on a more sophisticated machine, equipped with nine blades, that would allow the simultaneous decapitation of nine convicts, but his device, which was tried out the following year, was not quite ready to function. Thus, in an amateurish way, the French Revolution was already working covertly on the use of science and technology for murderous ends on a mass scale. Like some Moloch, the guillotine devoured indiscriminately the makers and the opponents of those dark days; even the neck of Dr Guillotin was condemned to the philanthropic blade he had invented and offered to France, and was spared only by the timely downfall of Robespierre.

Walk as far as Boulevard Saint-Germain and cross over. The statue of Danton at Carrefour de l'Odéon marks the site of Danton's home at what used to be n° 20 Cour-du-Commerce-Saint-André before the opening of Boulevard Saint-Germain. Danton had been living there since 1789 when, on 30 March 1794, the police burst into his large first-floor flat with a warrant for his arrest. Six days later he stepped on to the guillotine. Across the street, where now is n° 20 rue de l'Ecole-de-Médecine, stood the house of Marat, where he lived with his companion, Marie-Simone Evrard. It was a couple of minutes' walk to his printing-shop but of late, owing to some skin disease, he had been less active and spent several hours a day in his bathtub. At noon on 11 July 1793 a 25-year-old woman, arriving by coach from Caen in Normandy, alighted in Paris and went straight away to the Hôtel de la Providence, now on rue Hérold south-east of Place des Victoires (in the 1st arr.). Charlotte de Corday as she turned out to be, was a descendant of a sister of the playwright Pierre Corneille and an admirer of the *Girondins*. On July 13, she visited Marat's house and left a letter requesting to be received on a serious matter concerning France, after which she headed for Palais-Royal, where, at 177 Galerie de Valois, she bought a carving knife from Monsieur Badin for 2 francs. She then proceeded to her hotel, had dinner and then took a carriage back to Marat's house. Marie-Simone Evrard, however, would not let her in, but the determined Charlotte would not take no for an answer and, having returned to her hotel room, wrote Marat a second letter and returned to his house once more. Again Simone barred her way and the voices rose. Marat could hear them from his bathtub and interceded in favour of the visitor. Without a word, Charlotte went into his room, walked straight towards the bathtub, stabbed Marat right through his neck and down into his lungs, then pulled out the knife, laid it on the shelf and waited. She came to trial three days later, on 16 July, the day of Marat's funeral, when his embalmed body was carried through the streets of Paris alongside with his bathtub. Questioned about her deed, Charlotte Corday said: "I have not killed a man but a ferocious beast." The next day she was condemned to the guillotine and accepted her fate calmly, thanking her lawyer Chauveau-Lagarde (who was also to defend Marie-Antoinette) and asking him to pay her hotel bill.

Continue into rue de l'Ecole-de-Médecine, named after the school of surgery that stood at n° 5. 'The fraternity of surgeons in long robes' and the 'fraternity of surgeons in short robes' (i.e. barbers) were founded in the reign of Saint Louis and took up residence here. Surgery, being a manual activity, was separated from medicine till the middle of the 18th century. Indeed, although surgeons were educated members of society and barbers often illiterate, the two were considered of the same essence and were actually merged into a single fraternity in 1656, a merger that lasted nearly a hundred years. In 1691 they were given permission to build their anatomy amphitheatre, which still exists today, though at present it is used by the English department of the University of Paris III. When the school expanded, it was transferred across the street to n° 12, where there was more space. On 26 December 1774 Louis XVI laid the cornerstone of the new academy.

Across the street, inside the courtyard of n° 15-21 on your left (also part of the present school of medicine), stands the Gothic 15th-century dining-hall of the convent of the Cordoliers, the only vestige of that renowned order - or of any other order for that matter - to have survived in these parts. The Cordoliers, so called after the ropes they tied around their grey gowns, were founded in Italy by Saint Francis of Assisi and were one of the four great begging orders, even though they were in no want at all! Rather, they established a reputation as heavy, merry drinkers, but also for scholastic excellence. Enjoying the support of both the King and the Pope, they managed to hold their own against the rival University. Their church was one of the largest in the capital (100 by 30 metres) and deemed prestigious enough to pay host to Jeanne de Navarre, wife of Philippe le Bel. During the Revolution the convent was used as a gathering-place of the Club des Cordoliers, founded by Camille Desmoulins and frequented by the likes of Danton and Marat; here on 14 July 1791 these two were the first to demand the deposition of the King. Today this attractive and historic building, although in serious need of extensive restoration, is used for temporary exhibitions.

Cross over into rue Hautefeuille to your left. At n° 21, a charming 16th-century turret at the corner of rue Pierre-Sarrazin, evokes the medieval past of the neighbourhood. Not a trace is left, however, of the Jewish cemetery that in the Middle Ages occupied the site now bounded by Boulevard Saint-Germain, Boulevard Saint-Michel, rue Pierre-Sarrazin and rue Hautefeuille. The cemetery was closed down in 1306, when Philippe le Bel expelled the Jews, and its grounds were given to the Dominican Order. During the construction of the bookshop on the corner of Boulevard Saint-Germain and Boulevard Saint-Michel, in the middle of the 19th century, some of its 12th- and 13th-century tombstones were unearthed, which bore Hebrew inscriptions of the names of the deceased, sometimes also their occupation and their date of birth and/or death. In all likelihood more tombstones are lying under the buildings of the Boulevards, carrying the secret of an ancient community.

Retrace your steps and turn back into rue de l'Ecole-de-Médecine, left into rue Dupuyrten and left again into rue Monsieur-le-Prince, once known as rue des Fossés-Monsieur-le-Prince because it runs on the site of the old moat of Philippe-Auguste's walls. If the door at n° 45 is not locked, you may walk through the building to the back yard to see a chunk of the walls, now the back wall of the yard. During the Revolution the street was renamed rue de la Liberté; Monsieur le Prince, after all, was the great Prince de Condé, the staunch enemy of the Revolution. Note the magnificent Louis XV portal at n° 14, home, in the 19th century, to the French composer Saint-Saëns and, closer to us, to the Black American writer Richard Wright, who wrote *Black Boy* here and in 1959 was visited by Martin Luther King, Jr. At n° 41, the Polidor restaurant, once a 'canteen' frequented by James Joyce, still offers genuine, homely French cuisine served by genuine French waitresses, in genuine, unpretentious surroundings, all for a reasonable price. Most of the clients, however, are tourists avidly seeking local colour, while their local fellow beings are likely to be in a Tex-Mex or other such establishment. Opposite Polidor, at n° 22, is a charming 18th-century courtyard, shaded by a chestnut tree in the centre and surrounded by some artists' studios. A couple of sculptures add a further charming touch to this nook. There is another exquisite courtyard at n° 48, this time with a cherry tree, a rarity in Paris, and a profusion of ivy on the walls and busy lizzies on the ground. A charming, very narrow Louis XVI façade at n° 65 displays three allegorical sculptures of the Seasons. Spring, surprisingly rather than winter, was left out for lack of space.

Retrace your steps and turn right into rue de Vaugirard, which lay beyond Philippe-Auguste's city wall. A *jeu de paume*, Le Jeu de Paume de Bel-Air, was situated at n° 7-13, but by 1672 the game had lost its popularity, which enabled Lully to take over its vacant premises and move his opera here from rue Mazarine. At a time of fierce rivalry between theatre troupes, Lully, more than anyone, knew how to manoeuvre into prominence and gain a monopoly in his field. The following year he succeeded in ousting his dangerous competitor, le Théatre du Marais, which had been performing embryonic operas with spectacular machinery since 1647, and had been the craze of the town.

We now come to the beautiful Théâtre de l'Odéon at Place Paul-Claudel, overlooking the Luxembourg Gardens, but best appreciated from the main entrance at Place de l'Odéon, where it stands on its own in the middle of a semicircle, closing the elegant vista of rue de l'Odéon - a rare example of regal town planning in this part of Paris, surpassed only by the Palais du Luxembourg and the approach to it from rue de Tournon. No medieval heritage obstructed the architects in this area, which had been covered before 1774 by the magnificent grounds of the Prince de Condé's palace. The Place de l'Odéon is where the estate's impeccably tended garden *à la française* was then. Finding a permanent home for the *Comédiens du Roi* had become a crucial issue. For generations they had been packing up and transferring from one *jeu de paume* to the next because no church would have them on its parish. Their main sin was, of course, that their entertainment appealed to the parishioners more than anything the church could offer. As the priest of Saint-Germain-l'Auxerrois put it, "from the theatre one would have heard the organs, and from the church the violins." Eventually the troupe found shelter on rue de l'Ancienne-Comédie, where they stayed for nearly a century, but by 1770 their dilapidated premises had become a menace and the construction of a new building a necessity. Because the new theatre was erected in an unbuilt neighbourhood, special attention could be paid to the layout of the streets leading to the theatre, both to avoid congestion and on aesthetic grounds. The nature-loving Louis XVI, who came to the throne in 1774, deliberately chose a spot close to the Luxembourg Gardens so that "our subjects, before entering or upon leaving the show at the Comédie-Française, will have a place of promenade nearby, in the garden of Luxembourg." Wishing it to be a prestigious place, the King insisted it be built in the purest Classical style, emulating that of Greece, the cradle of Western theatre; it was also the largest theatre in the capital, holding 1913 seats, and the first to be lit by oil lamps. Likewise its architectural environment was carefully worked out, notably the style of the façades and the height of the buildings along the newly opened streets, so as to create an overall, elegant harmony. The streets in their turn were named after the great playwrights of France - Corneille and Molière (now Routrou) on either side of the building, Racine, Voltaire (now Casimir-Delavigne), Crébillon and Regnard fanning out on either side of the central artery, which itself was appropriately named rue du Théâtre-Français (now Odéon). This was a regal artery indeed, the first street in Paris to have pavements and gutters. An archway was built on either side of the theatre, over rue Corneille and rue Molière, to protect spectators and actors on rainy nights. The theatre hall was beautifully painted in light blue and white and, for the first time in France, benches were put in so that the less affluent members of the audience no longer had to stand through the performance.

The theatre was inaugurated on 9 April 1782 and two years later, on 26 April 1784, the subversive *Marriage of Figaro*, for which its author, Beaumarchais, had been sent to prison a year earlier, brought the house down. The Théâtre-Français was heading for a long career, or so it seemed if one failed to make allowance for the mounting progress of the Revolution, to which Beaumarchais himself had contributed by questioning the validity and immutability of the social order. Thus the Théâtre Français lasted only seven years... The Revolution led to splits and to the departure, among others, of the great Talma. Those actors and actresses who remained faithful to the royal troupe found themselves in prison and the theatre was closed down altogether between 1793 and 1794. A shaky period followed and in 1797, it was renamed the Odéon, after the musical theatre of ancient Greece. In 1799, however, it burnt down altogether and remained an abandoned ruin for eight entire years. By the time Chalgrin had restored the building in 1807, France was ruled by an emperor and when the theatre opened the following year, it was renamed after France's empress. Partly damaged by another fire in 1818, it was again reopened in 1819, restored to such glory that some considered it the most beautiful theatre in Paris, and second in France only to the theatre Victor Louis had built for Bordeaux.

The first half of the century was a time of hardship for the theatre despite the collaboration it received from the greatest actors of the time, including Frédérick Lemaître, Mlle George, Marie Dorval and Agar. Twice it had to close down. In 1862, the arrival of Sarah Bernhardt, freshly out of the Conservatoire and breaking loose from conservative traditions, gave it a boost, which culminated in 1872 when she took the lead role of the Queen in Victor Hugo's *Ruy Blas*. Ten years later Paul Porel, the theatre's director during the 1880s, also explored new paths and made the Odéon one of the best theatres in Paris. In 1884/5 *L'Arlésienne* with music by Bizet and libretto by Alphonse Daudet, brought the house down and over the next 15 years became the theatre's 'lifeline'. Poor Bizet, who died in 1875, was never to enjoy this triumph: both *l'Arlésienne* and his masterpiece *Carmen* were total flops at their first performances in 1872 and 1875 respectively. When the anti-conformist, avant-garde Antoine took over in 1906, he tried to remove the dust from the dark, severe 'antique vessel' by introducing young writers, such as Jules Romains and Georges Duhamel. However, Antoine never overcame financial difficulties and despite very warm reception of *Psyche* in 1914, he could not break even and submitted his resignation. In more recent years Samuel Beckett's *Waiting for Godot*, with the historic staging of Roger Blin and Beckett's *Oh, the Beautiful Days*, with its heart-rending interpretations by Madeleine Renaud and Jean-Louis Barrault, were unforgettable events. Having been involved politically in the 1968 student revolt, these two great actors and their troupe were exiled from the Latin Quarter and were allocated temporarily the old railway station of Orsay. When the station was turned into a museum, the couple packed up once more, crossed the Seine and settled near the Champs-Elysées in what used to be the fashionable ice-rink of Paris. By knocking about like this, they re-enacted the peripatetic life their colleagues led 300 years earlier. Today, in keeping with the historical evolution of our continent, the theatre plays host to visiting European troupes and has consequently been renamed Théâtre d'Europe.

The surroundings of the theatre are quiet these days, unlike in the 19th century when they were cluttered with bookstalls and newspaper stands, where papers could be rented for two hours to be read in the Luxembourg Gardens, and when letter-writers sold their skills to the less literate. Opposite the theatre, at n° 2 Place de l'Odéon, the terrace of the Méditerranée is an inviting setting for a fish meal, especially at night, when the theatre is beautifully illuminated. The aesthete Jean Cocteau appreciated the setting too and frequented the terrace in the 1950s. In return, the grateful establishment has used his drawings as decorations for its china. Camille Desmoulins had been living with his young wife Lucile on the second floor of the same building, when the emissaries of the Terror came to arrest him on 30 March 1794. Both husband and wife ended up on the guillotine. Until 1956 the Café Voltaire stood at n° 1 Place de l'Odéon, a stronghold of the intelligentsia in the 19th century, frequented among others by Eugène Delacroix and Alfred de Musset, later by political leaders such as Jules Vallès and Gambetta, who could be seen here smoking his pipe, still later by Paul Gauguin, Auguste Renoir, Paul Verlaine and Stéphane Mallarmé, and in due course André Gide, Paul Valéry and Léon-Paul Fargue. Before leaving Place de l'Odéon, take a last look towards rue Crébillon - named after a long-forgotten playwright - where an exquisite rustic house at n° 6 now shelters a charming café.

Walk down rue de l'Odéon. At n° 7, in her bookshop 'La Maison des Amis du Livre', Adrienne Monnier received and gave support to her writer friends Paul

Valéry, Paul Claudel and André Gide, among others. Emulating her French friend, the American Sylvia Beach in 1921 opened a bookshop across the street, at n° 12, the celebrated Shakespeare and Company. Here the 'lost generation' met - T.S. Eliot, Ezra Pound, Scott Fitzgerald, Sinclair Lewis, Sherwood Anderson, Hemingway - and of course James Joyce, whose *Ulysses* was first published here in 1922 thanks to the faith and energy of Ms Beach. Ms Beach had to close down during the Nazi occupation and in 1942 went into hiding in a students' hostel at n° 93 Boulevard Saint-Michel, (in the 5th arr.) which still exists.

Continue across Boulevard Saint-Germain and into rue de l'Ancienne-Comédie, on the site of the moat of the city walls, hence its previous name of rue des Fossés-Saint-Germain. Its present name commemorates the seat of the Comédie-Française, which was at n° 14, where a plaque reads, *Comédiens ordinaires du Roi de 1689 à 1770*. Here too the troupe had taken over an old *jeu de paume*, Le Jeu de Paume de l'Etoile, and replaced it with a magnificent theatre, sloping up elegantly from the stalls like an amphitheatre and lit by chandeliers. The drab façade of the present modern building corresponds roughly to the site of the curtain, and the courtyard to the stalls. An inscription on top of the façade reads, *La Comédie Française*. On the street façade is preserved Le Hongre's haut-relief of Minerva, tracing what she can see in the mirror of truth, just as Molière held out a mirror to his spectators to reflect their flawed nature. For nearly a hundred years all the great playwrights of the 17th and 18th centuries were represented here - Molière, Racine and Corneille, obviously, followed by Marivaux, Beaumarchais, Voltaire, Crébillon, Piron, Regnard, Rousseau, Diderot. Their works were performed by no less an impressive list of actresses and actors - Madame Dancourt, Armande-Béjart, Adrienne Lecouvreur, and their male counterparts, Poisson, Quinault, Grandval and Le Kain. In 1759 Henri-Louis Le Kain managed to get the three rows of benches encircling the stage removed: these had been habitually occupied by insufferable members of the fashionable set, pompous minor marquis who would exasperate the performers with their silly commentaries and incessant chatter.

At n° 13 is the main entrance to the Procope: its location just across the street from the Comédie-Française was the key to its fortune. Of course it had attractions of its own, the proximity of the *jeu de paume* (it was only replaced by the theatre five years later), the *boules* lanes in its back yard (now Cour-du-Commerce-Saint-André); but neither these nor the new sensational beverage introduced by Monsieur Procope (i.e. coffee), would have sufficed to create such long-standing success. When the troupe moved across the street, the Procope became the meeting-place of actors and playwrights and the socialites who came to see them, in other words, the showcase of the Comédie-Française. It was also the dreaded court of judgment where a playwright's reputation was made or demolished. In the 18th century it became the laboratory of ideological experiments that would lead to the French Revolution and the mean battlefield of personal confrontations (in which sharp-tongued Voltaire excelled in particular), the verbal scandal sheet of Paris. Above all, it was here that the compilation of the monumental *Encyclopédie* which was initiated by d'Alembert and Diderot. With the break up of the Revolution it was the turn of a new generation of men of action to take over, a convenient place as they often lived around the corner. It seems that some major assaults were launched by them from here in 1792, before this branch of the Revolution was chopped off. It is also believed that the Phrygian cap of the *sans-culottes*, so called after the cap worn by the enfranchised slaves of ancient Rome, made its first appearance here, worn by Citizen Julien.

In the 19th century the Procope remained the rendezvous of literati - Musset, George Sand, Balzac, Théophile Gautier came here in the first half of the century, Gambetta during the Second Empire, when he braved the law and began to smoke here his eternal pipe! Later still, Verlaine would be seen here drinking absinth. By then, however, it had become a private literary circle. New centres of gatherings had opened in the city, predominantly on the Right Bank, and the establishment went out of fashion. In 1890 the Procope closed down and landed eventually in the hands of the Assistance Publique. When it reopened timidly in 1952, Voltaire's table, which had served as a votive altar for the author's own ashes, and for the ashes of Marat and Le Peletier de Saint-Fargeau, did not suffice to restore the establishment its past prestige. After keeping afloat through several decades a new management took it over in 1988: by sprinkling it with some tourist kitsch, they have so far given it a new lease on life.

You will now arrive at the bustling, colourful Carrefour de Buci, bursting with flower stalls, once the bustling site of the city gate, the Porte de Buci. Continue into rue Mazarine, with its many bookshops and art galleries. Ahead is the lovely dome of the Institut de France. Turn right into Passage Dauphine, a charming haven paved with uneven cobblestones. A well-known language school has taken up residence here, and also a cosy *salon de thé* which serves delicious pastry. Rue Dauphine, at the end of the alley, commemorates the Dauphin and future Louis XIII and was opened by Henri IV. It is a continuation of the bridge of Pont-Neuf and Place Dauphine next to it. The Augustine monks protested that the new street would encroach on their grounds, but Henri IV was a man of vision in terms of town planning and refused to bend, saying he would use his guns to carry his project through, if he had to. In any case, he argued, the monks would draw an incomparably greater income from the houses along the new street than they did from their cabbage-beds. History proved him right: on the eve of the Revolution their order was one of the wealthiest in the capital. Rue Dauphine was one of the most elegant arteries in the capital, especially after 1763 when it was the first to substitute oil lamps to candles. Rue Christine, the continuation of Passage Dauphine, was named after the second daughter of Henri IV and Marie de Medici and is likewise lined with 17th-century houses. The one at n° 3 is now one of the best hotels on the Left Bank, the splendid Relais Christine, with its elegant courtyard in front and beautiful garden at the back, according to the canons of those days. Opposite the hotel is one of the best-known repertoire cinemas in the capital, magnet for lovers of classic films.

Retrace your steps into rue Mazarine and turn right. At the pretty corner of rue Jacques-Callot is the colourful terrace of the Mazarine bistro on the site of Le Jeu de Paume de la Bouteille, converted into a theatre in the 17th century, like so many others. A plaque on the wall tells us that this was the cradle of the opera, where the genre was first performed on 16 March 1671. The opera in question was *Pomone*, composed by Lully. On 28 June 1669 the King had given Lully's partner, l'abbé Perrin, official permission to perform operas and the year 1669 is still marked on the curtain of the opera house, although the Théâtre du Marais had already initiated the genre in the 1660s. Lully was soon to quarrel with Perrin and oust him; on 15 November 1672, he moved the opera to the Jeu de Paume du Bel-Air at 7-13 rue de Vaugirard, visited earlier. When Molière died the following year, the King ordered the merger of his troupe and that of the Marais on these vacated premises, which now became known as the Théâtre de Guénégaud. In 1680 the troupe of the Hôtel de Bourgogne was ordered to join them. From then on there was only one French troupe in Paris, La Comédie Française as it was renamed, which makes this site its cradle too. However, in 1687 the troupe was ordered to pack up yet again, this time under the pressure of the University, vexed by their presence next to the newly-founded Collège des Quatre-Nations. Fortunately, they found a new home on the present rue de l'Ancienne-Comédie. Rue Jacques-Callot replaced the alley that led to the theatre. Today it is full of charm, with slender lampposts and pleasant greenery. It is hard to believe that just over a century ago it was a dingy slum, described by Emile Zola in *Thérèse Raquin* as *"suant toujours d'une humidité âcre"* ("oozing with acrid dampness"), an aspect confirmed in Henri Mürger's *La Vie de Bohême*. N° 28 rue Mazarine was the home of Champollion where on 14 September 1822 he made his breakthrough discovery of the principle of deciphering Egyptian hieroglyphs. In 1944 the famous poet Robert Desnos was living across the street, at n° 19, when he was arrested and deported. He died in Theresienstadt (now Terezin in the Czech Republic) in 1945, on the eve of the liberation of the camp. Another *jeu de paume*, Les Métayers, was situated further up the street, on the site of n° 10/14. This was where the 21-year-old actor Poquelin opened L'Illustre Théâtre in 1643. He had just assumed the name of Molière by which he would become world-famous. His modest troupe of amateurs included four members of the Béjart family, Madeleine Béjart, who became his companion, being the only one of great talent. The rectangular premises (12m x 31m), the conventional setting of a *jeu de paume* were preserved and consequently the walls were painted black. The hall was 18m long, the stage 9 and the backstage 4. As you approach the Seine, rue Mazarine makes a sharp bend to the left, following the course of the counterscarp path of the city walls, which had to skirt the Hôtel de Nesle that stood alongside the river, roughly on the site of the present Institut de France.

The medieval Hôtel de Nesle was second to none, except perhaps to the Louvre on the opposite bank, the home of Jean, Duc de Berry and of his fabulous illuminated manuscript, *Les Très Riches Heures du duc de Berry*, his world-famous Book of Hours. The original defence tower had been erected around 1220 by Philippe Hamelin, the Provost of Paris, and was therefore known as the Tour Hamelin. A gate was soon added to the walls, roughly 30 m to the south, on the site of the present entrance to the Mazarine Library of the Institut de France (n° 23 quai de Conti). A plan on the façade of the eastern wing of the Institut de France indicates the precise location of the tower and gate. When later Simon de Clermont, the Lord of Nesle, built a palace next to them, they became known respectively as La Tour and La Porte de Nesle.

From 1308 on, when Philippe le Bel had bought the palace, it became the residence of various members of the royal family. Its waterside location, though pleasing, made it vulnerable to flooding and it therefore was provided with the first *quai* in the city (now quai de Conti), which was built in 1313 by Etienne Barbette, the road surveyor of Paris. Philippe le Bel's three sons, the future Louis X, Philippe V and Charles IV, married respectively Marguerite, Jeanne and Blanche de Bourgogne (the latter two were sisters and cousins of Marguerite). All three resided in the palace and seem to have used its tower for their amorous liaisons. One day, however, their sister-in-law Isabelle, Philippe le Bel's daughter and wife of Edward II of England, noticed three gentlemen wearing the three purses she had given the three princesses as gifts. Needless to dwell on the scandal that ensued, nor to enumerate the list the tortures inflicted on two of the lovers (which included, of course, castration) before they were finally decapitated and hanged by the armpits to be devoured by birds of prey. Marguerite and Blanche were shaved and dispatched to languish at the Château-Gaillard of Andelys (on route to Normandy), while Jeanne was locked up in the castle of Dourdan, south-west of Paris. Blanche was later forced to take the veil, Marguerite was suffocated between two mattresses by order of her husband Louis X, who wished to remarry, but Jeanne was offered the beautiful Hôtel de Nesle by her loving husband, Philippe V, who, moreover, generously passed away in 1322, leaving Jeanne free to lead a life of merry widowhood for the next seven years. Was she the queen who, as Brantôme wrote three centuries later, used to watch out from the tower for passers-by and, having sent for them and exhausted their sexual potency, had them tied up in sacks and precipitated from the top of the tower into the water to drown? Brantôme could not confirm this allegation but added that most Parisians believed the story to be true. Which is already corroborated by François Villon two centuries earlier who, in his moving poem *Ballade des dames du temps jadis* (1461), evokes the queen who ordered Buridan to be thrown in a sack into the Seine:

> *Semblablement où est la royne*
> *Qui commanda que Buridan*
> *Fust jecté en ung sacq en Seyne?*
> (Similarly where is the queen/Who ordered Buridan/To
> be thrown in a sack into the Seine?)

Buridan, who is supposed to have been her lover during those seven years and to have escaped death by falling on a boat loaded with hay, later became the rector of the University of Paris and outlived Jeanne by 30 years. The rival he injured subsequently, when he was involved in another liaison, later became Pope Clément VI.

From 1380 on, when Charles V's brother, Jean, Duc de Berry, settled here, the palace had its hour of glory, thanks entirely to the great culture and taste of the Duke. Across a dead arm of the Seine to the west, he built a lovely bridge with five harmonious arches, to link the *hôtel* with a new dwelling, Le Séjour de Nesle (on the site of today's Square Honoré Champion), a bejewelled fairytale palace, with four corner turrets topped with 'pepper-box' roofs, as witness old engravings. No wonder the victorious Duke of Bedford requisitioned it for his most eminent guests. Its fortunes declined in the course of the Hundred Years' War and Henri II ended up selling it. A century later, Mazarin's Collège des Quatre-Nations stood on its site as reported earlier, as well as an impressive library, where Mazarin's private collection was kept and which was open to the public twice a week. Louis Le Vau, to whom we owe most of the Ile Saint-Louis and much of the renovation of the Louvre, made this a magnificent monument indeed, with a chapel, topped by a dome, underneath which Mazarin's tomb was placed, and framed by two curving wings overlooking the Seine along the quai de Conti. 24 shops opened under the arcades, with astounding window displays of books, engravings, paintings, silverware and objets d'art, making this a mecca for discerning visitors, both French and foreign (mainly English) up to the Revolution. Among them Laurence Sterne who came to Paris in 1762 and 1765 and came to the quai de Conti under guise of clergyman Yorick, to browse in a bookshop, as he tells us in *A Sentimental Journey.* Four years later the Café Anglais opened at n° 1 the quai de Conti in 1769 to cater for his fellow countrymen. A place of literary gatherings, its patrons would find here their English papers, such as the *London Evening Post*, the *Westminster Gazette* or the *Daily Adviser*, sent over from the homeland.

With the build-up of terror in 1793, the premises were converted into a prison, where such respectable citizens as the historian Michaud, the painter David and Dr Guillotin were locked up together with 650 other prisoners. Under the chapel's dome now gathered the members of the dreaded *Comité du Salut Public*, in charge of the bloody purification of the *patrie*. Mazarin's mausoleum was naturally removed from the site, but was rescued by the archaeologist Alexandre Lenoir and transferred to his Musée des Monuments Français, where it went on display as an example of the work of the sculptor Coysevox. In 1806 the five Academies were transferred here from the Louvre to make up the Institut de France, and the chapel now became its hall. During its recent restoration, Mazarin's mausoleum regained its place under the dome, where it unquestionably belongs - partisan allegiance aside - if only for being the founder of the Institut's library, which now owns 350,000 volumes and thousands of manuscripts.

Next to the Institut de France, to the east, stands the elegant, stark building of the Monnaie, stunningly beautiful from across the river, particularly when illuminated at night. Commissioned by Louis XV in 1768, it was the work of a yet-unknown young mason and son of a carpenter, Jacques-Denis Antoine, who won the competition for the best design. It was built on the site of Mansart's Hôtel Guénégaud, said at the time to be the most splendid dwelling in the city. Unlike the present building, it ran perpendicularly to the river, its main entrance overlooking the future Collège des Quatre-Nations. Behind was a garden extending all the way to rue de Guénégaud, with fountains and beds of flower; in spring the air was filled with the fragrance of orange blossoms. Henri de Guénégaud had supported Louis XIV and Mazarin during the *Fronde* and could therefore afford to surround himself with luxury without giving offence to the King. In this splendid setting, Boileau and Racine gave readings of their early works and the opera *Pomone* was rehearsed here before its opening in the neighbouring Théâtre de Guénégaud in 1671. Mazarin's niece, widow of the Prince de Conti, exchanged her own mansion on quai Malaquais, further west, with the Hôtel de Guénégaud some time later, but the most illustrious member of the Conti family, who inherited it in the 18th century, had little interest in the place, especially after 1750 when he was appointed Grand Prior of the Temple, where he led a life of independence; so he sold it to the city's authorities who intended to move there from the Hôtel de Ville but then decided otherwise. The royal authorities, attracted by its convenient location, bought it from the city in 1758 to build a new mint, urgently needed in a fast-growing economy. It took, however, nearly 20 years to carry through the scheme. The present Mint is at Pessac near Bordeaux, but there is still very valuable metal stored here and security thus remains tight. The workshops can be visited on Mondays and Wednesdays between 2.15 and 3 pm only, but the coin museum, which has displays going back to the Merovingian kings in the 6th century, and the shop can be visited during normal daytime. The entrance to the shop is on rue Guénégaud.

SAINT-GERMAIN-DES-PRÉS

Our next walk leads us through the streets that lay west of the medieval city walls: modern Saint-Germain-des-Prés, undoubtedly one of the most desirable neighbourhoods in Paris, combining the charm of secluded nooks with a stunning proliferation of art galleries, interior decorators' shops, antique shops, ethnic arts and crafts shops, specialized and antiquarian bookshops, designers' clothes shops and others still, always on the arty side, always stylish and tasteful.

Begin on rue de Seine, behind the Institut de France. The attractive fountain at the junction of the two streets was designed by Evariste Fragonard, son of the famous painter. Across the street from the Institut de France was situated Queen Margot's early 17th-century palace, the entrance of which was at the present n° 6 rue de Seine. The refined, ravishing and highly cultivated Queen had been married against her will, aged 19, to her poor, provincial cousin, the loud-mouthed, coarse Henri, King of Navarre and soon to become Henri IV of France. It was a marriage she could tolerate only because they each went their own way. However, whereas the King's tumultuous love life was accepted, especially in his younger days, her own (which had begun when she was 11) created a scandal. Her mother, Catherine de Medici, used to say that "heaven had given her Margot to atone for her sins", and her brothers - three successive kings of France - François II, Charles IX and Henri III - were downright outraged. In 1583 Henri III created a scandal in the middle of a ball at the Louvre, when he showered insults on his sister and loudly recited the list of her lovers, after which he had her arrested and searched. In 1587, under the pressure of the court, Henri IV banished her to a *château* in the heart of France, an exile that lasted 18 years, during which time she consoled herself in the arms of those available. She also used her time to write her exciting *Memoirs*. Margot agreed to the annulment of her marriage so long as she could retain the title of Queen, even though it left Henri IV free to marry his favourite, Gabrielle d'Estrées ("that determined whore"). Fortunately the marriage was averted by Gabrielle's premature death in 1599, thus sparing the court a scandal (the royal code of ethics forbade outsiders in the nuptial bed) and another civil war, inevitable in the light of the number of illegitimate sons Henri IV had already scattered around the kingdom. The people of Paris saw in the death of Gabrielle d'Estrées the hand of God and the following year, despite certain rumblings of opposition, the marriage of Henri and Margot was annulled and Henri IV married Marie de Medici, by whom he had a legitimate heir to the throne, the future Louis XIII, who would perpetuate the nascent Bourbon dynasty. Margot remained Queen.

In 1605, she celebrated her 52nd birthday and her family thought it was safe to allow her back into the capital; but where would she reside? She had bought from the University a stretch of land along the Seine, all the way to rue des Saints-Pères, on the medieval enclave of the Pré-aux-Clercs, opposite her beloved Louvre, where she had spent her childhood. She had also bought the land beyond rue des Saints-Pères (now in the 7th arr.), and turned it into an exquisite garden, *le jardin de la Reine Marguerite*, which she graciously opened to the public. The palace itself was under construction and would not be ready for occupation for some time, so the Archbishop of Sens offered her the magnificent Hôtel de Sens in the Marais as a temporary home. Margot moved here from the in 1606, after a spectacular double love affair - proving her family wrong - which ended with the bloody death of both suitors. She spent here the last nine years of her life, a time of intermingled love, entertainment, culture and religious devotion, which left her riddled with debts. Louis XIII, to whom she had bequeathed her estate, had to sell it in order to pay them off. The estate was sliced up, altered and reconstructed over the years, which accounts for the presence of a 17th-century *hôtel* at the back of the courtyard of n° 6, postdating her death.

This end of rue de Seine and the streets that run out of it are lined with art galleries because of the proximity of the Ecole des Beaux-Arts. The painter Rosa Bonheur opened an art school for girls, at n° 10 bis rue de Seine, which still existed in 1910, ten years after her death. Across the street, at n° 13, was another entrance to the Jeu de Paume des Métayers. Turn right into rue des Beaux-Arts, created in 1824 on the former estate of Queen Margot to give access to the Beaux-Arts school ahead. This street too has many art galleries, the most famous being Albert Loeb's at n° 12; his father, Pierre, was one of the most renowned art dealers in Paris before World War I. Another famous dealer, Claude Bernard, at n° 9, sells the works of top-flight artists such as Giacometti, Bacon, Balthus and Hockney. The artists of the 1950s are represented by Patrice Trigano at n° 4. In the 19th century the sculptor Pradier lived at n° 4, writer Gérard de Nerval at n° 5 and the editor François Buloz at n° 6. Buloz's name is little known but his *Revue des Deux-Mondes*, with its characteristic salmon-coloured binding, was the most important literary magazine of the 19th century. Anatole France, in his autobiography, mentions this "hive of ideas" situated "in an out-of-the-way nook of faubourg Saint-Germain", where "everyone wrote, sang, philosophized and discoursed haphazardly, some for the glory of it, the greater number for pleasure." Buloz had flair for sensing talent and brought budding writers such as Alfred de Musset

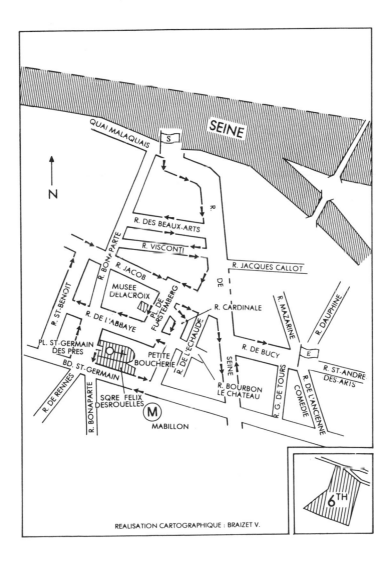

REALISATION CARTOGRAPHIQUE : BRAIZET V.

and Alexandre Dumas to the attention of the public. When Buloz moved with his wife to more spacious premises at n° 10, his collaborators would drop in and confide in his wife, an impressive list of callers which included Victor Hugo, Heinrich Heine, Louis-Adolphe Thiers and Prosper Mérimée (who happened to live in the same house); she listened to them in her drawing-room while doing her embroidery and they found her more approachable than her gruff husband. However, Buloz's gruffness concealed a sensitivity that came out in his correspondence with George Sand, his most faithful friend. Painter Corot and the physicist Ampère also lived at n° 10. N° 13 is one of the few luxury hotels of the Left Bank, simply called L'hôtel. In 1900, when poverty-stricken Oscar Wilde stayed here, it was a run-down, cheap place with appalling plumbing, called Hôtel Alsace. The writer lived here 'beyond his means' as he put it, and also died here, on 30 November of the same year. His grave is in the eastern cemetery of Père-Lachaise. His room in this hotel has been recreated, and constitutes a second Parisian shrine for the brilliant exile whom Britain had repudiated.

The Beaux-Arts school ahead, at 14 rue Bonaparte, occupies part of the convent built by Marguerite de Valois in 1608 on her estate. Being a truly devout person she had vowed to erect a temple to the Patriarch Jacob, whom she cherished for having been chosen by God. La Chapelle des Louanges was added, where 14 fathers of the Order of the Augustins-déchaussés sang the praises of Jacob, in relays of two, by night and day, to music composed by herself. However, annoyed that they sang out of tune, she evicted them after five years and replaced them with the apparently more musical Order of the Petits-Augustins, who gave their name to the convent. The enterprising archaeologist Alexandre Lenoir converted it into a museum, the Musée des Monuments Français, which allowed the chapel to survive the Revolution. The Ecole des Beaux-Arts settled here during the Restoration, annexing a couple of neighbouring mansions along the Seine to allow for expansion. Parts of the convent have survived to this day, as well as the cloister and the chapel.

Retrace your steps on rue des Beaux-Arts, turn right and continue along rue de Seine. At n°s 14 to 18 the Hôtel de La Rochefoucauld was the home of the La Rochefoucauld family, to which belonged François VI (1613-80), author of the *Maximes*. The intelligentsia of the time - La Fontaine, Corneille, Molière, Scarron - gathered here, sometimes to give readings of their works. This too was a grand estate extending all the way to rue Bonaparte. A plaque at n° 26 rue de Seine, on the corner house of rue Visconti, says that the writer Saint-Amant died here on 29 December 1621. This is essentially true but hardly the whole story, for Saint-Amant died not in his bed, as would be plausibly deduced, but in the cabaret Le Petit-Maure on this site, and it was not a natural death. Le Petit-Maure was the hangout of some of the famous writers of the day, who came to revel here over a pint of wine in good company. Its back yard was sometimes used for duels. The owner of the place was a personal friend of Saint-Amant. Saint-Amant was a highly-regarded writer, one of the first *Académiciens*, but when he rashly targeted the great Condé in a satirical verse, the latter had him dragged to the Pont-Neuf and thrashed vigorously, then dragged back to the cabaret, where he was dumped and left to die two days later, aged 67.

Across the street, at n° 31, an understated, elegant façade conceals a lovely courtyard. This was where Aurore Dupin first settled on her own, aged 27, after separating from her husband. In order to assert herself, she sported men's clothes and adopted the pen-name of George (with a British spelling) Sand. On this site a century later, in 1920, Raymond Duncan, the brother of the dancer Isadora Duncan, set up his academy dedicated to the revival of Ancient Greek culture. Apart from lectures on philosophy and Greek civilization, Greek arts and crafts, such as weaving and sandal-making, were also taught here. Raymond Duncan went around in a Greek-style robe and sandals and wore a wreath of leaves on his head.

Turn right into rue Visconti, a very narrow alley and still comparatively free of traffic. There was even less traffic in 1928, when Henry Miller brought his wife June here from his nearby hotel at 24 rue Bonaparte, to teach her how to ride a bicycle, so that they could go cycling in the south of France. There are several art galleries here today, among them, the one at n° 3 specializes in the theme of dancing. Rue Visconti opened in the 16th century, and situated in what was then a remote and therefore safer area, became the home of the Huguenots, and dubbed 'Little Geneva'. Here in 1559 their first synod was held, attended by delegates of 72 churches. When they convened again a few months later, they were surprised by the police, but all except four managed somehow to escape. Among these Huguenots was the famous architect Jean-Baptiste Androuet du Cerceau, who built the Pont-Neuf and was a friend of Henri IV's. His palatial home extended from the other end of rue Visconti, along rue Bonaparte, all the way to rue Jacob. A sincere Protestant, he preferred "to part with the friendship of the King, than to go to mass." The house that stands on its site today is an impressive 18th-century *hôtel*, where the Princesse de Rohan-Rochefort is said to have lived. Only three houses from the early period still exist - n°s 5, 7 and 9.

In the 17th and 18th centuries, when this part of the Left Bank became desirable, prominent figures lived in the street, too many to enumerate, but one was Adrienne Lecouvreur, a much idolized actresses of the Comédie-Française, who lived at n° 16 in the early 18th century. This was a glorious time for the aristocratic *faubourgs* on both banks of the Seine, when, thanks to the sophisticated, free-spirited Regent, who had turned his back on Versailles, Paris was again on the map. Adrienne Lecouvreur was certainly one of its stars, and had a long list of famous lovers, among them the great Maréchal Maurice de Saxe, the glorious hero of the battle of Fontenoy, and also the great-grandfather of George Sand. He may have been a great soldier, but his manners were unpolished, his education limited, and his spelling appalling. When he was offered a seat at the Académie, in recognition of his military feats, de Saxe refused the offer in writing, aware that he would be out of place among venerable *Académiciens*. His letter certainly corroborated his claim, scattered as it was with the most extravagant spelling mistakes. Mlle Lecouvreur, however, also frequented the most educated circles and Voltaire was among her close friends. He was on the first floor by her side on 23 March 1730 and closed her eyes when she died. No-one knew the exact cause of her death. Some said it was for love of the Maréchal, others that she was poisoned by one of her rivals. A century later, in 1826/7, at n° 17/19 across the street, Balzac lived in the early days of his career, trying his hand at different business ventures. He opened a printing-house, which brought in no money and which he handed over to the son of his much older friend and mentor Madame de Berny, in whose hands the business fared much better. This was probably where Stendhal's masterpiece *Le Rouge et le Noir* was first printed. Later Delacroix painted some of his great works in this building, notably *L'Entrée des Croisés à Constantinople*, *Hamlet* and *La Noce juive*, as well as portraits of some of his friends, such as George Sand and Chopin. Another famous actress from the Comédie-Française, Mlle Duclos, a generation older than Adrienne Lecouvreur, lived at n° 20. So did the writer Prosper Mérimée, when he wrote his famous *La Vénus d'Ille*. Racine spent the last seven years of his life at n° 24. Having led a peripatetic existence, mainly on the Left Bank, he settled here at the age of 53 in poor health and out of favour with Louis XIV, partly because the King had lost interest in the theatre, but also because he was a Jansenist at a time when they were outlawed. At least he did not die in destitution like Corneille but had a spacious apartment and a staff of 14 servants. He also had a carriage, two horses and a small post-chaise. Both he and his wife were devoted Christians and out of their seven children four intended to become nuns.

Retrace your steps and turn right again into rue de Seine. At n° 43, on the corner of rue Jacques-Callot, La Palette, a couple of minutes' walk from the Ecole des Beaux-Arts, is a stronghold of arty bohemia. The café has some exquisite ceramic decorations (signed Fouji: is it Fujita?) and it certainly has atmosphere, but it should be visited only by those who can tolerate a heavy veil of cigarette smoke and a surly welcome. Rue Jacques-Callot, named after the great Renaissance artist, is lined with trees and galleries and also celebrates art by way of an allegorical piece of sculpture on the pavement next to the Palette. Here, at n° 16, Man Ray's first exhibition, of photographs, paintings and sculptures, opened on 26 March 1926, in what was then known as La Galerie Surréaliste. Continue along rue de Seine and turn diagonally right into rue de l'Echaudé, a picturesque spot, where ancient narrow streets converge on a little patch of garden, with a decorative trellis climbing up a wall, some poplars, rose bushes and a little fountain. There are also some wonderful artistic shops. Rue de l'Echaudé was built along the ditch of the defence walls of the abbey of Saint-Germain and led to its gate (on the present n° 26). Charles V, aware of the impending English threat, ordered the abbey to be fortified. The walls, like those on the Right Bank, were pulled down only at the time of Louis XIV, when the victorious Sun King no longer felt the need to protect his city.

Turn right into rue Jacob, called after the Patriarch Jacob. This street too ran along the ditch of the abbey walls and beyond it, across the Pré-aux-Clercs. The beautiful shops and boutiques are enough to distract you from your historical exploration, but turn left into rue de Fürstemberg, named after Egon de Fürstemberg, the abbot who in 1691 reconstructed the abbey's brick-and-stone Renaissance palace. What is left of it now serves as a ravishing pink backdrop to the exquisite Place de Fürstemberg ahead, a bewitching gem by night, when its central street-lamp diffuses gentle light over the paving and over the four trees that cluster around it - one of the highlights of romantic Paris. Henry Miller thought differently, describing it as "A deserted spot, bleak, spectral at night, containing in the centre four black trees [...]; these four bare trees have the poetry of T.S. Eliot." Of course, in Henry Miller's time this was not yet the stronghold of luxury upholstery fabrics it is today, which would have filled him, presumably, with even greater horror! It must be said, however, that the showrooms' displays are in such impeccable taste that they only enhance the beauty of the place. When occasionally a busker will show up, he is sure to be inspired by the setting and play subdued music.

Place de Fürstemberg is on the site of the palace's main courtyard, which was turned into a square in the 18th century. The bright pink house, at n° 6/8 on the right-hand side, painted to look like bricks (brick was very expensive), served as stables and sheds for the palace's horses and carriages. In the courtyard of n° 6 are some vestiges of their early use. This charming courtyard, with its arched entrance, uneven cobblestones and creepers rambling out of windows, leads to the Musée (or *atelier*) Delacroix, located in the last home of the painter, where he died in 1863 at the age of 60.

Over 50 years later, in 1929, some prominent artists, Bonnard and Signac among them, founded a society to promote the memory of Delacroix and his work - *La Société des amis de Delacroix* - and the next year they rented the dilapidated premises, had them restored, and began to organize temporary exhibitions. In 1963 the Society managed to persuade the State to buy the premises to ensure their survival, and to turn them into a permanent museum, where drawings, sketches, studies and other documents chart the development of the artistic genius of one of the greatest - and often misunderstood - painters of France.

In January 1857 Delacroix was living in the artists' quarter of La Nouvelle-Athènes (in the 9th arr) when, after seven rejections, he was at long last elected to the Académie des Beaux-Arts. Having contracted very serious laryngitis in December, he had to remain indoors for three months and could not pay the traditional visits expected from a new *Académicien*. Nor until May could he teach or paint. He therefore threw himself wholly into writing and began his fascinating *Dictionary of the Fine Arts*, which he never was to complete.

On 16 March he was able to go out for the first time. The walk was an effort but it did him good. Because he now had to go to the Académie regularly and was also working on his murals for the church of Saint-Sulpice, on the other side of Boulevard Saint-Germain, he decided to return to the Left Bank, to avoid crossing Paris when in such poor health. But it was not simple to find available and suitable accommodation, although he thought his dealer Haro's place on the charming, somewhat shabby, provincial Place de Fürstemberg, might do for a studio. When he visited it ten days later, Haro was not very enthusiastic about the idea, believing it would be very difficult to convert the place into a studio. Haro was not the only obstacle - Dr Bégin, the tenant of the apartment next door also had to be persuaded to give it up: "I went to Paris, on tenter-hooks," he writes in his Journal, "to know whether M. Bégin would give me possession of the house so that we can begin the alterations."

Madame Bégin was also a problem: "My first anxiety was to meet him or his wife, and I cursed the driver for going slowly." When that obstacle was removed, Delacroix "rushed off in a great state of excitement to find Haro", soon to realize that the venture would be the devil's own job: "the builders are being diabolical; some of them are utterly unreliable, and the rest are either lazy or too expensive." He would also realize that Haro's apprehensions concerning the alterations of the premises were justified, since they caused "an immense amount of worry". Leaving his studio on rue Notre-Dame-de-Lorette the following December, was not easy either: "Even now that it's all bare and deserted, I still love this place [...] I cannot leave this humble place, these rooms, where for so many years I have been alternately melancholy and happy, without feeling deeply moved." But he adopted a positive attitude: "My new home is really charming. I felt rather depressed, after dinner, at finding myself transplanted, but I gradually became reconciled and went to bed quite happy."

Jenny Le Guillou, his tenacious Breton housekeeper, had naturally moved with him and as his health deteriorated, she increasingly took over, making short shrift of visitors, in particular of women. A portrait by Delacroix of the wilful Jenny is exhibited in the museum. Delacroix's *atelier* takes you back to that past, recreating a world now gone: the charming decorations of his apartment, the fire-place, the painter's personal belongings, documents and letters, his studio and all his painting materials make a visit here a moving and nostalgic experience. Outside, the green branches of old trees, filled with the song of birds, offer the kind of view you are so often denied because most Paris courtyards are kept locked by security-conscious residents in these days of mutual mistrust. These used to be the gardens of the abbey's infirmary and are now sliced up and belong to the different houses that were once the outbuildings of the palace. If you can make it early, on a fine morning, you will even share Delacroix's experience on his first morning here, on 29 December: "I awoke next morning to find the sun shining in the most welcoming way on the houses opposite my window. The view on to the little garden, and the cheerful look of the studio continue to give me great pleasure."

Rue Cardinale runs into rue de Fürstemberg on your left, a lovely picture with its tiny quaint wrought-iron balcony just where it makes a sharp bend. Walk into this old, narrow street with its assortment of picturesque old buildings. Some exciting shop windows have managed to infiltrate into this hidden nook, and by night the old street-lamps affixed to the houses create a wonderfully romantic atmosphere. Back in the 1920s, the wealthy Harry and Caresse Crosby, had spot ted out the street and set up the Black Sun Press (named after a poem by Archibald MacLeish) at n° 2, in the shabby shop of an excellent printer, Lescaret, who provided very tasteful, quality work. They published a substantial number of letters by Henry James and Marcel Proust, which Harry Crosby happened to inherit from a cousin; and an early story by D.H. Lawrence and some works of James Joyce. At the junction of rue Cardinale, Passage de la Petite-Boucherie, rue de Bourbon-le-Château and rue de l'Abbaye, two rustic, Montmartre-style, pale pink houses on your left make another lovely, quaint picture. So does the roof terrace on the corner of rue de l'Abbaye and rue de Fürstemberg on your right, with its riot of brightly coloured laurel bushes. Walk into rue de l'Abbaye. On your left is the brick palace of the abbey, a pale reminder of one of the city's most magnificent edifices at the time. Today, it is all partitioned, housing the classrooms and offices of the Catholic University, the Institut Catholique, and other establishments.

Originally built in 1589 by the Abbot Charles I de Bourbon, this was the second brick-and-stone building to have been erected in Paris (the first, the palatial mansion of the wealthy Italian, Scipion Sardini, on the eastern edge of the 5th, has long since disappeared), two decades before the Place des Vosges. Charles I de Bourbon was the Bishop of Rouen, the Abbot of Saint-Germain and the uncle of Henri IV, all of which points to the enormous political power wielded by some clergymen. Indeed, after the murder of Henri III in 1589, the Catholic Confederation (*La Ligue*) appointed him King of France, under the name of Charles X, a decision that was ratified by Parliament and remained in effect for two months. The Ligue had been commanded by the famous Duc de Guise, Henri le Balafré, whose family was second in power only to the King's - precisely the situation the Guise wished to reverse by supplanting the King. But Henri III tricked the Balafré into coming to Blois where he had him murdered in 1588; for this he paid with his own life at Saint-Cloud the following year. Meanwhile, having no direct descendants, he had appointed his brother-in-law, Henri de Navarre, heir to the throne, a decision rejected by the Ligue. In order to strengthen his position Charles de Bourbon, who was 67 at the time, asked the Pope for a dispensation to marry the widow of the Balafré and provide France with a dynasty *in extremis*. But before he could do so, he was taken prisoner by his nephew Henri de Navarre, whom he had fought at Fontenoy. Though treated well, he died in captivity. His appointment as King was annulled, which explains that the next Charles, over two centuries later, became Charles X rather than XI.

The abbey of Saint-Germain had always been a place of artistic splendour, of which nothing is left. Its 13th-century chapel, la Chapelle de la Vierge (level with today's n° 6 bis rue de l'Abbaye), a masterpiece of Gothic art, was wrecked during the French Revolution and finished off by the construction of rue de l'Abbaye. As the chapel was built by the same Pierre de Montreuil who designed the Sainte-Chapelle, one can measure the immense loss its destruction represented. Just beyond it was a beautiful cloister with an exquisite garden. Level with the present n° 12/14 was the 13th-century dining-hall, also the work of Pierre de Montreuil. His brilliant design of a vault unsupported by a pillar, created an uplifting, ethereal feel. Fifteen stained-glass windows completed the edifice, glorious when lit up by the sun. During the Revolution 15,000 tons of gunpowder were stored here, side by side with a huge stock of coal. No wonder it all ended up in a stupendous explosion and a gigantic fire! The flames devoured nearly everything, including the abbey's library above the dining-hall with its 50,000 volumes. Yet miraculously, most of its 7,000 manuscripts, 1,000 of which dated from before the 7th century, were saved and are now kept in the Bibliothèque Nationale. Among them was the original manuscript of Pascal's *Pensées*. Some fragments of the chapel's stained glass were also rescued and set into a modern stained-glass window inside the church, on your left. The little garden, just before the church, lies on the site of a 19th-century house where Alphonse Daudet lived when he wrote *Le Petit Chose*, in which he described these parts in detail. In the days of the abbey this was the south-west part of the cloister's garden. Some vestiges of the arcades of the medieval chapel are displayed here.

Turn left into the Place Saint-Germain-des-Prés. On your left is the entrance to the church, on your right, the terrace of the Deux Magots, overflowing with people in fine weather. Saint-Germain-des-Prés may have been put on the map of contemporary Paris in 1945, or to a lesser extent a decade or so earlier, but in fact, it entered the real history of Paris with its first foreign invasion. For this is where the Gauls assembled in 52 BC to defend the city against the invading Roman legions who were camping across the river. When the Revolution broke out, about 10,000 people were living around the abbey, a city within a city, and a wealthy one indeed, its domains reaching well into the present 15th arrondissement. Furthermore, for many centuries it remained under the direct tutelage of the Pope, which ensured its political independence. With the destruction of the abbey Haussmann was free to construct the present network of streets. The fact that the church was spared is extraordinary, it being the oldest church in Paris. It even retains some small columns from the first 6th-century basilica, the one that had honoured Saint Vincent before Saint Germain took over. They now decorate the second chancel.

The church was built between 990 and 1014 AD in the Romanesque style. When a new and larger choir was built in 1163, to accommodate the growing number of monks, together with a bell-tower (restored several times since) and a majestic portal, a magnificent ceremony took place, presided over by Pope Alexandre III, who had come up to Paris for the laying, a few weeks later, of the cornerstone of the cathedral of Notre-Dame. Maurice de Sully, the founder of Notre-Dame and Bishop of Paris, who had been expelled from the ceremony at Saint-Germain on 21 April, as described earlier, now had his revenge. During the Revolution the church was used as a refinery for saltpetre, which left it in a sorry state. Victor Baltard undertook its restoration, while Hippolyte Flandrin contributed the murals.

Before turning left into Boulevard Saint-Germain, you may wish to recapture the atmosphere of the post-war era, perhaps from the terrace of the Deux Magots. On the Boulevard Saint-Germain, to the right, is the celebrated Flore, haunt of Jean-Paul Sartre and Simone de Beauvoir during the dark years; across the street, the Drugstore Publicis replaces the Royal Saint-Germain. On the same pavement to the right is the Brasserie Lipp, whose setting has remained unchanged. To your left, the corner café on rue Bonaparte has modernized its furnishings but kept its name.

Continue on Boulevard Saint-Germain along the church and the little garden, Square Félix Desruelles. A spectacular enamelled sandstone portico is affixed to its eastern wall, manufactured by the celebrated Sèvres workshops for the 1900 Universal Exposition. The laying out of the Boulevard Saint-Germain transformed this section of Paris beyond recognition. It would take a great deal of imagination to picture the forbidding, massive prison of the abbey that stood across it (level with today's n°s 135 and 166) as recently as in 1857, when Haussmann had it razed to the ground. It was in this prison that the bloody massacres of

2, 3 and 4 September 1792 were triggered. Whoever masterminded the operation, it was cleverly handled by the Revolutionary authorities, who spread the rumour of a plot against 'the good people' of Paris, exciting 'the good people', goading them on, giving the alarm, ringing bells, distributing pamphlets... After a preliminary slaughter of 13 new detainees, who were grabbed by the mob on their way to the prison, 100 prisoners, among them many priests, were executed on the first day of the massacre, after a semblance of a trial. By the third day over 300 people had been executed, at or near the junction of the present rue Bonaparte and rue de l'Abbaye, then piled up in the abbey's gardens. Among them was one of Louis XVI's ministers and his first valet. The writer Beaumarchais, whose *Mariage de Figaro* had certainly contributed to the violent turn French history had taken, was lucky to have escaped the same fate, having been taken prisoner here during the mass arrests that had preceded the massacres, and released after four days, for a ransom of 30,000 francs.

Carried away by the smell of blood, the barbaric assailants continued their murderous deeds into the night, by torch light, and then on the following day, and yet again the following - an unspeakable savagery, stopped only when the number of 300 had been exceeded. Were they at last chilled by their deed? They certainly set out energetically to efface all traces of it, and a circular was sent to the prisons' *concierges* instructing them, "with water and vinegar, to wash the places in your prison that may be covered with blood and sand them over [...] Above all, hasten in the execution of this order, so that no trace of blood should be seen." The personal belongings of the victims were disposed of and the bodies transported in long lines of carts beyond the city walls, many of them to the Catacombs at Denfert-Rochereau (now in the 14th arr.). Wild bacchantes, an eye-witness reported, sitting or dancing on the heap of mutilated bodies, beat the rhythm on the bodies, shrieking 'Vive *la Nation!*'

Retrace your steps to rue de l'Abbaye and continue, past rue Bonaparte, to rue Saint-Benoît, whose name commemorates the Benedictine Order of the Abbey. Laid out on the site of its western ditch, the remains of a 14th-century tower are still hidden behind n° 15. Many poor *Germanopratins* lived in this street in the post-war years, often at the Montana or Crystal hotels. Marguerite Duras, author of *L'Amant*, also lived here and was the pivot of the communist clique. The *Petit Saint-Bénoit*, at n° 4 to your right, was their 'canteen' as also of Simone de Beauvoir and her friends. It has not changed an iota: the same furniture, the same handwritten menu, the same traditional dishes, the same low prices will welcome you... and credit cards, of course, are not accepted. Have a meal at the Petit Saint-Bénoît while you can: it may not be here on your next visit.

Turn left into rue Jacob and cross over. The street had already several hotels in the 18th century, where many foreign visitors stayed. Washington Irving stayed at

Hôtel d'Angleterre at n° 44 in 1804. The lovely 18th-century building now has a patio, where guests can have breakfast on fine days, and has been upgraded to a three-star *hôtel de charme* (the neighbourhood abounds in them). By contrast, in 1921, Sherwood Anderson paid 75 cents per night for a double room, and therefore recommended it to the newly-wed Hemingways when they arrived in Paris in December. N° 46 next door has a typical *Directoire* (end 18th-century) façade with its elegant niches housing Neo-classical allegorical figures. There is no hotel here at present, but it is possible that the early 18th-century house that stood here before was the Hôtel Modène that Laurence Sterne recorded in his *Sentimental Journey*. In 1777 Benjamin Franklin stayed for a month at the Hôtel de Hambourg at n° 52, while waiting for a permanent home. He then moved to Passy (now in the 16th arr.), where he remained for the seven-year duration of his stay. N° 56 at the time was the Hôtel d'York, where the peace treaty between England and the United States of America was signed at 9 am, on 3 September 1783, by the English representative, David Hartley, and his American counterparts, Benjamin Franklin, John Jay and John Adams. Adams actually came back with his family to stay here for a few days the following September, while looking for a permanent home. He too would move out west, to Auteuil, also in the future 16th.

Retrace your steps on rue Jacob and cross over. N° 35 opens into an exquisite alley, full of flowers and bushes, enhanced by quaint roof tops that huddle against one another above. This is the Galerie Triff, an oasis where magnificent kilims are for sale, displayed around a soothing pool. There is no obligation to buy, so just wander around and enjoy the sights and the tranquillity. On the corner of rue Bonaparte, the café-restaurant Au Pré aux Clercs commemorates the stretch of land that belonged to the University, through which rue Jacob was opened. Hemingway and Hadley used to eat here when they stayed at the Hôtel d'Angleterre and had a full meal *à la carte* for 6 francs. Today this is still an unpretentious place that offers decent fare at reasonable prices.

Unfortunately you cannot gain entrance to n° 28, Colette's home, which she described endearingly as dark and stuffy. You can, on the other hand, enter n° 20 during the day, but a fence bars you from the garden on your right, once the 'sanctuary' of Natalie Barney, the glamorous *Amazon* who used to ride in the Bois de Boulogne wearing a bowler hat and black bow tie. Weather permitting, French and American literati would gather in the shady courtyard, with its profusion of creeping ivy on the walls. A mock Greek temple, Le Temple de l'Amitié, created a hedonistic atmosphere and also provided shelter from the cold and rain. When Natalie first moved here in 1909, tea with cake and sandwiches were the rule, but when the 'expatriates' turned up in the 1920s, she had to resign herself reluctantly to serving champagne, and later whisky and gin. Paul Valéry used to read his works here but was quick to drop her once he was elected an *Académi-*

cien. Virgil Thomson and Georges Antheil performed their music here, and Antheil actually used Miss Barney's 'Greek' temple to rehearse his *Ballet mécanique*. The piece combined notes played on a piano with the sounds of machines and a ventilator, recreating in musical form the spirit of Dada, and provoked an immense scandal when it was performed in the strait-laced concert hall of the Paris Conservatoire, the stronghold of conservatism. Apart from her turbulent, Lesbian love affairs, literature was the main purpose of Natalie's life, 60 years of which she spent here. She founded an Académie des Femmes, as a reaction to the all-male Académie Française, but it did not come to much; nor did her other projects to help needy writers, notably T.S. Eliot.

Turn right into rue de Seine, which leads to the junction of rue de Buci and to another world. Here is the most exciting and most colourful market in the arrondissement. Along rue de Buci to your right are also some mouth-watering bakery and pastry shops. At the time of Henri IV this was already the most bustling spot on the Left Bank. On 2 September 1792 it was a fine recruiting-ground for volunteers for the defence of the motherland - *'la défense de la Patrie en danger'* - that is, for the three-day slaughter that was about to commence. The first four victims, four new detainees on their way to the prison of the abbey, were slain at this street junction by the delirious mob. Likewise, a barricade was erected here on the first day of the 1848 Revolution, to the fervent cries of *'Vive la République!'* Today this is a place of peace and fun, especially if the jazz musicians are about. The Hotel La Louisiane, the home of Simone de Beauvoir during the heyday of Saint-Germain-des-Prés, holds its own in the midst of the colourful fun, at n° 60 rue de Seine.

TO SAINT-SULPICE AND THE LUXEMBOURG

This walk takes us to the area of Saint-Sulpice, the one-time parish church of the borough of Saint-Germain and to the Luxembourg Palace and Gardens beyond. Start from the corner of Boulevard Saint-Germain and rue de Seine and head south. At the end of the street (which is worth exploring separately for its boutiques, art galleries and good bookshops) can be seen the elegant façade of the Palais du Luxembourg. Turn right into rue Clément, then left into rue Mabillon. You will be walking around the Marché Saint-Germain, recently renovated and, unfortunately, now devoid of local colour, a very pale replica of the world-renowned fair of days gone by and much reduced in size. Rue Clément led to the fair through a gate known as La Porte de Treille and rue Mabillon was known simply as rue de la Foire. In those days acrobats, tightrope dancers and animal tamers entertained all the social classes, including the King, who would mingle with the crowds. Henri III and his entourage of *mignons frisés* ('his curly-headed

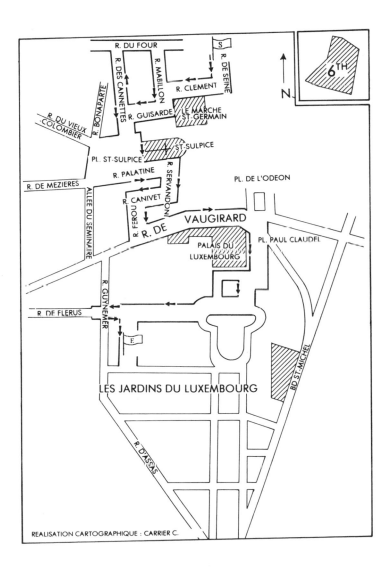

fairies') were ridiculed by jeering youths, skipping around his Majesty. The very thick crowds and the availability of wine led to violent brawls, scuffles, debauchery, prostitution and murders. The poet Scarron, who would come here in his notorious invalid's chair, wrote:

> Foire, l'élément des coquets,
> Des filoux et des tire-laine,
> Foire où l'on vend moins d'affiquets
> Que l'on ne vend de chair humaine [...]
> (Fair, the element of gallants ,/Of rogues and
> of robbers, /Fair where fewer trinkets are sold/
> Than human flesh)

It took only five hours for the fair to be consumed by a gigantic fire on the night of 16 - 17 March 1762. The flames even reached the church of Saint-Sulpice and damaged its Chapel of the Virgin. The new fair built in its place, never attained the same prestige; it was closed down during the Revolution and replaced by a market in the early 19th century. In 1898 it lost two thirds of its area and nearly a century later was threatened with total demolition. This was avoided *in extremis*, and the premises have been restored and still stand. An auditorium has been added to bring in more life and culture, but its soul is gone. The old, picturesque houses at n°s 6, 8 and 10 rue de Mabillon stand as witnesses of the colourful past, and the restaurant at n° 10 perpetuates the memory of the Compagnons Charpentiers du Devoir de Liberté (the carpenters' guild) through its decoration and its little adjoining museum.

Turn right into rue Guisarde, a lively, narrow street, which also led to the fair. Its name may derive from Guise, as the Duc de Guise, Henri le Balafré, may have had his headquarters in a *hôtel* here. Turn right into rue des Cannettes, yet another bustling street still on its medieval site, although today it is goods from the Wild West (and down towards Mexico) that seem to set the tone. But above the jumble of cowboy boots and other such accessories are still the bulbous façades of old houses and, above the portal at n° 18, an early 18th-century sculpted medallion representing four ducks *(cannettes)* swimming in a pond. It replaces an even earlier street sign that gave the street its name. N° 17 across the street has a lovely little niche with a statue of the Virgin and Child. N° 5 was the meeting place of local bohemians, Le Cénacle des Buveurs d'Eau, described by Henri Mürger in *La Vie de Bohème*. Turn left into rue du Four, named after the oven that people were strictly obliged to use for the baking of bread; offenders were fined, which was another means of levying taxes on the poor. At n° 33 a massive Louis XIII door leads to a charming, green courtyard all lined with creepers. An old well in the corner will recalls the days before Napoleon III's rule, when no running water was available in people's homes. Inside is an extraordinary spiral staircase, which has preserved its original, 16th-century, central wooden core. A beautiful twisted handrail carved out of the massive tree trunk is both practical and aesthetically pleasing.

Retrace your steps and continue to Place Saint-Sulpice. The spacious terrace of the Café de la Mairie, overlooking the rushing waters of Visconti's fountain in the centre of the square, makes it one of the popular cafés in the arrondissement. Named simply after the town hall of the 6th, which faces the church across the square, the café was already very popular in the early 1920s. In *A Moveable Feast* Hemingway described the pigeons perched on the statues of the four bishops on the fountain, and Henry Miller also mentioned them in *Tropic of Cancer*. Other 'expatriates' used to come here too from their nearby homes - Faulkner, Fitzgerald and Beckett - and in the next generation their French counterparts followed suit. The last meeting between Sartre and Camus took place here in 1951, after which the two quarrelled and parted company. Across the street Yves Saint-Laurent has been established successfully since the 1960s, when a new era of luxury opened in the 6th arrondissement.

Few artists or writers have had kind words for the unlovely church of Saint-Sulpice with its two jarring and conspicuous towers that pierce the sky - 'fat belfries', according to Henry Miller. The poet Raoul Ponchon, went further:

> Je hais les tours de Saint-Sulpice!
> Quand par hazard je les rencontre
> Je pisse
> Contre.
> (I hate the towers of Saint-Sulpice! Whenever I
> happen to come across them I piss on them).

But the French like things big, and the parish was swollen with pride in the 17th century, when it had the largest church on the Left Bank and the highest in the whole city, the northern tower rising 73 metres above the ground, 4 metres more than Notre-Dame. It was true that by the 17th century, the initial parish church, built in 1211, could no longer accommodate the growing number of parishioners. The parish priest, l'abbé Olier, had an ambitious enterprise in mind, and invited Anne of Austria in 1646 to lay the cornerstone. Gamard was commissioned to design the church but after nine years it was already deemed too small and the ubiquitous Louis Le Vau was asked to redesign and enlarge it. Le Vau died soon after, however, and funds for such a colossal monument were hard to find. Construction dragged on for over a century, overseen by six successive architects, the last being the famous Chalgrin. The southern tower was never actually completed.

One of the church's parishioners was Talleyrand, born in 1854 at 4 rue Garancière, just behind the church, and baptized here. Later he was sent to study in the seminary opposite the church (now the site of the square). Founded by l'abbé Olier in 1645, it was known as the Grand-Séminaire, as opposed to the Petit-Séminaire, built for less wealthy seminarists in 1686 at the entrance of rue Férou across the square. Young Talleyrand, however, was expelled from the institution for having repeatedly gone over the wall to his amorous rendezvous.

Saint-Sulpice

As you walk into the church, you will notice two great conches mounted on a marble socle, which were offered to François I by the Republic of Venice and serve as a spout. These were carved by Pigalle into the form of seaweed with tentacles entangled in the rock. Pigalle, who was particularly dedicated to religious art, also left a beautiful marble statue of the Virgin and Child at the opposite end of the church, in the Chapelle de la Vierge, damaged by the fire of the Fair in 1762. Pigalle's statue replaced an earlier one, which had been sent to the Mint during the Revolution and had been made, allegedly, from the silver cutlery that the artist Languet de Cergy spirited away from dinner parties, which explains why the statue had been nicknamed *Notre-Dame de la Vaisselle*. The most famous works of art in Saint-Sulpice, however, are Delacroix's mural paintings in the Chapelle des Deux-Anges, the first chapel on your right: *Heliodorus Driven from the Temple*, *Jacob Wrestling with the Angel* and *Saint Michael Slaying the Dragon* in the dome above. The painter dedicated eight years of his life (1853-1861) to these paintings, even when his health was declining. The Chapelle de Saint-Martin (recognizable by the mural depicting the saint) is incidentally the only place in Paris where the faithful are provided with sacred water. Another point of interest is the copper strip laid in the floor. In order to determine the spring equinox and thus the exact date of Easter Sunday each year, a hole was pierced in the window in the south transept crossing, through which a ray of sun reached the obelisk in the north transept. At midday on the relevant day, the ray of sun would travel along the copper strip and strike a given point on the obelisk. This method of calculation was worked out by the watchmaker Henri Sully in 1727, but of course it no longer holds good, the positions of the sun and stars having changed since. Note also the impressive Louis XV high altar in the Chapelle du Sacre-Coeur, in the north transept, and its huge organ, originally designed by Chalgrin and reconstructed by Cavaillé-Coll in 1862. With its 6,500 pipes, it is claimed to be the largest in Europe.

The two seminaries of Saint-Sulpice were swept away during the Revolution and a new seminary was built in 1820 on the southern side of the square, bounded by rue Férou to the east and rue Bonaparte to the west. A tree-shaded alley along rue Bonaparte, l'Allée du Séminaire, is a reminder of its presence. In 1906, after the vote for the separation of state and church, the government took over the seminary and handed it over to the Ministry of Finance. Nevertheless, the neighbourhood has remained the stronghold of Catholicism in the capital, hence the impressive number of specialized shops that sell religious items, ceremonial gowns and books.

The narrow, old streets that run south of the church are relatively free of traffic and crossed by few pedestrians. On a sunny weekend afternoon, a serene provincial peace prevails, interrupted only by the occasional chime of church bells. Turn left into rue Palatine, alongside the church. The street celebrates the Bavarian Princess, Anne, wife of the Condé, Monsieur le Prince (not to be confused with the more famous Princesse Palatine, the mother of the Regent who left an exciting correspondence about her son, his contemporaries and culinary matters). Condé's magnificent palace was situated roughly where the Théâtre de l'Odéon now stands, but his wife's *hôtel* is still at n° 15 in the neighbouring rue Garancière.

Turn right into rue Servandoni, a narrow, crooked street with elegant street-lamps affixed to its façades. Servandoni was the Italian architect in charge of the sets of the opera, and also one of the six architects who participated in the erection of the church of Saint-Sulpice. The imposing, severe façade is actually his contribution. On the corner building of rue Canivet you will see engraved in the stone the name of rue des Fossoyers ('gravediggers'), which the street was called when it led to the cemetery of Saint-Sulpice, then within the precinct of the seminary (roughly where the fountain now stands). Ahead of you on the right-hand side of the street is n° 14, a charming, old house with a bulbous profile, a slanting roof and windows cheerfully bursting with vegetation. It also has a massive door carved with two magnificent medallions, the one on the left representing Saint Anne teaching a disciple to read, the one on the right - in all likelihood - the architect Servandoni unrolling the plan of the church of Saint-Sulpice (Servandoni lived in this building). Inside, its courtyard has preserved its old paving and the walls are lined with creepers, muffling all noise At n° 15, across the street, a plaque commemorates the tragic naïveté of some idealists, for it was here that the great philosopher Condorcet, denounced for not having voted for the death sentence on Louis XVI, and tracked down by the Terror as a *Girondin*, was offered shelter in July 1793 by the generous widow of the sculptor François Vernet. Blind to the stark evidence of man's inhumanity that surrounded him, Condorcet went on with his *Esquisse des progrès de l'esprit humain* (!), for roughly eight months, until, worried about compromising his hostess any longer, he left her home in disguise on 25 March 1794. In no time he was caught and sent to prison, where he committed suicide on 6 April.

Retrace your steps into rue Canivet, whose name too is probably derived from a street sign, referring to the little knife used for making lace for the frames of religious pictures. A beautiful Louis XIII portal has survived at n° 2, leading to a leafy courtyard, where there is an old stone bench resting on two lions' heads. A rare Louis XIII wooden staircase still stands inside the building. Even the letterboxes are made of smooth old wood. Across the street, a beautiful Louis XV portal is surmounted by a lovely sculpted mask set in a shell. The windows were walled up by the landlord to avoid paying yet another tax. Rue du Canivet opens on to rue Férou, which runs along the wall of the old seminary. It was a shabby street in 1951, when Man Ray settled in a sculptor's studio at n° 2 bis, on his return to France. His wife, Juliet, was appalled by the premises which, she said, looked like a garage. But Man Ray was happy to be back in Paris and pleased with the "whitewashed place, flooded with light from skylights and windows on the three sides." Today rue Férou is an expensive street, located in one of the most desirable areas of Paris, which explains why there are plans to replace the adorable, one-storeyed house at n° 7 with a profitable modern block, with a car park underneath. An 18th-century *hôtel* at n° 6 displays a charming bas-relief, with chubby, playful cupids to suit the tastes of an idle society. Mademoiselle Luzy, a famous actress of the Comédie-Française, lived here between 1770 and 1785 and it was probably for her sake that Talleyrand went over the wall when he was studying in the neighbouring seminary. Hemingway, having left Hadley, came to live here with Pauline Pfeiffer in 1926, working at a time on *A Farewell to Arms*. He often went over to the Café de la Mairie and sometimes walked into the church with Pauline. The painter Fantin-Latour was living at n° 15 when Whistler visited him in 1858. Finding Fantin-Latour sitting up in bed, Whistler made a drawing of him huddled up in his overcoat. It is now in the Louvre. N° 17 next door conceals its charm behind a wall. Two old trees overhang the wall, extending their shade to the silent street on a hot summer's day, echoing Alphonse Daudet's description in his novel *Le Nabab* of the peaceful streets behind Saint-Sulpice, in the shade of its two big towers, which "seem detached from a provincial town [...] where big trees surmounting the walls rock to the sound of bells..."

The idyllic atmosphere comes to an abrupt halt at rue de Vaugirard ahead with its constant flow of traffic. Across the street the Musée du Luxembourg is housed in the west wing of the former palace. In 1750 the east wing was opened to the public, the first time such a step was taken in France. About 50 paintings from the King's collection were shown to visitors twice a week, on which occasion they were also admitted to the west wing to see Rubens's series of 24 paintings depicting the life of Marie de Medici (now in the Louvre). The present museum, however, was opened only in 1865, in the orangery that Alphonse de Gisors had built 30 earlier (now n° 19 rue de Vaugirard). Here were exhibited the works of the conventional, academic *Pompiers*, so appreciated by the bourgeoisie of the time and then considered modern art. The Impressionists were shown here only once they were semi-acknowledged, though not yet worthy of such institutions as the Louvre (where, incidentally, they were never exhibited, for in the 1920s the Jeu de Paume on the western edge of the Tuileries Gardens opened its doors to them instead).

Turn left into rue de Vaugirard. The Palais du Luxembourg, east of the museum, is now the seat of the French Sénat and can therefore be visited only on Sundays, between 9.30 and 11 am and between 2 and 4 pm. The entrance is at n° 15.

After the assassination of Henri IV, his Florentine widow, Marie de Medici, felt estranged at the Louvre and was homesick for Florence. For quite some time now, she had had her heart set on the Hôtel du Petit-Luxembourg, the home of François du Luxembourg, which he agreed to sell to her in 1611. The following year she purchased the adjoining houses to the east in order to build a vast palace that was worthy of a Medici Queen and would remind her of her childhood home, the Pitti Palace in Florence. Of course it would have been more sensible to complete the Tuileries Palace and move there, but there was no thwarting her extravagant, capricious whims. Nor did she have any qualms about dipping into the funds that her late husband had stored in one of the towers of the Bastille, for more urgent military purposes. The great architect Salomon de Brosse was commissioned to build an Italian-style palace but instead produced a typically French one. Whether he disregarded the Queen's instructions or was carried away by his own native inspiration, the Palais du Luxembourg, standing between its courtyard and gardens, according to French taste, bears only the remotest resemblance to the Palazzo Pitti. However, Salomon de Brosse surmounted its monumental portal with a pleasing dome and scattered fountains and grottoes in the garden after the Italian fashion. To flatter the Queen, Rubens was commissioned to paint a series of 24 narrative paintings on her life, for the west wing of the Palace. The fair-haired queen was still attractive enough to serve as a model, and plump enough to suit Rubens's penchant for well-padded bodies.

The Queen devoted most of her attention, however, to the garden, where she had 2,000 elms planted. Emulating the Romans of ancient Lutetia, she had an aqueduct built all the way from Arcueil (in the southern suburbs of Paris, now on the RER B line) to supply the fountains of her new Eden, which took Salomon de Brosse 11 years to complete. The palace took 15 years to complete (1615-1630), but barely had Marie de Medici settled in it than she was ousted and banished from France for having meddled in state affairs. She had underestimated the political mastery of her redoubtable opponent, Richelieu, the former friend she herself had promoted. She died in Cologne in total destitution. Her project for the east wing of another series of 24 narrative paintings by Rubens on the life of Henri IV, was therefore never carried out.

Louis XIII's brother Gaston d'Orléans moved to the palace in her place, followed after his death by various other members of the royal family. In the 18th century the daughter of the Regent and the Duchesse de Berry shared a life of careless frivolity here, so that when the Comte de Provence, the future Louis XVIII, received the palace from his brother Louis XVI, it was in serious need of repair. While waiting for restoration to be completed, he resided temporarily at the Petit-Luxembourg. But the Revolution was imminent and within four years the Comte de Provence had fled, Robespierre was reigning supreme and determined to eliminate the *Girondins* and the Palais du Luxembourg had been turned into a prison. 800 prisoners were kept here, a third of whom were guillotined, among them Danton and Camille Desmoulin. When the storm finally subsided the building was wrecked and overall renovation was necessary to make it suitable for its new function. It first served as an auditorium for the Directoire, then as a Senat, and during the Restoration as a Chamber of Peers. Repairs were begun in 1804 and were entrusted to the hands of Chalgrin. The main staircase was transferred to the west wing leading to a new auditorium on the first floor with a capacity of 80 seats. A new vestibule was also created. In 1836, another distinguished architect, Alphonse de Gisors, was commissioned to transform and enlarge the premises again. Hence the substantial extension projecting into the garden, a happy addition; built in the initial style of the Palace, it blends imperceptibly into the old building, while affording a magnificent view of the gardens from inside.

In 1852 the Palais du Luxembourg became the seat of the French Sénat, which is made up of 283 members and deals mainly with legislation and with changes to the Constitution. At times it may act as arbitrator between the government and the National Assembly. In case of vacancy, its President becomes acting President of the Republic. You can visit the library with its paintings by Delacroix, the Salle du Livre d'Or, which houses the panelling and paintings from the Queen's apartments, the Sénat's auditorium and the main staircase in the west wing, where Rubens's paintings were once on display. The President of the Sénat resides at the Petit-Luxembourg at n° 17 rue de Vaugirard, the *hôtel* Marie de Medici bought from François du Luxembourg in 1611 and gave to Richelieu, who lived here while waiting for the Palais-Royal to be completed. In recent years the Sénat has expanded across the street, above an attractive arcade, where beautiful reproductions from the Louvre's gift shop are on display. For once the general harmony has been preserved, with pleasing results. The portal of Anne of Bavaria's *hôtel* on rue Garancière has been successfully integrated into the new construction, at n° 36.

The Luxembourg Gardens are a stone's throw from the Sorbonne and are thus permeated with student and literary associations, for, although they were designed as part of the Palais du Luxembourg, they have long been annexed by the University and the people of the neighbourhood. Enter them through Place Paul Claudel, just after the Palace.

Over the generations, the gardens that Jacques Boyceau de la Bareaudière had laid out for Marie de Medici, emulating the Boboli Gardens of Florence, have been remodelled, most significantly in the 19th century - to suit new bourgeois tastes - but their general spirit, even some of their aristocratic aura, have been preserved. De la Bareaudière was a great artist, his reputation unfairly overshadowed by Le Nôtre. His work *Le Traité de jardinage selon les raisons de l'art et de la nature* is the first treatise on the French style of landscape gardening. Unlike Salomon de la Brosse, de la Bareaudière respected the Italian traditional plan for the garden, but little of it remains after the drastic alterations, among them, shifting the central axis 90 degrees. A substantial part of its area also disappeared with the rapid urbanization of Paris in the 19th century. Its two famous walks, La Vallée des Philosophes, much loved by J. J. Rousseau, and L'Allée des Soupirs, the sanctuary of lovers, were already gone before the Revolution.

In the early 19th century Chalgrin redesigned the gardens and created the present vista, which opens due south towards the Observatoire. This was feasible because the Order of the *Chartreux*, which had occupied the land south of the gardens, was expropriated after the Revolution. The entrance to their huge, magnificent domain was at the present n° 64 Boulevard Saint-Michel, previously occupied by a famous and sinister medieval castle, the Château de Vauvert. The origin of its name has been lost, but the castle was possibly the home in the late 10th century of the tragic King Robert II the Pious, who was banished from his palace on the Ile de la Cité and coerced by the Pope into renouncing his beloved wife Berthe for political reasons. For generations thereafter the place was said to be haunted by the Devil and no-one dared walk past it. The expression *aller au diable Vauvert* (to go on a dangerous journey), still in use, refers to that deeply-rooted fear. The *Chartreux* were not bothered by such superstitions and gratefully accepted the extensive grounds offered by Saint Louis, taking up residence on 21 November 1257. They came in a beautiful procession and may have frightened the Devil away, for he has never been seen since. When they left more than five centuries later, the Luxembourg Gardens became, for a brief spell, colossal on Parisian standards, extending all the way to Boulevard du Montparnasse. Soon, however, under the pressure of the real-estate market, chunks of land were chopped off its edges to allow for the widening of rue de Vaugirard and the opening of Boulevard Saint-Michel and rue de Médicis. The people were outraged: the imperial couple was booed at the Odéon, petitions were showered on the authorities (one of them bore 12,000 signatures!), but to no avail. The customary minimal concession was made in that Chalgrin's Avenue de l'Observatoire was allowed to survive.

The present gardens were created during the Second Empire. The English-style section to the south-west reflects the fashion of the time. In the middle of its rolling lawn stands, majestic, Le Duc's powerful stag. The fruit orchards on the southern edge also date from the 19th century, recalling the Order of the Chartreux, who cultivated succulent fruit, vegetables and vines in these blessed, sunny parts. Two tons of fruit are produced here yearly, including raspberries, blackcurrants, figs, over 200 varieties of pears and apples. The trees are a feast to the eye in early spring, when they are in bloom. A school of horticulture and an apiary initiate the city-dweller, in search of his rural roots, to the art of cultivating a fruit-tree or producing honey.

As you make your way into the gardens, do not leave out the Fontaine Médicis on your left, designed by the great Renaissance sculptor Jean Goujon, depicting Leda sitting by the Eurotas, next to a swan, the metamorphosed Jupiter. Tucked away amidst dark vegetation, this is the most romantically shaded nook of the gardens, a bliss during a heatwave. The fountain used to stand on the present rue de Médicis until the time of Haussmann, when it was transferred here. Continue till the famous central octogonal basin, the hub of the gardens, encircled by 50 sculpted female heroines of the history of France. They have watched over generations of little children who have come to float model boats on its shimmering waters and Latin Quarter students who have deserted their austere libraries to bask in the sun on one of the chairs ranked neatly around.

Continue due west to the exit and leave the park for a while. Ahead is rue de Fleurus, the most sought-after address among the 'expatriates' in the 1920s. N° 27 on your left was the home of Gertrude Stein between 1903 and 1937, a mecca "for those who were anybodies or on the way" – provided one had a recommendation when one was new, unless one was picked up by Gertrude Stein herself at Sylvia Beach's Shakespeare and C° on rue de l'Odéon. Gertrude Stein loved meeting new people, so long as she did not feel threatened by them. James Joyce was *persona non grata*; *as* Hemingway said, "If you brought up Joyce twice, you would not be invited back." Gertrude Stein once called him a fifth-rate political schemer, and did not fail to add that she, Gertrude Stein, was the main writer of the English language of the day. Likewise, she thought little of French writers, Jean Cocteau and Max Jacob being rare exceptions. She did, however, take up young Hemingway who devoted quite a few pages to her in *A Moveable Feast*. From the top of her pedestal she patronized him, taught him the facts of life and dismissed him and all his compatriots who had been through the War as 'a lost generation', a phrase she borrowed from a local garage owner - '*génération perdue*' - who had applied it to his young employee who had likewise been to the war. Journalists back home called the Americans in Paris 'expatriates', no less disparagingly. Hemingway and Stein first met in the Luxembourg Gardens. He could not remember exactly whether she already had a dog. Hemingway and Hadley loved the big studio on the ground-floor overlooking the courtyard, which "was like one of the best rooms in the finest museum except that there was a big fireplace and it was warm and comfortable...". On the walls hung paintings by Renoir, Cézanne, Picasso, Braque, Matisse, collected by Gertrude's brother Leo, a man of discriminating taste and flair. By that time Leo had already left for Italy and Gertrude was living with Alice Toklas and the two ladies became godparents to the Hemingways' baby son, Bumby. The rise of Nazi Germany lowered the curtain on 27 rue de Fleurus. The solid bourgeois building, now as then, is private property, but you may be able to get in if you duck the gaze of the *concierge*. The shady courtyard is exquisite.

Retrace your steps to the Luxembourg Gardens and head south. Here there is a small-scale replica of the Statue of Liberty and a tree of liberty, planted by the American Ambassador to Paris in June 1993 to commemorate the 200th anniversary of Franco-American friendship. We leave it to you to meander through the gardens, or just relax on one of the chairs before heading south for the last exploration in the arrondissement.

AROUND MONTPARNASSE

Our exploration of the southern part of the arrondissement starts in front of La Closerie des Lilas, the café on the corner of Boulevard du Montparnasse and Avenue de l'Observatoire. Despite its name, La Closerie has never had lilacs, not even when it was a stopping-place for the stage-coaches on their way to Fontainebleau. Instead it had plane trees, providing shade to the customers of the modest *guinguette* (an outdoor tavern) that first opened here in 1853. The lilacs belonged to another establishment across the Boulevard, from which La Closerie borrowed the name.

In 1905 La Closerie des Lilas was put on the map, when Montparnasse was launched from here as the centre of gravity of the world of art. The idea was the brainchild of two men, André Salmon and Paul Fort, who, launched a new magazine called *Vers et Prose*, and at the same time sent out invitations to artists to come to *La Closerie* and help promote that project. Endowed with overflowing imagination, André Salmon claimed to have sent out 23,000 letters, Paul Fort, a more modest 10,000. The numbers were probably nearer hundreds, but it is of no consequence, for the goal was achieved, whether through their initiative or not: Montparnasse did become the world's centre of art, and La Closerie des Lilas, swarming with customers sipping absinth, became the centre of gravity of Montparnasse - not that it had been overlooked in the 19th century, when Baudelaire, Verlaine, Strindberg, Oscar Wilde and many others frequented the original *guinguette*, conveniently situated on the edge of the Latin Quarter. It was on the occasion of the 1900 Universal Exhibition that it was refurbished and took on its present aspect, but the main café terrace then faced the Avenue de l'Observatoire.

In 1912 Paul Fort was elected '*Prince des Poètes*' and thereafter every Tuesday night he presided over an assembly of up to 200 writers, painters, musicians, critics and journalists, who converged on the place from all over, even from Montmartre. Francis Carco, Dorgèles, Léon-Paul Fargue, Paul Claudel, Picasso,

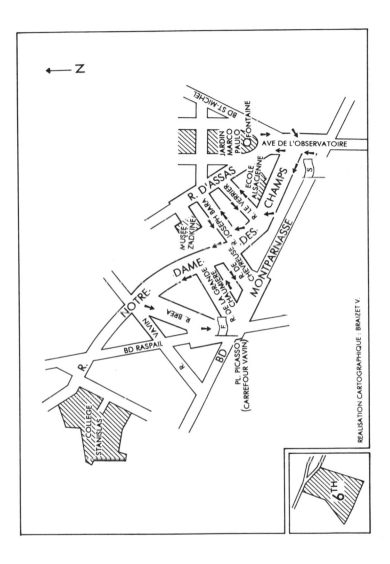

REALISATION CARTOGRAPHIQUE : BRAIZET V.

Max Jacob, Apollinaire, all engaged in passionate discussions here into the early hours of the morning, in a jovial hubbub, washed down with green absinth. Paul Fort, all in black, contrasted with the rainbow-coloured Delaunays. Alfred Jarry would turn up with a pistol. On one occasion he drew it, pointed it at the mirror and pressed... Turning to a horrified young woman he said, "Now that the mirror [a pun on '*glace*' meaning both 'mirror' and 'ice'] is broken, let us talk!" When the last customers were pushed out at 2 am, they would head for the Boul' Mich' (Boulevard Saint-Michel), where their heated discussions continued. By 1912 the entire colony of painters had also invaded the place, including Bonnard, Vlaminck, Derain, Léger and Modigliani. The latter was engaged in a fiery but short-lived relationship with the English poetess Beatrice Hastings, who arrived here dressed up as a Louis XV 'shepherdess'. But these were the last hours of glory of La Closerie des Lilas: within a year the colony had migrated to a new centre of gravity at the newly-opened Carrefour Vavin, one block further west.

When Hemingway, back from Canada with the newborn Bumby, discovered the Closerie in 1924, he found it quiet and melancholy, as depicted by Paul Fort in *Café des ombres*; but this suited Hemingway perfectly: he lived a few houses down, at n° 113 rue Notre-Dame-des-Champs, over a sawmill, and came here to escape the noise and concentrate on his writing, notably on his novel *The Sun Also Rises*. He did, however, socialise and meet friends, among them Scott Fitzgerald, who asked him to read his manuscript of *The Great Gatsby*, and John Dos Passos to whom he read parts of his own manuscript of *The Torrents of Spring*.

Outside the Closerie stands the statue of Maréchal Ney, Prince of the Moskova, one of France's greatest heroes during the Revolutionary and Napoleonic Wars, affectionately nicknamed '*le Brave des braves*'. During the Restoration, however, the authorities never forgave him for having joined forces with Napoleon during his Hundred Day return. The Tribunal of Peers, assembled at the Palais du Luxembourg, accused him of high treason and sentenced him to death, despite a brilliant defence by the renowned lawyers, Dupin and Berryer. On 7 December 1815, Ney was led to the present corner of Avenue de l'Observatoire and Boulevard du Port-Royal and shot by a firing squad, to the horror of many. His statue by Rude was inaugurated under a different regime, on 7 December 1853. It was erected on the site of his execution (level with n° 43 of Avenue de l'Observatoire), but with the opening of the railway station of Port-Royal it was moved to its present location, where Hemingway liked to contemplate it on the way to the Closerie: "my old friend, the statue of Marshal Ney with his sword out."

Before turning left into rue Notre-Dame-des-Champs, continue north along the Avenue de l'Observatoire for a glimpse at Carpeaux's impressive fountain, The Four Corners of the World, standing in the centre of the the Marco Polo Garden.

Walk into rue Notre-Dame-des-Champs. Today, the sawmill and n° 113 are both gone, and the street numbers now jump directly from n° 111 to to n° 115 bis. When Hemingway found the flat he informed Ezra Pound of it in a letter dated 10 February 1924: "We have trouved (found) an appt at 113 Notre Dame des Champs..." The street began originally as a winding country lane, leading to a chapel by the same name. At the time of Catherine de Medici it was used for the transport of stones from the quarries south of Paris to the building site of the Tuileries, her new palace under construction. In the second half of the 19th century, when artists, writers and professors began to move to these countrified parts on the edge of the Latin Quarter, rue Notre-Dame-des-Champs, lying in an area dotted with convents, assured them respectability. And yet, not much earlier Balzac had reported that "robbery was the least of dangers one encountered there." To the Right Bank bourgeois the entire area that lay across the river was a den of vice, and even as late as the early 20th century, Madeleine Renaud's mother was horrified when her daughter crossed the Seine to join the troupe at the Odéon theatre. As a matter of fact, the street was full of honest people living 'bourgeoisement', side by side with nuns and a lot of cheerful schoolchildren. At this end of the street, at n° 109, is still the entrance to the prestigious Ecole Alsacienne, which was founded in 1874. Emphasizing the humanities, openness and tolerance, but without sacrificing high academic targets, the school attracts members of the intelligentsia and of the arts who find here an alternative to the rigid education offered elsewhere. The school opened in Strasbourg (hence its name) as a Protestant establishment and was founded partly to resist Catholic hegemony. In the early days André Gide was among its students. At the other end of the street, at n° 22, the traditional Catholic Collège Stanislas is more in keeping with the values and aspirations of the average French middle classes. A well-known guidebook to the 6th arrondissement, published in 1986, devotes one line to the Ecole Alsacienne, but is effusive in its praise for the Collège Stanislas, concluding with a flourish: "How many of its pupils have suffered its harsh discipline which shapes the best minds!" Among its pupils was writer Roger Wild, who remembered having served at mass one day with a 14-year-old boy named Charles de Gaulle. This was back in 1904, the year de Gaulle passed his baccalauréat!

Walk into rue Le Verrier on your right, just for the pleasure of seeing some attractive houses, where fashionable artists lived at the end of the 19th century. Back on rue Notre-Dame-des-Champs, n° 86 was the last Parisian home of the American painter Whistler, who lived here from 1892 until his return to America 10 years later. His studio on the top floor offered a magnificent view of the Luxembourg Gardens, which largely compensated for the seven-floor climb up the narrow, twisting staircase. Turn right into rue Joseph-Bara, the mecca of Montparnasse in the 1920s, specifically n° 3 on your right. Its agglomeration of artists' studios climbs up erratically from street-level to the roof, in an otherwise bourgeois street. The top studios even have sunny terraces overlooking an enchanting courtyard at the back, nowadays barred to outsiders. Its typical pitched-grey roof and its attic, even its crooked gutter, add to the quaint charm. If the façade is cleaned up, it will retrieve the bright fresh aspect it had in 1913, when the painter Kisling moved here. His studio was in the attic under the roof, romantically picturesque, yet uncomfortable in hot or cold weather. However, this was luxury compared with what most fellow artists had to put up with across the Boulevard Montparnasse, in the 14th or 15th arrondissements. His attic became the social hub of Montparnasse, especially during the crazy years: Modigliani, Zborowski, Cocteau, Radiguet, Max Jacob and Pascin were all present when he threw parties. Pascin, Zborowski and Modigliani were living in the same house (Modigliani having been put up by his art dealer Zborowski, so that he should have where to work), and only had to climb up the stairs. André Salmon, on the other hand, moved out of n° 3 when he got married and settled with his wife across the street, on the ground floor of n° 6, then a recent building (1892). It still has a charming, sculpted, curly head of some Greek divinity over its entrance door, framed by branches of olive trees. Climbing the stairs to get to Kisling was no problem but tottering down after the wild parties was a different matter. Kisling was once heard to complain the next day: "They have peed on my sketches!" But he was a good-natured fellow, full of *joie de vivre* and everyone loved him for it.

Turn left into rue d'Assas. Across the street are the botanic gardens of the science faculty of the University and a picturesque rustic brick house that now belongs to it, reminiscent of a rural past. Continue to n° 100 bis on your left, the home and studio of the sculptor Ossip Zadkine, another oasis converted into a museum. Zadkine hated the life of destitution he was forced to live during his first years in Paris, and never idealized it. Fifteen years later, in 1924, he could afford to buy this picturesque, provincial house, tucked away behind the respectable rue d'Assas, from where he never budged. The place is a joy, richly endowed with the works he has bequeathed to the city of Paris and with its charming garden filled with the song of birds.

Retrace your steps along rue Joseph-Bara and turn right into rue Notre-Dame-des-Champs, then left into rue de Chevreuse. At n° 6 are the superb premises of Reid Hall, so called because it was originally sponsored by Mrs Whitelaw Reid, the wife of the American ambassador to France in the late 19th century. At the time this was the American University Women's Paris Club, a hall of residence for American women students, usually art students. Today it welcomes American students from various universities on a programme in Paris. The exquisite premises and garden must be the envy of many fine hotels and are open to the visitor who wishes to look around. At the corner of rue de Chevreuse and Boulevard du

Montparnasse, further on, is the restaurant *Le Batifol*, part of a chain that tries to maintain traditions by serving regular French dishes. However, it is a very pale substitute for the celebrated *Jockey*, the shrine of Montparnasse night-life between 1923 and 1927. The Jockey was decorated to look like a Wild West saloon. Nobody minded its cramped space, its cluttered mess - its cowboy-turned-pianist was an excellent performer and the two Hawaiian guitarists swept everyone into a langorous dance of blues. And Kiki, the most famous model and female character of Montparnasse, subjugated them with her harsh grating voice, as she sang her own composition which began as follows:

> Un apache avec sa lame
> M'a ouvert le ventre en long;
> ("An 'Apache' with his blade/Slit my belly open
> lengthwise;")

One could not exactly say that her verse soared to great poetic heights, but in that smoke- and alcohol-impregnated atmosphere everyone was thrilled. After the theatre shining limousines ejected the smart set in their evening garb, who came over to rub shoulders with bohemia.

Turn right into Boulevard du Montparnasse, then right again into rue de la Grande-Chaumière, named after a fabulous 19th-century open-air dance hall, across the Boulevard (in the 14th arr.). This little street became the indispensable school of the artists of Montparnasse, where they were allowed the freedom of expression denied them at the Beaux-Arts school, specifically at the Académie de la Grande-Chaumière at n° 14 and at Colarossi at n° 10. La Grande-Chaumière was the most famous of Montparnasse's art schools and when it opened in 1902 Whistler and Rodin were among its teachers. Later, all the Russian and Polish members of the Ecole de Paris received guidance here under Bourdelle. Furthermore, a 20-minute tuition session could be had for a modest 50 centimes. A 'models' fair' was held every Monday on the corner of Boulevard du Montparnasse and rue de la Grande-Chaumière, where artists came to choose models among a varied population of Italians from Calabria or Apulia (their elders in the 19th century had done likewise on Place Pigalle). While the men posed for allegorical figures that embodied contemporary values such as 'Work', the women were models for the 'Holy Virgin', 'Virgin and Child', but also for 'the Birth of Venus' and 'Bathers'. There was a fixed price of 5 francs for a three-hour session, a luxury that only the established artists could afford; struggling artists from Eastern Europe had to content themselves with girls picked up on café terraces, which was not necessarily a bad deal. A generation later Alberto Giacomeiti and Fernand Léger numbered among the Academy's teachers.

The Villa des Artistes hotel at n° 9 has been entirely renovated to suit a well-to-do clientele, offering air-conditioning, cable TV and a night valet, as well as a charming garden with a fountain at the back. The destitute artists who occupied its once run-down premises, then called Libéria, are remembered only in the name and the palette it uses as a logo. The unobtrusive Hôtel des Académies, which you passed by at n° 13, has retained more authenticity. That rue de la Grande-Chaumière has preserved its artistic atmosphere due to Pierre and Irène Charpentier who saved the Académie de la Grande-Chaumière by buying it in 1958, since when it has expanded into the neighbouring rue Jules-Chaplin (n° 2). The street's old shops have accordingly also survived and continue to supply paints, brushes, frames and canvasses. However, the Polish restaurant Wadja, the last remaining 'canteen' in Montparnasse, where Kisling used to dine for 3 francs 50, has recently closed down.

Back on rue Notre-Dame-des-Champs, turn left. The attractive building at n° 73 was the home of the painter Othon Friesz between 1914 and 1949, when he died. His huge studio had previously been occupied by Bouguereau, a highly-regarded *Pompier** painter and teacher at the conservative Beaux-Arts, who must have turned in his grave when his home was taken over by one of those wild painters known as *fauves* (=literally 'wild animals')! Continue to rue Vavin and turn left. Ahead is a lovely street junction, which has almost preserved its old setting intact. Four benches and six trees are neatly disposed around this provincial 'village square', with its Wallace fountain and old street-lamp. Even traffic has been kept within bearable limits. And although some elegant shops are making an appearance little by little, the food shops, café and *tabac* still predominate and add to the local colour of the place. A striking feature is the extraordinary building at n° 26, put up by the architect Sauvage in 1912. Entirely covered with white and blue ceramic tiles, like those that used to decorate the Métro stations, it has been dubbed *'Carreaux Métro'*. The café terraces are a fine place to enjoy a truly Parisian atmosphere, but not before walking up to Dominique, the Russian restaurant at n° 19 rue Bréa and to La Rotonde at the corner of Boulevard du Montparnasse and Boulevard Raspail.

After 60 odd years, Dominique is still going strong and is still in the hands of the original family, although the decorations in the window have been somewhat stylized of late, and the Russian dolls are arrayed in a more clinical fashion than hitherto. The restaurant was created to serve the 'white' Russian community that streamed to Montparnasse after the October Revolution. The Rotonde started as a shoe shop, which was bought by Libion in 1911, then turned into a café. Libion loved his ever-hungry artist clientele and pretended not to notice when a croissant or the tip of a baguette was spirited away, nor did he mind his customers sitting

---

*Uncreative academic painter in the second half of the 19th century

for hours in front of an empty cup. He even took out subscriptions to foreign newspapers on their behalf. On the other hand, he asked them to bring him their paintings, which he hung on the walls, thus creating this special atmosphere that soon distinguished Montparnasse. When, however, he extended his protection to the Russian Revolutionaries, such as Lenin and Trotsky, and refused to play informer to the police on the eve of the Russian Revolution, he brought about his own ruin. The police, looking for an excuse to close down his café, found one when they caught him buying American cigarettes for his '*artistes*'. He was also heavily fined. One day Libion was not at his place behind the bar: he had sold the Rotonde and moved to Denfert-Rochereau further south. Libion died, a broken man, not long after his protégé, Modigliani, and cheated out of the paintings the latter had given him. The Rotonde was never the same again, just another café.

rue Vavin

THE 7th ARRONDISSEMENT

Every year 2.5 million people converge on the 7th arrondissement to climb up the Eiffel Tower and over 125 million have done so since it was inaugurated in 1889. Parisians make up only 5% of the visitors and often under pressure from their children. Most turn their noses up at this emblem of touristy kitsch, as do quite a number of worldly foreigners. A hundred years ago, by contrast, people responded to the Tower with childlike spontaneity. On 31 March 1889, the second anniversary of the beginning of its construction, a 60-strong tailcoated, top-hatted and monocled party made the first official ascent. Prime Minister Gustave Tirard gave up at the first floor, followed by most of the others, but Gustave Eiffel persevered, urging the last 10 breathless participants on to the top, where, with Paris spreading at his feet, he was awarded the *Légion d'honneur* by the Minister of Trade, Gustave Lockroy. The honour, however, should have been shared by the two original designers, Koechkin and Nouguier, who were engineers in Eiffel's company and whose project had won the competition to build a striking monument for the 1889 Universal Exhibition. Officially, the Exhibition was to commemorate the centenary of the French Revolution and among the projects in competition was a gigantic guillotine in honour of the victims of the Terror. But, above all, by organizing the Exhibition, the Third Republic, beleaguered by anarchists, revisionists and Boulangistes, sought to boost patriotic feelings and achieve political cohesion. The Exhibition was to mark the recovery of the Republic and hail France's spectacular entry into modernity. It was to bestow upon her international prestige and dazzle the world with France's technological wizardry. Magnitude reigned supreme, superlatives were on every lip. The gigantic Galérie des Machines, but especially the Eiffel Tower, nicknamed 'La Colossale', was naturally the highlight of the Fair. Rising 318 metres above the ground, it was twice the height of the tallest construction hitherto ever built by man. Only in 1930 would the Chrysler building in New York challenge it and put an end to its supremacy, though never to its status as an emblem. Despite its gigantic dimensions, the Tower weighed only 7,000 tons, an awesome technical feat in itself. Yet, on 7 May 1889, the day of its solemn inauguration, none of the lifts worked!

Not everyone had greeted the project favourably - there was a lot of apprehension and harsh criticism against it. Some Parisians, endowed with exuberant imagination and too panic-stricken to worry about mathematical accuracy, were terrified that the 300-metre tower would sway and collapse, crushing the city all the way to Montmartre! But the main campaign against the Eiffel Tower was based on aesthetic grounds. Guy de Maupassant, after an impulse to pack up and move out of the capital, decided instead to eat in the second-floor restaurant, the only spot in Paris from where it could not be seen. He and 50 other celebrities from the world of arts and letters - Charles Gounod, Leconte de Lisle, François Coppée, Alexandre Dumas, Charles Garnier - signed a petition in the name of Art and Civilisation, against the 'monstrous construction', and showered on her multiple metaphors such as 'hollow candlestick', 'solitary riddled suppository', 'bald umbrella' and 'skeleton'. The more progressive members of the intelligentsia, thought differently. The painter Robert Delaunay, one of the champions of modernity, preferred the Tower to any other model, to judge by the number of paintings he devoted to her. As part of the World Fair, the Eiffel Tower was meant to be an ephemeral structure and only Eiffel's influential position enabled him to obtain a 20-year concession to exploit it. In 1909 the enemies of the Tower intensified their protest campaign, claiming that 'in any case she is useless' (the use of the female gender puzzled Irwin Shaw who saw it rather as a phallic symbol). Such an argument carried weight in those utilitarian days. Fortunately, its height was its salvation: wireless was beginning to be used to transmit messages, and the tall iron tower proved to be a marvellous antenna. The first news bulletin was broadcast from the Eiffel Tower in 1925 and in 1935 a score of excited enthusiasts picked up its first television broadcast, thrilled at the sight of a black disc bouncing on the screen!

The presence of this futuristic structure in the most backward-looking arrondissement may seem incongruous. Indeed, 150 families of the old nobility are still firmly established in their sanctuary of Faubourg Saint-Germain - the Duc and Duchesse de Harcourt on rue Vaneau, the Prince Guy de Polignac on rue Barbet-de-Jouy, the Duc and Duchesse de Noailles on the quai d'Orsay, the Prince and Princesse de la Tour d'Auvergne on Place du Palais-Bourbon, the Duc and Duchesse d'Orléans on Place Vauban... Walled within their magnificent 18th-century *hôtels, entre cour et jardin* (between a courtyard in front and a garden at the back), they still live in splendid seclusion, side by side, however, with the Republic that has usurped their rights and has robbed them of many of their splendid homes. Over 40 institutions and ministries, including the Prime Minister's headquarters at the Hôtel Matignon, now occupy the nobility's dwellings. As well as the Republic's tricolours, 24 foreign flags of embassies also fly over the arrondissement. These too are established in the nobility's former mansions and, like the Republican institutions, enjoy the heavy protection of the police. The presence of the police has turned the 7th into the safest arrondissement of Paris for the benefit of all its residents, aristocrats and commoners alike. For there is plenty to protect in this territory of top-ranking politicians and army officers (De

Gaulle's Paris base was on avenue de Breteuil), of diplomats, of successful writers and of *haute couture* designers, some of whom accumulate immense wealth behind the discreet façades, sometimes even extravagant luxury. One residence is said to have a bamboo forest inside, another a full-sized elephant carved in boxwood, another yet a dreamlike setting of *Beauty and the Beast*. This is also the centre of antique dealers most of whom are based in 'Le Carré Rive Gauche' in the heart of the Faubourg Saint-Germain, a rectangle bounded by quai Voltaire, rue de l'Université, rue des Saints-Pères and rue du Bac, where the greatest concentration of antique shops in Paris is to be found.

It all began in 543 with the foundation by Childebert of the early Christian shrine that from the 10th century on, was to become the formidable abbey of Saint-Germain (see chapter on the 6th arr.) The area around the abbey developed as a result of its presence and by the 13th century became a separate borough. It did not have aristocratic connotations until the 17th century, when Marguerite de Valois (also known as Queen Margot), forced out of the Louvre because of her uncertain social position, moved to her new palace on the corner of the present rue de Seine and the quai Malaquais. Its magnificent gardens extended north into what is now the 7th arrondissement, beyond rue de Bellechasse. When the estate was sold after the Queen's death to pay off her debts, local people mourned the gardens to which Queen Margot had generously allowed them access, but the real-estate developer Monsieur Barbier rubbed his hands with pleasure: within 14 years (1606-20) he had sliced up the entire property, opened new streets, erected new buildings and brought its value up twentyfold, not unlike his fellow developers in the Marais and on the Ile Saint-Louis (now in the 3rd and 4th arr.).

Among the first noble families to settle here were the Saint-Simon. The Duc de Saint-Simon, father of the writer of the *Mémoires*, took up residence at the Hôtel de Plessis-Châtillon on rue Saint-Dominique in 1650. Ten years later the Duchesse de Chevreuse, the famous heroine of the *Fronde*, moved to the Hôtel de Luynes, also on rue Saint-Dominique. At the same time, after the Counter-Reformation in the first half of the 17th century, there was a rapid development of monastic life and many religious institutions settled in the area, attracted by the large expanses of available land outside the city walls and hoping to enjoy the protection of the abbey of Saint-Germain. Among them was the Foreign Missions on the corner of rue du Bac and rue de La Fresnay, the only religious institution in the arrondissement to have remained on the same premises for over 300 years.

The second half of the 17th century was a favourable time for the future 7th because, for one thing, the abbey, anxious to increase its income, was selling off parts of its huge domain, at reasonable prices. This happened to coincide with the decline of the Marais, by now too noisy and crowded and quite a distance from the Louvre. The court's move to Versailles in 1682 sounded the Marais's death-knell. The centre of gravity of the privileged inevitably shifted west, notably to the Faubourg Saint-Honoré, close to the Louvre and on the way to Versailles. Many families would have willingly opted for the more countrified and therefore more appealing Faubourg Saint-Germain, had it been connected with the Right Bank by a proper bridge. At the beginning of the 17th century the two banks were connected only by a ferryboat, which had been put into service in 1564 to transport blocks of stones extracted from the quarries south-west of Paris to the building site of the Tuileries Palace. A country road was opened between the quarries and the river - now rue Notre-Dame-des-Champs, rue Saint-Placide, rue Dupin and, finally, rue du Bac which led to the ferry *(bac)* - allowing the transport to skirt the city. Not until 1632 was a bridge - the red painted Pont Rouge - thrown over this part of the Seine, just east of the old ferry, in line with the present rue de Beaune. It was a primitive, rickety bridge, unfit for vehicles, and often damaged or flooded. "The Pont Rouge has been washed away to Saint-Cloud," wrote Madame de Sévigné mockingly of its final doom. To cross the river one had to go all the way to the Pont-Neuf and, that being a place of ill repute, wary ladies such as Madame de Sablé would travel in their carriages as far as Notre-Dame in order to avoid it.

However, in 1689, when Jules Hardouin-Mansart's beautiful Pont Royal was completed on the site of the old ferry, the Faubourg Saint-Germain and the Tuileries were brought together. From then on it took only a couple of minutes to 'cross the waters', as the expression went, and a new era began for the Faubourg. Admittedly by now the centre of gravity of aristocratic life had shifted west to Versailles, but many believed this would be temporary. Besides, the more independent-spirited members of the nobility did not follow the King to Versailles, where he kept the courtiers in check, but preferred the intellectual freedom of the *salons littéraires* held in the town's sumptuous *hôtels particuliers*. Towards the close of the reign of Louis XIV, when the frivolous atmosphere in Versailles had been dampened by the King's illness and bereavements, as well as by the influence of the austere Madame de Maintenon, many courtiers, feeling increasingly constrained by the pomp and etiquette of court life, were eager to join their peers in the city.

The great migration back to Paris began during the Regency, which followed the death of the Sun King in 1715, when even the government left Versailles and resettled in the capital for a while. With the economic boom brought about by *La Compagnie de l'Inde* and the Louisiana adventure, Paris became a new Eldorado blessed with easy money and feverish speculation, which benefitted first and foremost the Faubourg Saint-Germain, the new stronghold of the fashionable set. Magnificent mansions sprang up throughout the neighbourhood, such as the Palais de Bourbon (now the National Assembly), built for the dowager Duchesse de Bourbon/Condé, the legitimized daughter of Louis XIV and Madame de Montespan, and the neighbouring Hôtel de Lassay, built at the same time by her lover, the Marquis de Lassay (now the residence of the National Assembly's president). The building spree slackened in the second half of the 18th century owing both to the increasing scarcity of land and to the Seven Year War; only a quarter of the houses in the Faubourg were built at the time of Louis XVI.

Meanwhile, the old nobility was shedding the last vestiges of its feudal veneer, whilst perpetuating its wealth by arranging marriages with *nouveau riche* families, which was already the case in the Marais in the 17th century: *"Il faut bien fumer ses terres"* ("One does have to manure one's land"), Madame de Sévigné had written at the time. A score of small 'courts' *(salons)* replaced the royal one, presided over by such clever ladies as the great rivals Madame Geoffrin, on Faubourg Saint-Honoré, and Madame du Deffand, on Faubourg Saint-Germain. Though by this time old and blind, the Marquise du Deffand had been powerful and compelling in her younger days and is said to have been the mistress of the Regent, Philippe d'Orléans. After her husband's death she retired to the convent of Saint-Joseph on rue Saint-Dominique, where she opened her celebrated *salon*, lavishly covered with buttercup-coloured moire. Princes and dukes were among her guests, as well as Montesquieu, Voltaire, d'Alembert and Fontenelle. Before his final return to the capital, the decrepit Voltaire wrote to Madame du Deffand, "I am coming back dead but I want to be resuscitated in order to throw myself at the feet of Madame *la Marquise du Deffand.* "

Influential visitors came also from across the Channel - David Hume, Lord Shelburn, Gibbon and, above all, Horace Walpole, for whom the 70-year-old Marquise felt a burning passion. Walpole, 20 years her junior, did not return her passion, but he felt a sincere friendship towards her and was greatly appreciative of her *salon*, which, he believed, as other foreigners did, embodied the essence of French spirit and intellect for which he had left the *salon* of her rival, Madame Geoffrin.

The politest society, however, according to contemporaries, gathered in the home of Julie de Lespinasse. Julie had been lady's companion to the old Marquise du Deffand but the latter threw her out when she discovered that she was the centre of attraction during the day, when the Marquise used to sleep (the Marquise's gatherings took place at night). Julie's friends, especially d'Alembert, helped her set up her own *salon* on the corner of rue de Bellechasse and rue Saint-Dominique.

While the discussions in the 17th-century *salons* were restricted to intellectual exchanges, in the 18th century new ideas were put forth and independent opinions debated around beautiful dinner tables in dining-halls, which were themselves an innovation. Thus, unknowingly, amidst the extravagant luxury of the Faubourg

Saint-Germain, a carefree, spoilt aristocracy was paving the way for its imminent downfall.

Ironically, it was in this area that the French Revolution actually preluded on the morning of 14 July, when the Hôtel des Invalides, the home Louis XIV had built for the war invalids in 1670, was raided for 32,000 guns, used to storm the Bastille a few hours later. Moreover, the Champ-de-Mars, the parade-ground of the royal Ecole Militaire, on the western edge of the present 7th arrondissement, was chosen by the new Republic for the celebration of the first Bastille Day in 1790, as well as for such revolutionary rituals as *La Fête de l'Etre Suprême* on 8 June 1794, a substitute for the day of Pentecost, by means of which Robespierre attempted to dispose of over 1,500 years of Christianity.

Somehow, none of the above actually altered the aristocratic character of the 7th; on the contrary, Napoleon, the ambivalent heir of the Revolution, ultimately preserved it. His modest social origins had left Napoleon with complex feelings towards the old nobility, a fascination tinted with jealousy. A child of Republican, egalitarian ideals, he had no sooner grabbed the reigns of power than he proceeded to create a new nobility whom he encouraged to settle in the aristocratic Faubourg, as also some of his closest relations, including his stepson Eugène de Beauharnais at the Hôtel de Torcy and his own brother Lucien Bonaparte at the Hôtel de Bricnne. It did not take these people long to settle into the property of the dispossessed nobility, but they lacked pedigree and therefore sought the friendship of the surviving old families who had retrieved their homes during the First Empire and were now trickling back to the Faubourg. On one occasion the Duc de Luynes was visiting Lucien de Bonaparte in his newly acquired Hôtel de Brienne, when he remarked on two of his old paintings hanging on one of the walls. Whether out of deference for the Duke or out of sheer indifference to art, the same evening Lucien Bonaparte had the paintings returned to their original owner at the Hôtel de Luynes.

In view of the above, it is hardly a coincidence that Napoleon is associated with the 7th arrondissement more than any other French ruler. Knowing more than anyone, how to integrate old values into new, he made this the area for the celebration of his military achievements, on which his modern state rested. His victorious armies and their heroes were honoured in the prestigious military establishments founded by his predecessors, the Invalides by Louis XIV and the Ecole Militaire (for the training of officers from a poor background) by Louis XV. Military ceremonies took place on the Champ-de-Mars, and the lion that Napoleon had plundered from Piazza San Marco in Venice now surmounted the spectacular fountain of the vast Esplanade des Invalides. (The lion was restored to Venice in 1815, after Napoleon's defeat.) Similarly, the guns captured in Vienna in 1803 were set up here and used in salutes. The famous order of the *Légion d'honneur* was founded at the Invalides in 1802 but moved to its present location at the Hôtel de Salm opposite Musée d'Orsay two years later. Above all, the chapel of the Invalides was to become the 'Elyseum of the brave', the final abode of France's war heroes, first and foremost of Napoleon himself, whose remains were brought here from Saint-Helena in great pomp on 15 December 1840, thus fulfilling the Emperor's wish to be buried "by the Seine, among the French people whom I have loved so." Thus the 7th arrondissement remains associated in the mind with Napoleon and with the military. The Hôtel des Invalides now houses the Musée des Armées and the Ministry of Defence occupies the Hôtel de Brienne, Napoleon's gift to his brother.

Napoleon, however, mingled with few members of the old nobility, nearly all of whom remained in exile until the Restoration. When the *émigrés* finally returned, times had changed and many had to renounce the luxury and glamour of their former lifestyles; some had to share or let out part of their homes and some ladies even had to make their own clothes... Unable to adjust to the rise of capitalism during the Second Empire, the Faubourg turned its back stoically on the court life of the Tuileries and retreated into its shell. But Haussmann's transformation of Paris, which accelerated during the Third Republic, was now reaching the 7th arrondissement. Most of the changes, fortunately, were in areas that had hitherto not been developed, predominantly west of the Esplanade des Invalides. Miraculously, neither the disastrous breach created by the opening of the Boulevard Saint-Germain, nor the damage caused by the Civil War of the *Commune* (when some beautiful mansions were burnt down, notably La Cour des Comptes, where the Musée d'Orsay now stands, and the Hôtel de Salm opposite, now the Musée de la Légion d'Honneur) were fatal to the arrondissement. But the social make-up of its population was bound to change, as most of the elegant blocks of flats along the new avenues were built for the well-to-do bourgeoisie.

With the arrival of the bourgeoisie the 7th was to enter the modern age, after all. The successive Universal Exhibitions held on the Champ-de-Mars - and beyond as they grew in size - were meant to trumpet France's economic and technical achievements to the world, not least to England! They were also meant to honour the new moneyed bourgeoisie. On the other hand, the large influx of visitors threatened to disfigure the subdued, outdated, elegant arrondissement and to disturb its serenity, but traditions die hard in the 7th and when the pavilions were dismantled, the crowds vanished and the 7th was restored unscathed to its privileged residents.

And they are certainly privileged. No other arrondissement enjoys such a central position in an uncongested area of broad avenues and greenery. As much as a third of it is covered with parks, gardens and squares, some, often the larger ones, being private, and the river is never too far away. Ironically, of the industrial intruders into this arrondissement, the most controversial is the only one to have survived. Somehow, as it rises conspicuously against the Paris sky, the Eiffel Tower remains in harmony with the perfect symmetry and the beautiful vista of the Champ-de-Mars and the Jardins du Trocadéro that roll down towards it on the opposite bank of the Seine. It took French genius for town planning to integrate this gigantic piece of Meccano into the landscape of an arrondissement that, more than any other, embodies the *Ancien Régime*.

WHERE TO WALK...

FAUBOURG SAINT-GERMAIN (THE EAST)

The 7th arrondissement covers a much larger area than the previous ones, but it is mainly the old Faubourg Saint-Germain that is of interest to the pedestrian. Its exploration should end with a climb to the top of the Tour Montparnasse (in the 15th arr.), which offers a spectacular aerial view of the Faubourg and an indication of how much of its area is still covered with gardens.

The opening of the Musée d'Orsay in 1987 brought the old Faubourg into the limelight and to the attention of 3 million visitors per year, but somehow it remains an area of discreet and refined dignity, impermeable to this crude age. On this walk, start from the corner of Boulevard Saint-Germain and rue des Saints-Pères. This is where rue Saint-Dominique began until 1866, when Haussmann opened the Boulevard Saint-Germain and destroyed the magnificent *hôtels* that stood in the way. Such was the fate of the Hôtel de Salvois (on the site of the present n° 188 Boulevard Saint-Germain and n° 48 rue des Saints-Pères), the home of the Saint-Simon family who were among the early settlers in the Faubourg. The Duc de Saint Simon, author of the justly famous and informative *Mémoires*, was born here in 1675.

Rue des Saints-Pères marks the eastern border of the arrondissement (the odd numbers belong to the 6th) and the eastern edge of the 'Carré Rive Gauche', the enclave of fabulous antique shops that extends between the river and the Boulevard Saint-Germain, as far as rue du Bac to the west. It also has leafy, hidden courtyards, architectural gems and a profusion of gorgeous, 18th-century, wrought-iron staircases. One such courtyard is situated at n° 16, the home of an antique dealer. Soon after you will cross rue de l'Université, reminiscent of the days when the University owned the strip of land between the abbey of Saint-Germain-des-Prés and the present National Assembly, known as the Pré-aux-Clercs. It was given to the University by Louis VII in the 12th century, but was a constant source of grievance to the abbey ever since, because of the students who came over from the Latin Quarter to cause a rumpus.

Turn left into rue de Verneuil, a haven of provincial drowsiness. Don't let the

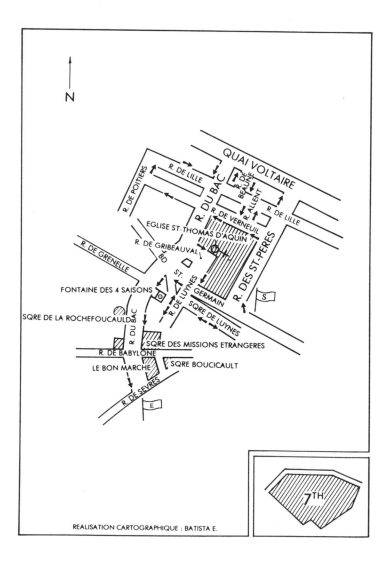

REALISATION CARTOGRAPHIQUE : BATISTA E.

excellent antique shops, with their beautiful old china, ceramic tiles and the wonderful smell of old wood that wafts from the harpsichord dealer's, distract you from the architectural beauty above - notably the elegant, curving profile of the old houses on the left-hand side of the street. Notice the original circular staircase at n° 13 and the picturesque corner of rue Allent, level with n° 15 - somewhat evocative of a sleepy village in Provence. Stroll into the peaceful rue Allent before continuing on rue de Verneuil. Beyond rue du Bac, rue de Verneuil is lined with succulent food shops and has been dubbed '*le hameau* ('hamlet') *de Verneuil*' for its village atmosphere. Hitherto it has catered to French locals, but a Vietnamese and an Indian restaurant have already started to change its *Vieille France* character. At n° 58 stands an extravagant-looking building, uncannily resembling a war memorial, dedicated to the memory of a little-known 18th-century figure, the Maréchal de Bercheny, also a Hungarian baron and Count. The 18th-century Hôtel d'Avejean across the street at n° 53/55 is prettier; it is named after its first landlord, the Marquis d'Avejean, who was a musketeer. During the Revolution, it was sold off in a lottery for 50 francs! Today this is La Maison des Ecrivains, which supports writers and organizes literary activities. There is a very pretty coffee shop in the flowery old courtyard, which is open to all and sundry. The next-door corner house of rue de Poitiers has an elegant façade with Italianate busts, a splendid staircase and a beautiful paved courtyard. The magnificent *hôtel* at n° 12 rue de Poitiers is now home to Ecole Polytechnique alumni (there are roughly 15,000 *Polytechniciens* working in France), whose status can also be measured by the menu posted in the archway!

Turn right into rue de Poitiers and right into rue de Lille. The brasserie *Le Télégraphe* at n° 41 was the home of the female employees of the post office in the 19th century. Though not renowned for its cooking, its spectacular Belle Epoque setting makes it a very popular restaurant.

Retrace your steps by way of rue de Lille, lined with old mansions all the way. Turn left into rue des Saints-Pères and turn left into the quai Voltaire, undoubtedly one of the beauty-spots of Paris: to your left is Hardouin-Mansart's elegant Pont Royal, and across the river, the Tuileries Gardens, Place du Carrousel and the Louvre. A beauty further enhanced by the fabulous antique shops and art galleries of world repute located in the magnificent *hôtels* of the *quai*. Balzac's hero, cousin Pons, already browsed here in the last century. On the other side of the *quai*, by the water, are the more humble, picturesque *bouquinistes*, where Rudyard Kipling liked to browse, like so many other writers and artists. Quite a number even took up residence here.

At n° 1, the Hôtel de Tessé, an 18th-century mansion with a wrought-iron balcony, was built for the widowed Comtesse de Tessé and her son, on the site of a previous *hôtel* which had burnt down in 1760, at the same time as the landlord, the 80-year-old Marquis de Bacqueville. This eccentric gentleman had gone off to the Opera, knowing full well that a fire had broken out in his house. When he returned from the show, he found the house in flames, but, wishing to rescue some papers, he walked straight inside and never came out again! Eighteen years earlier, emulating Icarus, he had taken off from the roof of his house, fitted with two pairs of wings, hoping to soar off to the skies. His brief flight ended on a wash-shed on the Seine, and he with a broken leg. The mansion next door was occupied at one time by Louise-Renée de Penacoët de Kéroualle, the artful mistress of Charles II of England, who had used her charms to climb the social ladder and become Duchess of Portsmouth. Louis XIV knew her strength, which came in handy in his dealings with England. After the death of Charles II the greedy Duchess removed as many works of art as she could handle from his magnificent collection and crammed them into her residence on quai Voltaire.

Anatole France spent much of his childhood in his father's bookshop at n° 9, where he claimed to have acquired his taste for the arts. Between 1829 and 1835 Delacroix lived on the 5th floor at n° 13, in an artist's studio advantageously facing the north, where the idea of his renowned painting *La Liberté Guidant le Peuple* may have germinated. Delacroix took over the studio from Horace Vernet, the famous battle-scene painter, when the latter was appointed director of the Villa Medici academy in Rome. Several years later, the painter Corot came to live here, while Ingres occupied a studio at n° 17. N° 19 was already a lodging-house when Baudelaire stayed in room n° 47 (which can still be seen) between 1856 and 1858, absorbed in his collection of poems, *Les Fleurs du Mal*. In the winter of 1861-2, Richard Wagner completed his *Die Meistersingers* at this hotel, where the Finnish composer Sibelius and the writer Oscar Wilde also stayed for a while. Between 1839 and 1849 Alfred de Musset stayed at n° 25. The best known house on the *quai*, however, is n° 27, the home of the Marquis Charles de Villette, where Voltaire died on 30 May 1778, at the age of 84. Voltaire had left the *quai* in 1723, finding it too noisy, but on 10th February 1778, he came back here to terminate his life, and Villette, his host and admirer, made sure he was given a room overlooking the quiet courtyard. In March his play *Irène* created a sensation at the Théâtre Français (The troupe was performing at the Palais des Tuileries at the time, their theatre on rue des Fossés-Saint-Germain, now Ancienne Comédie in the 6th arr., having closed down for safety reasons). A huge crowd pressed around Voltaire's triumphant coach on the *quai*, then called quai des Théatins, after the Order founded here by Mazarin in 1647. The Marquis de Villette had the quai illuminated for the occasion, and had the street sign *quai des Théatins* replaced by a plaque that read *quai Voltaire*. The authorities did not share the people's enthusiasm and the next morning the police were sent to remove the plaque. Nor was Voltaire appreciated by the church for that matter: when he died the priest of Saint-Sulpice refused to accept his body, which had to be transferred to Romilly, east of Paris. As for the Marquis de Villette's initiative to rename the *quai* after his admired friend, it only came into effect after the brutal fall of the *Ancien Régime*, on 11 July 1791, when Voltaire's remains were transferred to the Panthéon. On that occasion, "500,000 over-emotional Parisians" were reportedly gathered on the quai Voltaire, "weeping and rejoicing at the same time." The quai was strewn with flowers, while young girls, clad in white and adorned with garlands of roses, posed at n° 27. At their head stood the Marquise de Villette personifying some Greek goddess, in retaliation for the insult inflicted on Voltaire by the church 13 years earlier. The Marquis de Villette's efforts to immortalize his friend extended into every area of his life: when he died in 1793 it turned out that he had left a nine-month-old baby rejoicing in the name Voltaire-Villette!

Turn left into rue de Beaune for the sheer delight of a window-shopping spree, then come back to the *quai*. Five delectable sisters, the grand-daughters of the Duc de Mazarin, on their mother's side, lived at the Hôtel de Mailly-Nesle, at n° 29. One by one they succumbed to the charms of the gallant Louis XV, all but the third who was kept under tight guard by her husband, as confirmed in the following verse:

> L'une est presque en oubli, l'autre presque en poussière.
> La troisième est en pied, la quatrième attend,
> Pour faire place à la dernière...
> (One is almost forgotten, the other almost turned to dust.
> The third is on the active list, the fourth is waiting, to
> make room for the last...)

The last was to become the famous Duchesse de Châteauroux, upon whom the royal lover bestowed an annual pension of 80,000 pounds. The mob called her, more prosaically, *"La P... du Roi"* ('The King's Wh...') In 1744 she died suddenly, aged only 27, in her room on the first floor (it still exists). The second eldest daughter, had given the King a son and died just as mysteriously at age 28. The King did not grieve for long, for by the next year the Pompadour had completely captured his heart and embarked on a 19-year reign as his favourite, which ended only with her death in 1764.

Turn left into rue du Bac, the road to the ferry (*bac*) that carried the stones to the site where the Palais des Tuileries was being built. Alexandre Dumas's hero d'Artagnan lived on the site of n° 1 from 1659 to 1673, when he was killed during the siege of Maastricht. The Grey Musketeers whom he had commanded had their barracks along this part of rue du Bac (n° 13-17) and rue de Beaune, which is probably why he came to live here. D'Artagnan's two children were born here and he was held in such great esteem that King Louis XIV and Queen Marie-

Thérèse acted as godparents to his elder child, and the Grand Dauphin and the Grande Mademoiselle to the younger one.

Turn left into rue de Gribeauval, an elegant little street with some stunning luxury clothes shops, which leads to the pretty square and church of Saint-Thomas-d'Aquin, a peaceful haven, though not quite the beauty-spot it was before Haussmann's ruthless opening of the Boulevard Saint-Germain. The church, originally built as a Dominican noviciate, had its entrance on the now demolished part of rue Saint-Dominique, opposite the magnificent Hôtel de Luynes, from where it could be reached by way of a beautiful, tree-lined alley. Anne de Rohan-Montbazon, Duchesse de Luynes, was living at the Hôtel de Luynes when she came over to lay the cornerstone of the new monastery on 5 March 1682. The Revolution did away with the noviciate, but in 1804, when Christianity was no longer anathema, a huge congregation gathered around the front steps of the church, where Pope Pius VII gave them his blessing. It then became the parish church of the Faubourg's aristocracy, the returning *émigrés'* favourite place of worship. Turn right into rue de Luynes and continue beyond Boulevard Saint-Germain into the enchanting Square de Luynes, a reminder of past splendour. The Hôtel de Luynes was built in 1650 for the Duchesse de Chevreuse, widow of Charles de Luynes who had been Louis XIII's closest counsellor. It was one of the earliest and most magnificent mansions in the Faubourg and miraculously survived the fury of the Revolution, albeit stripped of many of its works of art. Some, however, were rescued by the zealous Alexandre Lenoir, who transferred them to the newly opened Musée des Monuments Français, (in the 6th arr.). The opening of Boulevard Saint-Germain deprived it of its front building and most of its courtyard, the opening of Boulevard Raspail swept away a good part of its gardens, and the main building, with its marvellous 18th-century halls, was replaced by blocks of flats. This time no one was to blame but the owners... The monumental staircase and its murals were saved and are now in the entrance hall of the Musée Carnavalet (in the 3rd).

Retrace your steps, turn left into Boulevard Saint-Germain and right into rue du Bac. Cross over to n° 46, which has a beautifully carved door surmounted by the letter B. Jacques-Samuel Bernard, Marquis de Coubert, the elder son of a famous financier, had inherited the fabulous sum of 33 million pounds, which enabled him to build this magnificent *hôtel* and indulge in a life of extravagance that ended in bankruptcy. Voltaire, who had been involved in his financial transactions, also got his fingers burnt in the process. The two magnificent wrought-iron staircases are still there, as well as the imitation-marble panelling. Only royalty and the high nobility could afford real marble which was too dear at the time, even for somebody as rich as Bernard. The gorgeous 18th-century knocker on the entrance door, like much other ironwork in Paris, has been spirited away somewhere. The back garden, although just a tiny fragment of the original grounds - another victim of the Boulevard Saint-Germain - remains a blissful oasis of green.

Cross the Boulevard Saint-Germain and continue along rue du Bac, a narrow, bustling street in this section, bursting with lush food shops which distract one from the street's architectural treasures. The site between n°s 68 and 80 was occupied by the Order of the Visitation Sainte-Marie in the second half of the 17th century, all gone with the Revolution. When the original, modest chapel was built in the 17th century, a humble girl, deliberately chosen for her poverty, was asked to lay the cornerstone. However, when the church was reconstructed in 1775, it was Marie-Antoinette who was asked to do so.

Turn left into rue de Grenelle, once the road leading from the abbey of Saint-Germain-des-Prés to the plain of Grenelle (now in the 15th arr.), a favourite hunting-ground. The name Grenelle derives from *garenne*, meaning 'warren'. The parallel rue de Varenne (a distortion of *garenne*) and the nearby rue de Bellechasse also reflect the use of the area for hunting. On your right, at n° 55/57, is Bouchardon's gigantic fountain known as La Fontaine des Quatre Saisons, where the four seasons of the year are represented by chubby cupids, decked in spring flowers, harvesting, revelling at grape-picking time (which is also hunting-time, hence a frightened rabbit making a dash to escape), sheltering under a blanket, and so on. Such an idyllic depiction of nature accorded with the tastes of the frivolous society of 18th-century France, unwary of the impending storm. Voltaire, however, was unimpressed by the fountain. For one thing, he found the street too narrow for this overbearing monument. He also nicknamed the fountain 'La Trompeuse' ('the deceiver') because it contained "so much stone for so little water..." This was probably a good thing given that the fountains in Paris were supplied with the filthy water of the Seine and were to blame for a couple of cholera epidemics. The fountain is also deceptive insofar as it is only a thin facing on the wall behind, a consequence of the meanness of the nuns of the Recollettes, who refused to give up more than this narrow strip of land, although their estate extended as far as rue de Varenne.

Back on rue du Bac their old premises can still be seen at n° 83/85, but are hardly recognizable. During the Revolution their chapel was found suitable for a theatre - Le Théâtre des Victoires Nationales - and the convent was therefore spared. The neighbouring convent of the Visitation was less fortunate and disappeared in the turmoil. The buildings that now stand at n°s 79 and 81 were erected during the Restoration. The delicate niches are typical of the architectural style of the time. Across the street, at n° 94, is a rare example of an Art Nouveau shop window, a style dubbed *style nouille* ('noodle') by the writer Paul Morand. At n° 98, on the corner of rue de Varenne, two golden angels on either side of the inviting golden head of Bacchus are a remnant of an old tavern, Les Deux Anges, previously known as La Cloche d'Or. In a room on the first floor a man called Cadoudal fomented a conspiracy against the First Consul and future Emperor. The conspiracy aborted and Cadoudal, together with 11 of his accomplices, perished soon after. Across the street, the Hôtel de Ségur at n° 97 is an early 18th-century house, built during the Regency for people devoted to easy living and libertinage, as can be seen from the mischievous masks on the walls overlooking the courtyard. Throughout the Second Empire it was the home of well-known people, among them the Ambassador of the United States.

In 1825 the Comte de Noe moved to the next-door *hôtel*, at n° 99. The Count was a man of high status, a peer of France, but he also had a rebellious son, Amédée de Noe, who had taken to drawing and was toying with the preposterous idea of making it his livelihood. Evicted from the paternal *hôtel*, Amédée carried off the cook and moved to the humble suburb of Batignolles-Epinette north of Paris (now in the 17th arr.). Shedding his previous identity, he assumed the name of his predecessor of ancient times, Cham (French for Ham), the accursed son of the Biblical Noah (Noé in French). Under this pen-name he became one of France's most famous caricaturists in the 19th century, contributing regularly to the satirical *Charivari*, alongside Daumier and Gavarni.

Next door, the elegant Hôtel de la Feuillade (n° 101) is a typical example of an 18th-century townhouse, built 'between courtyard and garden' *(entre cour et jardin)*. The Hôtel de Sainte-Aldegonde, across the street at n° 102, takes pride in its beautiful wrought iron and sculpted heads. This may have been the Swedish Embassy before the Revolution, where Madame de Staël moved after her marriage in 1775. The neighbouring n° 104 has a delightful garden at the back of the house, surpassed though by the Square de La Rochefoucauld at n° 108. A convalescent home was built here during the reign of Louis XIII. In the 18th century the establishment had 21 beds and patients could stay here up to 15 days before returning to their work. Soldiers, clergymen and lackeys were not admitted since they were provided for elsewhere. Located in an area noted for its pure air and tranquillity, the establishment was also reputed for its food, reported to be "healthy, abundant and clean" - certainly not the rule at the time!

The twin *hôtels* at n°s 118 and 120 have beautifully carved doors representing the four major continents, the work of Toro. Chateaubriand lived on the ground floor of the back building between 1838 and 1848, a poor, sickly old man. Every day, at precisely the same time, he would be seen walking over to the Abbaye-aux-Bois, at 16 rue de Sèvres, to visit his old friend Madame de Récamier. The neighbours would then set their watches accordingly... It is here that Chateaubriand wrote the last few lines of his *Mémoires d'Outre-Mer*:

En traçant ces derniers mots, ce 16 novembre 1841, ma fenêtre qui donne à l'ouest sur les jardins des Missions étrangères, est ouverte: il est six heures du matin. […] Je vois les reflets d'une aurore dont je ne reverrai pas se lever le soleil.

(Whilst writing these last words, this 16 November 1841, my window looking west over the gardens of the Foreign Missions is open: it is six in the morning […] I see the reflection of dawn, the sunrise of which I shall not see again)

However, Chateaubriand was not to die until seven years later, on 4 July 1848, when he was 80. The funeral service took place in the neighbouring chapel of the Foreign Missions, at n° 128, then an annexe of the parish church of Saint-Thomas-d'Aquin. In the congregation were Victor Hugo, Sainte-Beuve and Balzac, who left totally contradictory testimonies of the event. The seminary of the Foreign Missions was founded in the 17th century and is the oldest religious institution to have survived in the 7th arrondissement, La Salle des Martyrs, open to the public, illustrates the unspeakable sufferings of its missionaries in the Far East. The splendid gardens, invisible from the street, are unfortunately not open to the public except by special arrangement. A wall separates them from the gardens of the Hôtel Matignon, the residence of the Prime Minister, which are the largest private gardens in the capital.

As you reach rue de Sèvres you will come to the Bon Marché department store, which contrary to its name is no longer inexpensive. Noted for its household goods and haberdashery, until recently it catered predominantly to a solid bourgeois *Vieille France* clientele, who included the late Madame de Gaulle. It is also the only department store on the Left Bank, which fits with the tradition, dating back to the 12th century, that commercial activities were, until recently, concentrated on the Right Bank. The saying went: *La Rive Gauche pense, la Rive Droite dépense* ('the Left Bank thinks, the Right Bank spends').

When, in 1852, Aristide Boucicaut, a shop assistant at Au Petit Saint-Thomas, at n° 27/31 rue du Bac, was offered a partnership in a little hosiery shop, Au Bon Marché, on the corner of rue du Bac and rue de Sèvres, he little imagined that by 1863 he would be its sole owner. Nor could he have foreseen the staggering expansion of the establishment from an initial floor space of 30 sq. m to 26,000 within 60 years. Moreover, the new extended premises had an iron structure, the symbol of modernity, and were designed by Gustave Eiffel, then at the pinnacle of his fame (1889). The story of the Bon Marché is the success story of a man of enterprise in the second half of the 19th century, the age of triumphant capitalism.

These gigantic 'modern bazaars', as Emile Zola called them, paved the way for our consumer society, eliminating in the process many a helpless small trades-man. Pursuing his lifetime mission - the exploration of the mechanism of the soci-ety of his time - the relentless Zola set about to explore the world of the Bon Marché, probing into all its aspects and into every minute detail, and then recreat-ing it in his novel *Au Bonheur des Dames*. It was a perfectly lubricated piece of machinery, dedicated to the maximization of profit and served by cogs in a wheel, where only the mechanically fittest survived. In this world of sham, the irre-sistible weapon of advertising was used to lure the female client into the store where, dazzled by the overflowing accumulation of goods and ever-changing fashions, she was inevitably trapped.

Next to the Bon Marché is the Square Boucicaut, which commemorates the brilliant self-made-man, a possible place for a rest, albeit in one of the busiest junctions of the Left Bank. Off this square is rue de Babylone, where at n° 57 is a curio worth discovering, though quite a walk: a pagoda-shaped cinema, built in 1895/6 by one of the managers of the Bon Marché in the hope, so it is said, of winning back his unfaithful wife. Japanism was the rage, which should have pleased Madame, although the architect, Alexandre Marcel, was an authentic Frenchman. The Chinese legation, who rented the premises for a while, were not pleased to discover that some of the murals inside illustrated the victories of Japan over China in 1931 and never moved in. In 1935 it was turned into a cine-ma and has remained so since. The movie-goer will be advised to try and com-bine a visit to its picturesque *salon de thé* with a movie session. All the more so as this is the only picture-house to have survived in the 7th arrondissement.

FAUBOURG SAINT-GERMAIN (THE WEST)

The next itinerary runs through rue de Varenne, which, like the parallel rue de Grenelle, once led to the hunting-grounds further west (now the 15th arr.). This is a bastion of embassies and government institutions, often extending between the two streets, in magnificent 18th-century *hôtels*, resolutely closed to the public. The fronts of the buildings and the courtyards may sometimes be glimpsed but never the gardens. However, the fashion houses of the first section of rue de Grenelle, where Italian and Japanese designers have lately moved in, are worth seeing instead.

The Hôtel Matignon, at n° 57 rue de Varenne, is the residence of the Prime Minister and perhaps the most sumptuous mansion in the Faubourg. Its construc-tion began in 1721 for the Prince de Tingry, Christian-Louis de Montmorency, an exemplary soldier under Louis XIV and a future Maréchal de France, who sold it two years later to his niece's husband, Goyon de Matignon, the Comte de

Thorigny. The *hôtel* changed hands several times before it was taken over in 1808 by Talleyrand, who was already residing in the neighbouring n° 55. Here his famous cook, Carême, produced lavish dinner parties four times a week for 36 privileged guests. However, three years later Talleyrand chose to sell the *hôtel* to the state. Louis XVIII swapped it for the Palais de l'Elysée, the Right Bank property of the Duchesse de Bourbon, which has since become the residence of the President of the Republic. The Duke of Galliera bought it in 1852 and it was his widow who offered the Comte de Paris, the pretender to the throne, the use of the ground floor, where he gave a brilliant reception on the occasion of his daughter's engagement to the heir presumptive to the throne of Portugal, the Prince of Bragança. Displeased with this turn of events and suspecting that the forces of reaction were at work once more, the Third Republic passed a law expelling the princes of the House of Orléans from France, a law that remained in force until after the Great War. When the war broke out in 1914, the Prince d'Orléans perceived it his duty to return to France to join the army, but the authorities were not moved by his patriotism and imprisoned him! From 1888 to 1914 the Austrian Embassy was located here, the Duchess of Galliera having bequeathed it to the Austrian emperor, Franz Joseph. After the Great War it was sequestered and ultimately appropriated by the Republic. It has been the residence of the Prime Minister since 1935. Besides splendid interior decoration, the Hôtel Matignon has an immense garden with a bejewelled 18th-century folly, built as a music room and called Le Petit-Trianon.

Further down rue de Varenne, at n° 78, the Hôtel de Villeroi, is occupied today by the Ministry of Agriculture. Unfortunately, this lovely example of a Regency town house and its charming gardens are hidden from the street by newer government buildings. The *hôtel* was originally built for the famous actress Charlotte Desmares, a mistress of the Grand Dauphin and later of the Regent, by whom she had a daughter. Like many of her contemporaries, Charlotte Desmares went bankrupt and had to let out her *hôtel*. The Dutch Ambassador moved here in 1726 but died the following year. The English Ambassador, Horace Walpole, succeeded him, followed by Lord Waldegrave. Later the Comtesse de Tessé, Adrienne La Fayette's aunt, lived here and invited her friend Thomas Jefferson to stay here.

The Hôtel de Biron at n° 77 is now the Musée Rodin and is therefore open to the public, together with its lovely grounds! For this we must be thankful both to historical circumstances and to Auguste Rodin. Originally the *hôtel* was built for Monsieur Peyrenc, a wigmaker from Languedoc. Unlike his neighbour Charlotte Desmares, who had suffered from the sudden drop in the speculative market introduced by the Scotsman John Law, Monsieur Peyrenc had made such a staggering fortune that he could afford to employ the great architect Gabriel to draw up the plans for this mansion. It was certainly fit for royalty, since Louise de

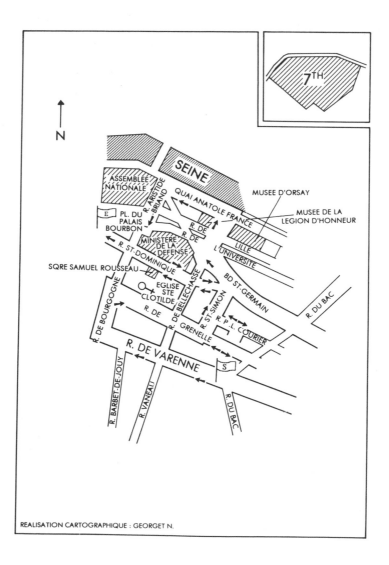

REALISATION CARTOGRAPHIQUE : GEORGET N.

Bourbon, the Duchesse du Maine and daughter-in-law of Louis XIV and Madame de Montespan, bought it from the wigmaker's widow in 1732. Its last owner, the Duchesse de Charost, sold it to a religious congregation in 1820, which eventually housed a school. When the congregation was dispersed in 1904 the school went public. With so much space becoming available, somebody had the idea of letting it out to artists at a moderate rent: thus Rainer Maria Rilke, Isadora Duncan, Rodin and Jean Cocteau became the privileged tenants of these enchanting surroundings. Cocteau was 19 when he arrived and remained for a year in this "large building, with five French windows opening into a park of 7 hectares in the middle of Paris, on Boulevard des Invalides...", as he reported in his *Portraits-Souvenirs*. His modest, meagrely furnished room had been previously the

Musée Rodin

solfeggio classroom of the school. From there he could see Rodin working in the unkempt garden, which was overgrown with wild briars, forget-me-not and weeds. When all was dark he could see a light in the window of the room where Rilke was working late into the night on *Les Cahiers de Malte Laurids Brigge*. When the state bought the Hôtel Biron in 1910 Rodin was given a life lease and it was agreed that a museum would be set up here to house his works which he was to bequeath to the state. The building and gardens have now been restored - some say too much - but certainly this is one of the most beautiful museums in the city, as far as premises and gardens go. A visit here should definitely be reserved for fine weather and leisurely sightseeing.

Turn right into rue de Bourgogne, up until recently one of the delightful streets in the arrondissement with its numerous succulent food shops. But one by one their shopkeepers have retired and closed down, carrying with them the soul of the street. The excellent Italian bookshop is still here, probably because of the proximity of the Italian Embassy, Consulate and school at n° 47 and 50 rue de Varenne. The Club des Poètes, at n° 30, is a cosy cabaret where poetry readings are given.

If you wish to look at some more 18th-century architectural gems, turn right into rue de Grenelle. On the corner of rue de Bourgogne and rue de Grenelle, on the site of n° 115, the adulated Adrienne Lecouvreur from the Comédie-Française, is said to have been buried secretly in 1730. Banished by the Church, like all other members of her profession, she was refused burial by the priest of Saint-Sulpice, in spite of Voltaire's angry protestations:

N'a même pas eu la faveur
De deux cierges et d'une bière
(was not even favoured with two candles and a bier)

That once admired body, he pursued, had to be carried by night to the river by three charitable souls, one of whom was his friend M. Laubinière. The years went by and eventually the Hôtel de Saumery was erected on this site. In 1786, an 86-year-old admirer of the actress, the Comte Ferrio d'Argental, fixed a commemorative plaque under its portal, which has been there ever since. But the remains of Adrienne Lecouvreur were never found, despite thorough search undertaken in 1797 at the instigation of the Comédie-Française.

The owner of the Hôtel de Villars at n° 116 at the time of Louis XVI was the Duc de Brissac, the governor of Paris. On 9 September 1792 the Duke was slain on the streets of Versailles, after which his head was sliced off and carried by the *patriotes* all the way to Louveciennes, to be displayed before his ex-mistress the Contesse du Barry. She took the head back to Paris and buried it in the gardens, where it was found accidentally in 1901, by which time the *hôtel* had been the

Mairie of the 7th arrondissement for nearly 40 years (1862). Little of the past splendour of the house has been preserved. Its mirrored gallery, 24 metres long and 8 metres high, was one of the finest in the capital. The elegant building next door, the Petit Hôtel de Villars, was built as an annexe during the Regency.

Hôtel de Rochechouart, at n° 110, a late 18th-century building, is today part of the Ministry of Education. The Duc de Saint-Simon died in 1755, aged 80, on the first floor of the Hôtel de Maillebois, at n° 102, to which he had retired to work on his *Mémoires*. N° 99/101, the Hôtel de Charolais, a house of faded splendour, was the home in the early 18th century of the Baron de Presle, who built the Hôtel Villeroi for his mistress, the actress Charlotte Desmares, conveniently across his own gardens. During the Second Empire the Princesse de Metternich held here a sumptuous *salon* of world renown. Since 1870 the premises have been occupied by the Ministry of Commerce and Industry. The Hôtel de Baufremont at n° 87 is a sheer aesthetic delight - somehow, it has hardly been touched by renovators and has retained the harmony of its original Regency architecture. The Hôtel d'Avaray at n° 85 was built at the same time and remained in the hands of the Avaray family for a remarkable 200 years. During his ambassadorship, Horace Walpole rented it from the Marquis d'Avaray for a couple of years, during which he hosted some lavish receptions upon his guests; these were the talk of the town. After the death of the last Duc d'Avaray in 1896, the *hôtel* was bought by outsiders, most recently in 1920 by the Dutch government for its Embassy.

During their visit to Paris in 1896, Tzar Nicholas II and his Tzarine stayed in the Russian Embassy at n° 79. The early 18th-century decoration of the lounges has survived, as has a splendid staircase. The Hôtel de Fürstenberg at n° 75, with its peach-coloured walls blending delicately into the curve of the street, is the work of Delisle-Mansart, who had been very active in the Marais. This is one of the earlier mansions in the Faubourg, dating from 1703, still in the time of Louis XIV. The Hôtel de Gallifet at n° 73 (main entrance being on rue de Varenne), has been occupied by the Italian Embassy since 1909. Talleyrand, the one politician who had managed to wriggle his way through revolutions and counter-revolutions, came to live here four times during four different regimes - during the Directoire and into the Consulat, during the First Empire, during the First Restoration and during the Second Restoration which followed Napoleon's brief return to power and his final defeat at Waterloo. He was not beloved by Napoleon who had defined him as "shit in a silk stocking".

Retrace your steps and turn right into rue Saint-Simon, which commemorates the great memorialist. Note the delightful profusion of greenery behind the gorgeous door at n° 102. Turn right into rue Paul-Louis Courier and right again into Impasse Paul-Louis Courier. A picturesque well and two pretty street-lamps add a romantic touch to this leafy nook. Note also the curious artist's studio at n° 7. Continue on rue Saint-Simon and turn left into Boulevard Saint-Germain, then left into rue Saint-Dominique. You will soon reach the Ministry of Defence which occupies the premises of the Dominican convent of Saint-Joseph at n° 10/12 and the Hôtel de Brienne at n° 14. Very little of it can be seen from the street, nor of its magnificent gardens overlooking rue de l'Université. The convent was originally built for poor orphan girls, to provide them with training and a future livelihood. Madame de Montespan not only took great interest in the convent and made charitable donations to it, but also retired to it when Louis XIV left her for Madame de Maintenon. From 1747 all the Parisian intelligentsia and many honoured foreigners gathered at Madame du Deffand's celebrated *salon*, held in this convent where she too had retired.

The Hôtel de Brienne is named after its last owner during the *Ancien Régime*, the Comte de Brienne. He was also the last Minister of War of the *Ancien Régime* and among the victims of the guillotine during the Terror of 1794. When the storm subsided his widow did not wish to keep the mansion and in 1802 it became the property of Lucien Bonaparte who filled it with a wealth of bibelots and paintings. It was in his house that the Duc de Luynes who had, as a matter of pragmatism, befriended the new regime, noticed and pointed out to his host two of his old paintings hanging on a wall, as mentioned earlier. That same night Lucien Bonaparte, had them returned to their original owner at the Hôtel de Luynes.

Across the street the Square Samuel-Rousseau, with its colourful flower-beds, recalls the composer César Franck who, from 1858 until his death in 1890, was the organist of the church of Sainte-Clotilde (on the other side of the square). A sculpture of the composer meditating can be seen in the square; an angel hovers above, symbolizing divine inspiration. The church is a 19th-century pastiche of Gothic architecture, built by Gau and Ballu (the latter being the architect of several Parisian churches, notably the Trinité north of the Opéra).

Turn left into rue de Bellechasse, which leads to the Musée d'Orsay on the corner of quai Anatole-France and to the Musée de la Légion d'Honneur, across the street. First have a look at n° 31 on your right, where Alphonse Daudet lived between 1885 and 1897 and where Proust claimed to have visited his widow, writing "*Je n'en sais d'aussi pleine du passé, de pensée, d'aussi pieusement consacrée par le souvenir que le 31 rue de Bellechasse*" ("I don't know of another so filled with the past, with thought, so piously consecrated by memory, as 31 rue Bellechasse"). The building is historic indeed since the mathematician Monge, the physician Villemin and the historian Bainville all died here. Gustave Doré had a studio at n° 27, which still bears the initials GD.

Paris loves novelty and converting a railway station into a museum, which, moreover, would house the immensely popular Impressionists, was bound to create a sensation. 11.5 million people visited the Musée d'Orsay within the first three years of its inauguration in February 1987. Even now there are at times discouragingly long queues for admission. Although the museum is devoted to all the forms of art that developed in France in the second half of the 19th century, and hosts other activities such as chamber-music concerts, most visitors come for the Impressionist collection, on which its reputation has been built, and to marvel at the audacious architectural conversion. This was always an admirable piece of architecture, a testimony to those glorious days when the railway station was the temple of modernity and the steam engine its object of worship, as witness Monet's paintings of *La Gare Saint Lazare* and Zola's novel *La Bête humaine*. However, this one was not inaugurated until 1900, on the symbolic date of 14 July, and was so beautiful that the painter Edouard Detaille suggested even then that it should be turned into a museum or art gallery. Like every self-respecting station, the Gare d'Orsay took pride in its hotel, of which the huge Belle Epoque dining-room was decorated with utmost care. The latter has been preserved on the first floor of the museum, complete with extravagant candelabras and a magnificent allegorical mural, *Allégorie des périodes du temps*, bringing to mind those pioneering days, when the travelling adventure began on the station platform. It also offers a beautiful view overlooking the Musée de la Légion d'Honneur in the Hôtel de Salm, and Place de la Concorde. The museum's interior is perhaps less successful: too many partitions and too many cumbersome items cramp what should have remained an unobstructed space, distracting the eye from the beautiful vaulted glass-and-iron ceiling and the wonderful station clock.

The Musée de la Légion d'Honneur has a fine collection of medals, crosses, pictures, manuscripts and other paraphernalia. The mansion was named after its first owner, Frédéric III, the Prince of Salm-Kyrburg, who, despite his sincere support of the Revolution, was accused of being "but the mask of patriotism" and was sent to the guillotine on Place du Trône, six days before the fall of Robespierre. His sister, the Princess Hohenzollern, bought the plot of land in the present 12th arrondissement known as the cemetery of Picpus, where his remains still rest, together with those of 1,300 other victims of the Revolution. He was possibly denounced by one of his creditors, for he was so heavily in debt that by the time the mansion was completed he no longer owned it but had become merely a tenant on the premises. Thomas Jefferson, who arrived in Paris in 1784, was a frequent guest at Lafayette's home at n° 123 rue de Lille, from where he could admire this beautiful *hôtel*. He showed it to the architect Charles Bullfinch and to the painter John Trumbull when they visited Paris, and above all to Pierre l'Enfant who is known to have been much inspired by the architecture of Paris in his design for the city for Washington DC.

Claude Lenthereau, a wigmaker who by the end of the Revolution called himself Marquis de Beauregard, became the next landlord of the Hôtel de Salm. He also bought the jewel-like Château de Bagatelle (now in the 16th arr.) on credit, while keeping the celebrated Mlle Lange on a pension of 10,000 pounds and holding unbelievably lavish banquets in his new home. Not everyone took him at face value and the *Feuille du Jour* of 9 August 1796 wrote:

> la sottise et l'impertinence d'un faquin parvenu [qui] pour effacer tout vestige de poudre originelle, se fait appeler le marquis de Beauregard.
> (the foolishness of a parvenu rascal [who] in order to efface any vestige of original powder [from wigmaking], called himself the Marquis de Beauregard).

He was eventually unmasked and condemned to be publicly exposed, branded and put in irons for four entire years. The Hôtel de Salm was set on fire during the *Commune*, but was fortunately beautifully restored. The Cour des Comptes (the revenue court), on the other hand, was utterly destroyed and replaced by the Orsay railway station.

Continue westwards along the *quais* to the Esplanade des Invalides. The Palais Bourbon at n° 33 quai d'Orsay, is the home of the National Assembly. Facing the Pont de la Concorde, it makes a perfectly symmetrical pendant to the Neo-classical church of the Madeleine on the opposite side of Place de la Concorde, across the river. Altogether, this is one of the most spectacular vistas of Paris, an urban expression of French order and Napoleon's legacy to the world. The Neo-classical façade of the building, however, is only a facing: the Emperor, a fervent admirer of Classical art, added it in 1806 to the 18th-century Palais-Bourbon to match the front of the Madeleine, then known as Temple de la Gloire.

The magnificent Regency palace was originally built for Louise-Françoise de Bourbon, the legitimized daughter of Louis XIV and Madame de Montespan, by such great architects as Gabriel, Ghirardini, Lassurance and Aubert. The latter three also built the next-door Hôtel de Lassay, for her friend and counsellor, the Marquis de Lassay, which is now the home of the President of the National Assembly. The Hôtel de Lassay consists essentially of a single, elongated, raised floor, with a row of elegant French doors along its front, surmounted by a sculpted balustrade carrying urns and clusters of chubby cupids - a masterpiece of Regency architecture, noteworthy for the purity of its lines and its elegant proportions. Inside, a succession of five spacious halls - still used for official receptions - were decorated with mirrors, carved doors and delicate paintings, all in keeping with the aesthetic taste of the time, which valued discreet simplicity of architecture contrasted with sumptuous interior decoration, to suit the lifestyle of their spoilt pleasure-seeking inmates. The best craftsmen of the land, notably those of the Faubourg Saint-Antoine, were commissioned to create embellishments to their new dwellings, which were more splendid than those at the time of Louis XIV but also smaller in dimension and more comfortable. Hence the growing use of mirrors - a rare commodity at the time of the Sun King - to create an illusion of space and also to embody the perpetual game of hide-and-seek, intrigue and of elusive love that so engrossed society at the time.

The Palais-Bourbon became the property of the Prince de Condé in 1764. Having extended his domain to the Seine and to the Esplanade des Invalides, he also annexed the Hôtel de Lassay. Needless to say, the entire estate was confiscated during the Revolution, but at least its owner was luckily able to emigrate in time. The interior architecture of the Palais-Bourbon was largely modified by Gisors and Lecomte to suit its new function as the French people's parliament. The entrance is from Place du Palais-Bourbon (reached by way of rue Aristide Briand, beyond Boulevard Saint-Germain on your left), a charming square of distinguished, understated harmony, in keeping with the subdued dignity of the Faubourg. Both the Palais-Bourbon and the Hôtel Lassay (at n° 120 rue de l'Université) are closed to the public except on special occasions or for arranged guided tours. Nevertheless, you can take in the atmosphere of the area by stopping at one of the very pleasant eating-places as an enjoyable way of ending the exploration of the old Faubourg.

FROM LES INVALIDES TO THE EIFFEL TOWER

The western part of the arrondissement is largely an area of open spaces, breath-taking vistas and world-renowned monuments. Following our route, therefore, requires energy and you may wish to leave out some of its sections. Most of the area is in any case covered with residential avenues which were built in the 19th century and are of little interest to the pedestrian.

Start from the Invalides, which is best appreciated from a distance, preferably from Pont Alexandre III; but the Invalides must be seen too from Place Vauban on the other side of the monument, where the church of the Dome (also known as the Royal Chapel) stands. For this is one of the most outstanding monuments in Paris, a masterpiece of 17th-century architecture, built by Jules-Hardouin Mansart.

The church's ample yet delicate, perfectly balanced proportions used to look stunning when approached from Avenue de Breteuil early on a fine morning, when its deep purple dome looked almost palpably mellow and pulpy and matched subtly the rest of the church, tinted pink by the rays of the sun. Not any more: when Paris was groomed for the bicentenary of the Revolution, someone

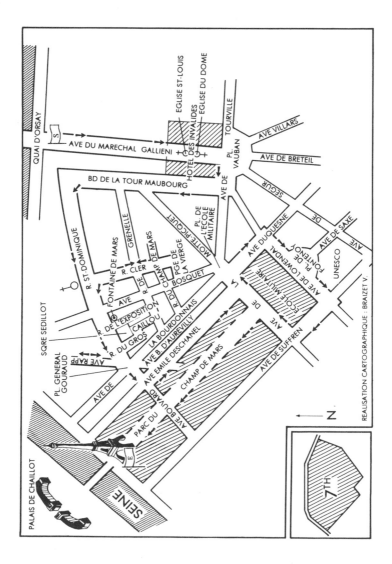

decided to dab shiny gold paint on its prestigious monuments, one of which was, alas, the dome of the Invalides, which now looks like a glittering, tawdry parvenue. Admittedly, the regilding of its gold leaves demanded great skill and was executed to the highest of standards, but was it really necessary to destroy the patina that only time can bestow? For at present it jars with the rest of the monument and, above all, has lost its miraculous outline, now blurred by so much glitter. At night, however, the dome, shimmering against the dark sky above the glowing walls of the floodlit monument, remains enchanting.

The church is one of the most visited monuments of Paris because its crypt houses Napoleon's tomb. Indeed, it is with Napoleon that most visitors associate the monument, although it was Louis XIV, assisted by his minister Louvois, who in 1670 founded the Hôtel des Invalides. Distressed by the sight of war cripples reduced to begging on the Pont-Neuf after loyal services rendered to His Majesty on the battlefield, Louis XIV felt he owed them a respectable shelter. The plight of crippled war veterans turned vagabonds had already preoccupied his grandfather, Henri IV, who in 1604 had provided shelter for them on the present rue Broca (5th and 13th arr.), an initiative continued by his son Louis XIII and his minister Richelieu, who built them the hospital of Bicêtre (now the 13th arr.). But the Sun King obviously tackled the issue on a much grander scale, and commissioned Libéral Bruant, one of the best architects of the day, to build a monument that was both colossal - its façade measures 195 metres across and the main courtyard, the Cour d'Honneur or Cour Royale, 102 meters by 63 - and subdued. In his *Lettres Persanes*, Montesquieu wrote *(Lettre LXXXIV)*.

> Je crois que c'est le lieu le plus respectable de la Terre.
> [...] Quel spectacle de voir rassemblées dans un même lieu toutes ces victimes de la Patrie, qui ne respirent que pour la défendre...
> (I believe this to be the most respectable place on earth [...] What a spectacle to see gathered in the same place all the victims of the motherland who breathe solely to defend her...)

By contrast, the tenants of the institution were unimpressed by the King's charitable intentions, which included full pension and free medical care in unimpeachable surroundings, and were not easily induced to barter their scanty independence on the Pont-Neuf for the inevitable constraints of a military institution. Indeed, they had good cause to be alarmed, for the daily reality fell short of the ideal: a harsh military discipline was imposed, of which infringements were punishable by anything from temporary deprivation of wine to downright imprisonment! They might also be submitted to public opprobrium on a wooden horse (a sort of trestle), with a placard describing the offence. If caught in the company of a woman of pleasure, the two would be exposed together, much to the delight of passers-by. On one occasion, a complaint about the poor quality of the soup sparked off an outburst of violence, which soon developed into a full-blown riot. Louvois spared no measures to crush the rebellion and had the most unruly rebel dispatched by a firing squad.

Louvois was not a modest man and had his eye on this place for his own sepulchre. His Majesty would not tolerate such impertinence and, according to Saint-Simon, had his remains removed to the chapel of the Capucines' convent (now Place Vendôme), which was destroyed during the Revolution. Louvois did at least succeed in perpetuating his name here in an astute, subtle way: as you enter the Cour d'Honneur look at the fifth garret to the right of the left-hand side pavilion; its bull's-eye window is framed by a wolf (*'loup'*) which looks (*'voit'*) intensely down on to the courtyard - a far-fetched pun, no doubt, but it had the merit of not ruffling the Sun King's pride. The tributes to the King were also discreet: an equestrian bas-relief representing him in the attire of a Roman emperor is in the tympanum of the central pavilion, which most visitors fail to see. Moreover, since the accompanying inscription, recording that 'Louis le Grand, in royal munificence for his soldiers and with great foresight, founded this edifice in 1675', is written in Latin only. This decoration, the work of Coustou, was actually added in 1735, at the time of Louis XV. It was damaged during the Revolution and the King's face you now see was made by Cartellier only in 1816, after Napoleon's defeat.

Napoleon, indeed, was determined to dispossess his predecessor of the Invalides and early in his career, in 1797, had already transferred the lion of the defeated Serenissima Republic to this stronghold of France's military glory and placed it on top of a fountain in the centre of the Esplanade. The choice of a fountain was not insignificant, for, having been dazzled by the fountains of Rome, he resolved to outdo them in his own capital. He had also hoped to bring back as a trophy the golden cross of the Kremlin and display it on top of the Dome of the Invalides, but history decided otherwise. The Venetian lion's Parisian career was short-lived and by 1815 it retrieved its position on the column in Piazza San Marco, where it still crouches. Napoleon need not have feared being in the shadow of the Sun King, for in matters military he ranked top in the hearts of the French. When he died, they readily damaged the gorgeous marble marquetry floor of the church of the Dome, decorated in the King's honour with *fleur-de-lis* and the figure XIV, to make room for the crypt and for his tomb and fulfil his wish to be buried "on the banks of the Seine, by the French people whom I have loved so much."

After seven years of negotiations with the English, the Emperor's ashes were brought from the island of Saint Helena to the Invalides on the 15 December 1840, having travelled to Le Havre, up the river Seine to the Pont de Neuilly, then on to Place de l'Etoile, down the Champs-Elysées to Place de la Concorde and across the river along the quai d'Orsay to their final destination at the Invalides. On that 15 December 1840 a heavy snow storm occurred and Victor Hugo, who was present at the funeral, reported how "... suddenly the guns exploded simultaneously on three different points of the horizon... In the distance the drums beat the salute. The Emperor's hearse appeared... The sun, veiled until that moment, appeared at the very same time. The effect was prodigious indeed."

The Emperor's body lay in state between the 16 and 25 December, when roughly 850,000 Parisians came to pay him homage, followed in January by many others who retraced the itinerary of the funeral procession as a sort of pilgrimage. It was another 20 years before Napoleon's ashes were moved to their permanent tomb made by Visconti, and placed in their dominant position in the crypt of the church. Another ceremony was held that day, 13 April 1861, attended by Napoleon III and his highest dignitaries. The Emperor lies within six coffins fitting into one another like Chinese boxes. A manuscript by J. Vacquier, kept in the museum, provides a full description of his position inside the coffin and his military dress. Apparently, despite the short stature of 'the little Corporal', his famous hat had to be placed on his thighs for lack of space. Next to him is a silver vase containing his heart; a silver box contains his stomach. Buried with him, like the personal effects of the Pharaohs, are gold and silver coins bearing his effigy, as well as the cutlery he used during his captivity on Saint Helena.

In the crypt of the church of the Dome lie such other military figures as Turenne, the great hero of Louis XIV's campaigns, and the Maréchal Foch, the hero of World War I. But Juin, Giraud and Leclerc, the heroes of World War II, rest in the crypt of the adjacent church of Saint-Louis-des-Invalides, also known as the Soldiers' Chapel. This was the original church of the institution, designed by Libéral Bruant and possibly completed by Mansart. The church of the Dome was added when this church proved too small and the two share the same choir. Before the Revolution they also shared a common altar. Among those lying in its crypt are the governors of the Invalides, military heroes such as Mac-Mahon and Jourdan (who became governor of the Invalides in 1830), as well as Rouget de Lisle, the captain from Strasbourg who in 1792 composed *Le Chant de guerre pour l'armée du Rhin*, the future sanguinary *Marseillaise*. His ashes were brought here on 14 July 1915. The church also boasts a magnificent 17th-century organ which was used in 1837, for the first performance of Berlioz's *Requiem*.

The Third Republic ignored Louis XIV's proclamation that the Invalides should forever remain a charitable institution, and instead installed its military administration there, consigning the war victims, barely 100 in number, to out-of-the-way quarters. A military museum, one of the largest and richest of its kind in the world, was created, of which the nucleus already existed in 1777, consisting of 43 models of major French fortifications made under the administration of Vauban, Louis XIV's *Haut Commissaire des fortifications*. The museum covers all aspects of warfare and traces its development from the palaeolithic age to World War II. It is all here: armoured chivalry from France itself, warfare in medieval Russia, China and Japan, the exotic glamour of the Ottoman Empire, the adventurous African experience, and also the grim reality of the trenches of World War I. Documentary films of the last two wars complete the visit. On summer nights, a spectacular *son et lumière* is given here (in all major languages), watched predominantly by tourists. The average Parisian will content himself with television broadcasts of military ceremonies filmed in the Cour d'Honneur of the Invalides.

West of the Esplanade des Invalides lies the more recent section of the 7th, previously named Le Gros Caillou ('big stone'), after the boundary stone of the domains of the abbeys of Saint-Germain and Sainte-Geneviève. Later the name was extended to the village that developed here during the 30-year construction of the Invalides and then made a living catering to the new institution. Its first shop was a butcher's on rue Saint-Dominique, which prospered greatly. In due course, the parallel rue de Grenelle accommodated the laundresses who did the washing for the Invalides' pensioners in the Seine. This was not up to the standard set by the discriminating clientele of the Faubourg, who preferred to send their linen to be washed in Holland. The area has retained its informal village atmosphere, even though today it is part of a generally expensive arrondissement, and rue Saint-Dominique, among others, is lined with shops and eating-places. The church of Saint-Pierre du Gros Caillou at n° 92 was the original parish church of the long-forgotten village. It took years of tough negotiations – including a petition to the King – for the inhabitants of the village to be granted an independent parish church, before which they had had to drag all the way to Saint-Sulpice (in the 6th arr.). Construction, however, proceeded very slowly and in fact the church was still not finished when the Revolution swept it away. The present church dates from 1822.

Even more than rue Saint-Dominique, it is the pedestrian rue Cler, to your left, that perpetuates the village atmosphere *par excellence* with its permanent market, held both mornings and afternoons. This is the most picturesque street in the 7th arrondissement - an explosion of genuine local colour, all the more exciting for being such a contrast with the rest of the area.

Back on rue Saint-Dominique you will come to the picturesque, arcaded corner of rue de l'Exposition, with its fountain, La Fontaine de Mars, one of several bequeathed to Paris by Napoleon. Mars, the god of war, is depicted being offered water by the goddess of health, Hygeia. Next to it, the homely restaurant La Fontaine de Mars, is an unpretentious place with genuine atmosphere - alas, so rare in modern Paris - and offering a warm welcome and with good, no-nonsense, traditional French cooking. Rue de l'Exposition, named for the Universal Exhibitions that started out in the nearby Champ-de-Mars, is also lined with small, pleasant eating-places.

Continue along rue Saint-Dominique to Place du Général-Gouraud, at the junction of Avenue de la Bourdonnais. If you are an Art Nouveau enthusiast, turn right into Avenue Rapp. At n° 29 is an astonishing building, built by Lavirotte and extremely reminiscent of the work of the Spanish architect, Gaudí. Retrace your steps and turn right into Avenue Bouvard and left into Avenue Deschanel until you come to the Ecole Militaire on Avenue de la Motte-Picquet. To your left is Place de l'Ecole Militaire.

Just as Madame de Maintenon founded the famous school of Saint-Cyr for the children of the impoverished nobility, Madame de Pompadour founded the Ecole Militaire to enable impoverished young men to become officers. Madame de Maintenon was certainly an example to be followed, she being the only King's favourite in French history to have become the King's wife. The no less ambitious Pompadour instructed Gabriel, who had already impressed the nobility with his Petit Trianon in Versailles, to build this new academy.

Turn right into Avenue Dusquesne and right again into Avenue Lowendal from where you can view the beautiful façade of the Ecole Militaire with its entrance on Place de Fontenoy. Also on Place de Fontenoy, facing the west wing of the Ecole Militaire, is the UNESCO building, designed jointly by Marcel Breuer (US), Pietro Nervi (Italy) and Bernard Zehrfuss (France) and built by the American Eugene Calisson. Its interesting "y" shape was quite revolutionary in 1955 when it was designed and, like all good architecture, is still effective. Works by Bezaine, Calder, Miro and Moore decorate it outside, and by Appel, Arp, Brassaï, Lurçat, Matta, Picasso and Tamayo inside, a prolific array in keeping with the post-war ambitions and hopes of UNESCO. The Japanese garden was designed by the famous Isamu Nogushi, who returned to Paris to restore it in 1988, just a few months before his death.

By skirting the Ecole Militaire you will reach the rectangular, orderly Esplanade and gardens of the Champ-de-Mars: ahead of you, in a perfect straight line with the centre of the Ecole Militaire, is the Eiffel Tower and, beyond, the perfect symmetry of the Trocadéro, from where the vista of the Champ-de-Mars is best appreciated. At these close quarters, however, you will enjoy the pretty nooks of its gardens that are unnoticed from a distance. They - and the inevitable grotto - make a romantic contrast with the Esplanade's overall symmetrical layout *à la française*. Willow, mulberry, alder and various other species of trees imported from China, the Himalaya and Virginia all contribute to the picture, especially in spring when the rhododendrons are in bloom.

The Champ-de-Mars was originally the parade-ground of the Ecole Militaire, used by the royal troops for the parades they had previously held at Sablons, west of Paris. Before then, this stretch of land was covered with kitchen gardens, like most outlying areas of the city. The Champ-de-Mars had beautiful grilled gates, and avenues of elm trees and hedgerows and was large enough for 10,000 soldiers to be lined up in battle formation, Among the cadets of the Ecole Militaire who paraded here was a poor Corsican who one day, in his turn, would inspect and distribute honours to the troops on the Champ-de-Mars.

An event of great novelty occurred here one fine morning in 1780, when two gentlemen ran in a horse-race for a bet, the first in a series of sports that in the course of the 19th century were imported from across the Channel, each of which became a fad. Oddly, this aristocratic sport, to which Marie-Antoinette gave an enthusiastic support, was adopted by the Revolution, except that the jockeys of those patriotic horse-races 'of public utility', wore tricoloured sashes. Principally it was Talleyrand who promoted the sport and strove to improve the breeds of horses. The Champ-de-Mars remained the racecourse of Paris till 1855, when the Longchamp in the Bois de Boulogne took over.

Those latter years of the 18th century were also the pioneering days of ballooning. The people of Gonesse, east of Paris, were panic-stricken when an 'unidentified flying object' descended on them from the heavens on 27 August 1783. A few weeks earlier, on 5 June, two brothers by the name of Mongolfier, from the village of Annonay, had already astonished the world, including the venerable members of the Academy of Science, by sending the first hot-air balloon one mile into the sky. Less amateurish than the Mongolfiers, the two Robert brothers understood the advantage of using hydrogen, which is 15 times lighter than air. The physicist J. A. C. Charles set about manufacturing enough hydrogen to fill the Roberts' first *Charlière* and on 27 August, the Roberts released this first unmanned hydrogen balloon from the Champ-de-Mars on an unprecedented flight of 15 miles, which lasted three quarters of an hour.

When on 2 March 1874 J.P. Blanchard arrived on the Champ-de-Mars with his outlandish 'airship' - a sophisticated balloon, equipped with four oars and a rudder - thousands came to watch. However, instead of floating east to La Villette, as he had intended, his machine headed in the opposite direction, and landed in Billancourt, due west... an event promptly satirized by the *chansonniers* :

7th ARRONDISSEMENT

Au Champ-de-Mars il s'envola
Au champ voisin il resta là
Beaucoup d'argent il ramassa
Messieurs, *'sic itur ad astra'*.

('From the field of Mars he took off /In the neighbouring
field he ended up / Much money did he amass / Gentlemen, *'sic itur ad astra'* [The Latin bit had been inscribed
on his balloon]).

But Blanchard persevered undaunted and the following January made the first
aerial crossing of the English Channel from Dover to Calais, together with the
American John Jeffries; after which he was seen floating across the skies of
Europe, to The Hague, Frankfurt, Basel and even as far as Berlin. In 1863 the
photographer Nadar took off from the Champ-de-Mars, accompanied by a number of prominent figures, in a huge balloon with a double-decker nacelle, called
Le Géant. On Nadar's second flight he got as far as Holland but was injured on
the landing.

The authorities of the Revolution chose the Champ-de-Mars as the site for the
first Bastille Day celebrations, then known as La Fête de la Fédération, presided
over by the ubiquitous Talleyrand, the man of all the parties. 300,000 fervent
patriots - including the Royal Family - were convened here on that 14 July 1790
for the uplifting ceremony. Citoyen La Fayette, standing up in the pouring rain,
took the Nation's oath, the first citizen to do so. By 1793 the Revolution had
become a bloody business and on one brief occasion the guillotine was set up
here to rid the nation of its abhorred enemy, Bailly. Bailly had been President of
the Constituent Assembly and Mayor of Paris between 1789 and 1791, but
became most unpopular when he ordered the troops to fire at the demonstrators
who had gathered on the Champ-de-Mars to claim the deposition of the King. The
crowds that gathered now to watch his execution, refused to have the sacred
Esplanade soiled by his foul blood and the infernal machine had to be dismount-
ed, then re-erected on the edge of the Esplanade (now corner of Avenue de la
Bourdonnais and the quai de Branly. While preparations were under way, poor
Bailly waited stoically, which further excited the blood-thirsty populace. By the
time he was ready to offer his head to the 'national razor', he was covered with
spittle and mud. On 8 June 1794, at the peak of the Terror, Robespierre came here
to preside over the Fête de l'Etre Suprême, an expression of homage to the new
god of the Republic, who, it was believed, would topple over a thousand years of
Christianity.

When royalty was reinstated in the 19th century, military parades alternated
here with horse-races. However, capitalism was fast superseding the *Ancien*

Régime and in 1855 the Champ-de-Mars was singled out to become the gigantic playground of the emerging capitalist society, the scene of successive *Expositions Universelles*, where British supremacy would be challenged and the world dazzled by French technological achievements. They began with an embryonic fair back in 1798, but as they became ever more colossal, they expanded along and across the river and became increasingly wearing on the feet. In 1900 an exciting novelty was installed - an electrically operated moving wooden platform to transport visitors through this gigantic forerunner of Disneyland. It went from the Champ-de-Mars to the Champs-Elysées, then to the Invalides and back to its starting-point. The 1889 fair was not quite that size yet, but its novelty and enchantment were even greater. The myriads of scintillating lights, the spellbinding exoticism of foreign lands and the bewitching magic of re-created fairy-tales astounded the visitor. As he was whisked off to the bazaars of Cairo, he was dazzled by the splendour of golden cupolas and intoxicated by the sensuous perfumes of Arabia, by languorous music and by erotic belly-dancing. The men ogled and the women went off to practise at home, in the hope of increasing their seductiveness. Above all, it was the gigantic scale of things that left visitors dumbfounded. There was the Galerie des Machines, measuring 420 x 115 metres and covering six hectares, with its 16,000 machines and, of course, the Eiffel Tower towering 318 metres above Paris and the world - unquestionably the two focal attractions of the fair. The Galerie des Machines was a disturbing experience though, which brought home harsh realities; as the writer Huysmans noticed, "People go out stupefied and ravished." On the other hand, the enormous mecano that pointed to the sky was quite thrilling, whether climbed on foot or ridden by elevator; and the view from the top, stretching over 120 km was stunning - never before had mortal eye embraced such horizons, except from a balloon.

By night luminous fountains with their sprays of golden water, their showers of rubies, and their streams of diamonds transformed the grounds of the fair into a dreamlike marvel... And since the fair commemorated the first centenary of the Revolution, patriotic touches were added. Thus one fountain bore the message: FRANCE ENLIGHTENING THE WORLD, while a tricoloured beam of light radiated over the city from the Eiffel Tower, itself stunningly illuminated. Expanding on the success of water and light effects in 1889, the organizers of the 1900 fair created 'Venetian' fêtes aboard illuminated boats on the Seine. The Château d'Eau (water tower) and especially the Palais de l'Electricité, were the highlights of the Champ-de-Mars, electricity being still a luxury at the time. At night a sheet of water, 9 metres wide, shimmering in all the colours of the rainbow, cascaded 25 metres in the water tower, against the backdrop of the incandescent Palace. Raoul Dufy's famous painting *Fée Electricité*, which served as a panel on the wall of the Palace, is now in the Museum of Modern Art of the City of Paris. Mirrors helped to create this world of illusion and enjoyed the public's favour and the world-famous Saint-Gobain glass should have been a key attraction but for some reason the exhibits were never delivered. The vacant space was offered to the Impressionists, which was of little help, as not a single one of their paintings was sold.

The golden age of Universal Exhibitions has gone, an ephemeral spark that fizzled out as a result of *ennui*, before being swept away by universal cataclysms. Not so the Eiffel Tower, its most controversial exhibit and paradoxically the most conspicuous survivor of the fairs, above all, the unassailable emblem of Paris. How ironic to recall that 300 prominent members of the intelligentsia of the time signed a petition against its erection, claiming it to be a crime against history and against Paris. Standing firmly on her four spread-out feet, the Iron Lady is there to stay. Even visitors familiar with the Empire State Building or the World Trade Center feel overwhelmed and uplifted as they approach it; all the more so, when they stop to think that 15,000 metal pieces held together in perfect balance by 2.5 million rivets (and 7 million rivet holes) and weighing a mere 7,000 tons, are all this gigantic structure amounts to - an extraordinary, technological feat. Hitler, however, was an exception who, when rushing through Paris in 1940, went to see it briefly and commented: "Is that all it is? It's ugly!" Some people find it gracefully feminine, even during the day when it cannot conceal its raw metal framework under luminous guise. Irwin Shaw, on the other hand, saw it as a phalic symbol. Cocteau's metaphor, 'The Iron Shepherdess', is perhaps the most apt, especially as the Tower has eight lightning conductors and thus actually protects Paris from lightning. It has been a source of inspiration to many: to the painter Robert Delaunay, to the singer Charles Trenet, to the film director René Clair (*The Crazy Ray*); more recently, the tower has also been used as a backdrop for Superman and for 007. In the James Bond movie *Live or Let Die*, a chase takes place in the second-floor restaurant during a performance given by T Jones, the bad female spy, a scene inspired perhaps by the story of the real Mata Hari. During World War I she led a double life as spy and nude dancer at the Eiffel Tower, but it was this that gave her away. Identified through its radio transmissions as H21, she was captured and shot on 15 October 1917. Nearly 50,000 words were received and transmitted from the Eiffel Tower during that war; this alone proved a very good reason not to demolish it.

The sporty community were also inspired by the Tower and came here to try their hand at different feats. Thus, emulating Icarus some eccentrics climbed it with their flying machines or parachuting gear. One such attempt by an Austrian called Reichelt in 1912 ended a few seconds after it had begun, when he hit the ground head first. In 1977 a French stunt man took off on a hang-glider from the first floor, while an English couple parachuted from the third. In the same year an

American pilot succeeded in flying between the legs of the Tower and lost his flying licence as a consequence. There were climbing contests and even a beauty contest in 1937 presided over by the Duke and Duchess of Windsor, when the minimum height required of entrants was 1.75 m, as a token of respect for the tall iron structure. Acrobats, cyclists, a ballerina and lovers have come here, but also hundreds of desperadoes determined to put an end to a wretched or meaningless existence. Some were locals and some had come up from the provinces; some even from overseas, by train or by plane to die at her feet. Of the 380 people who have hurled themselves from the Tower, only one escaped death - a young woman who in 1964 jumped from the first floor but landed on the roof of a parked car. That year the number of suicides rose alarmingly to an average of one per month, since when parapets have been installed around the Tower.

On a more cheerful note, do go to the top for an unforgettable view of Paris. Those who can, will not regret completing the experience with a dinner at the Jules Verne on the second floor, especially by night. You may have understandable reservations about falling into the ultimate tourist trap, but excellent cuisine is guaranteed and, with the western section of Paris floodlit at your feet, French talent for grandiose town-planning is displayed here at its best.

INDEX

Around and About Paris Volume 1, 2 & 3

Volume 2 takes you from the 8th to the 12th arrondissements, the area incorporated into Paris during the French Revolution.

Volume 3 covers the 13th to the 20th arrondissements which were annexed to Paris in 1860.

Thirza Vallois brings Paris to life in a way that enthralls her readers and provides them with a detailed knowledge of the city which exceeds that of most Parisians, while her fast moving style disguises a depth of historical fact that is normally only found in academic tomes.

Order Form

To order your copy, either check or insert the number of copies you want in the appropriate box and return this order form (or a photocopy of it) along with your cheque to the address below. Alternatively you can phone your order through on +44 (0973) 325 468 and pay by credit card.

☐ VOLUME 1: **From the Dawn of Time to the Eiffel Tower**
Arrondissements 1 to 7. Price £14.95 (available now)

☐ VOLUME 2: **From the Guillotine to the Bastille Opera**
Arrondissements 8 to12. Price £14.95 (available October 1995)

☐ VOLUME 3: **New Horizons: Haussmann's Annexation**
Arrondissements 13 to 20. Price £15.95 (available December 1995)
Add £2.90 per copy for post and packing

Send your order to; **ILIAD BOOKS,** 5 Nevern Road, London SW5 9PG

Name:...

Address:...

....

☐ Enclosed is my cheque payable to Iliad Books, amount:......................................

☐ Please bill my credit card. Specify type of card ....

Card No.. Expiry date...................................

Signature ....

310